THE SHAREWARE BOOK:
USING PC-WRITE®, PC-FILE+®, AND PC-CALC+®

SECOND EDITION

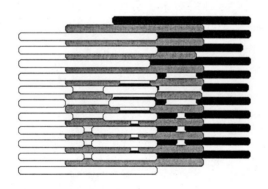

THE SHAREWARE BOOK:
USING PC-WRITE®, PC-FILE+®, AND PC-CALC+®

SECOND EDITION

Ramon Zamora, Frances Saito,
and Bob Albrecht

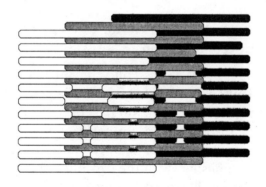

Osborne **McGraw-Hill**

Berkeley   New York   St. Louis   San Francisco
Auckland   Bogotá   Hamburg   London   Madrid
Mexico City   Milan   Montreal   New Delhi   Panama City
Paris   São Paulo   Singapore   Sydney
Tokyo   Toronto

Osborne **McGraw-Hill**
2600 Tenth Street
Berkeley, California 94710
U.S.A.

For information on translations and book distributors outside of the U.S.A., write to Osborne **McGraw-Hill** at the above address.

A complete list of trademarks appears on page 719.

The Shareware Book: Using CP-Write®, Pc-File+®, and PC-Calc+®, Second Edition

Copyright © 1990 by McGraw-Hill, Inc. All rights reserved. Printed in the United States of America. Except as permitted under the Copyright Act of 1976, no part of this publication may be reproduced or distributed in any form or by any means, or stored in a database or retrieval system, without the prior written permission of the publisher, with the exception that the program listings may be entered, stored, and executed in a computer system, but they may not be reproduced for publication.

1234567890 DOC 89

ISBN 0-07-881591-6

Information has been obtained by Osborne **McGraw-Hill** from sources believed to be reliable. However, because of the possibility of human or mechanical error by our sources, Osborne **McGraw-Hill**, or others, Osborne **McGraw-Hill** does not guarantee the accuracy, adequacy, or completeness of any information and is not responsible for any errors or omissions or the results obtained from use of such information.

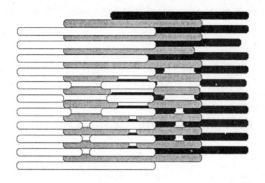

Contents at a Glance

Why This Book Is for You................................ 1

PART I

PC-Write

1: PC-Write: Getting Started 5
2: Letter to a Friend............................. 41
3: Business Correspondence....................... 73
4: Multi-page Documents 105
5: Screen and Page Format Control................ 135

PART II
PC-File+

- **6:** PC-File+: Getting Started 169
- **7:** Building a Mailing List Database 205
- **8:** Form Letters and Mailing Labels 265
- **9:** Database Calculations and Graphics 311

PART III
PC-Calc+

- **10:** PC-Calc+: Getting Started.................. 375
- **11:** Building a Spreadsheet..................... 421
- **12:** Going Camping with a Spreadsheet 463
- **13:** Importing, Graphing, and Other Features ... 507

PART IV
General Information for PC Users

- **A:** DOS Essentials 573
- **B:** ASCII Codes 591

PART V

PC-Write Resource Information

- **C:** PC-Write Command Summary.................... 601
- **D:** Files Used by PC-Write 621
- **E:** Creating a PC-Write Work Disk.................. 629
- **F:** Transferring Files Between PC-Write Version 3 and Other Programs............................ 637

PART VI

PC-File+ Resource Information

- **G:** PC-File+ Keystroke and Command Summary 647
- **H:** Files on the PC-File+ Disks 661
- **I:** Transferring Files Between PC-File+ and Other Programs.................................... 665

PART VII

PC-Calc+ Resource Information

- **J:** PC-Calc+ Keystrokes, Commands, and Functions . 671
- **K:** Files on the PC-Calc+ Disks.................... 687
- **L:** Transferring Files Between PC-Calc+ and Other Programs 691

PART VIII

Other Useful Resource Information

M: Transferring Files Between PC-Write, PC-File+, and PC-Calc+ 695
N: Other Shareware Programs 699
O: User Groups................................... 705

Index.. 723

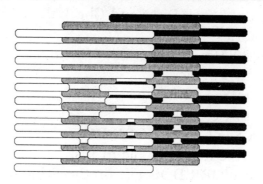

Contents

Introduction xxiii

Why This Book Is for You 1

Part I
PC-Write

1 **PC-Write: Getting Started** 5
   PC-Write, the Package 7
      The PC-Write Disk Sets 8
      Protect Your Disks.............................. 9
      Directories 12
      On-Disk Information........................... 13
   Make Copies of Your Disk Set 14
   Create PC-Write Work Disks....................... 16
      Two 3 1/2-inch Disk Drives 16
      Two 5 1/4-inch Disk Drives 18

	A Hard Disk Drive System...................	19
	Label Your Work Disks and Check the Directories	21
	PC-Write in 30 Minutes: A Guided Tour	22
	Start Your Engines	24
	Press F8 to See a Directory.................	25
	Press F1 to Get Help.....................	27
	Create a File Called WORK.DOC	29
	Save the WORK.DOC File to Disk............	32
	Print the WORK.DOC File on the Printer.......	35
	Summary	40
2	**Letter to a Friend**	**41**
	Start PC-Write..........................	42
	Browse the Directories	43
	Directory of the Disk in Drive A.............	44
	Directory of the Disk in Drive B.............	45
	Begin a Letter	47
	A Few Words About File Names	48
	The Editing Screen	49
	Start Typing	56
	Save Your Work and Return to DOS	59
	Continue Writing a Letter	60
	A New Way to Start PC-Write................	60
	Move Around the Editing Screen.............	63
	Finish Typing the Letter	66
	Save the Completed Letter	67
	Print the Letter and Exit to DOS.............	68
	Summary	70
3	**Business Correspondence**	**73**
	A Short Business Letter	74
	Load the Editing Program...................	74

	Editing Modes (Wrap+, Para+, and Wrap−)....	77
	The Automatic Paragraph Formatting Mode (Para+)...................................	79
	Type the Letter.................................	80
	Save and Print the Letter.......................	81
	Use New Tools to Modify the Letter.................	84
	Load the Editing Program and Select the TBT001.LTR File.............................	84
	Underline Names of Magazines	86
	More Font Characters	88
	Hide Font Characters	90
	Print in a Quality Font	90
	Move Blocks of Text	93
	Copy a Block of Text	96
	Delete a Block of Text	99
	Create a Letterhead...............................	101
	Summary	104
4	**Multi-page Documents**	**105**
	Create the LINE.NBR Practice File.................	106
	Print the LINE.NBR File	108
	Automatic Pages...............................	109
	Print Only Page 1..............................	110
	Print Multiple Copies	112
	Skip Page 1 and Print Page 2	114
	Page Breaks.....................................	115
	Repage	116
	Delete a Soft-Break Line	117
	Insert a Hard-Break Line	118
	Delete a Hard-Break Line	120
	Set Top and Bottom Margins	121
	Set the Top Margin............................	121
	Set the Bottom Margin.........................	122
	Multiple Line Spacing.............................	123

	Headers, Footers, and Page Numbers............	124
	A Header Dot Line	126
	A Footer Dot Line	128
	Page Numbers...................................	130
	Summary..	132

5 Screen and Page Format Control **135**
Default Screen and Page Formats 136
Change the Default Formats 138
    Create the COLUMN.NBR File 138
    Print the COLUMN.NBR File.................... 140
    Change the Printed Left Margin 141
    Editing the Ruler Line 143
    Edit the Edit Control File 155
    Edit the Print Control File 157
Split the Screen into Columns........................ 159
    The Two-Column Ruler Line 160
    Enter Text in the Left Column................. 162
    Enter Text in the Right Column 163
Summary.. 164

Part II
PC-File+

6 PC-File+: Getting Started **169**
PC-File+: The Package 170
Back Up Your PC-File+ Disks....................... 171
    Back Up the 5 1/4-Inch Disk Set 172
    Back Up the 3 1/2-Inch Disk Set 175
    Put PC-File+ on a Hard Disk................... 177
Format a Blank Database Disk 179

	Start PC-File+	180
	Get Help Anytime and Anywhere	181
	Set the Drive and Path of the Database	183
	Setting FILES=20 in CONFIG.SYS	185
	Files, Records, and Fields	186
	Get To Know PC-File+ in 30 Minutes	188
	Summary	204
7	**Building a Mailing List Database**	**205**
	Clone a PC-File+ Database	206
	The Shareware Book Convenience Disk	207
	Load PhoneLst into PC-File+	208
	The PC-File+ Utilities Menu	211
	Clone PhoneLst to Make MailList	214
	Modify Database Records	234
	Introducing PC-File+ Editing Keys	238
	Fill Out the MailList Data Records	242
	Generate a PC-File+ Report	245
	PC-File+ and Printers	251
	Explore the PC-File+ Utilities	255
	Make Global Changes to the Database	257
	Delete and Undelete Records	260
	Summary	262
8	**Form Letters and Mailing Labels**	**265**
	Using PC-File+ to Create a Form Letter	266
	The Letter Editing Window	267
	PC-File+ Mail Merge Commands	270
	Create the Form Letter	273
	Preview the Printed Letter	278
	Print the Letters	285
	Using PC-File+ to Create Mailing Labels	293
	Get Started with PC-Label	293

  Print Mailing Labels 303
  PC-Label's Many Labels 308
 Summary 309

9 Database Calculations and Graphics **311**
 The BookStor Database 312
  Create the BookStor Database 313
  Set Up the Calculation Fields 326
  Activate the Calculations...................... 334
 Let PC-File+ Graph Your Data 337
  Set Up Your Printer for Graphics 338
  Move the Graphics Files to the Data Disk 339
  Display BookStor Charts and Graphs 340
  Exit the Graphics Program 361
  Charting Two Fields of Data.................... 362
 Summary 372

Part III
PC-Calc+

10 PC-Calc+: Getting Started **375**
 PC-Calc+: The Package............................ 376
 Back Up Your PC-Calc+ Disks 377
  Back Up the 5 1/4-inch Disk Set................ 378
  Back Up the 3 1/2-inch Disk 381
  Install PC-Calc+ 383
 Start PC-Calc+ 393
  The PC-Calc+ Screen........................... 395
  Get Help Anytime and Anywhere 398
  Quit PC-Calc+ 402
 Getting to Know PC-Calc+ in 30 Minutes........... 405
 Summary 418

11	**Building a Spreadsheet**	**421**
	Load and Zap a Spreadsheet	422
	Build the Budget Spreadsheet	431
	Create Titles and Column Headings	433
	Create the Budget Category Labels	439
	Enter January Data	442
	Compute February Data	444
	Copy February Formulas into the March Column	446
	Edit March Formulas	449
	Add Up Each Month's Expenses	450
	Look at the Spreadsheet Formulas	454
	Use a Spreadsheet for "What If?" Questions	456
	Summary	460
12	**Going Camping with a Spreadsheet**	**463**
	Building the Backpack Spreadsheet	466
	Format Titles and Column Headings	470
	Enter the BACKPACK Data	475
	Print BACKPACK	488
	Install the Price Formulas	495
	Install the Weight Formulas	498
	Create Summary Totals	499
	Reformat the Price Summary Total	502
	Summary	504
13	**Importing, Graphing, and Other Features**	**507**
	Back Up the BACKPACK File	508
	Use the "Split Screen" Command	509
	Split the Screen Horizontally	510
	Split the Screen Vertically	516
	Use Split Screen Synchronization	518
	Sort Data on the Spreadsheet	521
	Print the Spreadsheet and Use Tables	529

Import Spreadsheet Data............................	536
Graph Spreadsheet Data	543
Activate the Graph Command..................	544
How to Read the Chart	547
The Graphics Menu............................	549
Leave the Graphics Program...................	560
Graph Multiple Columns	560
Summary	567

Part IV
General Information for PC Users

A	**DOS Essentials**..	**573**
	Starting DOS..	574
	Types of Systems	574
	Load DOS from Disk Drive A..................	575
	Load DOS on a Hard Disk System	577
	The Default Drive	579
	DOS Commands..	580
	The CLS Command.............................	581
	The DIR Command.............................	582
	The FORMAT Command.......................	585
	The DISKCOPY Command....................	587
	The COPY Command...........................	589
	The DEL Command.............................	590
B	**ASCII Codes**...	**591**

Part V
PC-Write Resource Information

C PC-Write Command Summary..................... **601**
  Starting PC-Write.................................. 602
    Create a New File Using the Opening Menu 602
    Create a New File Without Using the Opening
      Menu.. 603
    Create a New File, Bypassing the Initial Prompt.. 604
    Load an Existing File Using the Opening Menu .. 604
    Load an Existing File Without Using the Opening
      Menu.. 605
    Edit a File, Bypassing the Initial Prompt, with No
      Backup File................................... 606
    Start with a Directory on the Screen............. 606
  Managing Files in the Editing Screen 606
    Obtain a Help Screen 606
    Save a File and Exit the Edit Program 607
    Save a File and Continue Editing................ 607
    Exit Without Saving the File 607
    Load a Different File to the Editing Screen....... 607
    Display a Directory 608
    Name the File in the Editing Screen............. 608
    Delete a File.................................. 608
  Entering, Editing, and Formatting Text.............. 609
    Move the Cursor Around a File 609
    Toggle Automatic Reformatting and Wordwrap... 609
    Manually Reformat a Paragraph................. 610
    Toggle Between Pushright (Push) and Overwrite
      (Over).. 610
    Delete Characters, Words, and Lines 610

    Copy a Block of Text 611
    Delete a Block of Text 611
    Move a Block of Text 611
    Unmark a Marked Block 611
    Undelete a Block of Text 612
Changing the Ruler Line 612
    Display the Current Ruler Line on the Screen 612
    Embed a Ruler Line in a File 612
    Change the Left Margin in the Current Ruler
        Line 613
    Change the Right Margin in the Current Ruler
        Line 613
    Set a Tab Stop in the Current Ruler Line 613
    Split the Screen into Columns. 613
Formatting Printed Page Layout 614
    Select a Regular Print Font 614
    Turn Off a Font 614
    Set Multiple Line Spacing 616
    Set a Top Margin. 616
    Set a Bottom Margin. 616
    Add Leading Spaces to All Printed Lines (Left
        Margin). 616
    Toggle Between Show Mode and Hide Mode. 616
    Enter a Hard Page Break (Hard Break). 617
    Delete a Hard Page Break (Hard Break) 617
    Enter a Soft Page Break (Soft Break) 617
    Delete a Soft Page Break (Soft Break). 617
    Repage an Entire File 617
    Repage and Reformat an Entire File. 618
    Create a Header. 618
    Create a Footer. 618
    Print Automatic Page Numbers 618
    Print Header or Footer Text Flush Left 618

	Print Header or Footer Text Flush Right	619
	Center Header or Footer Text	619
D	**Files Used by PC-Write**	**621**
	Program Disk Files	
	(3 1/2-inch Disk or 5 1/4-inch Disk)................	622
	Utility Disk Files (5 1/4-inch Disk)....................	623
	Reference Disk Files (5 1/4-inch Disk)	625
	Utility/Reference Disk Files (3 1/2-inch Disk).........	628
E	**Creating a PC-Write Work Disk**	**629**
F	**Transferring Files Between PC-Write Version 3 and**	
	Other Programs.............................	**637**
	ASCII Files..................................	638
	Export an ASCII File from PC-Write	638
	Import an ASCII File to PC-Write..............	640
	WordStar Files	641
	Import a WordStar File to PC-Write............	641
	Export a File from PC-Write to WordStar........	642
	Files from Early Versions of PC-Write	642

Part VI
PC-File+ Resource Information

G	**PC-File+ Keystroke and Command Summary**	**647**
	Special Keys for Use When Typing	648
	Special Keys for Use in the PC-File+ Editor..........	650
	Editing Commands	651
	Smart Key Simulation Codes......................	652
	Edit Masks, Automatic Fields, Constants, and	
	Calculations................................	653
	Report Commands and Controls	657

H	Files on the PC-File+ Disks........................	661
I	Transferring Files Between PC-File+ and Other Programs..	665

Part VII
PC-Calc+ Resource Information

J	PC-Calc+ Keystrokes, Commands, and Functions....	671
	Different Ways to Start PC-Calc+	672
	PC-Calc+ Special Command Keys....................	673
	Keys that Move the Cell Pointer.....................	674
	Keys That Move the Cursor on the Edit Line.....	676
	PC-Calc+ Menu Command Summary	677
	PC-Calc+ Computational Functions	679
K	Files on the PC-Calc+ Disks	687
L	Transferring Files Between PC-Calc+ and Other Programs..	691

Part VIII
Other Useful Resource Information

M	Transferring Files Between PC-Write, PC-File+, and PC-Calc+..	695
	Transfer Files to and from PC-Write.................	696
	Transfer Files to and from PC-File+	697
	Transfer Files to and from PC-Calc+	698

N	**Other Shareware Programs**............................	**699**
	Word Processing Programs and Utilities	700
	Database Programs and Utilities.....................	702
	Spreadsheet Programs and Utilities..................	703
O	**User Groups**	**705**
	Index	**723**

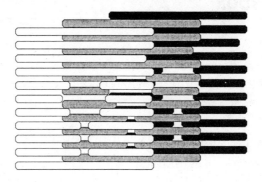

Introduction

In this book, each of the three shareware products is introduced through hands-on, tutorial sessions with your computer. As you explore the tutorial examples, you learn most of each product's key features. In addition, you see how the products can be used by yourself and others in both business and personal computing situations. The lower cost of shareware packages does not mean that the products are not powerful computing tools. As you will soon learn, products like the ones covered in this book represent state-of-the-art software technology—technology made affordable by the innovative shareware methods of product distribution.

About This Book

The Shareware Book gives you three easy-to-use, book-length tutorials plus a lot of helpful information about three major software packages:

- PC-Write, a full-featured word processing system
- PC-File+, a powerful database management program
- PC-Calc+, a sophisticated electronic spreadsheet

These products are part of the collection of "user-supported" software known as *shareware*. Under the shareware distribution concept, you get to "try before you buy." You can obtain evaluation copies of the three programs for practically the cost of the disks. Later, if you decide to use a product and would like complete documentation and technical support, you register your copy and pay a modest fee. Most of the fee goes directly to the author of the product and not into advertising budgets.

Tens of thousands of people have evaluated, used, and registered their copies of the shareware programs talked about in this book. Recently, all three products were upgraded extensively. Many old features were improved; many new features were added.

With this book, both long-time and first-time users of these shareware programs can learn how these newer versions of the programs work. The easy-to-follow tutorial approach that introduces each package shows you how to get started and leads you through fully integrated examples accompanied by many images of the products' screens. When you complete the tutorial sections, you will be able to generate professional-quality documents, create useful databases, and produce electronic spreadsheets with these three popular, reasonably priced, full-featured software products.

About the Three Shareware Packages

Recent surveys of how people use computers and what programs they use most frequently indicate that the top three activities on IBM PC and compatible computers involve

- Use of programs for word processing and for document preparation
- Maintenance of files of information with database management tools
- Calculation of data using electronic spreadsheet packages

The products highlighted in *The Shareware Book* encompass these three application areas and exemplify the kinds of software used by people in the surveys. These shareware products are not the most commonly used word processing, database management, and electronic spreadsheet programs, but they do represent a significant share of the software being used today.

PC-Write

Over 100,000 people around the world use PC-Write. PC-Write is published by QuickSoft, Inc., a company founded and run by Bob Wallace, one of the pioneers of the shareware industry.

PC-Write is one of the top ten full-featured word processors in use today. The program has enough power to produce a book (much of *The Shareware Book* was written using PC-Write), a multi-page report, a company newsletter, or a marketing brochure. PC-Write can also be used to write letters, make notes, and jot down ideas.

PC-Write helps you produce polished, high-quality printed materials. The program's page layout and extensive formatting commands give you control of the printed page. PC-Write's spelling checker helps you spot and correct spelling mistakes quickly.

QuickSoft, Inc., also offers a number of PC-Write utility programs that make it easy to use laser printer fonts, convert PC-Write files for use in other programs, and type documents in other languages such as French and Hebrew. Other programs help you check style, find grammatical errors, and improve the readability of your documents.

PC-File+

PC-File+ is a general-purpose database management package produced by ButtonWare, Inc. Jim Button, the founder and chief operating officer of ButtonWare, Inc., was also a shareware industry pioneer. He created the first version of PC-File back in the early 1980s. Over the years, the original PC-File program has been modified and expanded into the robust database management tool now called PC-File+.

All ButtonWare products have an estimated installed base of over 700,000 users throughout the world. For that reason, PC-File+ is available for use in over a dozen languages in addition to English.

PC-File+ combines power with ease of use so that you can build, maintain, and work with files containing dozens or thousands of pieces of information. Each complete entry in a PC-File+ database can contain up to 4000 characters of data. The program supports numerous commands that let you create and print reports, print mailing labels, produce form letters, graph data in a variety of formats, and generally search, sort, and perform calculations on any data elements.

PC-File+ also allows you to retrieve data from other database files as well as export and import data to and from files that can be read by other programs. For new database users, PC-File+ has a "teach mode" and many help screens that tell you exactly what to do at the point you ask for help.

Whether you use PC-File+ to maintain your personal address and telephone numbers or your company's personnel and inventory records, you will find PC-File+ easy to learn to use. And, when you need the power of a major database management tool, PC-File+ is ready to respond with all the features and capabilities you expect.

PC-Calc+

PC-Calc+ is also one of the ButtonWare, Inc., packages. It provides sophisticated computing at a truly affordable price. For less than the cost of several boxes of disks, you can be calculating and computing like a professional.

PC-Calc+ is an electronic spreadsheet package that helps you tabulate, organize, and calculate data by using the power, speed, and accuracy of your personal computer. Instead of writing equations yourself, you let the preprogrammed PC-Calc+ mathematical, statistical, financial, and business functions do the work. And when you finish specifying a spreadsheet and performing the required calculations, you use the many PC-Calc+ commands to print reports, plot your data and results, and export final data to other programs.

PC-Calc+ supports all the features you would expect in one of today's indispensable computerized calculational tools. The program offers extensive help messages, screen-splitting capabilities, full formatting options, and title-locking features. PC-Calc+ prints either the entire spreadsheet or selected sections to any printer, to your disk, or to the screen.

With PC-Calc+ you can create electronic spreadsheets with as many as 256 columns or 8000 rows of information, limited only by the size of your computer's memory.

How This Book Is Organized

The Shareware Book has four major sections: a tutorial section for each of the three shareware products, and a detailed set of appendixes. Each of the three shareware products (PC-Write, PC-File+, and PC-Calc+) has its own set of tutorial chapters, in which you learn how to start up and use the shareware program, and a part in the appendixes that provides summary information related to the program.

In most cases, you are expected to start with the first tutorial chapter for a particular product, proceed from there to the remaining tutorial chapters, and conclude by examining the associated appendixes as needed. Each block of tutorial chapters for the individual shareware products is completely self-contained and does not reference or rely on the tutorial chapters for the other products.

Getting Started Chapters

The introductory chapter for each shareware product shows you how to get started with that particular software package. The material in these chapters (Chapter 1 for PC-Write, Chapter 6 for PC-File+, and Chapter 10 for PC-Calc+) includes any required information about making backup disks, installing the programs, creating work disks, and starting up the programs for the very first time.

In addition, these introductory chapters also take you on a 30-minute tour of each product where you learn how to activate the main programs and perform tasks that create an initial document, a simple database, and your first electronic spreadsheet. Within each of these beginning chapter mini-tutorials, you learn the four or five most frequently used product commands and functions.

Tutorial Chapters

The main tutorial chapters for each of the shareware products lead you through the major product commands and features. In PC-Write's tutorial chapters, you begin by writing a simple letter in Chapter 2. In Chapter 3, you create more complex documents, such as a business letter. In Chapters 4 and 5, you explore PC-Write's extensive formatting and page-layout capabilities on documents that extend beyond a single page of text.

For PC-File+, you build a simple address file in Chapter 7. You use that file to produce form letters and mailing labels in Chapter 8. You conclude your explorations with Chapter 9, where you generate and plot data from a database used in monitoring the operations of a bookstore.

In Chapter 11, you use PC-Calc+ to create a simple electronic spreadsheet that fits on a single computer screen. Then, in Chapter 12, you explore building a unique, multi-screen spreadsheet for an application dealing with a journey back in time to 30,000 B.C. To conclude, in Chapter 13 you examine the PC-Calc+ sorting and graphing features, using the electronic spreadsheets you produced in the previous tutorial chapters.

All the tutorial chapters focus on two aspects of using the shareware packages: introducing you to as many product features and capabilities as possible, and showing how the software can be used to build meaningful applications for your home and business. When you complete the tutorial chapters for a particular shareware product, you are ready to use the program on your own. You will know enough about the package to start using it effectively for both your personal and business needs.

Appendixes

The appendixes in this book are organized into five subsections. The first two appendixes contain general information that you might find useful at any time, no matter which shareware package you are exploring. Appendix A contains brief and concise information about using DOS, the disk operating system on your computer. If you are a totally new user of personal computers, you may need to refer to Appendix A for information about using the various DOS commands.

Appendix B lists the standard ASCII codes. The table of codes correlates how your computer interprets the characters you see on your screen and on your printer, within the computer. You may need to refer to these tables occasionally.

Appendixes C through F are for use with PC-Write only. Appendix C contains the PC-Write command summary. A recap of the files and file conventions used by PC-Write appears in Appendix D. Appendix E discusses how to install PC-Write on several different computer configurations. Appendix F examines how to transfer files created by earlier versions of PC-Write into PC-Write version 3.

PC-File+ supplemental information can be found in Appendixes G through I. Appendix G contains the PC-File+ command summary and editing conventions. The PC-File+ file conventions are detailed in Appendix H. Appendix I tells you how to transfer files created by earlier versions of the PC-File program to PC-File+ version 3.

Appendixes J through L apply to the PC-Calc+ program. The PC-Calc+ command, function, and editing conventions appear in

Appendix J. PC-Calc+ file conventions and program names are listed and discussed in Appendix K. Files created by earlier versions of PC-Calc can be transferred to PC-Calc+ version 2 using the information in Appendix L.

The three remaining appendixes provide general information. Appendix M discusses how to move files between the three shareware products used in this book. Appendix N lists information about other shareware programs and services. Appendix O provides you with a representative list of user groups throughout the world.

Conventions Used in This Book

To assist the reader, several typographic conventions are maintained in all the sections of this book. The conventions help you to distinguish narrative text from items that you will be asked to type and from shareware program messages that are reproduced on these pages.

When you are asked to enter data you will see the word "Type:" on one line, the data to be typed on the next line (in boldface characters), and if needed, an instruction to press the key that terminates the data entry. The last item will often be on a third line. The entire data entry block will appear as follows:

Type:
the data goes here
and press ENTER

Any keys that you are asked to press will appear in small capitals, like the word ENTER in the last example. In many places throughout the tutorials, you will be instructed to press one or more keys to activate a menu or menu option. In those cases, you will see the word "Press" followed by the key or keys to be pressed. Each separate key press will be separated by a comma. Several examples follow:

Press ENTER
Press F10
Press F1, A, ESC, ENTER

The first example line instructs you to press the ENTER key. The second line asks you to press the F10 key, a function key on the keyboard. The third line instructs you to press four keys consecutively: the F1 function key, the key with the letter A, the escape key (ESC), and finally the ENTER key.

In cases requiring that you simultaneously press a set of keys as a combination, a hyphen (-) appears between the keys to be pressed. In general, when you are making combination key presses, you hold down the first key or keys in the sequence and press the final key to issue the combined keystroke. Examples of some combination keystrokes you might see are as follows:

Press CTRL-A
Press ALT-TAB
Press ALT-SHIFT-DEL

The first example asks you to hold down the CTRL key and then press the letter A. The second example instructs you to hold down the ALT key and press the TAB key. The final example asks you to hold down *both* the ALT and the SHIFT keys, and press the DEL key.

Messages being displayed by the shareware program appear as follows:

```
This is what a program message might look like.
```

Shareware screen messages are printed in this book in a font that resembles the display on the computer screen.

The Shareware Revolution

The shareware revolution began as the Freeware revolution. (Freeware is a trademark of Headlands Press, Inc.) In the early 1980s, Andrew Fluegelman created the first Freeware product, PC-Talk. He started out by giving the program away. He also put a request on the product's opening screen asking users to send him a small amount of money to help defray his future development costs. As Andrew received feedback from his Freeware user base he made changes and improvements to the original product. The demand for PC-Talk increased as the product improved and people heard about the concept of Freeware.

One of the people who heard about Freeware was Jim Button. At about the same time Andrew Fluegelman began sending out Freeware, Jim Button began distributing his first product, PC-File, as "user-supported software." One of Jim's first PC-File customers told him about PC-Talk and the similarity of marketing concepts. Jim and Andrew contacted each other and began to reference each other's products on their distribution disks.

The third person to enter this arena was Bob Wallace. Bob not only contributed a product to the revolution, PC-Write, but he pioneered the concept of paying commissions to users who get other people to register a copy of the product. Bob also coined the term "shareware" to encompass the kind of product distribution concepts begun by Andrew Fluegelman and Jim Button.

Today, shareware has come to mean a kind of distribution method that puts evaluation copies of software products into people's hands, easily and inexpensively. Generally, for only the cost of the disks, you can examine shareware products to see if they meet your needs.

Under the shareware agreements that are part of every shareware product, you can only use the evaluation copy for a reasonable time period. If you want to continue using the program beyond the evaluation period, you must register the program with the copyright holder.

Full product registration often brings you a box full of support literature, a current version of the software, technical support, newsletters, source code where available, commissions for some products when you get others to register, and many special discounts. Under the shareware distribution concept, your registration fees support product improvements and new product developments, not advertising and marketing budgets.

By registering your copies of the shareware products, you also become a participant in the shareware revolution—a vital link in helping further a concept that continues to make quality software products available to everyone at a reasonable price.

The book's authors fully support the concept of shareware and encourage you to participate in the shareware revolution. Locate the latest copies of PC-Write, PC-File+, and PC-Calc+, and use the exercises in this book to help you evaluate how these products can assist you in your home or office. When you complete your evaluations, register the products you plan to continue using. Then, give this book and a copy of the shareware disks to another person—someone who will join *you* in the shareware revolution.

If you wish to contact the authors about this book or other shareware programs and ideas, write to them at the following address:

The Shareware Teacher
c/o PC-SIG, Inc.
1030D East Duane Ave.
Sunnyvale CA 94086

Additional Help from Osborne/McGraw-Hill

Osborne/McGraw-Hill provides top-quality books for computer users at every level of computing experience. To help you build your skills, we suggest that you look for the books in the following Osborne series that best address your needs.

The "Teach Yourself" Series is perfect for people who have never used a computer before or who want to gain confidence in using program basics. These books provide a simple, slow-paced introduction to the fundamental uses of popular software packages and programming languages. The "Mastery Skills Check" format ensures your understanding concepts thoroughly before you progress to new material. Plenty of examples and exercises (with answers at the back of the book) are used throughout the text.

The "Made Easy" Series is also for beginners or users who may need a refresher on the new features of an upgraded product. These in-depth introductions guide users step-by-step from the program basics to intermediate-level usage. Plenty of "hands-on" exercises and examples are used in every chapter.

The "Using" Series presents fast-paced guides that cover beginning concepts quickly and move on to intermediate-level techniques and some advanced topics. These books are written for users already familiar with computers and software who want to get up to speed fast with a certain product.

The "Advanced" Series assumes that the reader is a user who has reached at least an intermediate skill level and is ready to learn more sophisticated techniques and refinements.

"The Complete Reference" Series provides handy desktop references for popular software and programming languages that list every command, feature, and function of the product along with brief but detailed descriptions of how they are used. Books are fully indexed and often include tear-out command cards. "The Complete Reference" series is ideal for both beginners and pros.

"The Pocket Reference" Series is a pocket-sized, shorter version of "The Complete Reference" series. It provides the essential commands, features, and functions of software and programming languages for users of every level who need a quick reminder.

The "Secrets, Solutions, Shortcuts" Series is written for beginning users who are already somewhat familiar with the software and for experienced users at intermediate and advanced levels. This series provides clever tips, points out shortcuts for using the software to greater advantage, and indicates traps to avoid.

Osborne/McGraw-Hill also publishes many fine books that are not included in the series described here. If you have questions about which Osborne books are right for you, ask the salesperson at your local book or computer store, or call us toll-free at 1-800-262-4729.

Other Osborne/McGraw-Hill Books of Interest to You

We hope that *The Shareware Book* will assist you in mastering telecommunications, and will also pique your interest in learning about other ways to better use your computer.

If you're interested in expanding your skills so you can be even more computer efficient, be sure to take advantage of Osborne/McGraw-Hill's large selection of top-quality computer books, which cover all varieties of popular hardware, software, programming languages, and operating systems. While we cannot list every title here that may relate to telecommunications and to your special computing needs, here are just a few books that complement *The Shareware Book*.

If you are just starting out with DOS, look for *DOS Made Easy* by Herbert Schildt, a step-by-step, in-depth introduction to PC-DOS and MS-DOS through version 3.3. Or see *DOS 4 Made Easy,* also by Herbert Schildt, if you use PC-DOS or MS-DOS version 4.0.

If you're looking for an intermediate-level book, see *Using MS-DOS* by Kris Jamsa, which covers all DOS versions through 3.3. It's a fast-paced, hands-on guide organized into 15-minute sessions that quickly cover basics before discussing intermediate techniques and some advanced topics. If you have DOS version 4, see *Using DOS 4,* also by Kris Jamsa.

For all PC-DOS and MS-DOS users, from beginners who are somewhat familiar with the program to veteran users, with any DOS version up·to 3.3, see *DOS: The Complete Reference, Second Edition* by Kris Jamsa. This book provides comprehensive coverage of every DOS command and feature. Whether you need an overview of the disk operating system or a reference for advanced programming and disk management techniques, you'll find it here.

If you're a spreadsheet beginner looking for a step-by-step introduction to Lotus 1-2-3, see *1-2-3 Made Easy* (for releases 1A, 2.0 and 2.01), *1-2-3 Release 2.2 Made Easy,* or *1-2-3 Release 3 Made Easy.* All are written by Lotus expert Mary Campbell.

For developing intermediate skills, look for *Using 1-2-3 Release 2.2* by The LeBlond Group or *Using 1-2-3 Release 3,* by Martin and Carole Matthews.

1-2-3: The Complete Reference, by Mary Campbell, is an ideal desktop encyclopedia for all Lotus 1-2-3 users, from beginners who know some basics to veteran users. This book provides brief, in-depth descriptions of every 1-2-3 command, function, and feature and covers 1-2-3 versions 1A and 2.0. If you have another version of 1-2-3, see *1-2-3 Release 2.2: The Complete Reference* or *1-2-3 Release 3: The Complete Reference.* Both are written by Mary Campbell.

Why This Book Is for You

Who can benefit from this book? In two words, almost anybody. This book's tutorial examples can be used by people who know practically nothing about computers and by computing professionals who want a quick tour of the shareware products' capabilities. The only assumption made is that you know a little about your computer's disk operating system, or DOS environment. For people who know nothing about DOS, the book provides an introduction to DOS.

For beginners, the step-by-step tutorials with numerous screen images provide a comprehensive, self-paced way to learn how the products work. Beginners also learn how the software gets used in both office and home situations.

For the professional, the same tutorials provide a streamlined, integrated way to learn how to get the products up and running and how the many features of the products fit together to produce usable applications. Professional computer users may find that the few hours spent going over the tutorials in this book will save many hours of time actually using the products. The tutorial examples present the products' features in an easy-to-digest, logical flow. Also, professionals who train new users in one or more of the shareware products may choose to direct people to this book first. The extensive tutorial sessions can save everyone hours of time learning key product features and capabilities.

When you complete each section of this book, you will discover that you have a thorough working knowledge of the presented shareware product. You will know enough about the product to proceed on your own confidently, using the product as one of your everyday home or office computing tools.

Learn More about Shareware

Here is another excellent Osborne/McGraw-Hill book that will help you build your computer skills and maximize the power of shareware.

If you're looking for the best way to get started in telecommunications with shareware or how to get more out of the on-line services available today, see *Dvorak's Guide to PC Telecommunications* by John C. Dvorak and Nick Anis. This book/disk package, written by the internationally recognized computer columnist John Dvorak with programming whiz Nick Anis, shows you how to instantly plug into the world of electronic databases, bulletin boards, and on-line services. The package includes an easy-to-read comprehensive guide plus two disks loaded with outstanding free software. It is of value to computer users at every skill level.

PART

1

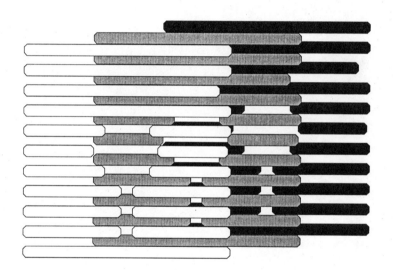

PC-Write

CHAPTER 1

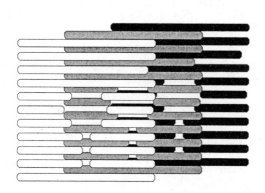

PC-Write: Getting Started

PC-Write is one of the top ten full-featured word processors on the market today. PC-Write allows you to create, edit, format, and print text-based documents. Using a computer and a program like PC-Write to perform all these tasks is called *word processing*.

You can use PC-Write to word process a letter, an essay, a newsletter, a textbook, or a novel. The authors used PC-Write to write some of the chapters in this book.

PC-Write has an impressive array of features to assist you in processing words, including a complete set of editing tools, a spelling checker, powerful formatting capabilities, and the ability to print text with headers, footers, footnotes, and end notes. You can edit text in multiple columns, and split the screen so that you can work on two documents at once. PC-Write is fast, flexible, and powerful.

In this chapter, you will begin to use PC-Write. In particular, you will

- Learn about the PC-Write disks, tutorial, and reference guide
- Learn how to print the PC-Write tutorial and users' guide from disk
- Learn about the WORKDISK file used to create a customized PC-Write work disk for your computer
- Use your work disk for a brief tour of PC-Write
- Create a simple PC-Write file, save it to a disk, and print it on your printer

It is assumed that you have some knowledge of the Microsoft Disk Operating System (*MS-DOS*), or of *PC-DOS*, the version of MS-DOS licensed to IBM. In particular, you should know the following DOS commands:

DIR	The directory command lists the names of all files on a directory
FORMAT	Formats a disk. A new disk must be formatted before it can be used. A previously used disk can be recycled, but do so with caution; formatting erases previously stored information from the disk
DISKCOPY	Copies everything on one disk to another disk
COPY	Copies named files, or groups of named files

For more information about DOS, see Appendix A, "DOS Essentials."

PC-Write, the Package

PC-Write is published by Quicksoft, 219 First Ave. N. #224, Seattle, Washington 98109. The complete PC-Write package consists of two books and a set of disks containing the many files that give you the power of PC-Write. The disk set consists of either two 3 1/2-inch disks or three 5 1/4-inch disks. The books are described briefly as follows:

- *PC-Write User's Guide* is a 480-page book that contains an introduction to PC-Write, an introduction to computers and DOS, a PC-Write tutorial, and comprehensive reference information.
- *PC-Write 3.0 Quick Guide* is a 64-page booklet designed to help you quickly find information.

If you have a PC-Write disk set, but do not have the above books, you can obtain them by registering your copy of PC-Write. Registration entitles you to the following:

- Registration number for support calls and commissions
- Hardbound user's guide with 480 pages of information about how to use PC-Write's many features and options
- Quick Guide and Quick Card for reference
- Current disk set (PC-Write is updated regularly)
- Telephone support for one year
- Quarterly newsletter with news and tips, for one year
- Two free disk sets with your choice of updates or utilities
- Source code available as an update, in Pascal and assembly
- $25 commission when someone uses your copy of PC-Write to register

- Special discounts on add-on products in the Quicksoft Catalog, such as grammar checkers, thesaurus, graphics, and fonts

Registration produces other benefits:

- **You support new PC-Write developments** Because users register, PC-Write is now one of the top ten word processors in popularity and capability, and it undergoes continual enhancement. Registration fees pay for the technical staff needed to provide technical support for PC-Write users and to create new updates.
- **You support the shareware concept** Shareware allows you to try the software before you buy it. You pay a reasonable price for your software. You avoid the frustration of copy protection. By supporting shareware publishers, you encourage other vendors to use the shareware approach.

If you need multiple copies of PC-Write for your company, school, or other organization, call Quicksoft about group and campus licenses at (800) 888-8088.

The PC-Write Disk Sets

The PC-Write disk set consists of either three 5 1/4-inch disks or two 3 1/2-inch disks. Both disk sets are briefly described in the sections that follow.

The 5 1/4-inch Disk Set If your computer uses a 5 1/4-inch disk drive, your PC-Write disk set should include the following three disks:

- **Disk 1 is the program disk** It contains the PC-Write main program file (ED.EXE), and the WORKDISK.BAT program used to create a PC-Write work disk for your computer.

- **Disk 2 is the utility disk** This disk contains a copy of the WORKDISK.BAT file and several other files used in the creation of a work disk.

- **Disk 3 is the reference disk** It contains the files necessary for installing the spelling checker and dictionary on your work disk. It also has the tutorial and Quick Guide in crunched (compressed) file format, along with the PRINTMAN.COM program, which uncrunches and prints the files.

The 3 1/2-inch Disk Set If your computer uses a 3 1/2-inch disk drive, you should have a PC-Write disk set with the following two disks:

- **Disk 1 is the program disk** It contains the PC-Write main program file (ED.EXE) and the WORKDISK.BAT program used to create a PC-Write work disk for your computer.

- **Disk 2 is the utility/reference disk** It contains a copy of the WORKDISK.BAT file and files used in the creation of a work disk. It also contains files for installing the spelling checker and dictionary. Disk 2 also includes the tutorial and Quick Guide in crunched (compressed) file format, along with a program (PRINTMAN.COM) that uncrunches and prints the files.

Protect Your Disks

To protect your disks from accidental erasure and over-writing, you should *write-protect* your disks. To write-protect your disks, follow the appropriate procedure for your disk set, as follows:

- If you have the 5 1/4-inch disk set, put an opaque (write-protect) tab over the write-protect notch on each disk. An example of a write-protect notch is shown in Figure 1-1.

- If you have 3 1/2-inch disks, slide the write-protect switch to the *no-write* position on each disk. When this switch covers the small opening, the disk can be written to and erased; when the

Figure 1-1.

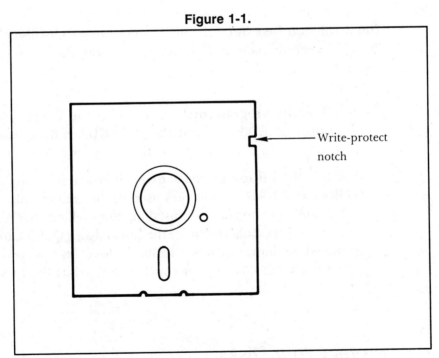

A write-protect notch on a 5 1/4-inch disk

small opening is uncovered, the disk is protected from erasure and cannot be written to. An example of the write-protect switch is shown in Figure 1-2.

Figure 1-2.

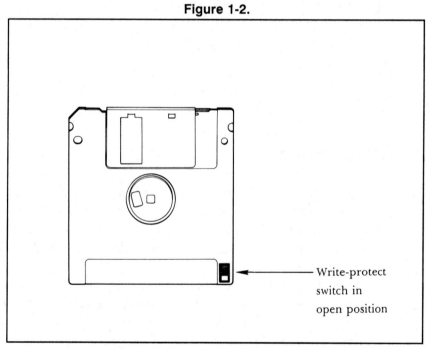

A write-protect switch on a 3 1/2-inch disk

Figure 1-3.

```
A>dir

 Volume in drive A has no label
 Directory of  A:\

GO        BAT        12   5-18-86   8:32p
READ      ME       1012  11-10-88   3:06p
GETYN     COM       161  11-11-88   6:25p
WORKDISK  BAT      6241   5-04-89   2:44p
INSTALL   DOC      5865   5-04-89   2:39p
ED        EXE    260912   4-30-89   5:23p
ED        HLP     72684   5-04-89   2:24p
ED        DEF        97  10-26-88   3:47a
ED        TRS      1017   5-04-89   2:22p
ED        SPC       886  10-25-88   2:02a
PROGRAM   DIR       950   5-04-89   2:56p
       11 File(s)      375808 bytes free
```

Files on the PC-Write program disk

Directories

Use the DOS DIR command to display the names of the files on each disk in your disk set. Figure 1-3 shows the directory of the files on the 3 1/2-inch program disk. The 5 1/4-inch program disk will list the same file names, but the number of bytes free will be much smaller.

You can use the DIR command to print the directory on your printer. This is especially useful for directories that are too long to display on one screen. Make sure that your printer is ready and that the DOS prompt for the appropriate directory and the cursor are on the screen (for example: A>_). Then, do the following:

Type:
dir > prn
and press ENTER

Use the DIR > PRN command to print the directories of all the disks in your PC-Write disk set. See Appendix D, "Files Used by PC-Write," for directory listings of all the disks in both disk sets.

 NOTE You can type DOS commands and file names in lowercase letters, uppercase letters, or any combination of both. For example, you can type the DIR command as **DIR, dir, Dir** or **diR** and type a file name as **WORKDISK.BAT, workdisk.bat,** or **Work-Disk.Bat**.

On-Disk Information

The program disk contains the GO.BAT file, a short program that provides information about PC-Write. If you run GO.BAT, it loads the READ.ME file to the screen. To run the GO.BAT program on a dual floppy system, put the program disk in drive A. (Throughout this book, unless otherwise indicated, it is assumed that you are using a dual floppy system with the program disk in drive A. If your system is set up differently, you will, of course, respond to a different prompt—the C prompt, for instance, if your program is installed on a hard disk.) At the A prompt (A>) do the following:

Type:
go
and press ENTER

Figure 1-4 shows the resulting screen.

GO.BAT uses the DOS TYPE command to display the READ.ME file on the screen. You can use the DOS TYPE command to display any ASCII file. To display READ.ME, do the following:

Type:
type read.me
and press ENTER

Figure 1-4.

```
A>go

A>type read.me
                    Introduction to PC-Write 3.0 by Quicksoft

Welcome to PC-Write! This screen tells how to begin. The PC-Write Tutorial
and Quick Guide, and the Help screens, will help you do simple editing and
get a feel for PC-Write. To print them, use the WORKDISK command or insert
the Reference diskette in the default drive and enter the command PRINTMAN.
You'll need to register, or get a full manual, to use PC-Write effectively.

The batch command WORKDISK uses the three PC-Write 5.25 inch disks (two 3.5
inch disks) to make a working diskette or hard disk directory, make backup
copies of the disks, and type or print the Tutorial and Quick Guide. To use
it, put the Program diskette in the A drive, make A the default drive, and
enter the command WORKDISK.  Then follow the directions.

To start PC-Write, enter the command ED at the DOS prompt. You will see a
full screen menu to get you started. You can also give the name of a file
to edit after the ED command, as in ED B:MYFILE.
```

PC-Write's GO.BAT program puts READ.ME on the screen

You should see the same display as that shown in Figure 1-4. Most shareware programs include a READ.ME file and a GO.BAT program to help users get started.

Make Copies of Your Disk Set

Before you do anything else, make copies of your PC-Write disks. Then, put the original disks in a safe place and use the copies to make your PC-Write work disks. To make copies of your original PC-Write disks, follow these steps:

1. Write-protect your original disks, as described in the earlier section "Protect Your Disks."

2. Use the DOS FORMAT command to format several blank disks which will become the copies of the original disks. To format a disk, if you are using a dual floppy system, put your DOS disk into drive A, and at the A prompt:

   Type:
   format b:
   and press ENTER

   You will see a prompt to insert a disk in drive B. Put a blank disk in drive B and press any key. When the disk in drive B has been formatted, DOS will prompt you with a message somewhat like this one:

   ```
   362496 bytes total disk space
   362496 bytes available on disk
   ```

   and a query about formatting another disk. Press N to stop the format operation; press Y to format another disk.

3. Use the DOS DISKCOPY command to make copies of each PC-Write disk. To begin this process, put your DOS disk in drive A and, at the DOS A prompt, do the following:

   Type:
   diskcopy a: b:
   and press ENTER

   You will see a prompt to insert the source disk in drive A and the target disk in drive B. The source disk is the original PC-Write disk; the target disk is a blank formatted disk which will become a copy of the original PC-Write disk. Put both disks in the indicated drives and press any key to continue the disk copying. DOS will guide you with prompts. Follow the directions you see on the screen.

4. Label the copies to correspond with the original disks. Be sure to include the PC-Write version number, for instance, version 3.02, and the date you made the copies.

For more information on formatting and copying disks, see Appendix A, "DOS Essentials."

After you have made copies of your original PC-Write disks, put the original disks (copy-protected, of course) in a safe place. Use the copies to work with PC-Write.

 REMEMBER As you learn how to use PC-Write, share the magic with friends. Make copies of PC-Write, give them to others, work together, and learn together.

Create PC-Write Work Disks

A PC-Write work disk is a disk that you use to create, edit, and print documents customized for your computer system. To make a work disk, use the WORKDISK.BAT program on the PC-Write program disk (disk 1 in the disk set). Do not use the original PC-Write disks for this purpose; use the copies you made previously.

You can make a customized work disk to use with various disk drive configurations, including the following:

- Two 3 1/2-inch disk drives
- Two 5 1/4-inch disk drives
- Hard disk drive and one or more floppy disk drives

These configurations are described in the sections that follow. You only need to read the section that corresponds to your system.

Two 3 1/2-inch Disk Drives

If you are using 3 1/2-inch disks, you can make a *self-booting* work disk. All of the work and program files will fit on this one disk. The self-booting disk contains the DOS *COMMAND.COM* file, which enables you to start your computer without loading DOS from another disk. To make a self-booting disk, use the FORMAT command with the *slash-s (/s)* option. Insert your DOS disk in drive A, and, at the A prompt:

Type:
format b: /s
and press ENTER

You will see a prompt to insert a disk in drive B. Put a blank disk in drive B and follow the instructions on the screen. When the formatting process is complete, you will see a message similar to this one:

```
Format complete
System transferred

    730112 bytes total disk space
     68608 bytes used by system
    661504 bytes available on disk
```

This message is followed by a query about formatting another disk. Press N to stop the format operation; press Y to format another disk.

You can use the DOS DIR command to verify that the formatting process has copied the DOS COMMAND.COM file to the disk. You can also test the disk by using it to boot up your computer. First, turn off the computer. Then, put the disk in drive A and turn the computer back on. The computer should boot up, just as it would from your DOS disk.

To make a work disk, put a copy of the PC-Write program disk in drive A and the self-booting disk in drive B. Then, do the following:

Type:
workdisk b:
and press ENTER

The computer runs the WORKDISK.BAT program from the program disk in drive A. The program will ask you a series of questions about your system and about your preferences for customizing a work disk. You can answer most of these questions by pressing the Y key for "yes" and the N key for "no." Many of the questions will prompt you with a suggested response. In most cases, you can choose the suggested response. Be sure to answer Y for "yes" when asked if you want the reminder lines displayed. Many illustrations in the PC-Write chapters show these reminder lines.

If you need to stop the run and start over, press the CTRL key and the BREAK key simultaneously. If your keyboard does not have a BREAK key, press the CTRL key and the C key.

For more information on making a work disk, see Appendix E, "Creating a PC-Write Work Disk," for an annotated walk-through of the WORKDISK.BAT program.

Two 5 1/4-inch Disk Drives

There is not enough space on 5 1/4-inch disks to have all the work disk files on one disk. Two disks are required—a primary disk containing the most often used files and a secondary disk containing less frequently used files. Do not make self-booting work disks. Use the FORMAT command, without the /s option, to format both disks. To format a disk, put your DOS disk in drive A and, at the A prompt, do the following:

Type:
format b:
and press ENTER

You will see a prompt to insert a disk in drive B. Put a blank disk in drive B and follow the instructions on screen. When the formatting process is complete, you will see a message similar to this one:

```
Format complete
    362496 bytes total disk space
    362496 bytes available on disk
```

Format two blank disks to use them for your work disks. Then, put a copy of the PC-Write program disk in drive A and a formatted disk in drive B.

Type:
workdisk b:
and press ENTER

The computer runs the WORKDISK.BAT program from the program disk in drive A. The program will ask you a series of questions about your system and your preferences for customizing a work disk. You can answer most of these questions by pressing the Y key for "yes" or the N key for "no." Many of the questions will prompt you with a suggested response. In most cases, you can make the suggested response. Be sure to answer Y for "yes" when asked if you want reminder lines displayed. Many illustrations in the PC-Write chapters show these reminder lines.

If you need to stop the run and start over, you can do so by holding down the CTRL key and pressing the BREAK key. If your keyboard does not have a BREAK key, hold down the CTRL key and press the C key.

If you want more information on making a work disk, see Appendix E, "Creating a PC-Write Work Disk," for an annotated walk-through of the WORKDISK.BAT program.

A Hard Disk Drive System

If you have a hard disk system, you can install PC-Write on your hard disk. Rather than making a separate work disk, run the

WORKDISK.BAT program to make a working directory on your hard disk. The *PC-Write User's Guide* suggests installing PC-Write in a directory called "PCW."

To create a directory called PCW, go to the prompt for your hard disk (assumed to be drive C).

Type:
mkdir\pcw
and press ENTER

This creates a PC-Write working directory called PCW. If you prefer, you may substitute a different name for PCW. Next, change to drive A as follows:

Type:
a:
and press ENTER

Put a copy of the PC-Write program disk in drive A. At the A prompt:

Type:
workdisk c:\pcw
and press ENTER

The computer runs the WORKDISK.BAT program from the program disk in drive A. You will be asked a series of questions about your system and your preferences for customizing a work disk. You can answer most of these questions by pressing the Y key for "yes" or the N key for "no." Many of the questions will prompt you with a suggested response. In most cases, you can choose the suggested response. Be sure to answer Y for "yes" when asked if you want reminder lines displayed. Many illustrations in the PC-Write chapters show these reminder lines.

If you need to stop the run and start over, hold down the CTRL key and press the BREAK key. If your keyboard doesn't have a BREAK key, hold down the CTRL key and press the C key.

If you need more information on making a working directory, see Appendix E, "Creating a PC-File Work Disk," for an annotated walk-through of the WORKDISK.BAT program.

Label Your Work Disks and Check the Directories

If you made a 3 1/2-inch work disk, label it "PC-Write Master Work Disk." Make copies of the master disk and use the copies for your work. You may label the copies "PC-Write Work Disk" and include the date and configuration information on the label. Figure 1-5 shows a sample label for a master work disk made for a Tandy 1000TL with a CM-11 color monitor and DMP-132 printer.

If you made a set of two 5 1/4-inch work disks, label them so that you know which is which, perhaps "Master Work Disk—Primary" and "Master Work Disk—Secondary." Make copies, and then use the copies for your actual work.

Figure 1-5.

```
PC-Write    version 3.02
Master Work Disk    7-10-89
Tandy 1000TL
CM-11 Color Monitor
DMP-132 Printer
Use only to make copies
```

Label for master work disk

Figure 1-6 shows the directory of a self-booting 3 1/2-inch work disk. Since this disk was formatted using the /s option, it contains the DOS COMMAND.COM file. Figure 1-7 shows the directory of a 5 1/4-inch work disk. It was formatted without using the /s option and, therefore, does not have the DOS COMMAND.COM file required for self-booting disks. Note that this 5 1/4-inch disk does not contain WORDS.MAS, which is the file that contains the word list for the spelling checker. You should be able to find WORD.MAS on the second 5 1/4-inch disk in your work disk set.

PC-Write in 30 Minutes: A Guided Tour

Learning just a little bit about PC-Write will enable you to do a lot of work. The more you use PC-Write, however, the more proficient you will become. Begin with a brief tour of PC-Write. During

Figure 1-6.

```
A>dir

 Volume in drive A has no label
 Directory of  A:\

COMMAND  COM    23612   7-21-87   3:00p
ED       EXE   268912   4-30-89   5:23p
ED       HLP    72684   5-04-89   2:24p
ED       DEF     1146   7-11-89  10:56a
JUSTIFY  TST     4054  11-09-88   8:49p
CHARS    TST      994  10-26-88   3:50a
PRINT    TST     2008  11-10-88   3:35p
PR       DEF     4368   7-11-89  11:16a
WORDS    MAS   189912  12-02-88  11:48a
        9 File(s)    202752 bytes free
```

Directory of self-booting 3 1/2-inch work disk

Figure 1-7.

```
A>dir b:

Volume in drive B has no label
Directory of  B:\

ED       EXE    260912   4-30-89   5:23p
ED       HLP     72604   5-04-89   2:24p
ED       DEF      1146   7-11-89  10:56a
JUSTIFY  TST      4054  11-09-88   8:49p
CHARS    TST       994  10-26-88   3:50a
PRINT    TST      2000  11-10-88   3:35p
PR       DEF      4368   7-11-89  11:16a
        7 File(s)     14336 bytes free
```

Directory of 5 1/4-inch primary work disk

this tour, it is assumed that you will use a work disk in disk drive A. If you are using a different drive, change all references to drive A to references appropriate to your system. For example, if you are using a hard disk, the A prompt would become C:\PCW>. During this brief tour, you will do the following:

1. Load the main PC-Write program.

2. Use PC-Write's directory screen to view the names of the files on the work disk.

3. Browse through PC-Write's on-line help system.

4. Create a small file called WORK.DOC.

5. Save the WORK.DOC file you created to the work disk.

6. Print the WORK.DOC file.

Start Your Engines

If you have a self-booting work disk, put it in disk drive A and start your computer. If you are not using a self-booting disk, load DOS to get the A prompt on the screen, and then put a work disk in drive A.

> Type:
> **ed**
> and press ENTER

The computer loads the PC-Write (ED.EXE) program and displays the opening screen, as shown in Figure 1-8.
 The opening screen lists the function keys F1, F2, F6, F7, and F8, and briefly describes what each function key does.
 The F2 key exits PC-Write and returns you to DOS.

> Press F2

You return to DOS and see the DOS A prompt on an otherwise blank screen. Use the F2 key whenever you are finished using PC-Write to make a graceful return to DOS. Now, load the ED.EXE program again.

> Type:
> **ed**
> and press ENTER

The PC-Write opening screen appears back on the screen, as shown in Figure 1-8.

Press F8 to See a Directory

The F8 key is used to display a directory of files on any disk drive. To display a directory:

Press F8

The top line on the screen shows the following message:

```
Directory to display:  can include * and ? (Exc:cancel): "A:\*.*"
```

Figure 1-8.

```
(To get these options later when you are editing, press the F1:System/help key)

        Welcome to PC-Write, Version 3.02, by Quicksoft!
        Please press one of the following function keys:

        [F1]  Help......Give information about PC-Write operations and features.

        [F2]  Exit......Return back to DOS, saving the file you were working on.

        [F6]  File......Enter the name of a file to edit or create.

        [F7]  Print.....Enter the name of a file to print.

        [F8]  Dir.......Get a directory of disk files, pick one to edit or print.
```

PC-Write's opening screen

The computer is ready to display all files on disk drive A. You can cancel the operation by pressing the ESC key. The ESC returns you to the opening screen shown in Figure 1-8.

    Press ESC

The opening screen returns. In general, the ESC key can be used to escape from one screen to the previous screen. Now call up a directory of the files on drive A.

    Press F8

The top line on the screen should appear as shown here:

```
Directory to display:   can include * and ? (Esc:cancel): "A:\*.*"
```

Notice the blinking cursor (_) under the "A" in "A:*.*." If you press the ENTER key, PC-Write will display a directory of all files (*.*) on drive A.

    Press ENTER

A directory screen appears with the names of all files on the work disk in drive A. Figure 1-9 shows the directory screen listing the files on a 3 1/2-inch work disk used by the authors.

When you are finished with the directory screen, use the ESC key to return to the opening screen:

    Press ESC

You should now be back at the opening screen shown in Figure 1-8.

Press F1 to Get Help

PC-Write has an extensive on-line help system. Pressing the F1 key moves you from the opening screen to the first help screen.

   Press F1

You will see the first help screen, as shown in Figure 1-10. The top line tells you two ways to leave this screen. You can press either ESC or F1.

   Press ESC

You return to the opening screen. Press F1 to go to the help screen, and then press F1 again to return to the opening screen. After you are satisfied that you can come and go as you please, go back to the help screen and do some browsing.

Figure 1-9.

```
Pick a file with the arrow keys, then press F6 to edit the file or F7 to print.


A:\*.*                          Last drive is E:         202752 bytes free

 COMMAND.COM    23612   7-21-87   3:00p
      ED.EXE   260912   4-30-89   5:23p
      ED.HLP    72684   5-04-89   2:24p
      ED.DEF     1146   7-11-89  10:56a
  JUSTIFY.TST    4054  11-09-88   8:49p
    CHARS.TST     994  10-26-88   3:50a
    PRINT.TST    2008  11-10-88   3:35p
       PR.DEF    4368   7-11-89  11:16a
    WORDS.MAS  109912  12-02-88  11:48a
```

PC-Write directory screen showing work disk files

The top ten lines of the help screen list the kinds of help that are available. "Basic editing" is highlighted. In the middle of the screen you see "Using help screens." It tells you how to move around in the help system. The "More: PgDn" message in the lower right corner of the screen tells you that more help is available by pressing the PGDN key. Press the PGDN key to see more information on "Basic editing."

The arrow keys (↓↑→←) move the highlight from "Basic editing" to the other topics. As you move the highlight down the list, the information in the lower part of the screen will change. Use the arrow keys to select a topic, and then use the PGDN and PGUP keys to scroll up or down one line at a time. Hold down the SHIFT key and press PGDN or PGUP to scroll the help information one page at a time.

When you finish browsing, press ESC to leave the help system, and return to the opening screen.

Figure 1-10.

```
Esc: Help off, cancel,  F1: Help off, to last menu,  Arrows: Select Help topic:
Basic editing   Deleting text    Formatting       Page layout     Shortcuts
Auto-numbering  DOS commands     Headers/footers  Paragraph style Shorthand
Box operations  Dot lines        Index/contents   Printer setup   Spell checker
Change margins  Enhancing text   Margins/tabs     Printing        Status line
Characters      Entering text    Marking text     Problem solving Switching files
Columns         File conversion  Measuring        Recording keys  Typewriter mode
Control files   File management  Merging          Repaging        Windows
Copy/move text  Find/replace     Misc.operations  Ruler lines     Support service
Cursor moves    Footnotes        Page elements    Shell to DOS    Shareware
BASIC EDITING

Using help screens
Use the four arrow keys, Home, End, and Tab key to select a topic.
Use the PgUp and PgDn keys to scroll a long help screen, like this one.
Shifted PgUp and PgDn keys scroll a screenfull at once.

File Operations
1. Create or load a file   A>ED filename
2. Enter text              type on keyboard
3. Save the text to disk   Press F1 F3
4. Edit the text           Bksp, Del, Ins
5. Print the file          Press F1 then F7
6. Save the file, exit     Press F1 then F2
                                                                More:PgDn
```

First help screen

Create a File Called WORK.DOC

From the opening screen, you can use the F6 key to enter the name of a file to edit or create.

    Press F6

The top line of the screen displays the following:

```
File to load or create (Esc:cancel F8:dir): "work.doc"
```

This line tells you that the computer is ready either to load a file called WORK.DOC from the default disk drive (assumed here to be drive A) or to create a new file called WORK.DOC. WORK.DOC is the default name supplied by PC-Write. PC-Write gives you the following options:

- Press the ESC key to cancel this screen.
- Press the ENTER key to load or create a file called WORK.DOC.
- Edit the file name WORK.DOC, then press ENTER.
- Type a new file name and press ENTER.
- Press F8 to see a directory of files.

Choose the second option and continue to load or create a file called WORK.DOC.

    Press ENTER

The computer searches the disk in drive A for the WORK.DOC file. Because WORK.DOC is not in drive A, the computer then displays the screen shown in Figure 1-11. You can ignore all but

Figure 1-11.

```
File not found; Esc to retype, or F9 to create "work.doc"
┌─────────────────────────────────────────────────────────────┐
│  Compliments of: Quicksoft [you can change this line with command ED +]  │
│                                                             │
│  PC-Write (R), Version 3.02, Released on: 12-Dec-88, Registration #(none).│
│     (C) Copyright 1983-1988 by Bob Wallace, Quicksoft, All Rights Reserved. │
│                                                             │
│  PC-Write is shareware in the U.S. and Canada. Please help us distribute it, │
│  by sharing unmodified copies of the disk set. Please don't copy the manual. │
│  PC-Write is not shareware outside the U.S. and Canada; don't copy it there. │
│                                                             │
│    If you use PC-Write often, please buy a registered copy, or a manual.   │
│                                                             │
│  Buying a registered copy provides you all of these benefits, for only $99: │
│    >  Hardbound copy of the 400 page PC-Write User Guide and Quick Guide. │
│    >  Current PC-Write diskette set, and your unique registration number. │
│    >  PC-Write support service for one year: includes telephone support, │
│       quarterly newsletter and two coupons for free updates or utilities. │
│    >  Discounts on writing and printing add-on products from our catalog. │
│    >  A $25 commission when someone registers and gives your reg. number. │
│    >  Sincere thanks; your support helps us continue to improve PC-Write! │
│  When you register, include registration #number above to credit its owner. │
│                                                             │
│  Quicksoft, 800/888-8088, 206/282-0452, 219 First Ave N, #224, Seattle WA 98109 │
│     Please call to order, or for more information.  Prices subject to change. │
└─────────────────────────────────────────────────────────────┘
```

Top line has "File not found..." message

the top line of this screen. The top line, as shown below, tells you what to do next.

```
File not found; Esc to retype, or F9 to create "work.doc"
```

You have the following two choices:

- Press the ESC key to cancel this screen and return to the previous screen.
- Press the F9 key to move on and create the file called WORK.DOC.

Choose the option to create a file called WORK.DOC, by doing the following:

Press F9

Figure 1-12.

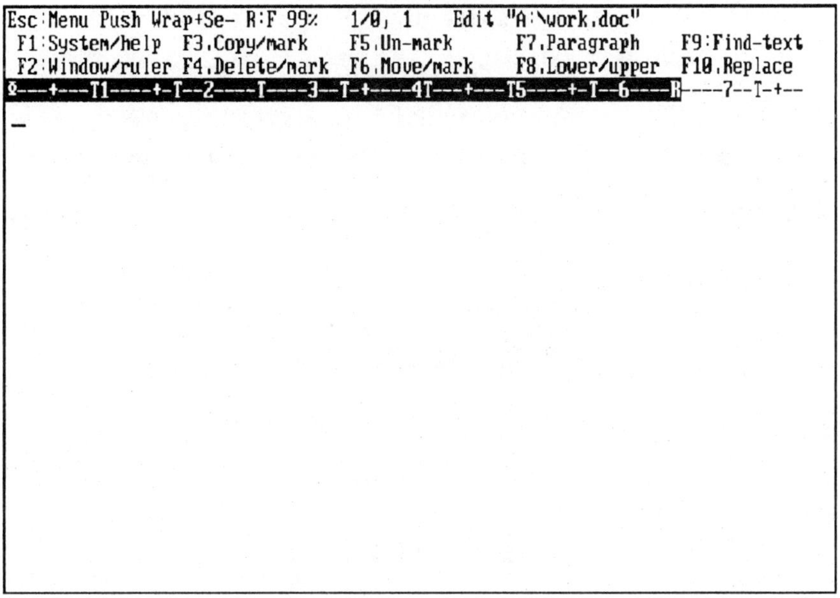

```
Esc:Menu Push Wrap+Se- R:F 99%   1/0, 1    Edit "A:\work.doc"
F1:System/help  F3.Copy/mark    F5.Un-mark     F7.Paragraph    F9:Find-text
F2:Window/ruler F4.Delete/mark  F6.Move/mark   F8.Lower/upper  F10.Replace
0---+---T1----+-T-2----T----3--T-+----4T---+---T5----+-T--6----R----7--T-+--
_
```

Ready to create WORK.DOC in the editing screen

You now see PC-Write's editing screen, as shown in Figure 1-12. The top four lines contain information to help you create and edit WORK.DOC. The remainder of the screen is available for typing.

The information at the top of the screen will be discussed in Chapter 2. For now, look only at the right end of the top line. It tells you that PC-Write has created a file called WORK.DOC on drive A, as shown here:

```
Edit "A:\work.doc"
```

An empty file named WORK.DOC has been created, or *opened,* on drive A. You now can type some text into the WORK.DOC file, as follows:

Type:
This is the work.doc file.
and press ENTER

The information you typed appears on the screen but is not yet saved to the file on disk. The top part of the screen should appear as shown here:

```
Esc:Menu Push Wrap+Se- R:F 99%    2/1, 1    Edit "A:\work.doc"
   F1:System/help  F3.Copy/mark   F5.Un-mark      F7.Paragraph    F9:Find-text
   F2:Window/ruler F4.Delete/mark F6.Move/mark    F8.Lower/upper  F10.Replace
   0---+---T1----+--T--2----T--+----3---T--+----4T---+---T5----+--T--6----R----?--T-+--
   This is the work.doc file.
   -
```

Save the WORK.DOC File to Disk

Before you save your work to the file on disk, you should get some system/help information:

Press F1

Help information appears on the top two lines of the screen, while your work remains on the remainder of the screen. The top part of the screen looks like this:

```
Esc F1:Help F2.Exit F3.Save F4.Command F5:Name F6:File F7:Print F8:Dir [no-save]
Esc:Cancel.  Arrows: select a menu option.  Shf F1: switch these lines on/off.

This is the work.doc file.
-
```

The top line lists nine menu choices that you can select by pressing either the ESC key or one of the function keys, F1 through F8. The word "Esc" is highlighted. You can use the right arrow key (→) to move the highlight to the right. The second help line provides information about the choice that is highlighted. When you reach the right end of the menu line, use the left arrow (←) key to move the highlight to the left.

You can select a menu item in the following ways:

- Use the arrow keys to highlight your choice, and then press ENTER.
- Press the function key next to your choice.
- Type the first letter of your choice (for example, type S to save).

Select the function key that is next to Save.

Press F3

The computer writes the information you typed to the WORK. DOC file in drive A. While the computer is saving your text, it momentarily displays the following message on the top line of the screen:

```
Writing "A:\work.doc", 30 bytes to write
```

When the save is complete, the editing screen returns, as shown here:

```
Esc:Menu Push Wrap↕Se- R:F 99%   2/1, 1    Read "A:\work.doc"
 F1:System/help  F3.Copy/mark    F5.Un-mark     F7.Paragraph    F9:Find-text
 F2:Window/ruler F4.Delete/mark  F6.Move/mark   F8.Lower/upper  F10.Replace
 0---+----T1----+-T--2---T----3--T-+----4T---+---T5----+-T--6----R----7--T-+-
This is the work.doc file.
-
```

Has the file really been saved on the disk in drive A? To verify that there is a file called WORK.DOC on drive A, call up the system/help menu and select the Directory item. First, call up the system/help menu:

Press F1

The top line of the screen shows the system/help menu, as follows:

`Esc F1:Help F2.Exit F3.Save F4.Command F5:Name F6:File F7:Print F8:Dir [no-save]`

You can select the Directory command (Dir) by pressing one key.

Press F8

The top line of the screen appears as shown here:

`Directory to display:  can include * and ? (Esc:cancel): "A:\*.*"`

To display the directory of all files on drive A (A:*.*), do the following:

Press ENTER

Figure 1-13 shows the directory of the 3 1/2-inch work disk. Note that there is a file called WORK.DOC, and that it contains 30 bytes.

REMEMBER Although the directory displays file names in uppercase letters, you can type them using any combination of uppercase and lowercase letters. Thus, "WORK.DOC" is the same as "work.doc."

The top two lines of the directory screen shown in Figure 1-13

Figure 1-13.

```
Esc F1:Help F2.Exit F3.Save F4.Command F5:Name F6:File F7:Print F8:Dir F9:Unsave
Esc:Cancel.  Fn-key: menu action above.  Arrows: Select file from those below.

A:\*.*                        Last drive is E:           201728 bytes free

    COMMAND.COM     23612   7-21-87    3:00p
        ED.EXE     260912   4-30-89    5:23p
        ED.HLP      72684   5-04-89    2:24p
        ED.DEF       1146   7-11-89   10:56a
     JUSTIFY.TST     4054  11-09-88    8:49p
       CHARS.TST      994  10-26-88    3:50a
       PRINT.TST     2008  11-10-88    3:35p
         PR.DEF      4368   7-11-89   11:16a
       WORDS.MAS   109912  12-02-88   11:40a
        WORK.DOC       30   7-10-89   10:44a
```

Directory now includes WORK.DOC file

tell you how to cancel this screen. To cancel the screen:

   Press ESC

You are returned to the editing screen, as shown here:

```
Esc:Menu Push Wrap+Se- R:F 99%   2/1, 1    Read "A:\work.doc"
  F1:System/help F3.Copy/mark   F5.Un-mark     F7.Paragraph    F9:Find-text
  F2:Window/ruler F4.Delete/mark F6.Move/mark   F8.Lower/upper  F10.Replace
  Ô---+--T1----+--T--2----T---3-T-+---4T---+--T5----+-T--6----R----7--T-+--
This is the work.doc file.
-
```

Print the WORK.DOC File on the Printer

You have created the WORK.DOC file and saved it to the work disk in drive A. The information you typed and saved to WORK.

DOC is still on the screen, which looks like this:

```
Esc:Menu Push Wrap+Se- R:F 99%   2/1, 1    Read "A:\work.doc"
   F1:System/help  F3.Copy/mark   F5.Un-mark    F7.Paragraph    F9:Find-text
   F2:Window/ruler F4.Delete/mark F6.Move/mark  F8.Lower/upper  F10.Replace
 0---+---T1----+--T--2---+---T---3--T-+---4T---+---T5----+--T--6-----R----7--T-+--
This is the work.doc file.
-
```

To print the contents of WORK.DOC, first make sure your printer is turned on and on-line. Then, get the system/help information on the screen, as follows:

    Press F1

The system/help menu appears at the top of the screen. Look for the option that reads F7:Print.

    Press F7

The top line on the screen tells you that the computer is ready to print the file called WORK.DOC, which is on drive A. This line is shown as follows:

```
File to print (Esc:cancel F8:dir): "A:\work.doc"
```

Note that at this point you could press the ESC key to cancel this option and return to the previous screen. You could also press the F8 key to see a directory of files. However, now you just want to complete the process of printing the WORK.DOC file on the printer.

    Press ENTER

The computer takes a few seconds to load the print program. While it loads the program, the computer displays the following message:

```
Loading print program, wait ...
```

The computer then checks to make sure the printer is ready. If everything is okay, it displays the following information on the top line of the screen:

```
Esc:Exit  F9:Print to disk file  F10:Printer is ready
```

The F10 key signals that the printer is ready.

    Press F10

The computer displays the screen shown in Figure 1-14. Near the bottom of the screen you can see the option to print everything in the WORK.DOC file, as shown here:

```
F10:Start continuous printing of pages (but stop if Esc key pressed).
```

To begin printing, do the following:

    Press F10

Even though WORK.DOC contains less than one page of text, the printer produces an entire page. The top of the page contains the contents of WORK.DOC, as shown here:

```
This is the work.doc file.
```

Figure 1-14.

```
Waiting.   Print from "A:\work.doc" to "PRN", Ready to begin.
F1.Help-screen  F3.Back-to-Edit  F5:Input-end    F7:Repeat-pages  F9.Page-stop
F2.Exit-to-DOS  F4.DOS-command   F6:User-input   F8:Skip-pages    F10.Continuous
Show help screen, giving dot commands and other information


    PC-Write (R), Version 3.02, Print Program.  Released on: 12-Dec-88.

    These keys are active when printing has been stopped for a command:

    F1: Show Help screen with Dot lines and font characters.
    F2: Exit to DOS, even if printing started from the edit program.
    F3: Go to Edit program, even if printing started from DOS.
    F4: Stay resident, but do a DOS command shell until DOS "exit" command.
    F5: Force end of current input file (if last input file, end printing).
    F6: Enter input text or Guide Lines (like .U, enter lines typed by user).
    F7: Repeat a page then stop, or repeat each page to print multiple copies.
    F8: Skip pages then stop, or skip pages each time to print every Nth page.
    F9: Print one page, then stop for another one of these commands.
    F10:Start continuous printing of pages (but stop if Esc key pressed).

    (C) Copyright 1983-1988 by Bob Wallace, Quicksoft, All Rights Reserved.
```

Waiting for printing instructions

The remainder of the page is blank. The paper in the printer is properly positioned to print another page. PC-Write automatically returns to the editing screen, as shown here:

```
Esc:Menu Push Wrap+Se- R:F 99%   2/1, 1    Read "A:\work.doc"
  F1:System/help F3.Copy/mark    F5.Un-mark      F7.Paragraph    F9:Find-text
  F2:Window/ruler F4.Delete/mark F6.Move/mark    F8.Lower/upper  F10.Replace
  0----+----T1----+---T-2----T---3-T-+----4T---+----T5----+--T--6----R----7-T-+--
This is the work.doc file.
-
```

Experiment. Type anything you want and view it on the editing screen. You can type the information shown in Figure 1-15. When

Figure 1-15.

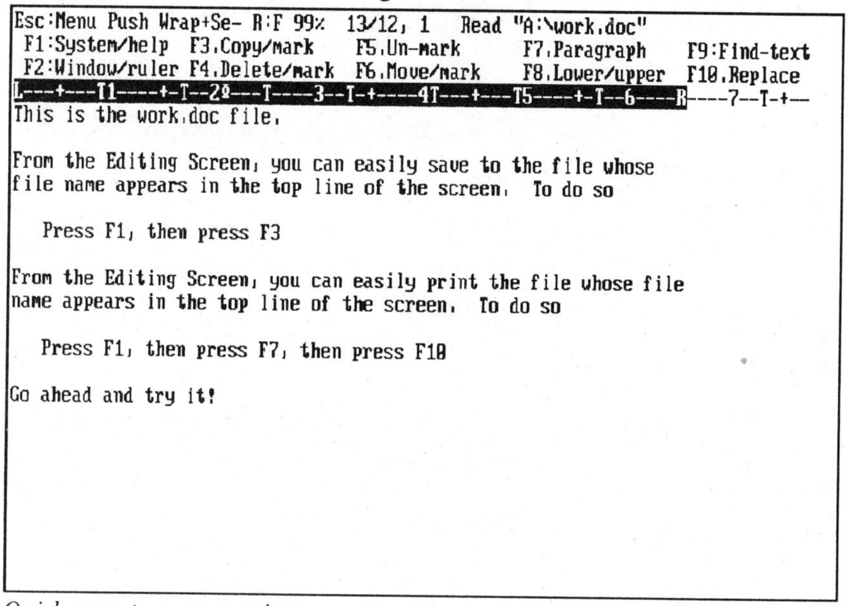

```
Esc:Menu Push Wrap+Se- R:F 99%  13/12, 1   Read "A:\work.doc"
 F1:System/help  F3.Copy/mark   F5.Un-mark      F7.Paragraph    F9:Find-text
 F2:Window/ruler F4.Delete/mark F6.Move/mark    F8.Lower/upper  F10.Replace
L---+---T1----+--T--28---T-----3--T-+----4T---+---T5----+-T--6---R----7--T-+--
This is the work.doc file.

From the Editing Screen, you can easily save to the file whose
file name appears in the top line of the screen.  To do so

   Press F1, then press F3

From the Editing Screen, you can easily print the file whose file
name appears in the top line of the screen.  To do so

   Press F1, then press F7, then press F10

Go ahead and try it!
```

Quick ways to save or print

you are finished typing, save your text to the WORK.DOC file on drive A, and then print it. Remember, to save the information displayed in the editing screen, simply press the following two keys in succession:

    Press F1, and then press F3

When you are finished using PC-Write, you should exit to DOS. From the editing screen, obtain the system/help menu lines at the top of the screen, by doing the following:

    Press F1

The system/help menu appears as follows:

```
Esc F1:Help F2.Exit F3.Save F4.Command F5:Name F6:File F7:Print F8:Dir [no-save]
Esc:Cancel,  Arrows: select a menu option,  Shf F1: switch these lines on/off,
```

You could press F2 to exit to DOS, but instead, use the → key to highlight F2, as shown here:

```
Esc F1:Help F2.Exit F3.Save F4.Command F5:Name F6:File F7:Print F8:Dir [no-save]
Save text if changed, exit back to DOS
```

The second line tells you what will happen if you select this menu item.

Press ENTER

You are returned to DOS. The screen is blank except for the A prompt in the upper left corner of the screen.

Summary

In this chapter, you began exploring PC-Write. You learned about the PC-Write disks and supporting documentation. You made copies of the original disks, and then used the copies to make work disks. Using a work disk, you went on a brief tour of PC-Write. You loaded the PC-Write main program (ED.EXE) and used a few of its capabilities. You used PC-Write's directory command to see the names of the files on your work disk. You browsed the extensive help system. You created a file called WORK.DOC, saved it to your work disk, and printed it on your printer. Finally, you made a graceful exit from PC-Write back to DOS.

CHAPTER 2

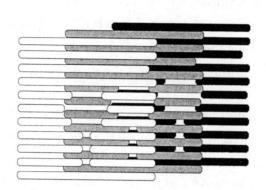

Letter to a Friend

PC-Write has many tools and features. In this chapter, you will learn about some of them by writing and editing a letter to a friend. A sample letter is supplied. You can use this letter or create one of your own.

It is assumed that you are using a computer system with two disk drives, drive A and drive B, with a PC-Write work disk in drive A and a data disk in drive B. If you are using a hard disk system, make appropriate substitutions for the disk drive designators, A and B.

In this chapter, you will do the following:

- After loading DOS, insert a work disk in drive A and a formatted data disk in drive B.
- Load the PC-Write editing program.
- Look at the directories of the disks in both drives A and B.
- Create a file called KATHY01.LTR on drive B.
- Enter text with intentional errors, and then use several editing tools to correct the errors.
- Save a partially created letter and return to DOS.
- Start PC-Write by including the name of the file you want when you load the editing program.
- Learn several ways to move the cursor around the screen.
- Complete the letter to a friend, save it, and print it on the printer.

Start PC-Write

In the discussion that follows, it is assumed, again, that you are using a system with two disk drives, A and B, and that your PC-Write work disk is in drive A and a data disk in drive B. The data disk is formatted and empty, that is, it contains no files. You will create data files and save them to the data disk in drive B.

Load DOS. At the A prompt, load the PC-Write editing program:

Type:
ed
and press ENTER

PC-Write's opening screen appears, as shown in Figure 2-1. You

Figure 2-1.

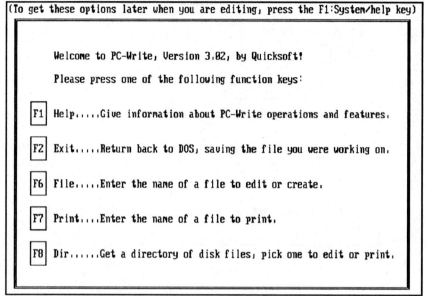

PC-Write's opening screen

have already explored the options listed on the opening screen during your brief tour of PC-Write in Chapter 1. In this chapter, you will learn more about these options and be introduced to several other capabilities of PC-Write.

Browse the Directories

As a beginner, you are encouraged to begin a work session by looking at the directories of the disks in drives A and B. This discussion assumes that drive A contains a work disk and drive B contains a formatted disk with no files stored on it.

Figure 2-2.

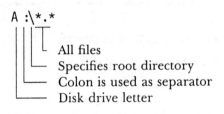

(1) *.* means all file names with all file name extensions.
(2) The root directory is the main directory on any disk. It is automatically created when you format a disk.

For more information, see Appendix A, "DOS Essentials"

Explanation of A:.**

Directory of the Disk in Drive A

Check the directory of your work disk in drive A:

    Press F8

The following line appears at the top of the screen:

`Directory to display; can include * and ? (Esc:cancel): "A:\*.*"`

The "A:*.*" displayed at the end of the line tells you that the computer is ready to list the names of all files on the *root directory* of the disk in drive A. See Figure 2-2 for a detailed explanation of the meaning of A:*.* and the root directory.

You can either press the ESC key to cancel the current option and return to the opening screen, or you can press ENTER to see a directory of files on the disk in drive A.

    Press ENTER

Figure 2-3.

```
Pick a file with the arrow keys, then press F6 to edit the file or F7 to print.


A:\*.*                          Last drive is E:            201728 bytes free

 COMMAND.COM     23612    7-21-87    3:00p
      ED.EXE    260912    4-30-89    5:23p
      ED.HLP     72684    5-04-89    2:24p
      ED.DEF      1146    7-11-89   10:56a
  JUSTIFY.TST     4054   11-09-88    8:49p
    CHARS.TST      994   10-26-88    3:50a
    PRINT.TST     2008   11-10-88    3:35p
       PR.DEF     4368    7-11-89   11:16a
    WORDS.MAS   109912   12-02-88   11:48a
     WORK.DOC       30    7-19-89    6:15a
```

Directory of all files on the disk in drive A

Figure 2-3 shows a directory of files on the work disk used by the authors of this book. This is a 3 1/2-inch disk. It contains the DOS COMMAND.COM file and therefore is self-booting. It also contains the WORK.DOC file created in Chapter 1.

When you are finished looking at the directory of files on the disk in drive A, press the ESC key to return to the opening screen:

   Press ESC

The opening screen shown in Figure 2-1 appears.

Directory of the Disk in Drive B

The disk in drive B should be a formatted disk containing no files. Verify this by viewing the directory of files on the disk:

Press F8

You again see the following line at the top of the screen:

Directory to display; can include * and ? (Esc:cancel): "A:*.*"

The computer is ready to display a directory of all files on the disk in drive A. However, you want to see a directory of all files on the disk in drive B. You can switch to drive B by changing A:*.* to either B:*.* or to just B:*.*. There are several ways to change directories, but only one way is shown here. Do the following slowly and watch what happens on the screen:

Type:
B:*.*   (It is okay to type **b:*.***)

As soon as you begin to type, the previous information (A:*.*) disappears and is replaced by the information you type. Before you press ENTER, the information you type might appear in quotation marks as shown here:

"B:*.*"

or

"b:*.*"

If the information shown on your screen is incorrect, you can use the BACKSPACE key, DELETE key (also called the DEL key), the ← key, and the → key to fix it. When the information on the screen is correct, press the ENTER key to obtain the directory:

Press ENTER

Figure 2-4 shows a directory of the disk in drive B. Since this formatted disk does not contain any files, no file names appear in the directory. Later in this chapter, you can display this directory again to see the names of files you created and saved to the data disk in drive B.

Figure 2-4.

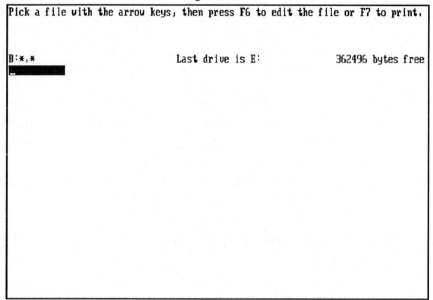

The formatted disk in drive B has no files

Now that you have seen a directory of the files (none) on the disk in drive B, escape from this screen and return to the opening screen.

Press ESC

You are returned to the opening screen shown in Figure 2-1.

Begin a Letter

You can use PC-Write to put your thoughts into words. You will find that it is very easy to change your mind, and then change the words. It is also easy to make corrections and insert afterthoughts into text you have already written.

Imagine that you have a friend named Kathy. Your friend Kathy is entering graduate school. With your encouragement, she has just bought a laptop computer. Bundled with the computer is an "all-purpose" package of applications, including a simple word processor. However, the word processor does not have the power Kathy needs to survive and thrive in graduate school.

Shareware to the rescue! You decide to write Kathy a letter, or perhaps a series of letters, to share your shareware experience. You decide to name these letters with the file names KATHY01.LTR, KATHY02.LTR, and so on. You are pretty sure you will not write more than 99 letters; otherwise you might name the files KATHY001.LTR, KATHY002.LTR, and so on.

A Few Words About File Names

When you write a letter or document with PC-Write, you also create a file. You must provide a file name that conforms to the conventions for naming DOS files. A file name can have up to eight characters followed by a period (.) and up to three additional characters. The characters following the period are called the *file name extension*. For example, the file name WORK.DOC consists of the name WORK followed by a period (.) and the file name extension DOC which indicates that the file is a document.

Since you are just beginning to use PC-Write, you should think now about ways to name files, especially file name extensions. The following extensions are suggested:

LTR	for letters	(KATHY01.LTR for the first letter to Kathy)
ESA	for essays	(MOZART.ESA for an essay about Mozart)
LST	for lists	(SHOPPING.LST for a shopping list)
CAT	for catalogs	(CAMPING.CAT for information from a camping catalog)

Choose file name extensions that suit *your* style. File name extensions are useful for organizing files when your data disk contains many files.

The Editing Screen

You will do your actual writing in the editing screen. From the opening screen, you can get to the editing screen by pressing the F6 key and supplying imformation as requested. Do it now.

    Press F6

The top four lines of the opening screen provide you with information on actions that are currently possible, as shown here:

```
File to load or create (Esc:cancel F8:dir): "work.doc"
F1.Help        F3.Set-drive    F5.Prior-series F7.Next-series  Esc.Cancel
F2.Set-prefix  F4.Set-path     F6.Copy-cursor  F8.Directory    Enter.Accept
Type filename (include * or ? for directory)  F9.Accept /s    F10.Accept /e
```

The top line on the screen tells you that the computer is ready to load or create a file called WORK.DOC. Since no disk drive is specified, the default drive A is automatically selected.

    However, you do not want to load or create the WORK.DOC file. Instead, you want to create a new file, KATHY01.LTR, on disk drive B. Note the blinking cursor (_) under the "w" in "work.doc." You can easily change WORK.DOC to another file name and designated disk drive. Do the following, but do not press ENTER yet.

    Type:
    B:KATHY01.LTR   (It is okay to type **b:kathy01.ltr**)

As soon as you begin typing, the name WORK.DOC disappears and is replaced by the information you type. The top line should appear as follows, with the cursor blinking under the righthand quotation mark.

```
File to load or create (Esc:cancel F8:dir): "B:KATHY01.LTR"
```

If you make a typing mistake, use the ← and → keys to move the cursor to the mistake, and then use the BACKSPACE and DELETE keys to erase any unwanted characters. When everything is correct press the ENTER key to accept the file name.

>Press ENTER

A screen containing Quicksoft advertising appears. You can ignore everything except the top line, which is shown here:

```
File not found; Esc to retype, or F9 to create "B:KATHY01.LTR"
```

Of course, you did not expect the computer to find a file called KATHY01.LTR, rather, you want to create this file.

>Press F9

The editing screen appears. The editing screen is mostly blank, so that you can fill it with words. The top four lines appear as shown here:

```
Esc:Menu Push Wrap+Se- R:F 99%    1/0, 1    Read "B:KATHY01.LTR"
F1:System/help  F3.Copy/mark   F5.Un-mark    F7.Paragraph   F9:Find-text
F2:Window/ruler F4.Delete/mark F6.Move/mark  F8.Lower/upper F10.Replace
0----+---T1----+-T--2---T---3-T-+----4T---+---T5----+-T--6---R----7-T-+-
-
```

The top line is the status line. It provides information on the status of actions occurring in the editing screen. For example, you can glance at the status line and see that the computer is ready for you to edit the file on disk drive B called KATHY01.LTR. This file has now been opened on the disk in drive B, but it is empty. It exists as a name in the directory, but contains no words or characters. You can verify this by looking at the directory of all files on the disk in drive B. First, though, you must display the proper menu in the top line by using the F1 key.

Press F1

The system/help menu appears as shown:

```
Esc F1:Help F2.Exit F3.Save F4.Command F5:Name F6:File F7:Print F8:Dir [no-save]
Esc:Cancel, Arrows: select a menu option, Shf F1: switch these lines on/off,
```

You can now press the F8 key to select the directory.

Press F8

The top line tells you which directory the computer is ready to display. If it says it is ready to display the directory of all files on the disk in drive B ("B:*.*"), press ENTER. However, it might tell you it is ready to display the directory of all files on the disk in drive A, as shown here:

```
Directory to display; can include * and ? (Esc:cancel): "A:\*.*"
```

In this case, change A:*.* to B:*.*, as follows:

Type:
B:*.*
and press ENTER

Figure 2-5 shows the directory of all files on the disk in drive B. The file name KATHY01.LTR is shown, along with the number of bytes it contains (0), and the date (7-27-89) and time (10:58a) it was created. You can now escape from this screen, return to the editing screen, and type the letter.

Press ESC

Figure 2-5.

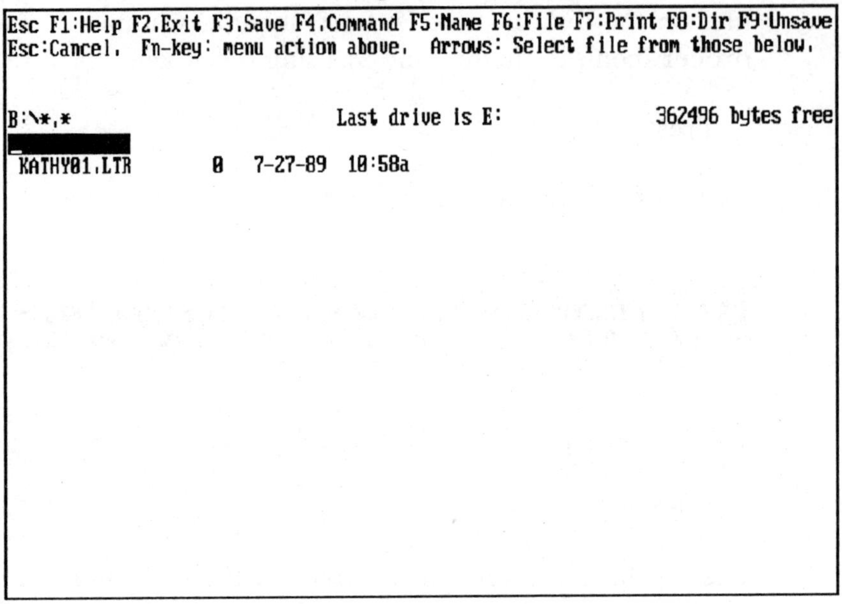

```
Esc F1:Help F2.Exit F3.Save F4.Command F5:Name F6:File F7:Print F8:Dir F9:Unsave
Esc:Cancel,  Fn-key: menu action above,  Arrows: Select file from those below,

B:\*.*                        Last drive is E:              362496 bytes free
─
 KATHY01.LTR         0    7-27-89   10:58a
```

The empty KATHY01.LTR file is on the disk in drive B

The editing screen is displayed.

The Status Line The status line contains much cryptic information, as shown here:

```
Esc:Menu Push Wrap+Se- R:F  99%  1/0, 1    Edit "B:KATHY01.LTR"
```

You can ignore most of this information for now. The following are brief descriptions of two items on the status line:

    1/0, 1   The cursor is on line 1 of the work area, no lines have been typed, and this is page 1 of the document. This information will change as you type your documents

Wrap+   *Word wrap* is on. You do not have to press ENTER when you approach the end of a line as you do with a typewriter. Just keep typing. PC-Write will automatically start a new line when necessary, and it will do so without breaking a word at the end of a line. If the last word on a line will not fit, word wrap simply wraps it to the beginning of the next line

PC-Write has another handy feature called *automatic paragraph formatting*. You are encouraged to use this feature unless you have a good reason not to do so. Turn on the automatic paragraph formatting by holding down the SHIFT key and pressing the F7 key.

Press SHIFT-F7   (Hold down SHIFT key and press F7)

Look at the status line shown below. Where it used to say "Wrap+," it now says "Para+."

```
Esc:Menu Push Para+Se- R:F 99%   1/0, 1    Edit "B:KATHY01.LTR"
```

The presence of "Para+" in the status line indicates that both automatic paragraph formatting and word wrap are on. You will see "Para+" in action when you make changes to previously typed information, especially when you delete old information or insert new information.

If you press SHIFT-F7 again, "Para+" will change to "Wrap−," as shown here:

```
Esc:Menu Push Wrap-Se- R:F 99%   1/0, 1    Read:B:KATHY01.LTR"
```

The presence of "Wrap−" in the status line indicates that both automatic paragraph formatting and word wrap are off. Press SHIFT-F7 to change "Wrap−" to "Wrap+," and then press SHIFT-F7 again to change "Wrap+" to "Para+."

In general, pressing SHIFT-F7 causes PC-Write to cycle through the following three editing modes:

Wrap−   Word wrap and automatic paragraph formatting are both off. Do not use this mode now

Wrap+   Word wrap is on and automatic paragraph formatting is off. Do not use this mode now

Para+   Automatic paragraph formatting and word wrap are both on. This is the mode you want to use now

Press SHIFT-F7 until the status line shows ("Para+"), indicating that automatic paragraph formatting and word wrap are both on.

The Ruler Line   The fourth line from the top of the editing screen is the ruler line, as shown here:

The ruler line determines the left and right margins for text on the screen. The ruler line shown in the previous illustration allows up to 65 characters per line, beginning in column 1 (left edge of screen) and ending in column 65.

The letter "R" marks the right margin of the text area, and is where word wrap occurs. Any word that extends beyond this point is automatically wrapped to the beginning of the next line.

This ruler line was established by the WORKDISK.BAT program during the setup run. (See Chapter 1 for a description of setup.) To obtain this ruler line, answer yes to the following setup instruction:

```
Press Y to get one inch margins by default; N for no margins. (y/n)
```

This ruler line will provide one-inch margins when you print on 8 1/2-inch-wide paper with a 10-character per inch print font. Of course, you must properly position the print head of your printer in order to get exact one-inch margins on both the right and left sides of the paper.

It is okay if the ruler line on your screen is different from the one shown in the previous illustration. The text you type will be narrower or wider than the illustration, and the margins during printout will be different. Later in this book you will learn how to set the ruler line to whatever margins you want.

Figure 2-6.

```
Dear Kathy,

Congratulations on being accepted to graduate school! I knew by
the way you were totally immersed in your studies last year and
the great grades you got, that there was no way grad school
wouldn't accept you. We're all so proud of you!

Second congratulations: you bought a computer! All those early
morning hours, groggily retyping papers on your typewriter, were
unnecessary, dark-age torture. Your Tandy Laptop is an excellent
choice, especially for a student. Its DeskMate software does
just about everything, but when you need more, Shareware to the
rescue!

I'm sending you a Shareware version of PC-Write, a word processor
that should meet all your needs.

Good luck. Have fun. Tell me what you think.

Call if you have questions.

Love,

Fran
```

A letter to a friend

Start Typing

Before you begin typing, make sure that the editing screen is in the automatic paragraph formatting mode. You should see "Para+" in the status line. If not, press SHIFT-F7 until "Para+" appears. The editing screen should appear as shown:

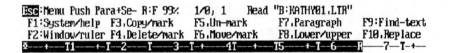

Figure 2-6 shows a practice letter for you to type. As shown in Figure 2-6, the letter is correctly typed. However, as you type it you will make a few deliberate errors so that you can fix them later.

When you type a paragraph of two or more lines, do not press ENTER at the end of each line. Just keep typing, and word wrap will work for you. Press ENTER at the end of a paragraph and at the end of single lines. Begin typing as follows:

Type:
Dear Kathy,
and press ENTER

Press ENTER again to insert a blank line between "Dear Kathy," and the text that follows. Next, type the first paragraph of the letter, including the mistakes, as shown here:

```
Congradulations on being accepted to graduate school!  I knew by
way you were totally immersed in your studies last year and the
the great grades you got, that ther was no way grad school
woudn't accept you.  We're alll so proud of you!
```

At the end of the paragraph:

Press ENTER, ENTER

The second **enter** inserts a blank line between the first and second paragraphs. The screen should now appear as shown in Figure 2-7. You typed seven lines, including two blank lines. The cursor is at the beginning of the eighth line of the text area. The status line keeps track of this information. Near the center of the line you see: "8/7, 1." This tells you that the cursor is on line 8, that 7 lines have been typed, and that this is page 1.

The paragraph shown in Figure 2-7 contains several typing mistakes. It is okay if you added some of your own as you typed the paragraph. PC-Write has powerful tools you can use to fix errors.

Figure 2-7.

```
Esc:Menu Push Para+Se- R:F 99%   8/7, 1    Edit "B:KATHY01.LTR"
 F1:System/help F3.Copy/mark   F5.Un-mark     F7.Paragraph    F9:Find-text
 F2:Window/ruler F4.Delete/mark F6.Move/mark   F8.Lower/upper  F10.Replace
 8---+---T1----+-T--2----T----3--T-+----4T---+---T5----+-T--6----8----7--T-+--
Dear Kathy,

Congradulations on being accepted to graduate school!  I knew by
way you were totally immersed in your studies last year and the
the great grades you got, that ther was no way grad school
woudn't accept you.  We're alll so proud of you!

-
```

Salutation and first paragraph—with several mistakes

In the first line, "Congratulations" is misspelled as "Congradulations." Use the ↑ key to move the cursor to the line, and then use the → key to put the cursor under the "d" in the misspelled word, as shown here:

Cursor

Press the DELETE key to delete the letter at the cursor position. Text to the right of the cursor will move one place to the left, and you will see the following:

Cursor

Now type a **t**. The text under and to the right of the cursor is pushed to the right to make room for the newly inserted "t." The word is now spelled correctly, as shown:

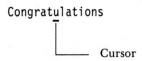

Cursor

Line two is missing the word "the" at the beginning of the line. Use the arrow keys to move the cursor under the "w" in "way." Watch the screen as you type **the** and a space to see automatic paragraph formatting occur. Since the "the" you inserted at the left pushed the "the" at the end of the line beyond the "R" in the ruler line, it was moved down to the next line, as shown:

```
the the great grades you got, that ther was no way grad school
```

Note the extra "the" at the beginning of the line. Also, the word "there" is misspelled. First, put the cursor at the space just to the right of either "the," and then press BACKSPACE four times to delete the extra "the" and space. You can also delete the word by placing the cursor under the "t" and pressing DELETE four times.

Now, fix the misspelled word "ther." Place the cursor on the space to the right of "ther," and type an **e**.

The last line of the paragraph has two mistakes: "woudn't" and "alll." Place the cursor under the "d" in "woudn't," and type an **l**. Then, move the cursor to the space just to the right of "alll," and press the BACKSPACE key.

Save Your Work and Return to DOS

You have completed the editing exercises for this example. Now, fix any other mistakes you may have made in typing the paragraph. After you are finished editing, it is a good idea to save your work to the disk.

Press F1

The system/help menu appears, as shown here:

```
Esc F1:Help F2.Exit F3.Save F4.Command F5:Name F6:File F7:Print F8:Dir F9:Unsave
Esc:Cancel.  Arrows: select a menu option.  Shf F1: switch these lines on/off.
```

The top line indicates that you can press the F3 key to save the work in the editing screen.

Press F3

As the disk spins, the information on the screen is saved to the file. While the save operation is in process, a message similar to the following appears briefly at the top of the screen:

```
Writing "B:KATHY01.LTR", 267 bytes to write
```

You have completed the section on beginning a letter to a friend. It is time to take a break. Later, you can retrieve the partial letter from the disk and complete it. Now, exit from PC-Write and return to DOS.

   Press F1, and then press F2

You are returned to DOS at the A prompt. Continue to the next section to learn more about PC-Write.

Continue Writing a Letter

In this section, you will continue the letter to a friend, shown previously in Figure 2-6. First load DOS, and then put your work disk in drive A and the data disk containing the KATHY01.LTR file in drive B.

A New Way to Start PC-Write

You already know that you want to edit the file KATHY01.LTR contained on the disk in drive B. You can include this information when you tell the computer to load PC-Write's editing program. At the DOS A prompt, do the following:

Type:
ed b:kathy01.ltr   (or type **ED B:KATHY01.LTR**)
and press ENTER

Remember to type a space between **ed** and **b:kathy01.ltr**. The computer loads the editing program and displays the screen shown in Figure 2-8. The top line of this screen describes your current options, as follows:

```
Press Esc if no backup, F9 to write backup file "b:kathy01.&1t"
```

This line tells you that the editing program located the KATHY01.LTR file on the disk in drive B and is now offering you two choices. You can press F9 to create a backup file with a slightly

Figure 2-8.

```
Press Esc if no backup, F9 to write backup file "b:kathy01.&1t"
  Compliments of: Quicksoft [you can change this line with command ED +]
PC-Write (R), Version 3.02, Released on: 12-Dec-88, Registration #(none).
   (C) Copyright 1983-1988 by Bob Wallace, Quicksoft, All Rights Reserved.
PC-Write is shareware in the U.S. and Canada. Please help us distribute it,
by sharing unmodified copies of the disk set. Please don't copy the manual.
PC-Write is not shareware outside the U.S. and Canada; don't copy it there.
   If you use PC-Write often, please buy a registered copy, or a manual.
Buying a registered copy provides you all of these benefits, for only $99:
  > Hardbound copy of the 400 page PC-Write User Guide and Quick Guide.
  > Current PC-Write diskette set, and your unique registration number.
  > PC-Write support service for one year:  includes telephone support,
    quarterly newsletter and two coupons for free updates or utilities.
  > Discounts on writing and printing add-on products from our catalog.
  > A $25 commission when someone registers and gives your reg. number.
  > Sincere thanks: your support helps us continue to improve PC-Write!
When you register, include registration #number above to credit its owner.
Quicksoft, 800/888-8088, 206/282-0452, 219 First Ave N, #224, Seattle WA 98109
     Please call to order, or for more information.   Prices subject to change.
```

Ready to continue writing a letter to a friend

different name. The file name extension for the backup file would be &LT instead of LTR. You can press ESC if you do not want a backup file. However, it is a good idea to make a backup file in case something goes wrong while you are editing the original file. Tell the computer to create a backup file as follows:

    Press F9

The computer writes a backup file to the disk in drive B, and then displays the original file on the editing screen so that you can edit it. The cursor is blinking in line 1, column 1, under the "D" in "Dear," as shown in Figure 2-9.

If you wish, look at the directory of files on the disk in drive B. You will see that it now contains the original file called

Figure 2-9.

```
Esc:Menu Push Wrap+Se- R:F 99%   1/7, 1    Read "b:kathy01.ltr"
 F1:System/help F3.Copy/mark    F5.Un-mark      F7.Paragraph    F9:Find-text
 F2:Window/ruler F4.Delete/mark F6.Move/mark    F8.Lower/upper  F10.Replace
0---+---T1----+-T--2----T----3--T-+----4T---+---T5----+-T--6----R----7--T-+--
Dear Kathy,

Congratulations on being accepted to graduate school!  I knew by
the way you were totally immersed in your studies last year and
the great grades you got, that there was no way grad school
wouldn't accept you.  We're all so proud of you!
```

The letter is on the editing screen

KATHY01.LTR, as well as the backup file called KATHY01.&LT. To check the directory on the disk in drive B:

Press F1, F8, ENTER

After browsing through the directory, press ESC to return to the editing screen shown in Figure 2-9.

Move Around the Editing Screen

Use the information on the screen shown in Figure 2-9 to learn more about moving the cursor quickly around the screen. You have already used the arrow keys to move the cursor in small steps, as follows:

To move the cursor down one line, press the down arrow key (↓).

To move the cursor up one line, press the up arrow key (↑).

To move the cursor one character position to the right, press the right arrow key (→).

To move the cursor one character position to the left, press the left arrow key (←).

You can hold down an arrow key to zoom the cursor in the direction of the arrow. Use the arrow keys to zoom around the screen so that you see what happens when the cursor reaches the top line of text, the left edge of the screen, the right end of text, and the bottom of the text on the screen.

Move to the Beginning of a Word You can move the cursor in bigger increments. For example, you can move it to the next or previous word. Position the cursor at the beginning of the first line in the paragraph, as shown here:

```
Congratulations on being accepted to graduate school! I knew by
|
└──── Cursor
```

To move the cursor to the beginning of the next word, "on," do the following:

    Press CTRL-→   (Hold down the CTRL key and press the right arrow key)

The cursor immediately jumps to the beginning of the next word, as follows:

```
Congratulations on being accepted to graduate school! I knew by
                 |
                 └──── Cursor
```

To move the cursor to the beginning of the previous word:

    Press CTRL-←   (Hold down the CTRL key and press the left arrow key)

Practice moving the cursor one word at a time, both to the left and to the right.

Move to the Beginning or End of a Line   Use the HOME and END keys to quickly move the cursor to the beginning (left margin) of a line or to the last character at the end of a line, as follows:

    To move the cursor to the beginning of a line, press HOME

    To move the cursor to the end of a line, press END

Place the cursor anywhere on a line and try out the HOME and END keys.

Move to the Top or End of a File You can quickly move the cursor to the top or to the bottom of a text file displayed on the screen. This is especially useful when a file has more lines of text than can be displayed at one time on the screen. The method to use may vary with the type of keyboard on your computer.

First, try jumping to the top, or beginning, of text on the screen.

If there is a GREY PLUS (+) key on the right side of your keyboard, do the following:

> Press SHIFT-GREY PLUS   (Hold down the SHIFT key and press the GREY PLUS (+) key)

If your keyboard has an F12 key, try this method:

> Press SHIFT-F12   (Hold down the SHIFT key and press the F12 key)

If neither of the above methods works, try this method:

> Press ALT-WHITE PLUS   (Hold down the ALT key and press the WHITE PLUS key. This key is located in the top row of the main part of the keyboard. Do not use a SHIFT key.)

Find the method that works on your computer. You can use a similar method to jump to the end of the file. Jumping to the end of the file will put the cursor on the last character you typed (which could be a blank line at the bottom of the text area).

Try the following methods to find the one that works on your computer:

If there is a GREY MINUS (−) key on the right side of your keyboard, do the following:

> Press SHIFT-GREY MINUS

If your keyboard has an F11 key, try this method:

> Press SHIFT-F11

If neither of the above methods works, try the following:

Press ALT-WHITE MINUS   (Hold down the ALT key and press the WHITE MINUS key. This key is in the top row of the main part of the keyboard. Do not use the SHIFT key.)

Finish Typing the Letter

Position the cursor at the end of the file displayed on the screen. There should be a blank line between the last line of the paragraph and the cursor, as shown here:

```
wouldn't accept you.  We're all so proud of you!
```

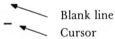
Blank line
Cursor

If you do not see a blank line, press ENTER to obtain one. Then, type the rest of the letter, as shown below. As you type, try to make a few mistakes so that you can practice your new editing skills.

```
Second congratulations:  you bought a computer!  All those early
morning hours, groggily retyping papers on your typewriter, were
unnecessary, dark-age torture.  Your Tandy Laptop is an excellent
choice, especially for a student.  Its DeskMate software does
just about everything, but when you need more, Shareware to the
rescue!

I'm sending you a Shareware version of PC-Write, a word processor
that should meet all your needs.

Good luck.  Have fun.  Tell me what you think.

Call if you have questions.

Love,

Fran
```

When you finish typing the entire letter, the screen should appear similar to the one shown in Figure 2-10. Since the letter has too many lines to fit on the screen, you do not see the entire letter. To view the rest of the letter, zoom the cursor to the top of the file, and then back to the bottom.

Save the Completed Letter

Proofread the letter in the editing screen and make any corrections or other changes. Then, save the completed letter to the disk in drive B by pressing the following two keys in succession:

    Press F1, F3

Figure 2-10.

```
Esc:Menu Push Wrap+Se- R:F 99%  25/24, 1    Edit  "b:KATHY01.LTR"
 F1:System/help  F3.Copy/mark    F5.Un-mark      F7.Paragraph   F9:Find-text
 F2:Window/ruler F4.Delete/mark  F6.Move/mark    F8.Lower/upper F10.Replace
R---+---T1-----+-T--2----T---3--T-+----4T---+--T5----+-T--6----R----?--T-+--
wouldn't accept you.  We're all so proud of you!

Second congratulations:  you bought a computer!  All those early
morning hours, groggily retyping papers on your typewriter, were
unnecessary, dark-age torture.  Your Tandy Laptop is an excellent
choice, especially for a student.  Its DeskMate software does
just about everything, but when you need more, ShareWare to the
rescue!

I'm sending you a ShareWare version of PC-Write, a word processor
that should meet all your needs.

Good luck.  Have fun.  Tell me what you think.

Call if you have questions.

Love,

Fran
_
```

The editing screen after completing the letter

The computer saves the file in the editing screen to the disk in drive B. You can verify this by looking at the directory of files on that disk. You should see the names of two files, KATHY01.&LT and KATHY01.LTR. KATHY01.&LT is the backup file created at the beginning of this work session. KATHY01.LTR is the completed letter you just saved.

Print the Letter and Exit to DOS

While the letter is still in the editing screen, you can print it out on the printer. First, position the paper in your printer so that the print head is at the top of a page, either at or near the perforations that separate pages. Then, press the following two keys in succession:

    Press F1, F7

You will see the following line at the top of the screen:

File to print (Esc:cancel F8:dir): "b:kathy01.ltr"

Do the following:

    Press ENTER

The top line changes to the following:

Esc:Exit F9:Print to disk file F10:Printer is ready

Make sure that the printer is ready and that the paper is positioned correctly. Then, do the following:

    Press F10

The computer displays the print screen shown in Figure 2-11. This screen contains a considerable amount of information about printing. Browse through this information and look for the line that says:

F10:Start continuous printing of pages (but stop if Esc key pressed).

The F10 key will print an entire document. Start continuous printing of pages as follows:

    Press F10

The printer prints out a hard copy of your letter. When the printer finishes printing, the editing screen returns.

Figure 2-11.

```
Waiting.   Print from "b:KATHY01.LTR" to "PRN". Ready to begin.
F1.Help-screen  F3.Back-to-Edit F5:Input-end    F7:Repeat-pages F9.Page-stop
F2.Exit-to-DOS  F4.DOS-command  F6:User-input   F8:Skip-pages   F10.Continuous
Show help screen, giving dot commands and other information

      PC-Write (R). Version 3.02. Print Program.  Released on: 12-Dec-88.

      These keys are active when printing has been stopped for a command:

      F1: Show Help screen with Dot lines and font characters.
      F2: Exit to DOS, even if printing started from the edit program.
      F3: Go to Edit program, even if printing started from DOS.
      F4: Stay resident, but do a DOS command shell until DOS "exit" command.
      F5: Force end of current input file (if last input file, end printing).
      F6: Enter input text or Guide Lines (like .U, enter lines typed by user).
      F7: Repeat a page then stop, or repeat each page to print multiple copies.
      F8: Skip pages then stop, or skip pages each time to print every Nth page.
      F9: Print one page, then stop for another one of these commands.
      F10:Start continuous printing of pages (but stop if Esc key pressed).

      (C) Copyright 1983-1988 by Bob Wallace, Quicksoft. All Rights Reserved.
```

The print screen has many options

Your work is finished, so you can take a well-deserved break. Exit to DOS by doing the following:

Press F1, F2

You return to the DOS A prompt.

Summary

In this chapter, you learned how to use some of PC-Write's features and tools in writing a letter to a friend. You began with your work disk in drive A and a formatted data disk in drive B. (Hard disk users should substitute appropriate hard disk directory designations for drives A and B). You loaded PC-Write's editing program and checked the directories on both disk drives.

After browsing through the directories, you began a writing session in the editing screen. You learned about the status line and how to turn on and off features such as word wrap and automatic paragraph formatting.

You created a new file called KATHY01.LTR on the disk in drive B, and then began a letter to Kathy to put in the file. During this work session, you typed the first part of the letter, replete with intentional errors, and then used some of PC-Write's editing tools to correct the mistakes. Then, you saved the corrected partial letter to the disk, exited PC-Write, and returned to DOS.

You learned a different way to begin a work session, by including the name of the file you want to edit when you load the PC-Write editing program (for example, ED B:KATHY01.LTR). You also made a backup file with a slightly different name. Making a backup file is recommended whenever you are going to make major changes to a file.

You learned several ways to move the cursor around the screen. Now you can quickly move the cursor anywhere in a file in order to make an editing change.

After learning how to zoom the cursor around the screen, you completed typing the letter, saved the final version to the disk, and printed the letter on the printer. You learned a lot in this chapter, so it might be a good idea to quickly review your work.

CHAPTER 3

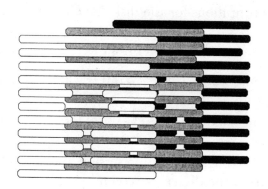

Business Correspondence

In writing a personal letter to a friend, you set the style. However, in business correspondence, you may wish to conform to letter formats that are commonly accepted in business. Two sources of information on business correspondence formats are listed as follows:

Geffner, Andrea B., *Business Letters the Easy Way,* Barron's Educational Series, Hauppauge, New York, 1983.

Sabin, William A., *The Gregg Reference Manual,* McGraw-Hill, New York, New York, 1985.

It is assumed that you are using a computer system with two disk drives, drive A and drive B, with a PC-Write work disk in drive A and a data disk in drive B. If you are using a hard disk system, make appropriate substitutions for the disk drive letters "A" and "B."

In this chapter, you will do the following:

- Learn more about word wrap (Wrap+) and automatic paragraph formatting (Para+).
- Write a short business letter, using PC-Write tools you already know.
- Learn another way to begin an editing session, by selecting the file to be edited from the directory screen.
- Learn how to underline text.
- Learn how to print an entire document in a letter-quality font.
- Learn how to move, copy, and delete blocks of text.
- Learn how to create a letterhead.

A Short Business Letter

For your first business letter, you will type the letter shown in Figure 3-1. This letter is from an individual, Laran Stardrake, to the circulation people of a magazine called *The BASIC Teacher*. Laran intends to write frequently to *The BASIC Teacher*, so she assigns the file name TBT001.LTR to this first letter.

Load the Editing Program

Since you already know the file name (TBT001.LTR) of the file you want to create, you can include it when you tell the computer

Figure 3-1.

```
P. O. Box 1635
Sebastopol, CA 95473-1635
January 2, 1990



The BASIC Teacher
2814 - 19th Street
San Francisco, CA 94110

Attention:  Circulation Department

Dear People:

I am a new subscriber to The BASIC Teacher. My first issue
(January, 1990) arrived last week. Well, actually, 101 copies
arrived.

Enclosed is a shareware copy of PC-File +, an excellent database
program. I use it to keep track of people who request my
occasional newsletter, DragonSmoke, and recommend it for your
use.

The BASIC Teacher is great, just what I need for self-study in
learning GW-BASIC and QuickBASIC. However, I live in a modest
apartment and don't have room to store 101 copies of each issue.
One copy is sufficient.

Sincerely,



Laran Stardrake
```

A short business letter

to load PC-Write's editing program. At the DOS A prompt, do the following:

Type:
ed b:tbt001.ltr   (or type: **ED B:TBT001.LTR**)
and press ENTER

Remember to insert a space between **ed** and **b:tbt001.ltr**.

The computer loads the editing program. After the editing program is loaded, the top line on the screen should appear as shown here:

```
File not found; Esc to retype, or F9 to create "b:tbt001.ltr"
```

If the disk drive designation and file name (B:TBT001.LTR) are not correct, you can press the ESC key, make any desired changes, and then press ENTER. The top line shown in the previous illustration will return. When everything is as you want it, you can begin to create the file.

Press F9

The editing screen appears, as shown in the following illustration:

```
Esc:Menu Push Wrap+Se- R:F 99%   1/0, 1    Edit "b:tbt001.ltr"
  F1:System/help F3.Copy/mark   F5.Un-mark    F7.Paragraph    F9:Find-text
  F2:Window/ruler F4.Delete/mark F6.Move/mark  F8.Lower/upper  F10.Replace
  0---+---T1----+-T--2---T--+--3--T-+----4T---+---T5----+-T--6----R----7-T-+--
  -
```

The status line at the top shows that the editing screen is in the word wrap mode (Wrap+). The ruler line is set with the left margin in column 1 and the right margin in column 65. The letter

"R" marks the right margin. The cursor is on line 1, column 1 of the editing area below the ruler line and the cursor marker (☿) is in column 1 of the ruler line. When the cursor moves right or left, the cursor marker moves with it. If the cursor is not in column 1, you will see the letter "L" marking the left margin in column 1 of the ruler line.

Tab stops are marked with the letter "T." Press the TAB key to move the cursor and the cursor marker (☿) to a tab stop. Tab stops are set in columns 9, 17, 25, 33, 41, 49, 57, 65, and 73. If the cursor is at the left margin, you could press the TAB key four times to put the cursor in column 33. You might do this, for example, to indent the return address to the middle of the page.

In this chapter, you will use the ruler line as shown in the previous illustration. In Chapter 5, you will learn how to change the ruler line, the margins, and tab stops.

Editing Modes (Wrap+, Para+, and Wrap−)

In Chapter 2, you learned about word wrap and automatic paragraph formatting. The status line tells you what mode is selected, as follows:

Wrap+	Word wrap is on, automatic paragraph formatting is off
Para+	Word wrap and automatic paragraph formatting are both on
Wrap−	Word wrap and automatic paragraph formatting are both off

Use the SHIFT-F7 key combination to cycle from Wrap+ to Para+, from Para+ to Wrap−, and from Wrap− to Wrap+.

The Word Wrap Mode (Wrap+)   You will usually use the word wrap mode to enter new text. To type short lines, such as the lines in the return address, press ENTER after each line. To type paragraphs, however, do not press ENTER at the end of each line. Keep typing, and word wrap will wrap words that would otherwise extend beyond the right margin to the beginning of the next line. Press ENTER only at the end of the paragraph.

If you edit text in word wrap mode, the text will not be automatically reformatted. There may be lines in which text extends beyond the right margin ("R" in the ruler line) and lines which are too short. This problem is easy to fix. Position the cursor at the beginning of a paragraph you want to reformat, and then press the F7 key. Only that paragraph is reformatted. You must use F7 to reformat each paragraph.

Do not try to reformat the return address with the F7 key. If you do, the word wrap mode will try to combine all the lines of the return address into a single paragraph. For example, suppose the return address and the date appear as shown here:

```
P.O. Box 1635
Sebastopol, CA 95473-1635
January 2, 1990
```

If you position the cursor on the first line and press F7, the three lines will be combined into a single line, as follows:

```
P.O. Box 1635 Sebastopol, CA 95473-1635 January 2, 1990
```

The word wrap mode recognizes a single short line followed by a blank line as a one-line paragraph. It will not try to combine such a line with text that follows the blank line. It will also recognize indented short lines as paragraphs, even if they are not followed by blank lines. For example, if you indent the return address and date, the F7 key will not reformat them as one line.

The Automatic Paragraph Formatting Mode (Para+)

In the Para+ mode, word wrap and paragraph formatting both occur automatically. A short line followed by a blank line is recognized as a paragraph. An indented line is also treated as a paragraph. You can use the ENTER key to end these lines.

However, the Para+ mode does not allow you to type consecutive short lines that begin at the left margin and end when you press ENTER. The second line will be moved to the first line as soon as you type one word followed by a space. To see this happen, put the editing screen in Para+ mode and type the following return address:

```
P.O. Box 1635
Sebastopol, CA 95473-1635
```

Type the first line and press ENTER. Then, slowly type the second line as you watch the screen. As soon as you type the space following "Sebastopol," automatic formatting occurs. The second line is moved up to the first line, as shown here:

```
P.O. Box 1635 Sebastopol,
```

There is an easy method to prevent unwanted automatic reformatting. Instead of using ENTER to end a short line, use the ALT-K key (hold down ALT and press K). The ALT-K key inserts an end-of-paragraph mark (¶) at the end of the line.

Try using this method with the letter shown in Figure 3-1. Make sure that the editing screen is in Para+ mode, and then type the return address and the date. Press ALT-K to end each line. When you finish, the return address and date should appear on the screen as shown here:

P. O. Box 1635¶
Sebastopol, CA 95473-1635¶
January 2, 1990¶
-

The three address lines are now immune from automatic paragraph formatting. You need to use ALT-K only on short lines that are not followed by a blank line. For typing the rest of the letter, proceed in word wrap mode.

Type the Letter

If the editing screen is not already in Wrap+ mode, press SHIFT-F7 until you see "Wrap+" on the top line. If the return address is not already on the screen, type it as shown in Figure 3-2.

Figure 3-2.

```
Esc:Menu Push Wrap+Se- R:F 99%    4/3, 1    Edit "B:tbt001.ltr"
  F1:System/help  F3.Copy/mark   F5.Un-mark     F7.Paragraph    F9:Find-text
  F2:Window/ruler F4.Delete/mark F6.Move/mark   F8.Lower/upper  F10.Replace
  0---+---T1----+-T--2----T----3--T-+----4T---+---T5----+-T--6----R----7--T-+--
P. O. Box 1635
Sebastopol, CA 95473-1635
January 2, 1990
-
```

Begin with the return address and date

Press ENTER four times to create some blank space, and then type the rest of the letter. When you finish, your screen should appear similar to the one shown in Figure 3-3.

Save and Print the Letter

Save the letter to the disk in drive B. You can do this with the following two keystrokes:

Press F1, F3

The file is saved to the disk and remains on the editing screen.
To print the letter on the printer, do the following:

Press F1, F7

Figure 3-3.

```
Esc:Menu Push Wrap+Se- B:F 99%  35/34, 1   Edit "b:tbt001.ltr"
 F1:System/help  F3.Copy/mark    F5.Un-mark     F7.Paragraph    F9:Find-text
 F2:Window/ruler F4.Delete/mark  F6.Move/mark   F8.Lower/upper  F10.Replace
R---+---T1----+-T---2----T---3--T-+----4T---+---T5----+-T--6----R----7--T-+--
I am a new subscriber to The BASIC Teacher. My first issue
(January, 1990) arrived last week. Well, actually, 101 copies
arrived.

Enclosed is a shareware copy of PC-File +, an excellent database
program. I use it to keep track of people who request my
occasional newsletter, DragonSmoke, and recommend it for your
use.

The BASIC Teacher is great, just what I need for self-study in
learning GW-BASIC and QuickBASIC. However, I live in a modest
apartment and don't have room to store 101 copies of each issue.
One copy is sufficient.

Sincerely,



Laran Stardrake
_
```

The editing screen after the letter is completed

The top line reads as follows:

```
File to print (Esc:cancel F8:dir): "b:tbt001.ltr"
```

The computer is ready to print the file named in the top line.

    Press ENTER

After loading the print program, the computer displays the following information on the top line:

```
Esc:Exit  F9:Print to disk file  F10:Printer is ready
```

Make sure that the printer is ready and that the paper is properly positioned. Then, continue the print process by doing the following:

    Press F10

You now see the Print menu, as previously described in Chapters 1 and 2. The top line, shown as follows, tells you that the computer is waiting for final instructions.

```
Waiting.   Print from "b:tbt001.ltr" to "PRN".   Ready to begin.
```

This line tells you that the computer is ready to print the file B:TBT001.LTR to the printer ("PRN"). The rest of the Print menu provides information on the current status of the function keys F1 through F10. The one you want now is F10, which causes the entire document to be printed.

    Press F10

While the letter is printing, the top line displays the following information. (Since the letter is short, the information appears for a short time.)

```
Esc:Stop. Continuous. Print from "b:tbt001.ltr" to "PRN". Printing page 1.
```

Note that you can press the ESC key to stop the printing. When the entire file has been printed, you are returned to the editing screen.

You can save a little time by using a shortcut method to print the file to the printer—pressing three keys in succession. Use this method now to print another copy of the letter.

   Press F1, F7, F10

The file is printed, and you are returned to the editing screen. Proofread the letter and correct any mistakes. Practice using the editing tools you learned in Chapters 1 and 2. For example, you can practice adding and deleting words.

Before you begin editing, change from the word wrap mode (Wrap+) to the automatic paragraph formatting mode (Para+). Remember, use SHIFT-F7 to change modes from Wrap+ to Para+, from Para+ to Wrap−, and from Wrap− to Wrap+. Press SHIFT-F7 until the status line displays Para+, indicating that the editing screen is in the automatic paragraph formatting mode.

   Press SHIFT-F7

This causes automatic paragraph formatting to occur, according to the settings displayed in the ruler line. As you make corrections or changes, formatting will occur automatically.

In Chapter 2, you learned how to delete words by using the BACKSPACE and DELETE keys. There is a quicker way to delete a word.

Position the cursor on the first letter of the word you want to delete, and then hold down the CTRL key and press the ESC key. The word disappears, and text to the right of the deleted word moves left to fill the empty space.

You can also delete a word by putting the cursor to the right of the word. Hold down the CTRL key and press the BACKSPACE key. This deletes the word to the left of the cursor.

When you are finished practicing, exit to DOS. From the editing screen, you can return to DOS by pressing the following two keys in succession:

    Press F1, F2

Use New Tools to Modify the Letter

In this section, you will learn how to begin an editing session by selecting the file to be edited from the directory screen. Then, you will make some changes to the file.

Load the Editing Program and Select the TBT001.LTR File

Make sure your PC-Write work disk is in drive A and the disk containing the TBT001.LTR file is in drive B. Load the editing program without naming the file, as follows:

    Type:
    ed
    and press ENTER

When the PC-Write opening screen appears, do the following to display a directory:

   Press F8

The top line of the screen indicates that the computer is ready to display the directory of files on drive A. However, you want the directory of files on drive B. Edit the top line so that it reads as follows:

```
Directory to display;  can include * and ? (Esc:cancel): "B:*.*"
```

Press ENTER to get the directory of all files on drive B (B:*.*). A sample directory is shown in Figure 3-4. It contains the names of two files, KATHY01.LTR and TBT001.LTR.

Figure 3-4.

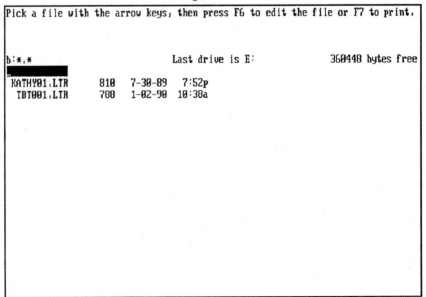

Directory of files on the disk in drive B

Use the ↓ key to highlight the name of the file you want to edit, TBT001.LTR. Note the top line of the directory screen shown in Figure 3-4. You could press the F7 key to print the highlighted file. However, you want to load the file into the editing screen and make some changes.

Press F6

A screen full of information appears. You can ignore most of the information on this window, except for the top line, shown here:

`Press Esc if no backup, F9 to write backup file "B:\TBT001.&LT"`

Since you are going to make several changes to the file, it is a good idea to make a backup file. The backup file will have a name identical to the original file name, except that the file extension will be changed from LTR to &LT.

Press F9

The computer writes the backup file, and then displays the original TBT001.LTR file in the editing window. You can now begin to make changes.

Underline Names of Magazines

The BASIC Teacher and *DragonSmoke* are publications. It is common practice to underline names of publications in the body of a letter (but not in the address). You can use *font characters* to underline text when it is printed on the printer. A font character appears on the screen as a graphics character. For example, the underline font character looks like this: ꞈ .

To type the underline font character (↨), press ALT-U. To underline a section of text, insert the underline font character just before and just after the text to be underlined.

Tell the computer to underline "The BASIC Teacher" in the first line of the letter. First, position the cursor under the "T" in "The," as shown here:

```
I am a new subscriber to The BASIC Teacher.  My first issue
```

The cursor is at the beginning of the section of text you want underlined. Insert the underline font character.

Press ALT-U

The underline font character (↨) appears at the cursor position. The cursor and the text under and to the right of the cursor are pushed one space to the right. The line looks like the following illustration:

```
I am a new subscriber to ↨The BASIC Teacher.  My first issue
```

The computer now knows where to begin the underlining, but does not know where to stop. If you printed the letter now, the line would appear as follows:

```
I am a new subscriber to The BASIC Teacher.  My first issue
```

However, you want only "The BASIC Teacher" to be underlined. Move the cursor to the period following "Teacher" and type another underline font character. The line should appear on the screen as follows:

```
I am a new subscriber to ↨The BASIC Teacher↨.  My first issue
```

If you print the line, only "The BASIC Teacher" will be underlined, as shown here:

```
I am a new subscriber to The BASIC Teacher.  My first issue
```

Modify the letter so that "The BASIC Teacher" and "Dragon-Smoke" are underlined everywhere they appear in the body of the letter. If you want to delete a font character, you can do so in the same way you delete any character. Either position the cursor on the font character and press DELETE; or position the cursor to the right of the font character and press BACKSPACE.

More Font Characters

PC-Write has an assortment of font characters that you can use to enhance your printed documents. Table 3-1 is a list of font characters reproduced from the manual. For more information, look up "Font characters" and "Enhancing text" in the index of your *PC-Write User's Guide*.

The enhancements shown in Table 3-1 are for non-laser printers and depend on the capabilities of your printer. Here are some things to remember in using font characters:

- Insert the font character before and after the character, word, or entire line to be enhanced.
- Font characters affect only one line at a time. If you want to enhance more than one line, insert font characters at the beginning and end of each line.

Go ahead and try some of the enhancements listed in Table 3-1. For example, pick a word and make it boldface (ALT-B). Print a word in 12-cpi Quality mode (ALT-Q). Does your printer support italics? Find out by using the italic font character (ALT-I). Try

Table 3-1.

Enhancement	Press	Font Character
Boldface	ALT-B	☻
Compressed (15 cpi usually, Fast mode)	ALT-C	♠
Double wide (5 cpi usually, Fast mode)	ALT-D	▶
Elite (12 cpi Fast mode)	ALT-E	♥
Fast (10 cpi Fast mode)	ALT-F	⌐
Higher (superscript)	ALT-H	↑
Italics (underline if no italics)	ALT-I	§
Lower (subscript)	ALT-L	↓
Marine blue (color printers)	ALT-M	•
Overstrike ("/" over text [for legal work])	ALT-O	‼
Pica (10 cpi Quality mode)	ALT-P	♣
Quality (12 cpi Quality mode)	ALT-Q	▬
Red (color printers)	ALT-R	▲
Second Strike (bold, strikes character twice)	ALT-S	☺
Underline (looks underlined on monochrome)	ALT-U	⊥
Variable (Proportional or other)	ALT-V	♦
Double Underline ("Double U" [for accounting])	ALT-W	↕
Yellow (color printers)	ALT-Y	▼

Enhancing Printout: Keys to Press and Font Characters

an enhancement within an enhancement, such as underlined boldface. Type the boldface font character followed by the underline font character at the beginning of the text to be enhanced, and then type the underline font character followed by the boldface font character at the end of the text. Thus, the underline font characters are nested inside the boldface font characters. An example is shown here:

☻§Attention:§☻

Hide Font Characters

Font characters can be either visible or invisible on the screen. Generally, you will want to make font characters visible when you are editing, but invisible when you are just reading text on the screen. Since a visible font character occupies a space on the screen, you will want to make it invisible when creating a table or lining up text in vertical columns. Use the ALT key and the SPACEBAR key to make font characters either visible or invisible, as follows:

If font characters are visible, hold down the ALT key and press the SPACEBAR key to make them invisible.

If font characters are invisible, hold down the ALT key and press the SPACEBAR key to make them visible.

The ALT-SPACEBAR key combination acts as a *toggle switch* to make font characters visible or invisible. When you make them invisible, they disappear from the screen, and the text appears as if the font characters are not there. Of course, the font characters remain in the file that is stored either in the computer's memory or on a disk.

Visible or invisible, font characters perform their tasks when you print a document to the printer. Printing with font characters invisible on the screen produces exactly the same printed document as printing with font characters visible on the screen.

Print in a Quality Font

PC Write usually prints using the standard print font of your printer. This is sometimes called the *draft mode*. However, when your letter is in final form, you may want to print it either in a *letter-quality font* or *near letter-quality font,* if your printer has this capability.

For most printers, PC-Write supports two draft-quality fonts, *Elite* and *Fast,* and two letter-quality fonts, *Pica* and *Quality.* Each font is identified by a font letter, as shown:

Font	Font Letter	Description
Elite	E	Draft quality, 12 characters per inch
Fast	F	Draft quality, 10 characters per inch
Pica	P	Letter quality, 10 characters per inch
Quality	Q	Letter quality, 12 characters per inch

The default font is Fast (F)—draft quality at 10 characters per inch. However, you may select another font. In the following exercise, you will select the Pica (P) font and then print the letter.

First, position the cursor at the beginning of the file (at the beginning of the text on the screen). Remember, there are three possible key presses that move the cursor to the beginning of the file, depending on your keyboard: SHIFT-GREY PLUS(+), SHIFT-F12, and ALT-PLUS(+). The cursor appears under the first letter of the first line of text, as shown here:

P. O. Box 1635

To begin selecting a font, do the following:

    Press ALT-G   (Hold down ALT and press G)

This highlights the text from the cursor position to the end of the line. Next, type a *dot command* to select the Pica (P) font.

    Type:
    .R:P
    and press ENTER

The top two lines in the edit area now appear as shown here:

Figure 3-5.

```
P. O. Box 1635
Sebastopol, CA 95473-1635
January 2, 1990



The BASIC Teacher
2814 - 19th Street
San Francisco, CA 94110

Attention:  Circulation Department

Dear People:

I am a new subscriber to The BASIC Teacher.  My first issue
(January, 1990) arrived last week.  Well, actually, 101 copies
arrived.

Enclosed is a shareware copy of PC-File +, an excellent database
program.  I use it to keep track of people who request my
occasional newsletter, DragonSmoke, and recommend it for your
use.

The BASIC Teacher is great, just what I need for self-study in
learning GW-BASIC and QuickBASIC.  However, I live in a modest
apartment and don't have room to store 101 copies of each issue.
One copy is sufficient.

Sincerely,



Laran Stardrake
```

Letter printed in PC-Write's Pica font

.R:P
P. O. Box 1635

You have marked the beginning of a block of text to be printed using the Pica font. To print the entire file in Pica, do the following:

Press F1, F7, F10

Figure 3-5 shows the entire letter as printed on a Tandy DMP 132 dot matrix printer. Note that names of publications are underlined.

After printing the letter, remove the dot command (.R:P). Position the cursor anywhere within the dot command, and then do the following:

Press CTRL-Y   (Hold down CTRL and press Y)

The CTRL-Y key combination deletes an entire line. You have deleted the line containing only the dot command.

PC-Write has many dot commands you can use to control the way your documents are printed. The dot commands are listed in the index of the *PC-Write User's Guide,* under the heading "Dot lines."

Move Blocks of Text

After reading the printed letter, Laran decided she would like to switch the second and third paragraphs. PC-Write provides an easy way to do this.

Position the cursor between the first and second paragraphs of the letter. The cursor should be on the left margin of the blank line between the two paragraphs, as shown here.

```
arrived.

Enclosed is a shareware copy of PC-File+, an excellent database
```

Next, use the F6 key to mark this as the beginning of a block of text to be moved.

> Press F6

Note the top line on the screen. The word "Marking" is highlighted. Use the (↓) key to mark the entire second paragraph.

> Press ↓ five times

Each time you press ↓, the cursor moves down one line and highlights the line. You should end with the entire paragraph highlighted and the cursor on the blank line below the paragraph, as shown here:

```
Enclosed is a shareware copy of PC-File +, an excellent database
program.  I use it to keep track of people who request my
occasional newsletter, DragonSmoke, and recommend it for your
use.

The BASIC Teacher is great, just what I need for self-study in
```

You have now marked the block of text you want to move. Do the following to tell the computer you have finished marking text:

> Press F6

Look at the status line at the top. Instead of saying "Marking," it now says, "Marked." You are ready to actually move the text.

Move the cursor to the end of the third paragraph. The cursor should be on the left margin of the blank line just below the third paragraph, shown as follows:

```
The BASIC Teacher is great, just what I need for self-study in
learning GW-BASIC and QuickBASIC.  However, I live in a modest
apartment and don't have room to store 101 copies of each issue.
One copy is sufficient.
_
```

To move the previously marked text to the cursor position, you will press F6 one more time.

Press F6

The second and third paragraphs have been switched and appear as shown in Figure 3-6. Note that the text that was moved is still marked (highlighted). Finish the process by using the F5 key to unmark this text.

Press F5

Remember, to move a block of text, follow these steps:

1. Position the cursor at the beginning of the block of text and press F6. The word "Marking" appears in the status line.

2. Use the arrow keys to mark the block of text you want to move. As you use the arrow keys, the text to be moved is highlighted.

3. When you have marked all the text you want to move, press F6. In the status line, the word "Marking" changes to "Marked."

4. Move the cursor to the place where you want to move the marked text, and then press F6. The marked text moves to the cursor position.

Figure 3-6.

```
Esc:Menu Push MARKED.  R:F 99%  29/38, 1   Edit "b:TBT001.&LT"
  F1:System/help  F3,Copy/mark    F5,Un-mark      F7,Paragraph    F9:Find-text
  F2:Window/ruler F4,Delete/mark  F6,Move/mark    F8,Lower/upper  F10,Replace
0---+---T1----+-T--2----T---3--T-+----4T---+---T5----+-T--6----R----7--T-+--
San Francisco, CA 94110

Attention: Circulation Department

Dear People:

I am a new subscriber to The BASIC Teacher.  My first issue
(January, 1990) arrived last week.  Well, actually, 101 copies
arrived.

The BASIC Teacher is great, just what I need for self-study in
learning GW-BASIC and QuickBASIC.  However, I live in a modest
apartment and don't have room to store 101 copies of each issue.
One copy is sufficient.

▓Enclosed is a shareware copy of PC-File +, an excellent database▓
▓program.  I use it to keep track of people who request my      ▓
▓occasional newsletter, DragonSmoke, and recommend it for your   ▓
▓use.                                                             ▓
-
```

The marked text has been moved to its new position

5. Press F5 to unmark the text.

After reading the new version of the letter, Laran decided she preferred the letter in its previous form. You can either move the third paragraph to its original position as the second paragraph, or you can move the current second paragraph below the current third paragraph. Remember to press F5 to finish the move and unmark the block of text.

Copy a Block of Text

When you move a block of text, it is deleted from one location and inserted in another location. You can also copy a block of text. Copying retains the text in its original location and places a copy in another location. Try copying the first paragraph of the letter. You will use the F3 key to mark the paragraph for copying.

Position the cursor on the first letter of the first line of the paragraph, as shown here:

```
I am a new subscriber to The BASIC Teacher.  My first issue
```

Press F3

The word "Marking" appears on the status line. Use the ↓ key to move the cursor down and mark the lines of the paragraph, as follows:

Press ↓ three times

As the cursor moves down, each line of the paragraph is marked and highlighted. The marked paragraph and the cursor should appear as follows:

```
I am a new subscriber to The BASIC Teacher.  My first issue
(January, 1990) arrived last week.  Well, actually, 101 copies
arrived.

The BASIC Teacher is great, just what I need for self-study in
```

You have marked the lines you want to copy. Next, tell the computer you are finished marking.

Press F3

In the status line, the word "Marking" changes to "Marked." The paragraph is marked and ready to be copied to the cursor position. You could now move the cursor anywhere in the file and copy the marked text to that place. For this exercise, leave the cursor where it is and proceed with the copying process.

Press F3

The marked paragraph is copied to the cursor position. It is still marked. The original paragraph remains in its original position. You now see the paragraph in two places, as shown here:

```
I am a new subscriber to The BASIC Teacher.  My first issue
(January, 1990) arrived last week.  Well, actually, 101 copies
arrived.
I am a new subscriber to The BASIC Teacher.  My first issue
(January, 1990) arrived last week.  Well, actually, 101 copies
arrived.
```

Since the text that was copied is still marked, you can make another copy by pressing the F3 key, as follows:

Press F3

Another copy of the paragraph appears. Figure 3-7 shows the entire screen as it appears with two copies plus the original paragraph. The first three paragraphs are now identical. You could, of course, continue pressing F3 until there are 101 copies of the first paragraph—a not very subtle way to make a point! Instead, end the copying process by unmarking the marked text, as follows:

Press F5

This completes the copying process. Remember, to copy a block of text:

1. Use the F3 key to mark the beginning and end of the block of text to be copied.

2. Move the cursor to the place where you want the copy to appear.

3. Press F3 to make the copy.

4. When you are finished copying, press F5 to unmark the marked text.

Delete a Block of Text

You can delete an entire block of text. The process is similar to that of moving or copying a block of text. First, mark the block of text to be deleted, and then press a key to delete it. If you delete

Figure 3-7.

```
Esc:Menu Push MARKED, R:F 99%  25/40, 1   Edit "b:TBT001.8LT"
  F1:System/help  F3.Copy/mark    F5.Un-mark      F7.Paragraph    F9:Find-text
  F2:Window/ruler F4.Delete/mark  F6.Move/mark    F8.Lower/upper  F10.Replace
  0---+---T1----+-T--2----T----3--T-+----4T---+---T5----+-T--6---R----7--T-+--

The BASIC Teacher
2814 - 19th Street
San Francisco, CA 94110

Attention:  Circulation Department

Dear People:

I am a new subscriber to The BASIC Teacher.  My first issue
(January, 1990) arrived last week.  Well, actually, 101 copies
arrived.
I am a new subscriber to The BASIC Teacher.  My first issue
(January, 1990) arrived last week.  Well, actually, 101 copies
arrived.
I am a new subscriber to The BASIC Teacher.  My first issue
(January, 1990) arrived last week.  Well, actually, 101 copies
arrived.
-
The BASIC Teacher is great, just what I need for self-study in
learning GW-BASIC and QuickBASIC.  However, I live in a modest
```

Two copies of the first paragraph have been made

a block of text, and then regret your action, you can easily undelete it to make it reappear. Follow these steps to delete a block of text:

1. Move the cursor to the beginning of the block and press F4.

2. Use the arrow keys to mark the text to be deleted, and then press F4 again. The text is deleted and disappears from the screen.

Use the method described to delete the extra copies of the first paragraph of the letter. This returns the letter to its original appearance, before you practiced making copies of a block of text.

When you delete a block of text, it is moved to a *hold area* and it remains there until you either delete another block of text or exit from the editing program. The hold area allows you to *undelete* previously deleted text. This is handy if you change your mind or if you later want to insert deleted text somewhere in the file. Use this undeleting method to recover the text in the hold area, as follows:

1. Move the cursor to the position in which you want to insert the text from the hold area.

2. Press CTRL-F4. This inserts the marked text at the cursor position.

3. Press F5 to unmark the text and complete the undeleting operation.

The text in the hold area remains intact. You can insert it into the file anywhere you wish. You can also move a block of text or copy a block of text without affecting text being held in the hold area. However, if you delete another block of text, that block replaces any previously held block.

Create a Letterhead

You can create a letterhead, save it to a disk, and then use it at the beginning of each letter. You might want to make different letterheads for different types of letters. Laran Stardrake's letterhead is shown here, with each line centered on the page.

```
             Laran Stardrake
              P. O. Box 1635
          Sebastopol, CA 95473-1635
               707-555-1234
```

You will create this letterhead and save it as a file called LSHEAD.LTR. From the editing screen, begin a new file by pressing the following two keys in succession:

    Press F1, F6

The top line prompts you for the name of the file to load or create. If you began this process while the TBT001.LTR file was on the editing screen, the top line will appear as follows:

```
File to load or create (Esc:cancel F8:dir): "B:TBT001.LTR"
```

You want to create a new file called LSHEAD.LTR. Therefore, change the file name in the top line to match the following:

```
File to load or create (Esc:cancel F8:dir): "B:LSHEAD.LTR"
```

Next press ENTER. The computer searches disk drive B for the LSHEAD.LTR file and, not finding it, displays the following top line:

```
File not found; Esc to retype, or F9 to create "B:LSHEAD.LTR"
```

Press F9 to create a new file called LSHEAD.LTR. The editing screen appears with the file name B:LSHEAD.LTR at the right end of the status line. Type the letterhead in the upper left corner of the editing area, as shown here:

```
Laran Stardrake
P. O. Box 1635
Sebastopol, CA 95473-1635
707-555-1234
```

Next, center each line of the letterhead. To center a line, put the cursor on the first character of the line, and then press the SHIFT-F8 key combination. Do this for each line. When you are finished, the letterhead should appear as shown in Figure 3-8.

Figure 3-8.

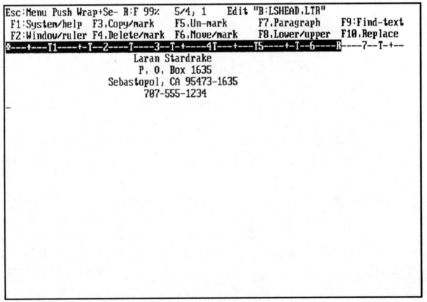

Laran Stardrake's letterhead

If the letterhead is not exactly as you like it, you can make any changes you want. Then, save the letterhead as follows:

Press F1, F3

To print the letterhead on the printer to see how it looks, press F1, F7, and then F10. To print it in a letter-quality font such as Pica or Quality, use ALT-G and the appropriate dot command, either .R:P for Pica or .R:Q for Quality.

After you have created the letterhead, you can type a short letter. Before you do, however, change the file name of your letter from LSHEAD.LTR to PRACTICE.LTR. Begin the name change like this:

Press F1, F5

This tells the computer that you want to change the name of the file in the editing screen. The top line prompts you for the file name, as follows:

```
Name to use for saving (Esc:cancel F8:dir): "B:LSHEAD.LTR"
```

Use the F1 and F5 keys to change the current file name, B:LSHEAD.LTR, either to B:PRACTICE.LTR or to a name of your choice. If you choose B:PRACTICE.LTR, the top line should look like this:

```
Name to use for saving (Esc:cancel F8:dir): "B:PRACTICE.LTR"
```

Press ENTER, and the editing screen will appear with your file name in the status line and the letterhead in the editing area. Go ahead and type your letter. When you have finished typing the letter, press F1 and F3 to save it. To print the letter, press F1, F7, and F10.

In the future, any time you want to type a letter, you can load the editing program so that it begins with the LSHEAD.LTR file (the letterhead) on the editing screen. You can do this either by typing **ed b:lshead.ltr** at the DOS A prompt, or by loading the editing program, and then retrieving the LSHEAD.LTR file from the directory screen.

Summary

In this chapter, you applied writing tools which you learned in previous chapters to writing a short business letter. You learned more about PC-Write's editing modes, word wrap (Wrap+), and automatic paragraph formatting (Para+).

After typing a first draft, saving it, and printing it, you learned how to use some new PC-Write tools to modify the letter. You learned about font characters used to enhance printout, and you used the underline font character to underline words in the printed document. You then learned how to use a dot command to print the entire letter in a letter quality font called Pica. (The exact appearance of such a letter, of course, depends on the capabilities of your printer.)

PC-Write allows you to easily move, copy, and delete entire blocks of text. You learned how to mark a block of text, and then to either move it or copy it to another location in the document. You also learned how to delete the marked text. Deleted text is stored in a hold area, in case you change your mind and want to undelete it.

You ended this chapter by creating a letterhead and saving it for future use. A sample letterhead (Laran Stardrake's) was supplied, but perhaps you made your own letterhead instead. You also learned how to begin a letter writing session by first loading your letterhead file, and then changing the name of the file to name the letter.

CHAPTER

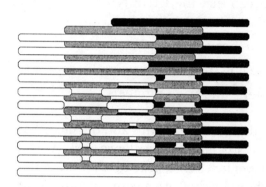

4

Multi-page Documents

In preceding chapters, you created short files which could be printed as single-page documents. In this chapter, you will create longer files and learn how to print multi-page documents. In particular, you will learn how to do the following:

- Create a file called LINE.NBR containing the numbers 1 through 73, with one number per line.
- Use PC-Write's automatic page break feature to print the LINE.NBR file as a two-page document.
- Print only the first page of the document.

- Print multiple copies.
- Skip the first page and print only the second page.
- Insert page breaks so that the LINE.NBR file is printed as a three-page document.
- Set top and bottom margins.
- Print with multiple line spacing (for example, double spacing).
- Add headers, footers, and page numbers.

The files used for the examples in this and the next chapter are available on *The Shareware Book* Convenience Disk. You can load the files from the Convenience Disk instead of entering them from the keyboard. You should either use a copy of your Convenience Disk for this purpose, or copy the files from the Convenience Disk to your PC-Write data disk. For example, to copy the LINE.NBR file, put your Convenience Disk in drive A and your data disk in drive B. At the DOS A prompt:

Type:
copy line.nbr b:
and press ENTER

Create the LINE.NBR Practice File

In order to learn about printing multi-page documents, you need a file that is long enough to print two or more pages on the printer. A handy file for this purpose is a document consisting of consecutive numbers, with one number per line. The number 1 is on line 1, number 2 is on line 2, number 3 is on line 3, and so on. In this exercise, you will create the LINE.NBR file consisting of the numbers from 1 to 73, with one number per line.

Load PC-Write's Edit program and include the name of the new file to be created:

Type:
ed b:line.nbr   (or type **ED B:LINE.NBR**)
and press ENTER

PC-Write's opening screen appears with the name of the file you want to create (b:line.nbr) on the top line. Press F9 to obtain the editing screen shown here:

```
Esc:Menu Push Wrap+Se- R:F 99%    1/0, 1    Read "b:line.nbr"
 F1:System/help F3.Copy/mark      F5.Un-mark      F7.Paragraph    F9:Find-text
 F2:Window/ruler F4.Delete/mark   F6.Move/mark    F8.Lower/upper  F10.Replace
 L0--+---T1----+-T--2----T---3--T-+----4T---+----T5----+-T--6----R----7-T-+--
 -
```

Type the number **1** and press ENTER, then type the number **2** and press ENTER, then type the number **3** and press ENTER, and so on. After you type the number **7** and press ENTER, the screen should appear as shown in Figure 4-1.

Continue this process until you have entered the number 73 on line 73. The screen should appear as shown in Figure 4-2.

You have created the LINE.NBR file. This file consists of 73 lines containing the numbers 1 to 73 — one number per line. The cursor is on line 74. The center of the status line reads "74/73, 1." Note that PC-Write considers this still to be page 1. This is because PC-Write considers a file that is in memory or on a disk to be on one page unless you specify otherwise. However, when you print this file to the printer, it will print on two pages.

Before moving on, save the file (press F1, F3). Then, proceed to the next section and learn about various ways to print the LINE.NBR file on the printer.

Figure 4-1.

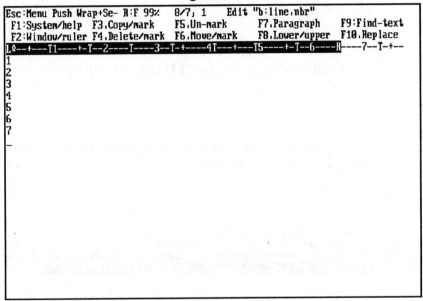

The LINE.NBR file after entering the first seven numbers

Print the LINE.NBR File

Now that you have created the LINE.NBR file, you can use it to learn more about PC-Write's printing capabilities. You will begin by simply printing the file and seeing PC-Write's automatic pagination.

In this section, it is assumed that you will print on 8 1/2- by 11-inch paper, that your printer uses six lines-per-inch vertical spacing, and that is prints 66 lines on a page. PC-Write reserves a six-line, one-inch margin at the bottom of each page. The authors' work disk is set up to also print a margin of six blank lines, or one inch, at the top of each page. Your top margin may have a different setting, depending on how you set up your work disk with PC-Write's WORKDISK.BAT program. Do not worry if your

Figure 4-2.

```
Esc:Menu Push Wrap+Se- R:F 99%  74/73, 1   Edit "b:line.nbr"
 F1:System/help  F3.Copy/mark   F5.Un-mark      F7.Paragraph   F9:Find-text
 F2:Window/ruler F4.Delete/mark F6.Move/mark    F8.Lower/upper F10.Replace
L8--+---T1-----+-T--2----T----3--T-+----4T---+--T5----+-T--6---R----7--T-+--
54
55
56
57
58
59
60
61
62
63
64
65
66
67
68
69
70
71
72
73
-
```

The editing screen after creation of the LINE.NBR file

top margin is different or if your pages break at a different line than in the examples. You will learn how to control margins and page breaks later in this chapter.

Automatic Pages

Position the paper in your printer so that it is ready to print on the first line of a blank page. Print the LINE.NBR file:

    Press F1, F7, F10

The printer begins printing page 1, and the screen displays the following top line:

Esc:Stop. Continuous. Print from "b:line.nbr" to "PRN". Printing page 1.

After printing page 1, the computer prints page 2. The top line of the screen changes from "Printing page 1" to "Printing page 2." When page 2 has been printed, the printing process ends. Note that the print head on the printer is positioned to print another page. The editing screen still displays the LINE.NBR file. The file has been printed as a two-page document. The two pages, as printed on the authors' system, are shown in Figure 4-3.

The printed pages shown in Figure 4-3 are printed as follows:

Page 1 is printed with six blank lines as the top margin, followed by the first 54 lines of the LINE.NBR file, and then followed by six blank lines for the bottom margin, for a total of 66 lines.

Page 2 is printed with six blank lines as the top margin, followed by the rest of the LINE.NBR file, lines 55 through 73, followed by 41 blank lines, including the six-line bottom margin, for a total of 66 lines.

If the LINE.NBR file contained 150 lines, it would be printed on three pages, with the first 54 lines on page 1, the next 54 lines on page 2, and the remaining 42 lines on page 3. If you set different margins while making your work disk, your version might print 60 lines per page instead of 54. Later in this chapter, you will learn how to set the top and bottom margins.

Print Only Page 1

The F1, F7, and F10 keystroke sequence causes an entire file to be printed. There are several other print options. To access these options, bring up the Print menu, as follows:

Press F1, F7, ENTER

Figure 4-3.

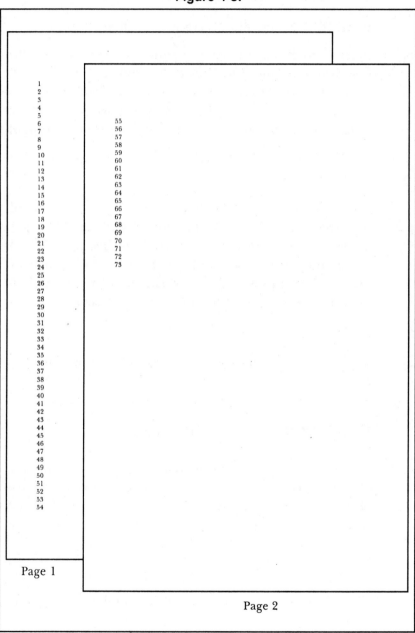

Page 1 and page 2 of the LINE.NBR file

The top line appears as shown here:

```
Esc:Exit  F9:Print disk drive  F10:Printer is ready
```

Press F10 to display the Print menu on the screen. The Print menu is shown in Figure 4-4. Notice that you can use the F7, F8, F9, and F10 function keys to perform different kinds of printing tasks. You can also obtain a help screen (F1), return to the Edit program (F3), or leave PC-Write and return to DOS (F2). Try pressing F9 to print only one page:

>Press F9

The printer prints one page, beginning at the top of the LINE.NBR file. After printing one page (page 1), the top line informs you that the computer has "Finished page 1." It is waiting for another print command. Next, press F3 to return to the Edit program. From the editing screen, you can print only page 1 by pressing the following three keys in succession:

>Press F1, F7, F9

The computer prints page 1, and then stops. The Print menu remains on the screen.

Print Multiple Copies

It is assumed that the Print menu is on the screen, and that the computer is waiting for a print command. Unless you tell it otherwise, the computer asumes you want to print one copy of each page. You can use the F7 key to print more than one copy, as follows:

>Press F7

The top line will prompt you for the number of copies to print, as shown here:

```
Number of times to repeat last page (Esc:cancel) "1"
```

Figure 4-4.

```
Waiting.   Print from "b:line.nbr" to "PRN". Ready to begin.
F1.Help-screen  F3.Back-to-Edit F5:Input-end    F7:Repeat-pages F9.Page-stop
F2.Exit-to-DOS  F4.DOS-command  F6:User-input   F8:Skip-pages   F10.Continuous
Show help screen, giving dot commands and other information

    PC-Write (R), Version 3.02, Print Program.  Released on: 12-Dec-88.

    These keys are active when printing has been stopped for a command:

    F1: Show Help screen with Dot lines and font characters.
    F2: Exit to DOS, even if printing started from the edit program.
    F3: Go to Edit program, even if printing started from DOS.
    F4: Stay resident, but do a DOS command shell until DOS "exit" command.
    F5: Force end of current input file (if last input file, end printing).
    F6: Enter input text or Guide Lines (like .U, enter lines typed by user).
    F7: Repeat a page then stop, or repeat each page to print multiple copies.
    F8: Skip pages then stop, or skip pages each time to print every Nth page.
    F9: Print one page, then stop for another one of these commands.
    F10:Start continuous printing of pages (but stop if Esc key pressed).

    (C) Copyright 1983-1988 by Bob Wallace, Quicksoft. All Rights Reserved.
```

The Print menu

The cursor is blinking on the number 1 enclosed in quotation marks ("1"). If you press ENTER, one copy will be printed. Instead, change the "1" to a "2":

Type:
2
and press ENTER

The top line changes and gives you two options. You can either press F9 to print only one page two times, or press F10 to print each page two times. The top line is shown here:

Esc:cancel   F9:Print this page 2 times and stop   F10:Print each page 2 times

Try both of these options. When you press F9, the computer prints two copies of page 1, and then stops. When you press F10, the computer prints two copies of page 1, then prints two copies of page 2, and then stops.

Skip Page 1 and Print Page 2

Return to the Edit program (press F3). Suppose you want to print only page 2. From the editing screen, go to the Print menu by pressing four keys in succession. After pressing each key, look at the top line to see the information displayed there.

    Press F1, F7, ENTER, F10

You should see the Print menu, with the top line as shown here:

```
Waiting. Print from "b:line.nbr" to "PRN". Ready to begin.
```

Use the F8 key to skip one or more pages. The computer is ready to print from the beginning of the file. You can skip page 1 and then print page 2. Do the following to begin the operation:

    Press F8

The top line gives you the following three options:

```
Esc:Cancel F8:Skip to page number F9:Skip n pages F10:Print every nth page
```

You can use either the F8 key to skip *to* page 2, or the F9 key to skip one page (page 1) and arrive at page 2.

    Press F8

The top line prompts you for the page number to skip to:

```
Page number to skip to: "1"
```

Do the following to skip to page 2:

Type:
2
and press ENTER

The top line changes to the one shown here. Note that it says, "Skipped page 1."

```
Waiting. Print from "b:line.nbr" to "PRN". Skipped page 1.
```

The computer has skipped page 1 and is waiting to print page 2. You can press F9 to print only one page. If the document contained more than two pages, you could press F10 to begin continuous printing from page 2 to the end of the document. Now, press F9 to print page 2 of the LINE.NBR file.

Suppose that you have just printed a 10-page document, and then you made some changes to pages 9 and 10. You do not need to print the entire document again. You can skip to page 9, and then print from there to the end.

Page Breaks

A page break is a place in your file that marks where a new page will begin when you print the file on the printer. If your work disk is set to start a new page after 54 lines of text, then automatic page breaks will occur after line 54, line 108, line 162, and so on. The automatic page breaks inserted by PC-Write are called *soft breaks*. You can tell the computer to display soft-break lines on the screen. You can also delete these lines. The process of inserting and deleting visible soft page break lines is called *Repaging* in the *PC-Write User's Guide*.

Repage

Start with the LINE.NBR file in the editing screen. Then, position the cursor at the beginning of the file, on line 1. The status line reads "1/73, 1," that is, the cursor is on line 1 of a 73-line file. Do the following to repage the entire file:

    Press ALT-F7   (to get the Pagebreak menu)
    Press F5   (to get a menu for repaging the entire file)
    Press F5   (to repage the entire file)

The status line now reads "1/54, 1" instead of "1/73, 1." Move the cursor down to line 54. Between lines 54 and 55, a soft-break character (♀) is followed by the number 2, as shown here:

54
♀2
55

The soft-break line located between lines 54 and 55 marks the beginning of page 2. If you put the cursor on the soft-break character (♀), the status line reads "0/19, 2," meaning that you are on line zero of 19 lines on page 2. Move the cursor down some more lines and watch the status line change.

A soft-break line can appear in two modes, the *Show mode* and the *Hide mode*. The Show mode displays the soft-break character (♀) and the page number on the screen. The Hide mode hides the soft-break character, and the break line consists of the page number followed by a dashed line. You can use the ALT-SPACEBAR key combination to toggle between the two modes (hold down ALT and press SPACEBAR). Do the following to change from the Show mode to the Hide mode.

    Press ALT-SPACEBAR   (Hold down ALT and press SPACEBAR)

The break line between lines 54 and 55 now appears as shown here:

```
54
2----------------------------------------------------------------------------
```

Press ALT-SPACEBAR again to toggle back to the Show mode with the soft-break character (♀) visible. Remember, these break lines are nonprinting. They appear on the screen only to show you where page breaks will occur when you print the file to the printer.

Delete a Soft-Break Line

You can easily remove a soft-break line by positioning the cursor on the line and using the CTRL-ENTER key combination. The soft-break line disappears and the text lines close up. Delete the soft-break line between lines 54 and 55. Put the cursor at the start of the break line, and then do the following:

    Press CTRL-ENTER   (Hold down CTRL and press ENTER)

Since the LINE.NBR file has only 73 lines, the repaging operation inserted only one soft-break line. If the file were longer, repaging would insert a soft-break line between lines 54 and 55, between lines 108 and 109, and so on. If you want to delete all soft page breaks, you can do it a line at a time by using CTRL-ENTER. However, it is quicker to use one keystroke sequence that deletes all page breaks. Look at the top line after pressing each key as you do the following:

    Press ALT-F5   (to get the Conversion menu)
    Press F7   (to get page break options)
    Press F10   (to remove soft breaks)

All soft-break lines are removed from the file. Later, you will use a similar keystroke sequence to remove hard breaks, which are described in the next section.

Insert a Hard-Break Line

You can insert a hard-break line anywhere in a file to cause a new page to begin. Use the ALT-T key combination to insert a hard break. Insert hard breaks in the LINE.NBR file so that page 2 begins at line 26 and page 3 begins at line 51. Put the cursor on the "2" in "26" in line 26, and then do the following:

    Press ALT-T   (Hold down ALT and press T)

The computer inserts a blank line between line 25 and line 26, and then prints the following highlighted pair of graphics characters to mark the hard break:

The graphics characters (♀✹) inserted between lines 25 and line 26 mark the hard break. A new page begins with line 26. Move the cursor to line 51 and insert another page break (press ALT-T). Next, repage the file (press ALT-F7, F5, and F5). This causes page numbers to appear just to the right of the hard-break characters. For example, page number 2 appears with the hard-break characters between lines 25 and 26, as follows:

Print the LINE.NBR file (press F1, F7, and F10). You should see three pages printed, with lines 1 through 25 on page 1, lines 26 through 50 on page 2, and lines 51 through 73 on page 3.

A hard-break line can appear in two modes, the Show mode and the Hide mode. The Show mode displays the hard-break graphics characters (♀☼) on the screen. The Hide mode hides the graphics characters, and the entire break line consists of a double dashed line. You can use the ALT-SPACEBAR key combination to toggle between the two modes (hold down ALT and press SPACEBAR). Do the following to change from the Show mode to the Hide mode:

Press ALT-SPACEBAR

The break line between lines 25 and 26 should appear as shown here:

```
25
2================================================================================
26
```

Press ALT-SPACEBAR *again* to toggle back to the Show mode with the hard-break graphics characters visible. Remember, these break lines are nonprinting. They appear on the screen only to show you where page breaks will appear when you print the file on the printer.

Practice some of the other printing modes discussed previously in this chapter. For example, skip *to* page 3 and print it. Or, skip page 1 and print pages 2 and 3. After you experiment with different ways to print the file, proceed to the next section to learn how to delete hard breaks.

Delete a Hard-Break Line

You can remove a hard break as easily as you insert one. When you put the cursor on the hard-break line and use the CTRL-ENTER key combination, the hard-break line disappears, and the text lines close up. Delete the hard break that is located between lines 25 and 26. Put the cursor at the start of the hard-break line, and then do the following:

    Press CTRL-ENTER   (Hold down CTRL and press ENTER)

This deletes the hard break between lines 25 and 26. The hard-break line between lines 50 and 51 remain intact. If you printed the file, it would be printed on two pages, with lines 1 through 50 on page 1 and lines 51 through 73 on page 2.

Delete the hard break between lines 50 and 51. Put the cursor on the hard-break line and press CTRL-ENTER. The file is now the same as it was before you added hard breaks.

Suppose you insert a hard break between lines 70 and 71, and then you print the file. Three pages will be printed, with lines 1 through 54 on page 1 (automatic paging), lines 55 through 70 on page 2 (hard break), and lines 71 through 73 (the rest of the file) on page 3.

Go ahead and experiment with hard breaks. Put them where you want them. When you are finished, delete all hard breaks, thus returning the file to its original condition. You can do the following to delete all hard-break and soft-break lines in a file:

    Press ALT-F5   (to get the Conversion menu)
    Press F7   (to get page break options)
    Press F9   (to delete all page breaks)

Delete all break lines, returning the LINE.NBR file to its original 73 lines, and then save the file (press F1, F3). Proceed to the following section to learn how to set top and bottom margins.

Set Top and Bottom Margins

You can set the top margin and bottom margin for every printed page. To set margins, you use the ALT-G key combination followed by a Dot line that specifies the type and length of the margin. To see how this works, you will set both top and bottom margins of the LINE.NBR file to three lines (1/2 inch).

Set the Top Margin

Position the cursor at the top of the LINE.NBR file, and then set the top margin to three lines, as follows:

    Press ALT-G
    Type:
    .XT:3
    and press ENTER

The Dot line .XT:3 is now at the top of the file, before line 1 of the text, as shown here:

```
.XT:3
1
2
3
```

You have set the top margin to three lines. If you print the LINE.NBR file, each page will begin with three blank lines. Proceed to the next section to set the bottom margin to three lines.

Set the Bottom Margin

If the cursor is not already at the beginning of the text (on the number "1"), move it to line 1. Then, set the bottom margin to three lines, as follows:

    Press ALT-G
    Type:
    .XB:3
    and press ENTER

Both Dot lines .XT:3 and .XB:3, are now at the top of the file, before line 1 of the text, shown as follows:

```
.XT:3
.XB:3
1
2
3
```

If you print the file, each page will be printed with a three-line top margin and a three-line bottom margin. Since each page contains 66 lines, there is room for 60 lines of text. Print the LINE.NBR file (press F1, F7, and F10) to verify the page length. The document should print as two pages, as shown in Figure 4-5.

You can delete a Dot line in the same way that you delete any text. An easy way is to put the cursor on the line containing the dot command, then press CTRL-Y to delete the entire line. Use this method to delete the Dot lines in the LINE.NBR file.

Suppose you want to print each page with a six-line top margin and a 10-line bottom margin. Put the cursor at the top of the file and do the following:

    Press ALT-G
    Type:
    .XT:6

and press ENTER
Press ALT-G
Type:
.XB:10
and press ENTER

The Dot lines and the top of the file now look like this:

```
.XT:6
.XB:10
1
2
3
```

Print the file to verify the margin settings, and then delete both of the Dot lines.

REMEMBER The Dot line used to set a top margin is of the form .XT:*length,* where *length* is the number of lines you want for the top margin. The Dot line used to set a bottom margin is of the form .XB:*length,* where *length* is the number of lines you want for the bottom margin.

Multiple Line Spacing

Unless you specify otherwise, printed text is single-spaced. You can use a dot command to change the line spacing to double-spaced, triple-spaced, or whatever spacing you want. Change the spacing to double-spacing. Put the cursor at the top of the file, and then do the following:

Press ALT-G
Type:
.M:2
and press ENTER

The Dot line .M:2 tells the printer to advance two lines after printing each line. This causes the printed text to be double-spaced. The Dot line is inserted at the top of the text to be double-spaced, as shown here:

1
2
3

If you want to triple-space text, use the Dot line .M:3. In general, the line spacing dot command is of the form .M:*lines*, where *lines* is the number of lines the printer advances after printing a line. Therefore, the number of blank lines between printed lines is equal to *lines*−*1*, or one less than the value of *lines*.

Delete this Dot line as you would delete any line. Put the cursor on the line and press CTRL-Y.

Headers, Footers, and Page Numbers

A *header line* is a line that appears at the top of every page. A *footer line* is a line that appears at the bottom of every page. You can use headers and footers for the title of a document, page numbers, or anything else you want to put at the top or bottom of a page. To tell the printer to put a header and a footer on every page, use the following Dot lines: .H for a header and .F for a footer. Following the Dot line, type a colon (:) and the text you want in the header or footer.

Figure 4-5.

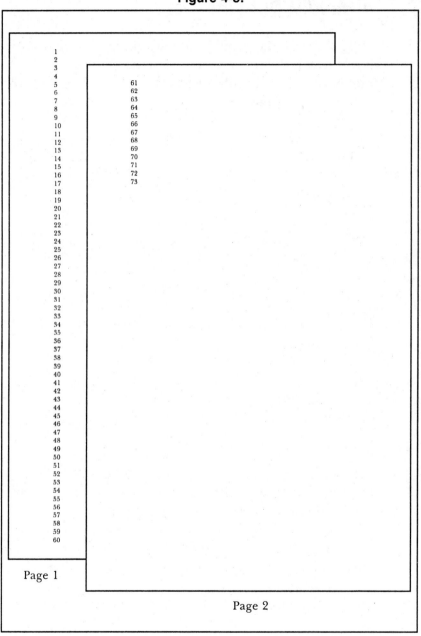

Top and bottom margins set to three lines

A Header Dot Line

Make sure that the LINE.NBR file is in the editing screen and that it is in its original form consisting of the numbers 1 to 73, with one number per line. Put the cursor on the first line. You should see "1/73, 1" in the middle of the status line. Enter a header Dot line as follows:

> Press ALT-G
> Type:
> **.H:Header**
> and press ENTER

The header Dot line should appear at the top of the file, as shown here:

```
.H:Header
1
2
3
```

Print the file. Page 1 will be printed with a six-line top margin, followed by the header line, followed by the first 53 lines of the file (the numbers 1 through 53), and then followed by the six-line bottom margin. Page 2 is printed with the six-line top margin, followed by the header line, followed by lines 54 through 73 of the file, and then followed by a series of blank lines (including the bottom margin) to the end of the page.

Note that 53 lines, instead of 54, are printed on page 1. This happens because the header line is printed where the first line of the file would otherwise appear. Also note that there are no blank lines between the header line and the first line of the file (the number 1). The first few lines of page 1 appear as shown here:

```
Header
1
2
3
```

If you want to separate the text from the header line, insert a blank header line, as shown here:

```
.H:Header
.H:
1
2
3
```

The blank header Dot line (.H:) causes a blank line to be printed after the header line on each page. Since these two header lines occupy two lines, only 52 lines of the text will be printed on each page. You can change this, of course, by setting a different top margin or bottom margin.

You can enter any text you want in the header Dot line. For example, the header Dot lines shown here will print "The LINE.NBR File" followed by two blank lines on each page:

```
.H:The LINE.NBR File
.H:
.H:
1
2
3
```

You can delete header Dot lines as you would delete any text line.

Put the cursor on the Dot line and press CTRL-Y. After returning the LINE.NBR file to its original condition, save the file to the disk.

A Footer Dot Line

Place the cursor on the first line of the LINE.NBR file and add a footer Dot line, as follows:

>   Press ALT-G
>   Type:
>   **.F:Footer**
>   and press ENTER

The footer Dot line should appear at the top of the file, as shown here:

```
.F:Footer
1
2
3
```

Print the file. You will see "Footer" printed at the bottom of each page. If your work disk is set to print 54 lines of text, then the word "Footer" will appear on the 54th line of page 1, as shown here:

```
51
52
53
Footer
```

Page 2 consists of lines 54 through 73 of the file, followed by blank lines for a total of 53 lines, and then followed by the footer. The footer is printed just before the bottom margin. If you want the footer to appear closer to the actual bottom of the physical page, change the bottom margin.

You may want to print a blank line just before the footer. To do this, insert a blank footer Dot line (.F:) just before the footer Dot line that includes the footer text. Place the cursor on the current footer Dot line (.F:Footer), and then press ALT-G. The current footer Dot line moves down one line to make room for a new dot line.

Type:
.F:
but don't press ENTER

You do not need to press ENTER. In fact, if you do press ENTER, a line space will open up between the blank footer Dot line (.F:) and the footer Dot line that contains the footer text (.F:Footer). The top of the editing area should look like this:

```
1
2
3
```

Print only page 1 of the file (press F1, F7, and F9). If your work disk is set to print 54 lines per page, the bottom of the printed part of the page will look like this:

```
51
52

Footer
```

After printing only page 1, the computer stops, with the Print menu on the screen. Press F3 to return to the editing screen.

Suppose that you want to print 54 lines of text with both a header and a footer. You also want one line space after the header and before the footer. To do this, you need to change both the top and bottom margins to four lines. You can accomplish all of this by placing Dot lines at the beginning of the LINE.NBR file, as shown here:

Print page 1 to check your work. It should contain a four-line top margin, the header and one blank line, lines 1 through 54 of the file; one blank line and the footer, and a four-line bottom margin.

Page Numbers

When you create a multi-page document, you probably will want to print a page number on each page. PC-Write can automatically print page numbers either in the header or in the footer. To print automatic page numbers, enter three dollar signs ($$$) in the Dot line to show where you want the page numbers to appear. For example, do the following to insert page numbers in a header:

Press ALT-G
Type:
.H:The LINE.NBR file, Page $$$
and press ENTER

If you wish, you can also include a blank header dot line so that the top of the editing area looks like the following:

```
.H:The LINE.NBR File, Page $$$
.H:
1
2
3
```

If you print the file, the top of page 1 will appear as follows:

```
The LINE.NBR File, Page 1

1
2
3
```

Page 2 will begin in the same way, except that it will be numbered "Page 2." If the file printed 37 pages, the pages would be properly numbered from 1 to 37 in the header lines.

You can also place the page numbering command ($$$) in a footer Dot line. If you wish, you can also include information to center the page numbers. Delete the header dot lines, and then insert footer Dot lines so that the top of the editing area appears as shown here:

1
2
3

Print the file to verify that this works. The three dots on either side of the dollar signs cause the page numbers to be centered. You should see the number 1 printed near the center of page 1 and the number 2 printed near the center of page 2.

There is much more to learn about headers, footers, and page numbers. Be sure to read about them in the *PC-Write User's Guide*.

Summary

In this chapter, you learned about printing documents of two or more pages, multi-page documents. You first created a practice file called LINE.NBR, which consists of the numbers 1 through 73, with one number per line. You printed this file as a two-page document, using a keystroke sequence that you learned in previous chapters (F1, F7, F10). If your work disk is set to print 54 lines on a page, you saw lines 1 through 54 printed on the first page, and lines 55 through 73 on the second page. If your work disk is set to print 60 lines per page, you will see lines 1 through 60 of the file on page 1, and lines 61 through 73 on page 2.

You learned how to print only page 1, and how to skip page 1 and print only page 2. You also learned how to print multiple copies of a page. From the editing screen, you printed only page 1 by using the keystroke sequence F1, F7, F9.

Instead of using the default pagination, you inserted page breaks in the file in order to control where each page begins. The automatic breaks are called soft breaks; the page breaks you insert are called hard breaks. You learned how to repage a file so that all breaks appear in the file either as graphics characters (Show mode) or as dashed lines (Hide mode).

Instead of using the default top and bottom margins, you used a Dot line to specify the margins. Setting your own margins allows you to control the appearance of your printed document.

The default line spacing used by PC-Write is single spacing. However, you learned to use a dot command line to change to double-spacing, triple-spacing, or whatever spacing you want.

Finally, you learned how to use Dot lines to tell PC-Write to print a header or footer on each page. You also learned how to include automatic page numbering in either a header or a footer, or both.

CHAPTER

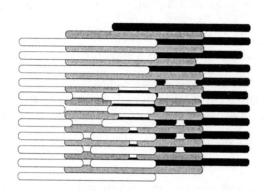

Screen and Page Format Control

Your PC-Write work disk has several *default settings* that control the appearance of text on the screen and the way text is printed to the printer. In the preceding chapters, you learned how to override some of these default settings by using Dot lines and font characters. In this chapter, you will learn more about default settings and how to change them to suit your purposes. In particular, you will do the following:

- Learn about the edit control file (ED.DEF), which controls the appearance of text on the screen.

- Learn about the print control file (PR.DEF), which controls the way text is printed to the printer.
- Create a practice file called COLUMN.NBR.
- Learn how to edit the ruler line in the editing screen.
- Learn how to imbed a ruler line in a file so that it is stored as part of the file.
- Learn how to edit the ED.DEF file in order to make permanent changes to default settings.
- Learn how to edit the PR.DEF file in order to make permanent changes to default settings.
- Learn how to divide the screen into two or more columns, and then edit them independently.
- Create a file called FCC001.NSL that has two columns, edit it, and print it.

The COLUMN.NBR and FCC001.NSL files used in this chapter are on *The Shareware Book* Convenience Disk. If you have this disk, you can load these files from the Convenience Disk instead of entering them from the keyboard. Since you will be editing these files, use a copy of your Convenience Disk for this purpose, or copy files you want to use from the Convenience Disk to your PC-Write data disk.

Default Screen and Page Formats

Two files on your PC-Write work disk control the appearance of text on the screen and the way text is printed on the printer. The edit control file (ED.DEF) controls the appearance of text on the screen. The print control file (PR.DEF) controls the way text is printed on the printer.

The ED.DEF and PR.DEF files contain the default settings that determine such things as where text begins and ends on the screen, and where left, right, top, and bottom margins occur when you print text to the printer. When you use the WORKDISK.BAT program to make a work disk, you determine several of these default settings by your answers to setup questions. In this way, you customize the ED.DEF and PR.DEF files to your requirements. As you gain experience with PC-Write, you might want to make work disks with different default settings for different purposes. Of course, you can override the default settings by including formatting commands such as Dot lines and font characters in your files.

During setup of the work disk, the authors generally used the suggested answers to setup questions. For example, the authors recommended answering "yes" to the question about one-inch margins. Here are some of the default settings for the work disk used by the authors:

- A page has 66 lines, spaced 6 lines per inch. Therefore, page length is 11 inches.

- The default top and bottom margins are each 6 lines, or 1 inch.

- The default type font is Fast (F), draft quality at 10 characters per inch.

- The left margin is 10 spaces wide. Using the default type font of 10 characters per inch, this gives a 1-inch left margin.

- Text on the screen is controlled by the ruler line. The default ruler line has a left screen margin at column one and a right screen margin at column 65. Word wrap occurs at the right margin (column 65). This gives a text width of 6 1/2 inches when printed using the default type font of 10 characters per inch. Text printed on 8 1/2-inch-wide paper will have a default left margin of 1 inch and a right margin of 1 inch.

In preceding chapters, you learned how to override some of the default settings. In this chapter, you will learn how to change the ruler line and the left margin for text you print on your printer.

Change the Default Formats

In this section, you will create a small practice file called COLUMN.NBR, and you will use it to learn how to edit the ruler line and change the way text is printed to the printer. In the previous chapter, you used the LINE.NBR file to change the *vertical* appearance of a printed page, using page breaks, headers, and footers. In this chapter, you will learn how to change the *horizontal* appearance of text on the screen and printed on the printer.

Create the COLUMN.NBR File

Load PC-Write's Edit progam and create the file shown in Figure 5-1. This file is called COLUMN.NBR. It consists mostly of odd numbers and spaces. Each digit appears in every tenth column. For example, the digit "1" appears in columns 1, 11, 21, 31, 41, 51, and 61, and the digit "3" appears in columns 3, 13, 23, 33, 43, 53, and 63. Note that the digit "5" appears in column 65, where word wrap occurs.

Spaces occur in even-numbered columns. Without spaces, of course, word wrap would never happen! The COLUMN.NBR file is intentionally contrived to make it easy for you to count characters and see where word wrap occurs as you use the ruler line to make text on the screen wider or narrower.

Figure 5-1.

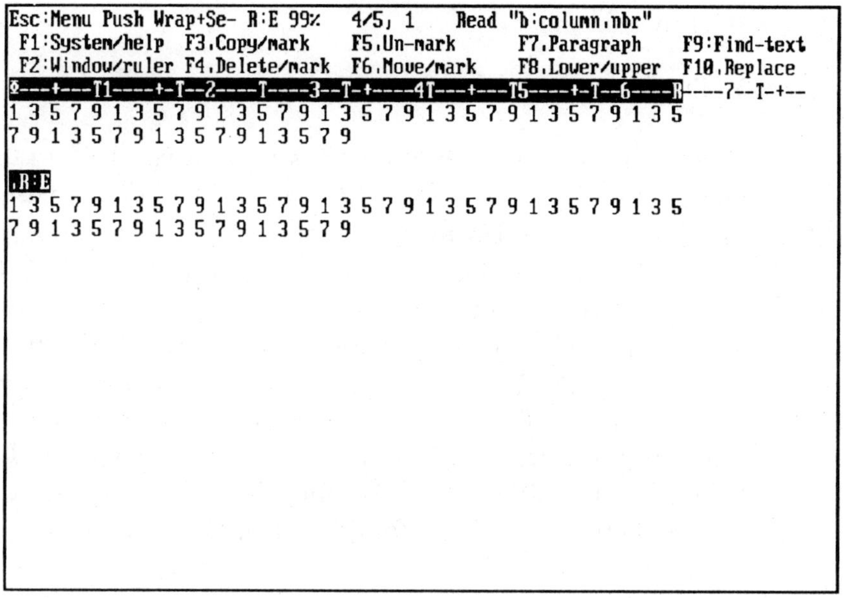

```
Esc:Menu Push Wrap+Se- R:E 99%   4/5, 1    Read "b:column.nbr"
 F1:System/help  F3.Copy/mark   F5.Un-mark      F7.Paragraph    F9:Find-text
 F2:Window/ruler F4.Delete/mark F6.Move/mark    F8.Lower/upper  F10.Replace
R---+---T1----+-T-2----T----3--T-+----4T---+---T5----+-T-6---R----7--T-+--
1 3 5 7 9 1 3 5 7 9 1 3 5 7 9 1 3 5 7 9 1 3 5 7 9 1 3 5 7 9 1 3 5
7 9 1 3 5 7 9 1 3 5 7 9 1 3 5 7 9

.R:E
1 3 5 7 9 1 3 5 7 9 1 3 5 7 9 1 3 5 7 9 1 3 5 7 9 1 3 5 7 9 1 3 5
7 9 1 3 5 7 9 1 3 5 7 9 1 3 5 7 9
```

The COLUMN.NBR practice file

Create this file the easy way. Type the first two lines of numbers, then obtain the other two lines by copying the first two lines. You can use the following steps to copy a block of text:

1. Put the cursor on the first character of the first line and press F3. You will see the word "Marking" in the status line.

2. Press the ↓ key twice to mark the two lines you want to copy.

3. After marking the two lines, press F3. The word "Marking" in the status line will change to "Marked."

4. Move the cursor to the place where you want to insert the copy. You might have to press ENTER to create a blank line between the marked text and the place where you want the copy to

appear. When the cursor is where you want it, press F3. The copy is in place.

5. Press F5 to unmark the marked text.

The editing screen's reminder lines remind you how to use F3 to mark text for copying—"F3.Copy/mark"—and to use F5 to unmark text—"F5.Un-mark."

Now, insert the Dot line .R:E, as shown in Figure 5-1. Put the cursor where you want the Dot line to appear and press ALT-G. Then, type the Dot line. Check the appearance of your screen against Figure 5-1, make any corrections, and save the file.

The Dot line .R:E causes the text that follows it to be printed in the Elite font, draft quality, at 12 characters per inch. The text above this Dot line is not preceded by a Dot line, so it will be printed in the default type font, Fast (F), at 10 characters per inch.

Print the COLUMN.NBR File

Before printing the file, carefully align the print head on your printer, so that printing will begin at the actual left edge of the paper. Doing this will enable you to actually measure the left margin after you print the file.

Print the file. Figure 5-2 shows a printout of the file. The page begins with the default top margin of 6 lines. Next come the first two lines of text, each printed with a 10-space left margin. Note that the first line has 65 characters of text (digits and spaces). These lines are printed with the default 10 characters-per-inch draft quality font.

The second pair of lines is printed in the Elite font, draft quality, at 12 characters per inch, as specified by the Dot line .R:E in the file. Note that the margin is narrower than in the top pair

Figure 5-2.

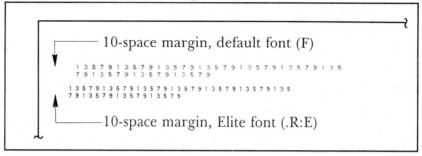

Printout of the COLUMN.NBR file

of lines. The margin consists of 10 spaces printed at 12 characters per inch. Although the first line of the pair still contains 65 characters, it is narrower because it is printed at 12 characters per inch.

Change the Printed Left Margin

The default left margin for the printed copy is 10 characters wide. You can use a Dot line to override the default left margin and set it to a different number of spaces. To set the left margin, press ALT-G, and then type a .X Dot line. Use this method to set the printed left margin to zero (0) spaces. Put the cursor at the beginning of the file, and then do the following:

Press ALT-G
Type:
.X:0
and press ENTER

After you enter the Dot line, the top of the file should look like this:

.X:0
1 3 5 7 9 1 3 5 7 9 1 3 5 7 9 1 3 5 7 9 1 3 5 7 9 1 3 5 7 9 1 3 5
7 9 1 3 5 7 9 1 3 5 7 9 1 3 5 7 9

Make sure that your printer is set to begin printing at the left edge of the paper, and then print the file. All lines should be printed with no left margin, as shown in Figure 5-3.

REMEMBER The Dot line to set the printed left margin is of the form .X:*number,* where *number* is the number of spaces you want in the left margin. For example, if you are printing in a 12-character-per-inch font (Elite or Quality) and want a 1-inch left margin, use the Dot line .X:12.

Do not delete the Dot line .X:0. Leave it at the top of the file and proceed to the next section.

Figure 5-3.

```
1 3 5 7 9 1 3 5 7 9 1 3 5 7 9 1 3 5 7 9 1 3 5 7 9 1 3 5 7 9 1 3 5
7 9 1 3 5 7 9 1 3 5 7 9 1 3 5 7 9
1 3 5 7 9 1 3 5 7 9 1 3 5 7 9 1 3 5 7 9 1 3 5 7 9 1 3 5 7 9 1 3 5
7 9 1 3 5 7 9 1 3 5 7 9 1 3 5 7 9
```

Printout after changing left margin to zero

Editing the Ruler Line

The ruler line controls the horizontal placement of text on the screen. The default ruler line on the authors' work disk is shown here:

```
1 3 5 7 9 1 3 5 7 9 1 3 5 7 9 1 3 5 7 9 1 3 5 7 9 1 3 5 7 9 1 3 5
7 9 1 3 5 7 9 1 3 5 7 9 1 3 5 7 9
```

The ruler line determines the left and right limits for text on the screen. The ruler line shown in the preceding illustration allows up to 65 characters per line, beginning in column 1 (left edge of screen) and ending in column 65.

The letter "L" marks the left end of the text area. The letter "R" marks the right end of the text area, where word wrap occurs. Any word that extends beyond this point is automatically wrapped to the beginning of the next line. The part of the ruler line from the left margin (L) to the right margin (R) is highlighted.

The cursor marker (Φ) is in column 7. You can see the cursor under the first 7 in the first line of text. When you move the cursor left or right, the cursor marker moves with it. Press HOME to move the cursor to column 1; the cursor marker moves with the cursor and covers the "L" in column 1. Press END to move the cursor to the right end of the text. If the cursor moves to column 66, then you know that the end of text contains an invisible space. The word following the space was wrapped to the next line.

Tab markers (T) are in columns 9, 17, 25, 33, 41, 49, 57, and 73. There is also a tab stop in column 65, but it is covered by the right margin marker (R). Press HOME to move the cursor to column 1, and then use the TAB key to tab to all the tab markers. You will see the cursor marker stop in column 65. Press TAB again to reach the tab stop in column 73.

Columns that end in the numeral 5 are marked with a plus sign (+), unless preempted by a more imporant character. You can see plus signs in Columns 5, 15, 35, 55, and 75. However, in columns 25, 45, and 65 the plus sign is preempted by a more important column character.

You can edit the ruler line and position the left margin (L), right margin (R), and tab stops (T) wherever you want them. Note that the markers are all uppercase letters. When you enter markers, be sure to type them in uppercase.

You can display the ruler line anywhere on the screen. Put the cursor where you want the ruler line to appear and use the F2 key to display it. The third line from the top of the editing screen reminds you of this, as shown here:

```
F2:Window/ruler
```

Try it. Move the cursor two lines below the bottom of the file and display the ruler line, as follows:

Press F2

The ruler line appears at the cursor position, as shown in Figure 5-4. The top part of the screen provides information on editing the ruler line, most of which you can ignore. However, in the line that begins with "Right Margin Letters," note the phrase "Ragged (normal)." You will soon reset the "ragged" right margin. But first, remove the ruler line:

Press F2

If the ruler line is displayed at the cursor position within the editing area, pressing F2 removes it. You can press F2 to display the ruler line wherever you want it; you can also press F2 to remove it.

Figure 5-4.

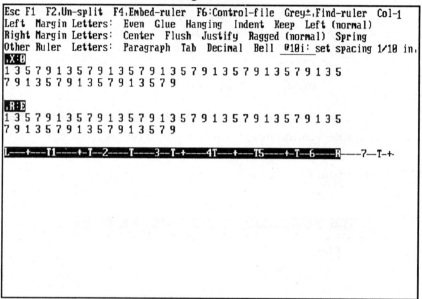

The ruler line displayed in the editing area

Change the Right Margin You will now display the ruler line on the top line of the file and change the right margin from column 65 to column 60. Put the cursor on the top line, and then do the following:

   Press F2

The ruler line appears at the cursor position, temporarily covering the top line of the file, as shown here:

The cursor is now blinking in the ruler line. You can move it anywhere in the ruler line and make changes. Move the cursor to column 60 (under the 6), and set a new right margin, as follows:

Type:
R   (must be an uppercase R)

You do not need to press ENTER. As soon as you type **R**, it is accepted as the new right margin. The "R" that was in column 65 changes to "r." The ruler line is now highlighted from column 1 to column 60, as shown here:

```
L---+---T1----+-T--2----T----3-T-+----4T---+---T5----+-T--R---r----?-T-+-
1 3 5 7 9 1 3 5 7 9 1 3 5 7 9 1 3 5 7 9 1 3 5 7 9 1 3 5 7 9 1 3 5
7 9 1 3 5 7 9 1 3 5 7 9 1 3 5 7 9
```

You can leave the "r" in column 65. Since it is now in lowercase, it has no effect on the ruler line. Only uppercase letters are effective. Since the "r" falls in a column ending with 5, you could replace the "r" with a plus (+), but that isn't necessary. Make sure that your ruler line matches the preceding illustration, and then remove it from the editing area and return to the normal editing screen, by doing the following:

Press F2

The status line, reminder lines, and ruler line appear at the top of the editing screen, as shown in Figure 5-5. The ruler line is now set with a right margin (R) in column 60. However, the text in the editing area remains unchanged. To make it conform to the new ruler line, you must reformat each paragraph. Put the cursor at the left end of the first line of text (on the "1") and reformat the first paragraph as follows:

Press F7

Figure 5-5.

```
Esc:Menu Push Guide,    R:F 99%    0/5, 1    Edit "b:column,nbr"
F1:System/help  F3,Copy/mark      F5,Un-mark      F7,Paragraph    F9:Find-text
F2:Window/ruler F4,Delete/mark    F6,Move/mark    F8,Lower/upper  F10,Replace
L---+---T1----+-T--2----T----3--T-+----4T---+---T5----+-T--R°---r----7--T-+--
.X:0
1 3 5 7 9 1 3 5 7 9 1 3 5 7 9 1 3 5 7 9 1 3 5 7 9 1 3 5 7 9 1 3 5
7 9 1 3 5 7 9 1 3 5 7 9 1 3 5 7 9
.R:E
1 3 5 7 9 1 3 5 7 9 1 3 5 7 9 1 3 5 7 9 1 3 5 7 9 1 3 5 7 9 1 3 5
7 9 1 3 5 7 9 1 3 5 7 9 1 3 5 7 9
```

The ruler line has a new right margin

Use the F7 key to reformat the second paragraph. The text should now appear as shown in Figure 5-6. If you enter new text at the bottom of the file, then word wrap will occur at column 60. Move the cursor to a couple of lines below the bottom of the file and type a long line, anything you want. You will see word wrap occur at the right margin setting (R) in column 60.

As shown in Figure 5-6, the file is ready to be printed, with no left margin (.X:0). The first two lines will be printed in the default font. Since the last two lines are preceded by the Dot line .R:E, they will be printed in the Elite font. A sample printout of the file is shown in Figure 5-7.

Change the Left Margin For most purposes, it is best to leave the left screen margin in column 1, and then use Dot lines to set left margins for printing. However, if you want to change the ruler

Figure 5-6.

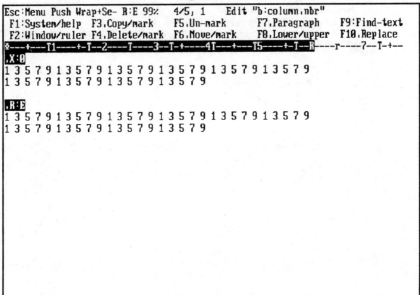

Text is reformatted (F7) to conform to the new ruler line

Figure 5-7.

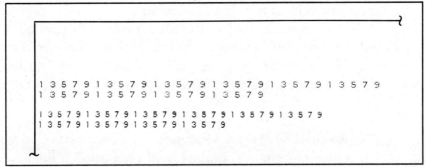

Printout with ruler line right margin in column 60

line's left margin, you can do it as easily as changing the right margin. Put the cursor where you want to display the ruler line, press F2, and then type an uppercase **L** where you want the left margin. The ruler line shown below has the left margin in column 10 and the right margin in column 60.

```
1 3 5 7 9 1 3 5 7 9 1 3 5 7 9 1 3 5 7 9 1 3 5 7 9 1 3 5 7 9
1 3 5 7 9 1 3 5 7 9 1 3 5 7 9 1 3 5 7 9
```

You cannot use the F7 key to reformat text that is to the left of the left margin. Instead, you must put the cursor at the beginning of each line and type spaces to move the text to the new left margin. After moving the text, position the cursor so that the cursor marker does not cover the left margin marker in the ruler line. The ruler line and the top part of the text should look something like this:

```
        1 3 5 7 9 1 3 5 7 9 1 3 5 7 9 1 3 5 7 9 1 3 5 7 9 1 3 5 7 9
        1 3 5 7 9 1 3 5 7 9 1 3 5 7 9 1 3 5 7 9
```

Note that the text now extends to the right of the right margin. Use the F7 key to reformat this paragraph so that it looks like that shown here:

```
1—+-&-↑L—---+-T—2-----T-----3--T-↑-----4T---+----T5----+-T--R----r-----7—T-+—
.X:0
        1 3 5 7 9 1 3 5 7 9 1 3 5 7 9 1 3 5 7 9 1 3 5 7 9 1
        3 5 7 9 1 3 5 7 9 1 3 5 7 9 1 3 5 7 9 1 3 5 7 9
```

Put the cursor on any text line and press HOME. The cursor will move to the new left margin. If you want to type text to the left of the left margin, then use the ← key to position the cursor. When word wrap occurs at the right margin, the wrapped word will be placed on the next line, beginning at column 10. Go ahead and try it. Put the cursor somewhere below the text now on the screen, press HOME, and start typing. You will see word wrap occur at the right margin, and the wrapped word will appear at the left margin.

Print the file. Although the left margin is set to zero, the printed page has a 10-space left margin because of the 10 spaces that you inserted to the left of the left margin in the ruler line. If you had typed text to the left of the ruler line left margin, then you would see that text printed.

The changes you have made to the ruler line are temporary. When you exit from PC-Write and return to DOS, all the changes will be lost. When you reload the PC-Write editing program (ED.EXE), you will again see the default ruler line. If you want to make your changes permanent, you can imbed a ruler line in a file so that it is loaded into the editing screen along with the file. You will learn how to imbed a ruler line in the next section.

Before proceeding to the next section, practice editing the ruler line. Return the ruler line to the default settings. Put an uppercase "L" in column 1 and an uppercase "R" in column 65. This will cause the "L" in column 10 and the "R" in column 60 to change to lowercase. Replace the letter "l" in column 10 with the number "1" and the "r" in column 60 with the number "6." The ruler line should now be in its original (default) form, as shown in Figure 5-1 at the beginning of this chapter.

Imbed a Ruler Line in a File Remember that letter from Laran Stardrake to *The BASIC Teacher*? Laran decided that she would like to print that letter in the Quality font, with a 1-inch left margin and a text width of 6 1/2 inches. The quality font prints at 12 characters per inch. Therefore, Laran needs a printed left margin of 12 spaces and a text width of 78 characters (6 1/2 × 12 = 78). An easy way to accomplish this is to set the left and right margins in the ruler line to columns 1 and 78, respectively, and then use the Dot line .X:12 to set the printed left margin.

Load the TBT001.LTR file into the editing screen by first pressing F1 and then pressing F6. The top line will prompt you for the file name, as shown here:

```
File to load or create (Esc:cancel F8:dir): "b:column.nbr"
```

Change "b:column.nbr" to "b:tbt001.ltr" and press ENTER. You will be asked if you want to make a backup file. Press F9 to make a backup file. Soon you will see the TBT001.LTR file in the editing screen, as shown in Figure 5-8.

Figure 5-8.

```
Esc:Menu Push Wrap+Se- R:F 99%   1/34, 1   Edit "b:tbt001.ltr"
   F1:System/help  F3.Copy/mark    F5.Un-mark      F7.Paragraph    F9:Find-text
   F2:Window/ruler F4.Delete/mark  F6.Move/mark    F8.Lower/upper  F10.Replace
 0---+---T1----+-T--2-----T----3--T-+----4T---+----T5----+-T--6----R----7--T-+--
P. O. Box 1635
Sebastopol, CA 95473-1635
January 2, 1990



The BASIC Teacher
2814 - 19th Street
San Francisco, CA 94110

Attention:  Circulation Department

Dear People:

I am a new subscriber to ‡The BASIC Teacher‡.  My first issue
(January, 1990) arrived last week.  Well, actually, 101 copies
arrived.

Enclosed is a shareware copy of PC-File +, an excellent database
program.  I use it to keep track of people who request my
```

The TBT001.LTR file in the editing screen

Change the right margin in the ruler line to column 78. The ruler line should now appear as shown here, with the left margin in column 1 and the right margin in column 78:

Use the F7 key to reformat the three paragraphs of the body of the letter. Do not reformat the return address or the address of *The BASIC Teacher*. After reformatting, the letter should appear as shown in Figure 5-9.

Now, add Dot lines at the top of the file to specify the Quality type font and a left margin of 12 spaces. Remember, you must

Figure 5-9.

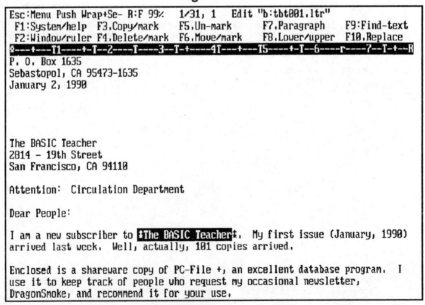

The TBT001.LTR file after reformatting

press ALT-G to begin each Dot line, and then type the Dot line and press ENTER. The Dot lines and the first line of text are shown here:

P. O. Box 1635

To imbed the ruler line in the file, put the cursor on the top line of the file and press two keys in succession, as follows:

Press F2 then press F4

A copy of the ruler line appears at the top of the file, as shown here:

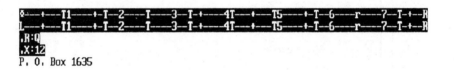
P. O. Box 1635

The second ruler line, the copy, is now part of the file. You can move the cursor to this ruler line and edit it as you would edit any text. If you want to make any changes, do so now, and then save the file. From now on, when you load this file into the editing screen, the ruler line will accompany it.

Make sure your printer is ready to print at the beginning of a page, and then print the TBT001.LTR file. A sample printout is shown in Figure 5-10.

You can imbed a ruler line anywhere in a file, and you can put as many ruler lines in a file as you want. Each ruler line controls the text below it, until another ruler line is encountered. Thus,

Figure 5-10.

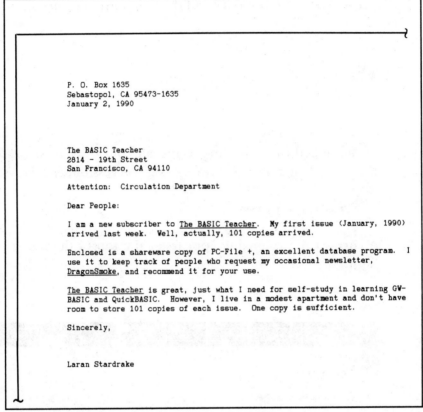

The TBT001.LTR file printed in Quality font with a 12-character left margin

you can use different formats in different parts of a file. Once you have imbedded a ruler line, you can position the cursor on the ruler line and edit it just like any text. To remove a ruler line, put the cursor on the ruler line and press CTRL-Y.

Now, exit from the Edit program and return to DOS. Next, you will learn how to make permanent changes in the edit control file (ED.DEF) and print control file (PR.DEF). You can customize these files by setting your own default settings.

Edit the Edit Control File

In this section, you will learn how to edit the edit control file, called ED.DEF on your work disk. Use a copy of your work disk so that you can retain your original default settings. Insert the work disk in drive A and load the Edit program and the ED.DEF file, as shown here. (The /e that you type tells PC-Write that you are loading the ED.DEF file for the purpose of editing it.)

Type:
ed ed.def /e
and press ENTER

The beginning of the authors' ED.DEF file is shown here. (Your ED.DEF file may be different, depending on your computer.)

```
!ed.*
!pr.def
```

The part of the ED.DEF file that you want to edit is at the bottom of the file. Move the cursor to the bottom of the file (press SHIFT-GREY MINUS, ALT-MINUS, or on some computers SHIFT-F11). The last four lines of the authors' ED.DEF file are shown here:

The ED.DEF file contains the default ruler line and three Dot lines. The Dot lines specify a 10-space printed left margin (.X:10), a 6-line top margin (.XT:6), and a 6-line bottom margin (.XB:6). If your file has these lines, then you can edit them so that they appear as shown in the following illustration. Change the first .X line and the ruler line so they appear as shown. If your file does not contain the Dot lines shown, then add them. In the illustration, arrows point to the changes you should make. Remember, you can edit these lines just as you would edit any text.

After you have made the changes specified in the illustration, save the edited file. The work disk containing the modified ED.DEF file now has new default settings that will be invoked the next time you load the editing program. To verify that the defaults have been changed, exit the editing program, return to DOS, and then reload the editing program. Include the KATHY01.LTR file as you load the editing program:

Type:
ed b:kathy01.ltr /e
and press ENTER

Figure 5-11 shows the KATHY01.LTR file in the editing screen. Since the file was created using a different ruler line, the text does not conform to the new default ruler line on this work disk. Use the F7 key to reformat the three paragraphs that comprise the body of the letter, and then save the file.

Remember that this work disk now has a default ruler line with the left margin in column 1 and the right margin in column 78. It also has a printed left margin setting of 12 spaces.

Figure 5-11.

```
Esc:Menu Push Wrap+Se- R:F 99%   1/24, 1  Read "b:kathy01.ltr"
  F1:System/help F3.Copy/mark    F5.Un-mark    F7.Paragraph   F9:Find-text
  F2:Window/ruler F4.Delete/mark F6.Move/mark  F8.Lower/upper F10.Replace
  0---+---T1----+-T--2----T----3--T-+----4T---+---T5----+-T--6----+----7--T-+--R
  Dear Kathy,

  Congratulations on being accepted to graduate school!  I knew by
  the way you were totally immersed in your studies last year and
  the great grades you got, that there was no way grad school
  wouldn't accept you.  We're all so proud of you!

  Second congratulations:  you bought a computer!  All those early
  morning hours, groggily retyping papers on your typewriter, were
  unnecessary, dark-age torture.  Your Tandy Laptop is an excellent
  choice, especially for a student.  Its DeskMate software does
  just about everything, but when you need more, ShareWare to the
  rescue!

  I'm sending you a ShareWare version of PC-Write, a word processor
  that should meet all your needs.

  Good luck.  Have fun.  Tell me what you think.

  Call if you have questions.
```

The editing screen with the new default ruler line

Edit the Print Control File

You can edit the print control file in the same way that you edit the ED.DEF file. Load the PR.DEF file for editing. Press F1, press F6, and then type the name of the file you want. The first line of the authors' PR.DEF file looks like this:

(Radio, DMP-130/130A, IBM mod. M 12/06/88)

If you have a different printer, of course, then you will see a different first line. Move the cursor to the end of the file, where you will see the defaults for printer control. The defaults for the authors' PR.DEF file appear as eight Dot lines, and they are listed and described in Table 5-1.

Edit the Dot lines in your PR.DEF file so that the default settings specify the Elite font and a 12-space left margin. If the Dot lines in your file are the same as those shown in Table 5-1, change .R:F to .R:E, and change .X:10 to .X:12. Save the edited file and exit the editing program.

Your work disk now has new default settings in the ED.DEF and PR.DEF files. Load the editing program and the KATHY01.LTR file, and then print the KATHY01.LTR file. The letter should print out in the Elite font, with a 12-character (one inch) left margin, as shown in Figure 5-12.

Table 5-1.

PR.DEF Dot Line	Description
.L:66	Sets the page length to 66 lines
.XT:0	Sets the top margin to zero lines, overridden by another Dot line below
.XB:6	Sets the bottom margin to six lines
.R:F	Selects Fast (F) as the default type font
.S:6	Sets line spacing to six lines per inch
.X:10	Sets the left margin to 10 spaces
.XT:6	Sets the top margin to six lines, overrides the earlier top margin Dot line (.X:0)
.XB:6	Sets the bottom margin to six lines; overrides the earlier bottom margin Dot line (.X:6), even though it sets the bottom margin to the same number of lines

NOTE The last three Dot lines (.X:10, .XT:6, and .XB:6) are put into the PR.DEF file if you answer "Y" to the question about 1-inch margins when you make your work disk. If you answer "N," these Dot lines do not appear in PR.DEF.

Dot Lines in the Authors' PR.DEF File

Figure 5-12.

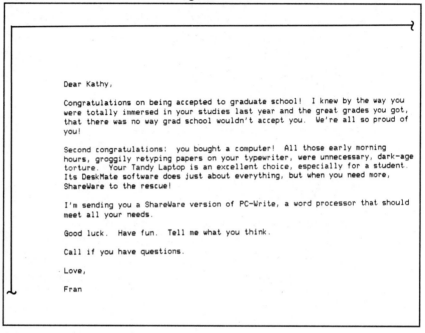

Printout using the edited PR.DEF file

Split the Screen into Columns

The Family Computer Club is a club for families who are new users of computers; it is a club for beginners. The club specializes in home education and personal productivity. It is a new club and has just had its first meeting. Suppose that you have been volunteered to create, edit, and publish the *Family Computer Club Newsletter*.

You decide to use a two-column format on 8 1/2- by 11-inch paper. You also decide to use the Quality type font, which prints at 12 characters per inch. With this in mind, you decide to make each column 3 inches (36 characters) wide. You want a 1-inch (12 characters) left margin and a half-inch (6 characters) space between columns. (The space between columns is called *gutter space*.) As you can see from the following, the text width is 78 characters:

Left column	36 characters
Gutter space	6 characters
Right column	36 characters
Total	78 characters

One of the features of the newsletter will be a page containing brief reviews of books and shareware. You decide to list books in the left column and shareware in the right column. To learn how to set up this two-column format, first create a new file called FCC001.NSL (FCC for Family Computer Club, 001 for issue number 1, NSL for newsletter). Start with the editing screen, as shown here:

```
Esc:Menu Push Wrap+Se- R:F 99%   1/0, 1    Edit "b:fcc001.nsl"
 F1:System/help  F3.Copy/mark    F5.Un-mark       F7.Paragraph   F9:Find-text
 F2:Window/ruler F4.Delete/mark  F6.Move/mark     F8.Lower/upper F10.Replace
 0---+---T1----+-T-2----T---3-T-+----4T---+---T5---+-T-6----E----7-T-+---
```

The Two-Column Ruler Line

The word "column" has two meanings. Previously in this book, it has been used to refer to any space across the screen that contains a single character. In this section, "column" will also mean a column in the sense of a newspaper or newsletter column. Keep this dual use of the word "column" in mind as you continue reading.

Screen and Page Format Control

Ch 5

In order to create two independent columns on the screen, you will split the ruler line into two parts, each part with its own left and right margins. To do this, you will type an uppercase "V" in the column (print position) where you want to split the screen, and then put a left margin (L) and right margin (R) in each half. Begin by displaying the ruler line in the text area:

Press F2

The ruler line appears in the editing area as shown here:

```
Esc F1  F2,Un-split  F4,Embed-ruler  F6:Control-file  Grey±,Find-ruler  Col-1
Left  Margin Letters:  Even  Glue  Hanging  Indent  Keep  Left (normal)
Right Margin Letters:  Center  Flush  Justify  Ragged (normal)  Spring
Other Ruler Letters:   Paragraph  Tab  Decimal  Bell  @10i: set spacing 1/10 in,
L---+---T1----+-T-2----T---3-T-+---4T---+--T5---+-T-6---R---?-T-+-
```

With the cursor in the ruler line, edit the ruler line, as follows:

1. Move the cursor to column 39 and type **V**. This separates the screen into two independent editing windows.

2. Move the cursor to column 36 and type **R**. This sets the right margin for the left half (column) of the screen.

3. Move the cursor to column 42 and type **L**. This sets the left margin for the right half (column) of the screen.

4. Move the cursor to column 78 and type **R**. This sets the right margin for the right half (column) of the screen.

5. Move the cursor to column 65 (under the "r") and type **+**. The plus sign is used to mark every 5th column, unless it is preempted by a more important symbol.

That completes the ruler line editing. The ruler line should now appear as shown here:

```
L---+---T1----+-T--2----T----3--T-+R--V4TL---+---T5----+-T--6----+----7-T-+--R
```

Make any corrections, and then press F2 to remove the ruler line from the text area.

The ruler line is now set for two-column work. Use the arrow keys to move the cursor to the left and right as you watch the ruler line. If the cursor is to the left of the "V," the ruler line is highlighted from the left margin in column 1 to the right margin in column 36. If the cursor is to the right of the "V," the ruler line is highlighted from the left margin in column 42 to the right margin in column 78. Try using the HOME and END keys. They move the cursor to the far left and right, respectively, within the area highlighted in the ruler line.

Enter Text in the Left Column

Position the cursor at the left edge of the screen, just below the ruler line. Then, type two Dot lines, as follows:

    Press ALT-G
    Type:
    .R:Q
    and press ENTER

    Press ALT-G

Type:
.X:12
and press ENTER

You have selected the Quality type font and a 12-space left margin for printout. The ruler line and Dot lines look like this on the screen:

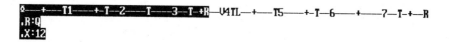

The title of the left column is "BOOKS." The first book entry is the *PC-SIG Encyclopedia of Shareware*. Enter the information shown in Figure 5-13. Note that the text is word wrapped at column 36 in the left half of the screen.

Enter Text in the Right Column

Move the cursor to the right half of the screen, to the right of "V" in the ruler line. Position the cursor on the same line as "BOOKS," and at the left margin of the right column (print column 42). Enter the text in the right half of the screen as shown in Figure 5-14. As you type, note that word wrap occurs in column 78. Words are wrapped to the left margin at column 42.

Make any corrections, save the file, and print it. Figure 5-15 shows a printout of the FCC001.NSL file.

You can edit the two columns independently of each other. Try deleting text in each column. Use the F7 key to reformat within each column. Then, put the deleted text back in and reformat again.

Figure 5-13.

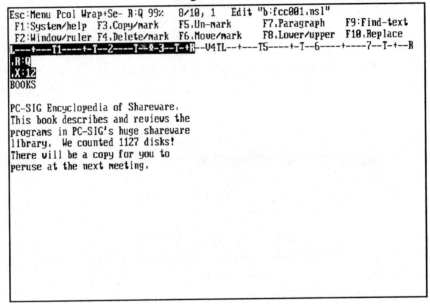

Text has been entered in the left column

You might want to enhance the look of the printed copy by making the column headings ("BOOKS" and "Shareware") boldface. Also, underline the titles *PC-SIG Encyclopedia of Shareware* and *Word Processor for Kids*. Go ahead and experiment. Make changes and see what happens. You can find more information in the "Working with Columns" section of the *PC-Write User's Guide*.

Summary

Your PC-Write work disk has several default settings that control the appearance of text on the screen and the way text is printed to the printer. In Chapters 1, 2, and 3, you used these default

Screen and Page Format Control **165**

Ch 5

Figure 5-14.

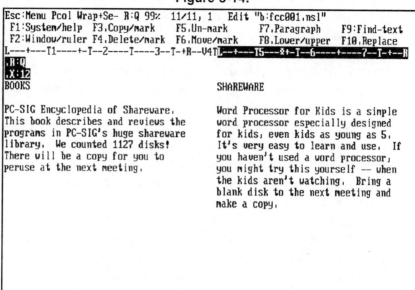

Text has been entered into both columns

Figure 5-15.

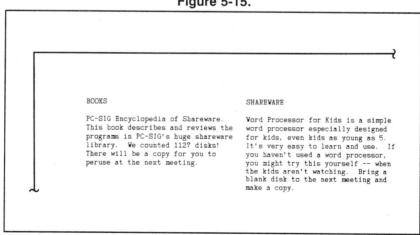

Printout of the two-column FCC001.NSL file

settings to create personal and business letters. In Chapters 4 and 5, you learned how to override default settings and gain more control over the look of text on the screen and as printed on the printer.

You learned how to make temporary changes while working within the edit program on the editing screen. Temporary changes are lost when you exit the edit program and return to DOS.

The appearance of text on the screen and text that is printed is controlled by two files on your work disk, the edit control file (ED.DEF) and the print control file (PR.DEF). You learned how to edit these files and change the default settings. You can now easily make work disks customized for your different purposes.

This chapter included a brief introduction to working with columns. You can split the screen into two columns, and then create and edit them independently of each other. You can extend these principles to working with three or more columns.

Now that you have learned a lot about PC-Write, you can browse through the *PC-Write User's Guide* and learn more. When the need arises, you can look for topics in the table of contents and the index, and then read the sections that help you answer your questions.

PART II

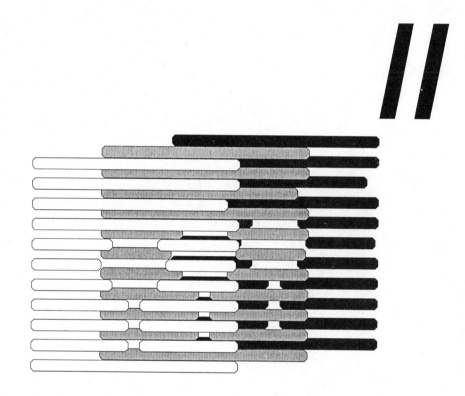

PC-File+

CHAPTER

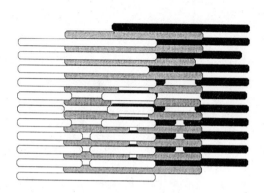

PC-File+:
Getting Started

This chapter shows you how to start using PC-File+, a general purpose database management program. PC-File+ gives you the ability to create, store, maintain, organize, and manipulate collections of information, or databases. With PC-File+, you can also print reports based on the data you collect and graph the data in a variety of formats.

What kinds of databases could you manage with PC-File+? To name only a few possibilities, you can use PC-File+ to manage

- Phone and mailing lists
- Lists of business contacts

- Inventory records (books, tapes, coins)
- Lists of customers
- Purchase orders
- Recipes
- Home and personal records

In this chapter, you will use PC-File+ to create and manipulate a simple list of people's names and telephone numbers.

Before you begin, check your package of PC-File+ materials and disks to verify PC-File+ (version 3) will run on your computer system. Also, be sure that you make backup copies of your original PC-File+ disks.

PC-File+: The Package

PC-File+ version 3 is published by ButtonWare, Inc., P.O. Box 96058, Bellevue, Washington 98009. If you purchased a licensed copy of PC-File+, you received a typeset user's manual, some informational flyers that describe version 3 changes, features, and capabilities, and the disks that contain the PC-File+ programs and resource files.

The PC-File+ programs and resource files come on either a disk set of three 5 1/4-inch disks or a disk set of two 3 1/2-inch disks.

If you have an unregistered copy of PC-File+, ButtonWare assumes that you are evaluating the program. Under the shareware agreement that accompanies any usage of PC-File+, after a reasonable evaluation period you must either discontinue using the program or purchase a licensed copy.

One major advantage to purchasing your own copy of PC-File+ is that you receive the ButtonWare *PC-File+ User's Manual*, a printed reference over 250 pages long. Otherwise, the manual is only available in electronic form from computer clubs, user groups, bulletin boards, and approved shareware disk vendors. If you locate an electronic version of the manual, plan to expend a lot of time, ribbon ink, and paper printing your own nontypeset, unbound version of the manual.

A second advantage is that you receive a *current* version of the product. Shareware products are regularly updated and improved. You should use only the latest and best available version of PC-File+.

When you purchase a licensed copy of PC-File+, you also get a third advantage: one year of technical support and access to the ButtonWare Bulletin Board to help you resolve technical questions about PC-File+. So, if you have an evaluation copy of PC-File+ and believe you have a need for the program, go ahead and license a copy and support the shareware revolution.

Back Up Your PC-File+ Disks

PC-File+ requires at least 384K of memory in order to operate correctly. In addition, PC-File+ needs either two double-sided disk drives or one double-sided disk drive and a hard disk, plus an 80-column monitor display and DOS 2.0 (or later version). To print reports or graphs, you also need a printer.

PC-File+ comes on either three 5 1/4-inch disks or two 3 1/2-inch disks. If you have not already done so, back up your PC-File+ disks. To make backup copies of the original PC-File+ disk sets do one of the following:

- Follow the instructions in the *PC-File+ User's Manual*.
- If you are working with a dual floppy system, boot up your computer with a DOS disk and answer the date and time questions. When the DOS prompt appears, proceed with one of the following step-by-step procedures according to the size of your disks.

Back Up the 5 1/4-Inch Disk Set

If you have 3 1/2-inch disks, please skip to the next section, "Back Up the 3 1/2-Inch Disk Set."

The PC-File+ 5 1/4-inch disk set consists of three disks, labeled DISK ONE, DISK TWO, and DISK THREE. Table 6-1 lists the program and resource files on each disk.

To back up this disk set, you will need three blank (formatted or unformatted) disks. With the A prompt showing and a DOS disk in drive A:

Type:
diskcopy a: b:
and press ENTER

You will be prompted to insert a source disk in drive A and a target disk in drive B. Remove the DOS disk and put the PC-File+ DISK ONE disk in drive A (source disk) and a blank disk in drive B (target disk). When you have the disks inserted in the drives:

Press ENTER

Table 6-1.

DISK ONE (PC-File+ main program disk)
READ.ME	File of information about PC-File+ and shareware concepts
PCF.EXE	PC-File+ main program
PCF.HLP	Help messages
PCFILE.PRO	PC-File+ control file; used to control screen colors, printer functions, and so on
VENDOR.DOC	Shareware guidelines for vendors

DISK TWO (PC-File+ label and graphics programs disk)
PCLABEL.EXE	The PC-File+ mailing label program
PCG2.EXE	The PC-File+ graphing program
MSHERC.COM	File to set up a monochrome monitor with a Hercules Graphics Card

DISK THREE (Miscellaneous programs and files)
CARD	PC-File+ reference card
CHANGES	List of changes to PC-File+ version 3 over earlier versions
PRODUCTS	ButtonWare order form
RESPONSE	User response form
TECHINFO	Notice of how to get technical information about PC-File+ formats
FPRPT.EXE	Program to print database definition reports
PCFIX.EXE	Program to help you repair a damaged database
PEOPLE*.*	Eleven files that constitute an example PC-File+ database. Of all the file names on the disk, the first asterisk (*) is either blank or a number (1 through 6). The second asterisk is one of the following file extensions: DTA, HDR, INX, KEY, PRO, REP

5 1/4-inch Distribution Disks' Contents

The computer will make a copy of DISK ONE. When the copy operation is complete, remove the target disk from drive B and label it. Remove DISK ONE from drive A and then do the following:

    Press Y

Once again, you see a prompt asking you to insert a source disk in drive A and a target disk in drive B. Put PC-File+ DISK TWO in drive A and a blank disk in drive B.

    Press ENTER

A copy of DISK TWO will be made. When the copying operation ends, remove the target disk from drive B and label it. Remove DISK TWO from drive A and then do the following:

    Press Y

You are again prompted to insert a source disk in drive A and a target disk in drive B. Put PC-File+ DISK THREE in drive A and a blank disk in drive B. Insert the two disks into the drives and do the following:

    Press ENTER

A copy of DISK THREE will be made. When the copying operation ends, remove the target disk from drive B and label it. Remove DISK THREE from drive A, and then do the following:

    Press N

The disk copying terminates, and the A prompt reappears. You have made copies of all three original PC-File+ 5 1/4-inch disks. Put the originals in a safe place and use the copies for your explorations. Skip over the following section, "Back Up the 3 1/2-Inch Disk Set."

Back Up the 3 1/2-Inch Disk Set

If you need to make copies of your 5 1/4-inch disk set, refer to the previous section, "Back Up the 5 1/4-Inch Disk Set."

The PC-File+ 3 1/2-inch disk set consists of two disks, labeled DISK ONE and DISK TWO. Table 6-2 lists the program and resource files on each disk.

To back up this disk set, you will need two blank (formatted or unformatted) disks. With the A prompt showing and a DOS disk in drive A do the following:

Type:
diskcopy a: b:
and press ENTER

You will be prompted to insert a source disk in drive A. Remove the DOS disk and put the PC-File+ DISK ONE disk in drive A (source disk). When you have the disk inserted in the drive:

Press ENTER

After a while, you see a prompt asking you to insert the target disk. Remove the source disk (DISK ONE) and put a blank disk into drive A. Then, do the following:

Press ENTER

Watch the prompts and continue to remove and insert the requested disks. When the copy operation is complete, you will be asked if you want to copy another disk. Remove the target disk from drive A and label it. Put DISK ONE aside, and then do the following:

Press Y

Once again, you see a prompt to insert a source disk in drive A. Put the PC-File+ DISK TWO disk in drive A (source disk). When you have the disk inserted in the drive:

Press ENTER

Table 6-2.

DISK ONE (PC-File+ main program disk)

READ.ME	File of information about PC-File+ and shareware concepts
PCF.EXE	PC-File+ main program
PCF.HLP	Help messages
PCFILE.PRO	PC-File+ control file; used to control screen colors, printer functions, and so on
VENDOR.DOC	Shareware guidelines for vendors
CARD	PC-File+ reference card
CHANGES	List of changes to PC-File+ version 3 over earlier versions
PRODUCTS	ButtonWare order form
RESPONSE	User response form
TECHINFO	Notice of how to get technical information about PC-File+ formats
FPRPT.EXE	Program to print database definition reports
PCFIX.EXE	Program to help you repair a damaged database
PEOPLE*.*	Eleven files that constitute an example PC-File+ database. Of all the file names on the disk, the first asterisk (*) is either blank or a number (1 through 6). The second asterisk is one of the following file extensions: DTA, HDR, INX, KEY, PRO, REP

DISK TWO (PC-File+ label and graphics programs disk)

PCLABEL.EXE	The PC-File+ mailing label program
PCG2.EXE	The PC-File+ graphing program
MSHERC.COM	File to set up a monochrome monitor with a Hercules Graphics Card

3 1/2-inch Distribution Disks' Contents

After a while, you see a prompt asking you to insert the target disk. Remove the source disk (DISK TWO) and put a blank disk into drive A. Then do the following:

   Press ENTER

Follow the prompts and continue to remove and insert the requested disks. When the copy operation is complete, you will be asked if you want to copy another disk. Remove the target disk from drive A and label it. Put DISK TWO aside, and do the following:

   Press N

When you press N, the disk copying terminates and the A prompt reappears. You have made copies of the two original PC-File+ 3 1/2-inch disks. Store the originals in a safe place and use the copies for your explorations.

Put PC-File+ on a Hard Disk

If you are not using a hard disk drive, skip this section and go to the following section, "Format a Blank Database Disk."

   Unlike a number of other software packages, PC-File+ does not use or require an "install" program. If you plan to use PC-File+ with a hard disk drive, all you have to do is copy all of the PC-File+ programs and resource files into a subdirectory on the hard drive.

1. Boot up your computer and make sure the DOS prompt is the appropriate one for being logged onto your hard drive. For example, if your hard drive is assigned to drive C, you should see the C prompt on the screen.

2. Make sure you are at the root directory:

   Type:
   cd
   and press ENTER

3. Create a subdirectory with the following name or a name of your choice:

   Type:
   md \pcf
   and press ENTER

4. Change the directory to the subdirectory you just created:

   Type:
   cd \pcf
   and press ENTER

5. Put PC-File+ DISK ONE in drive A, and do the following:

   Type:
   copy a:*.*
   and press ENTER

   All the files on DISK ONE will be copied into the subdirectory \PCF.

6. Remove DISK ONE from drive A. Put PC-File+ DISK TWO into drive A, and do the following:

   Type:
   copy a:*.*
   and press ENTER

7. If you are using the 3 1/2-inch disk set, you are finished copying PC-File+ files into the subdirectory. If you have the 5 1/4-inch disk set, remove DISK TWO from drive A. Put PC-File+ DISK THREE in drive A, and repeat the operation:

   Type:
   copy a:*.*
   and press ENTER

When all of your PC-File+ files are copied to the hard disk drive, proceed to the next section, where you will format a blank database disk.

Format a Blank Database Disk

In all of the subsequent examples in this part of the book, it is assumed that the user is working on a computer with two floppy 5 1/4-inch disk drives. If you have two 3 1/2-inch drives, you can follow most of the examples in this book without modification. Occasionally, screen messages will vary slightly from those shown in the text because of the larger storage capacities of the 3 1/2-inch disks.

If you are using PC-File+ with a hard disk, you will have to modify the PC-File+ disk drive designations and path name requests used in the examples in this book to correspond to the way PC-File+ has been installed on your hard disk. In general, here is the correspondence between a system with two floppy drives and a hard drive system with one floppy drive:

Two Floppy Drives	**One Floppy Drive**
Path A:	Path C:\PCF
Path B:	Path A:

When you first start PC-File+, it prompts you to create a new database on a blank *formatted* disk. If you do not have a formatted disk available, PC-File+ cannot proceed on systems with only floppy drives. To format a disk, put a DOS disk into drive A, and at the A prompt:

Type:
format b:
and press ENTER

You will see a prompt to insert a disk in drive B. Put a blank disk in drive B and press any key. When the disk in drive B has been formatted, you see a message somewhat like this one:

```
362496 bytes total disk space
362496 bytes available on disk
```

You also see a query about formatting another disk. You need only one blank disk to do the exercises in this book. However, if you want to format more disks, press Y and then ENTER, and follow the prompts. When you are ready to stop the format operation:

> Press N, ENTER

Put a label on one blank formatted disk to identify it as a PC-File+ database disk, and get ready to start PC-File+.

Start PC-File+

If you have not already done so, boot up the computer with a DOS disk. Once the A prompt appears, put a copy of PC-File+ DISK ONE in drive A and a blank formatted disk in drive B.

> Type:
> **pcf**
> and press ENTER

PC-File+ displays a title screen like that shown in Figure 6-1. Under the large PC-File+ logo you should see a line that says "PC-File+ Version 3."

PC-File+: Getting Started **181**

Ch 6

Figure 6-1.

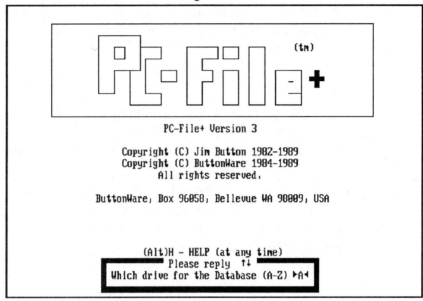

PC-File+ title screen

 CAUTION If you do not have PC-File+ version 3, the screens, examples, and directions used in this book will not work with your version. The examples in this book work only with version 3.

At the bottom of the title screen, you see a message telling you to press ALT-H to get help at any time. Also at the bottom is a "Please reply" portal requesting the *drive designation* for the database to be created on the formatted blank disk.

Get Help Anytime and Anywhere

PC-File+ contains a number of *context-sensitive* help messages. Context-sensitive help messages provide information about the current request on the screen and the actions you can take. For example, PC-File+ is now asking you for the drive designation of the database. Try the PC-File+ help feature:

   Press ALT-H   (hold down the ALT key and press the H key)

Pressing ALT-H produces a PC-File+ help window related to the information being requested in the "Please reply" portal. Figure 6-2 shows you what this context-sensitive help message looks like.

NOTE If your copy of PC-File+ does not contain the help messages' file, PC-File+ will produce an error message and let you continue. All distribution copies of PC-File+ disks include the help message file.

Figure 6-2.

```
                      ←↑↓→
         ┌─────────────────────────────┐
         │Help: See page(s) 128        │
         │                             │
         │Which disk contains the file?│
         │                             │
         │The diskette drive on the left│
         │   or top is usually drive A │
         │The diskette drive on the right│
         │   or bottom is usually drive B│
         │The hard disk                │
         │   is usually drive C        │
         └─────────────────────────────┘
```

PC-File+ drive request help message

At the top of the help message window are four arrows, one for each of the four directions: left, up, down, and right.

    Press ↑   (the up arrow on the keyboard)

When you press ↑, the help window moves up the screen. Try it! Move the help window around the screen with the cursor control (arrow) keys.

The arrows at the top of the window tell you which cursor control keys are active when the window is displayed. Moving the help window up the screen will completely display the "Please reply" portal. Notice the two arrows on the "Please reply" portal: ↑ and ↓. The arrow keys only move this portal up and down the screen.

The help window shown in Figure 6-2 tells you that the question being asked is "Which disk contains the file?" The word *file* refers to the database or data files that you will create. Some common disk drive designations are provided, and the line near the top of the help window displays the page number of the user's manual that might be of additional help.

To make the help window disappear, press any key.

Set the Drive and Path of the Database

After you exit the help window, do the following:

    Press B

The "Please reply" portal changes size, and a new question asks for the DOS path name for the database.

    Press ALT-H

Figure 6-3 contains the help message that PC-File+ displays for the current request. Since you will want to leave the path name blank, the first line of the help message is appropriate. Press any key to make the help message disappear and then:

Press ENTER

When you press ENTER to tell PC-File+ that you want no path name, the program might respond with the following error message:

```
...you should use FILES=20 in CONFIG.SYS...
```

If you see that message, press any key to remove it. If you do not get the error message, you see a screen with the following message:

```
We'll need to define a database. Please give it a name.
```

Figure 6-3.

```
                    ←↑↓→
        ┌─────────────────────────────┐
        │ Help: See page(s) 33        │
        │                             │
        │ If you don't have a hard disk, │
        │ you probably want to leave this blank. │
        │                             │
        │ If you have a hard disk, you can state │
        │ the "path" to the subdirectory that    │
        │ contains your data.         │
        │                             │
        │ example:    \mydata         │
        └─────────────────────────────┘
```

PC-File+ path name help message

Whether you see the error message or not, you should exit from PC-File+ here by pressing the following keys:

Press ESC, ESC

When you press ESC twice, PC-File+ terminates and returns you to the A prompt.

NOTE If you did not see the PC-File+ error message you can skip over the following section, "Setting FILES=20 in CONFIG.SYS" and go on to "Files, Records, and Fields."

Setting FILES=20 in CONFIG.SYS

After you exit from PC-File+, remove the copy of PC-File+ DISK ONE from drive A. Put a DOS disk into drive A.

PC-File+ opens several different files during a database management session. To make sure PC-File+ can open all the files it needs, you must tell your system how many files to expect. Putting a FILES=20 line into the system's CONFIG.SYS file tells your system to expect up to 20 files to be open at the same time. You can set FILES to a larger number, but FILES=20 will be enough for the examples in this book.

If your DOS disk already has a CONFIG.SYS file, you can use your word processing program to insert the line "FILES=20" into the existing file. From the A prompt:

Type:
dir
and press ENTER

A directory of your DOS disk appears on the screen. If the directory contains a file called CONFIG.SYS, use your word processor to add FILES=20 to CONFIG.SYS. (You may have to put the DOS disk in drive B and insert your word processor disk in drive A.)

If no CONFIG.SYS file exists, type the following two lines to create the file. Press ENTER at the end of each line.

Type:
copy con:config.sys
files=20
and then press F6, ENTER

When F6 is pressed, the characters "^Z" appear on the screen. When the last ENTER is pressed, a message "1 File(s) copied" appears, along with the A prompt.

After you change your CONFIG.SYS file (either with a word processor or by creating a new file), make sure the DOS disk is in drive A. Then reboot the computer as follows:

Press CTRL-ALT-DEL   (Hold down CTRL and ALT and press DEL)

When the A prompt appears, remove the DOS disk, put your copy of PC-File+ DISK ONE in drive A, and restart PC-FILE+:

Type:
pcf
and press ENTER

The PC-File+ title screen will reappear as shown in Figure 6-1.

Files, Records, and Fields

Before you start to use PC-File+, you might want to review a few common database terms and ideas.

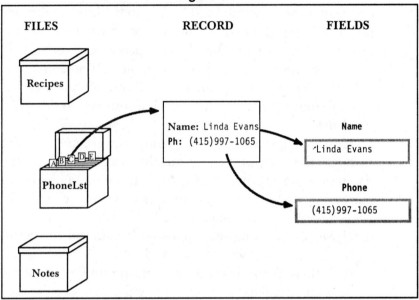

Figure 6-4.

Files, records, and fields

A *database* is any collection of data or information that has been stored or organized in some meaningful way. A database does not have to be in a computer. For example, you probably keep a phone list of the people you know. You might keep the names and phone numbers on a piece of paper you put in your wallet, on a set of index cards, in a book that has different pages for each letter of the alphabet, or on a flip-file that can be placed near the phone. No matter what form you use, the result is that you have a database to refer to when you need a particular telephone number.

Suppose you keep your telephone numbers on a set of index cards in a metal box, as shown in Figure 6-4. You keep one name and number per card. You have also organized the set of cards by the letters of the alphabet and put tabs in the box, one for each letter.

The entire collection of names and phone numbers in the box constitutes the database *file*. The tabs in the box are the *index* to the file. The index gives you an organized way to look for the *records*, the individual cards in the file. On each record or card, there are at least two *fields:* one field for the name of a person and a second field for that person's primary telephone number. If the person has a second telephone number, that number could be put into a third field.

Most database files within a computer are given *names* so that you, and the computer programs that access the files, can tell one database from another. In Figure 6-4, the open box bears a label marked "PhoneLst." If all three boxes were closed, the labels would help you to quickly find the box you need. Naming databases in the computer helps both you and the computer to locate the data you want to see and use.

With these preliminary definitions in mind, it is time for you to name your first database file, specify the fields you want on each record in the file, and begin to create data entries for each of the fields.

Get To Know PC-File+ in 30 Minutes

The following exploration introduces you to the basic PC-File+ features needed to create, search, and print a small database. You will create a telephone list composed of people's names and telephone numbers. You can expect to spend about 30 minutes on the entire exploration. To create your first database with PC-File+, follow these steps:

1. Make sure you have gone through the earlier sections of this chapter, that you have created a copy of PC-File+ DISK ONE, and that you have a blank formatted disk available.

2. If your computer is not turned on, put a DOS disk in drive A and reboot the system. (If your computer is already turned on with the A prompt showing, go to step 5 in this procedure.)

    The computer will go through its normal startup activities and then display a message asking you to provide the new date:

    Enter new date:

3. Type the date and press ENTER, or just press ENTER. The computer will then request that you provide a new time:

    Enter new time:

4. Type the time and press ENTER, or just press ENTER. The A prompt should appear along with the blinking cursor.

    A>_

5. Remove the DOS disk from drive A. Put your copy of PC-File+ DISK ONE into drive A and insert the blank formatted disk (the database disk) in drive B. When the two disks are in the drives:

    Type:
    pcf
    and press ENTER

6. The PC-File+ version 3 title screen appears. At the bottom of the screen is a "Please reply" portal asking for the disk drive designation for the database.

    Which drive for the Database (A-Z) >A<

    The cursor blinks underneath the letter "A" that lies between the two arrowheads (shown as > and < in this book). Since your database file will be created on drive B, do the following:

    Press B

7. The "Please reply" portal message changes to a path name request:

   ```
   What path for the data? >_
   ```

   For this example, you do not need to use a path name.

   Press ENTER

8. The title screen disappears, and the following message shows at the top of the screen:

   ```
   We'll need to define a database. Please give it a name.
   Type a name
   >_       <
   ```

   Type:
   PhoneLst
   and press ENTER

 REMEMBER If you feel confused or want more information during any of these activities with PC-File+, you can access the help system as follows:

   Press ALT-H

PC-File+ can help you with its many context-sensitive help screens.

9. The following message appears near the middle of the screen:

   ```
   B\:PhoneLst is a new file.
   ```

   Underneath this message is the following "Please reply" portal asking if you want to define, that is, create, the new database file named B:\PhoneLst:

   ```
   Do you want to define it? Y/N >Y<
   ```

The request line contains two allowable answers: Y for yes and N for no. Y is set as the default response. Since you do want to define the database:

Press Y or ENTER

10. Figure 6-5 shows the next screen. The Fast method of screen design automatically positions the fields on the display. You have to provide only the names and sizes of the fields. The Paint method of screen design lets *you* decide where fields are to be placed. For this introductory exploration, you will select the Fast method of defining a database:

Press F or ENTER

Figure 6-5.

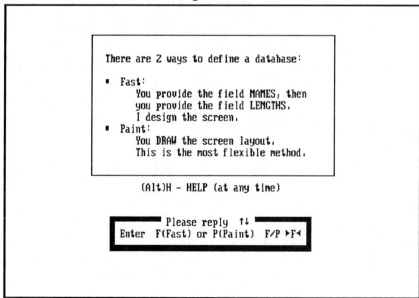

Database definition options screen

11. When you press F, PC-File+ displays a screen where you can type in the field names for your database records. Each field that you name on this screen will appear on every database record. Figure 6-6 shows what the field definition screen looks like before you enter the names of fields. Each field position is enclosed in a set of brackets [] except for the field containing the cursor. The blinking cursor sits in the first field position which is in the top left corner, enclosed by two arrowheads. Here you can type a name for this first field.

```
>_          <
```

12. In this example, use "Name" for the field that contains a person's name and "Phone" for the field that holds that person's telephone number.

Figure 6-6.

```
Enter the field NAMES in their relative positions.
You can place the names anywhere on the screen.
 >          <     [         ]   [         ]   [         ]   [         ]
[         ]      [         ]   [         ]   [         ]   [         ]
[         ]      [         ]   [         ]   [         ]   [         ]
[         ]      [         ]   [         ]   [         ]   [         ]
[         ]      [         ]   [         ]   [         ]   [         ]
[         ]      [         ]   [         ]   [         ]   [         ]
[         ]      [         ]   [         ]   [         ]
[         ]      [         ]   [         ]   [         ]
[         ]      [         ]   [         ]   [         ]
[         ]      [         ]   [         ]   [         ]
[         ]      [         ]   [         ]   [         ]
[         ]      [         ]   [         ]   [         ]
[         ]      [         ]   [         ]   [         ]
[         ]      [         ]   [         ]   [         ]
[         ]      [         ]   [         ]   [         ]
[         ]      [         ]   [         ]   [         ]
Please respond. (F10) when complete. (Alt)H for help.
```

PC-File+ field definition screen

Type:
Name
and press ENTER

If you need to make corrections to your typing, use ↑ to put the blinking cursor back in the first field. Then, either use the backspace key to erase characters or reposition the cursor using the left or right arrow keys, and type over the characters on the screen. When you are finished making corrections, you can either press ENTER or the ↓ key. The section screen area should look like this:

```
[Name      ]
>_           <
```

13. Enter the name of your second field, "Phone":

    Type:
    Phone

    The screen area now looks like this:

    ```
    [Name      ]
    >Phone_      <
    ```

    You can tell PC-File+ that you are finished entering field names by pressing the F10 key:

    Press F10

14. PC-File+ now asks you to define the *display length* for each field you have named. The display length is the number of characters you want displayed when the field is shown on the screen. *Regular fields* are fields that have the same values for display length and actual length. Regular fields can have a display length of up to 65 characters.

    The last field on a record is called a *superfield*. For this database, the field Phone is the superfield. A superfield can contain and display up to 1665 characters, the exact number depending on the number of fields you have defined. Since the PhoneLst database has two fields, PC-File+ gives the following message on the second line of the current display:

```
The " superfield" maximum size for this database is 1585
```

For this database, you will use regular fields, and the display lengths will be smaller than 65 characters. You will set the Name field to a display length of 35 and the Phone field to a display length of 15. The cursor sits between the arrowheads following the word "Name," waiting for you to enter the Name field display length.

Type:
35
and press ENTER
Then type:
15

The display where you typed these values should look like this:

```
Name        [35]
Phone       >15_ <
```

To tell PC-File+ that you have defined the display lengths:

Press F10

15. When you press F10, PC-File+ displays the screen shown in Figure 6-7.

   PC-File+ wants you to tell it whether the fields you defined are regular fields or *window fields*. If the display length of a field is shorter than the actual number of characters in the field, the field is called a window field.

   In this example, you want to specify regular fields. The field Name contains up to 35 characters and the field Phone contains up to 15 characters. For each of these fields, there will be no difference between displayed and actual length.

   Press N or ENTER

16. PC-File+ now displays the following message near the top of the screen:

   The fields will be accessed from left to right,
   and top to bottom as you drew them on the screen.

   A "Please reply" portal asks the following question:

   Would you like to change this sequence? Y/N >N<

   PC-File+ allows you to control the way data gets entered into fields for each record. Unless you say otherwise, the order for data entry is the same as the order shown on the screen (Name first, Phone second). For this example, you will keep the order shown on screen. Make the following response:

   Press N or ENTER

Figure 6-7.

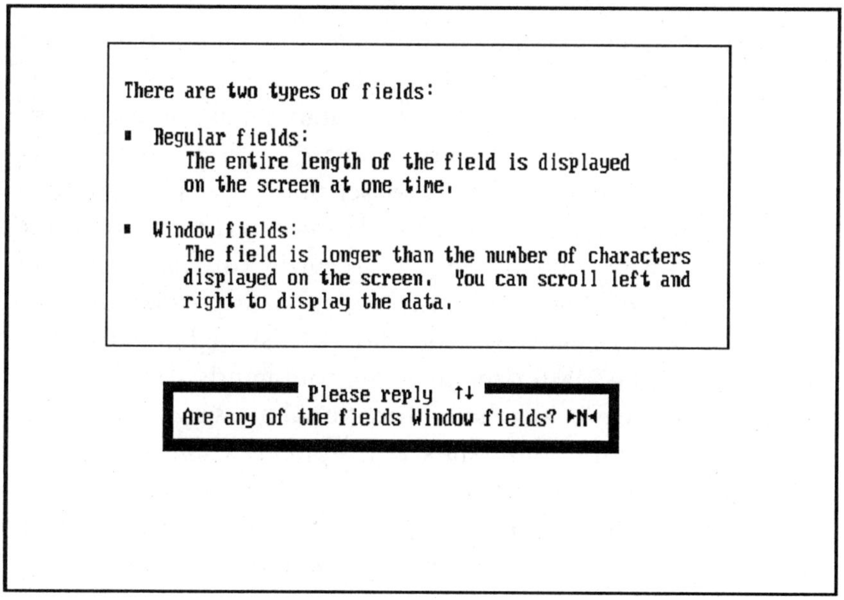

```
There are two types of fields:

■ Regular fields:
     The entire length of the field is displayed
     on the screen at one time.

■ Window fields:
     The field is longer than the number of characters
     displayed on the screen. You can scroll left and
     right to display the data.


         ▀▀▀▀▀▀▀ Please reply ↑↓ ▀▀▀▀▀▀▀
         Are any of the fields Window fields? ►N◄
```

Field type query screen

17. PC-File+ now displays a "Please reply" portal asking you to supply a description for the database:

Database description:>_

You can type a description for the database that is longer than the database name. The description will help you remember what is in the database. (PC-File+ displays both database names and descriptions when it shows you a list of database files.)

For this example, type the following description (or whatever you want to say about this file):

Type:

PhoneLst is my first PC-File+ database
and press ENTER

PC-File+ clears the "Please reply" portal and displays the following message near the center of the screen:

Creating Database..

18. PC-File+ creates the PhoneLst database file on the disk in drive B. When it is finished, PC-File+ displays the PC-File+ Master menu for the new database, as shown in Figure 6-8.

The name of your database appears near the top of the screen, along with the description that you typed. PC-File+ tells you that the database has no (0) records. It also shows the approximate number of records you have the capacity to create. (The total number of records possible depends on the room available on your floppy disk or hard disk.)

The Master menu active commands appear in the boxed-off areas below the informational messages. The Master menu has more commands that appear when you actually enter data into your database.

To tell PC-File+ that you are ready to enter data, choose the "Add a new record" command:

Press F1 or A

19. When you press F1 or A, the Master menu disappears and you see a data entry screen with the following heading:

Record number 1   A

The record number at the top of the screen tells you that you are about to enter data on the first record in the file. The "A" at the top right corner of the screen tells you that you are using the "Add a new record" command.

The cursor is positioned in field 1 of record 1 (Name). To enter data into the field:

Type:
Linda Evans
and press ENTER

Figure 6-8.

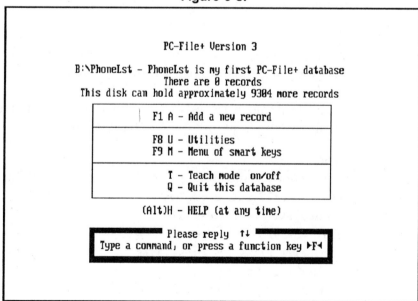

36PC-File+ Master menu

The cursor moves into the Phone field. Enter Linda's phone number:

Type:
(415)997-1065

You can make corrections by using the cursor control keys to move between fields. When you have entered the data correctly:

Press F10

20. When you press F10, PC-File+ displays a "Please reply" portal asking:

    O.K. to ADD? Y,N,or X(stop asking) >Y<

    You have three options: "Y" for "yes," "N" for "no," and "X." Choosing "X" tells PC-File+ to add the record you just created (Linda's name and telephone number) and to stop asking if you want to add future records.

    Press X

    When you press X, record number 1 is added to the PhoneLst database, and a blank record number 2 appears.

21. Create four more records by typing four more names and telephone numbers into the database, as follows:

    Type:
Donut Heaven and press ENTER	(record 2)
(415)996-1171 and press F10	
Donut Haven and press ENTER	(record 3)
(415)998-2025 and press F10	
Strawberry Pizza and press ENTER	(record 4)
(707)899-1212 and press F10	
Ultimate Pizza House and press ENTER	(record 5)
(707)898-7777 and press F10	
and then press F10 again	(record 6)

Figure 6-9.

```
                    PC-File+ Version 3

    B:\PhoneLst - PhoneLst is my first PC-File+ database
                     There are 5 records
        This disk can hold approximately 9304 more records

            ┌─────────────────────────────────────┐
            │      F1 A - Add a new record        │
            │      F2 F - Find a record           │
            ├─────────────────────────────────────┤
            │      F4 G - Graphs                  │
            │      F5 L - Letter writing          │
            │      F6 R - Reports                 │
            │      F7 S - Sort                    │
            │      F8 U - Utilities               │
            │      F9 M - Menu of smart keys      │
            ├─────────────────────────────────────┤
            │      T - Teach mode on/off          │
            │      Q - Quit this database         │
            └─────────────────────────────────────┘

                 (Alt)H - HELP (at any time)

            ┌──────────── Please reply ↑↓ ────────┐
            │ Type a command, or press a function key ►F◄ │
            └─────────────────────────────────────┘
```

Expanded Master menu

The last time you press F10, on the blank sixth record, PC-File+ terminates the "Add" command and displays the expanded form of the Master menu.

22. Figure 6-9 shows how the expanded Master menu might appear on your screen. If you entered all of the data records in step 21, the message "There are 5 records" will appear above the boxed-off command list.

Several new commands appear on the Master menu. These new commands reflect the fact that your database now has records in the file. Select the "Find a record" command:

Press F2 or F

The "Find a record" command search options list appears as shown in Figure 6-10. You will use the first option, "Search for data (find)."

Figure 6-10.

"Find a record" command search options

Press S or ENTER

23. PC-File+ can search files in several ways. The "Please reply" portal now asks you what type of search you wish to make:

    S(Simple search), C(Complex search), Q(Quit)   S/C/Q >S<

    Choose the "Simple search" method, as follows:

    Press S or ENTER

    Your screen now displays the following message and data entry fields:

    ```
            Please supply the search data below
    ================================================================
     Name >*******************************<
     Phone [**************]
    ```

PC-File+: Getting Started **201**

Ch 6

Suppose you want to find Linda Evans's telephone number. To do so, type her name into the Name field and press F10:

Type:
Linda Evans
and press F10

When you press F10, the first record in the database, with "Linda Evans" in the Name field, appears on the screen. A list of the "Find a record" command browse control keys appears in the lower right corner of the screen. Ignore that list for now, and tell PC-File+ to find the next record that contains the data "Linda Evans":

Press F or ENTER

A "Please reply" portal appears in the middle of the screen telling you that no other records were found with "Linda Evans" in the first field position. Do the following:

Press ENTER

When you press ENTER the "Please reply" portal goes away. PC-File+ backs up to the message that asks you what type of search you want to make.

24. Start the search again:

Press S or ENTER

When you see the "supply the search data" message with two fields of asterisks, do the following:

Type:
donut
and press F10

Record number 2 containing the name and telephone number of Donut Heaven should appear on the screen. Notice that PC-File+ matched this record, even though your search data entry was in lowercase letters and you did not type the complete name. But what about the record for Donut Haven?

Press F or ENTER

Record number 3 containing the name and telephone number for Donut Haven appears. To find out if there are any more records with "donut" in the first five character positions of field 1, do the following:

Press F or ENTER

No more records! PC-File+ found both records in the file that had the word "donut" in the first five character positions of field 1.

25. PC-File+ can help you search electronic database records in ways that are often not possible with conventional paper and pencil database files. For example, do the following:

Press ENTER, ENTER

You go back to the "supply the search data" screen, where the two fields of asterisks appear. Suppose you want a pizza but cannot remember the name of the pizza places in your telephone directory. If you enter the letter "p" (for pizza) in the Name field, PC-File+ will look for a name that has "p" in the first character position, but will find no entries. You want a pizza badly. What can you do?

On the screen containing two fields of asterisks, type the *tilde* (~) character and the word "pizza" into field one:

Type:
~**pizza**
and press F10

In an instant, PC-File+ displays record number 4, the name and telephone number for Strawberry Pizza. Not your favorite pizza place? Then, do the following:

Press F or ENTER

The record for Ultimate Pizza House jumps to the screen! The tilde (~) in front of the word "pizza" instructs PC-File+ to scan all the data records, to look for a match anywhere within the specified data field, and to display the records where matches occur.

26. This step concludes your introduction and initial exploration of how you can use PC-File+ to create a database. You might like to continue exploring the PC-File+ "Find a record" command and other Master menu options on your own. Remember:

Press ALT-H

Figure 6-11.

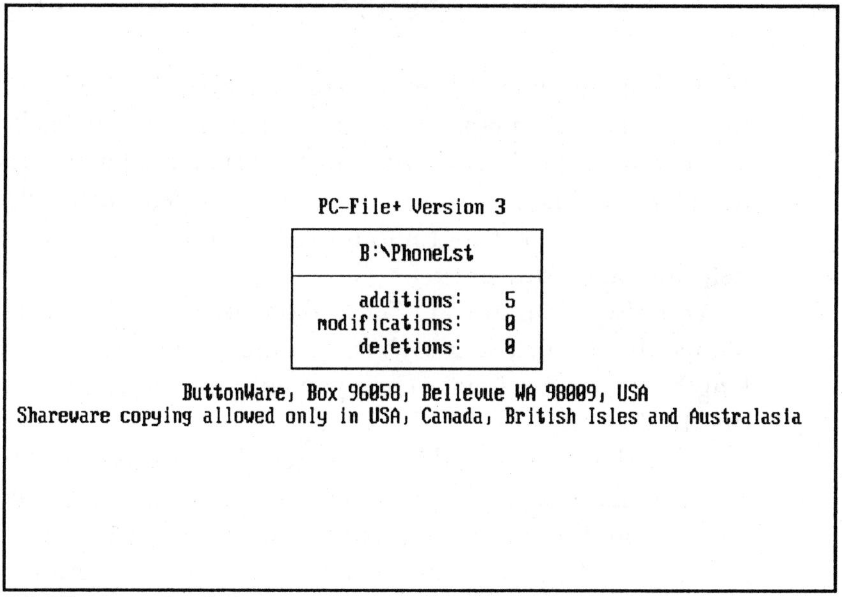

```
                    PC-File+ Version 3
                  ┌─────────────────────┐
                  │     B:\PhoneLst     │
                  ├─────────────────────┤
                  │      additions:  5  │
                  │    modifications: 0 │
                  │      deletions:  0  │
                  └─────────────────────┘
            ButtonWare, Box 96058, Bellevue WA 98009, USA
   Shareware copying allowed only in USA, Canada, British Isles and Australasia
```

PC-File+ termination screen

at any time to get help. When you press ALT-H, the program displays messages that are either related to what you are being asked to do or related to the last action that PC-File+ has taken.

When you want to exit from the PC-File+ program, press ESC as many times as needed to make the Master menu reappear.

Then do the following:

Press Q, Q   (twice from the Master menu)

This ends your session with PC-File+. When you leave PC-File+, you will see the PC-File+ termination screen message, as shown in Figure 6-11.

Summary

In this chapter, you began an exploration of PC-File+, a general purpose database management program. You made backup copies of your original distribution disks and created a blank formatted disk on which to store your databases. You learned how to start the PC-File+ program and how to use its context-sensitive help message feature.

You also created a PC-File+ database called PhoneLst. You named the two fields on each record in the file and set the display lengths for the two fields. Then you entered five data records into the database.

Once the data records were entered, you used the PC-File+ Master menu and "Find a record" command to search the database and to extract records based on the search criteria you supplied. When you completed your search operations, you learned how to end your PC-File+ session.

CHAPTER 7

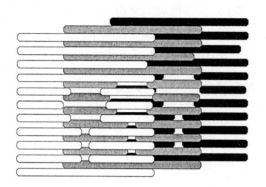

Building a Mailing List Database

In this chapter, you will build a mailing list database that contains complete address information as well as names and telephone numbers.

In Chapter 6, some introductory PC-File+ features and operations were used to build the simple PhoneLst database. Next, you will learn several new PC-File+ commands and capabilities while you expand the PhoneLst datebase. When you finish this chapter, you will know how to do the following:

- Generate a new database from an existing one by using the PC-File+ Clone command. *Cloning* allows you to define a new file that is similar to an existing database and to copy data from the existing file into the new file as the new database is created.

- Use the "Paint" method of screen design to specify the field names, sizes of fields, and location of fields for the records in your new database.

- Utilize some of the many PC-File+ editing commands to help you enter, edit, and manipulate information on the screen.

- Print simple reports from your database, both to the printer and to the screen.

- Modify records in your new database both individually (record-by-record), and globally (where you make changes to all the records at once).

- Delete and undelete records in the database.

- Explore selected PC-File+ built-in utilities that facilitate the job of maintaining a database.

Clone a PC-File+ Database

When you clone an existing PC-File+ database, you create a new database from the old one and copy selected data from the old file into the new file. As you perform the cloning operation, you can make the following changes and additions to the new database:

- Alter the appearance of the data entry screen and the location of fields on the screen. You can add graphic and text elements that enhance the screen and clarify the data entry tasks.

- Extend or shorten field lengths.
- Add new fields to the database and delete old fields.

Because of the alterations you can make as you clone a file, your new database may differ from the original file. *Copying* a database, on the other hand, gives you an exact replica of the original database. The copy has the same number of records, the same number and size of fields, the same data, and the same data entry screen. A clone of a database may be completely different from the original in all aspects.

The Shareware Book Convenience Disk

To begin the cloning operation and the generation of a new database, first load the PhoneLst database created in Chapter 6.

NOTE If you have purchased *The Shareware Book* Convenience Disk, use a copy of the PhoneLst database from that disk. Using that version of the file will ensure that your screen examples and database information are similar to what appears in this book. If you do not have the convenience disk, and you think your version of PhoneLst differs from the one developed in Chapter 6 (you added more records, left fields blank, and so on), you may want to go back through the section in Chapter 6 called "Get to Know PC-File+ in 30 Minutes" and create another version of PhoneLst for use here.

To copy the PhoneLst database from the convenience disk, put the disk in drive A and a formatted database disk in drive B. (This disk can be the one you used in Chapter 6, or any other formatted disk that has enough room for both the PhoneLst files and the files you will create in this chapter.) With the A prompt showing, do the following:

Type:
copy phonelst.* b:
and press ENTER

The copy operation produces the following messages:

```
PHONELST.HDR
PHONELST.INX
PHONELST.DTA
        3 File(s) copied
```

When PC-File+ creates a database, it creates several different files on the database disk. The file with the HDR extension contains information about the database structure. PC-File+ uses this information to display records and fields, to create the data entry screen, and to tell you which database you are viewing.

The file with the INX extension contains the index to your database. PC-File+ uses the index data to keep track of records, to perform find and sort operations, and in general to manipulate and display selected database records.

The actual data in your database is contained in the file with the DTA extension. The names and telephone numbers you entered into the PhoneLst database are stored in this file.

Load PhoneLst into PC-File+

At the A prompt put a copy of PC-File+ DISK ONE in drive A and the database disk containing the PhoneLst files in drive B.

Type:
pcf
and press ENTER

Figure 7-1.

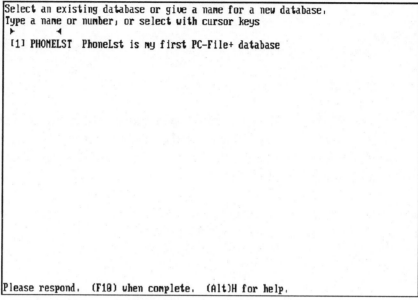

PC-File+ database selection screen

When the PC-File+ version 3 title screen appears, enter the drive designation and an empty path name for the PhoneLst database, as follows:

   Press B
   and
   press ENTER

PC-File+ examines the disk in drive B. If PC-File+ finds the database files with the extensions HDR, INX, and DTA, the program displays a selection screen, as shown in Figure 7-1.

To select a database, you can either type the name of the database or enter the number of the database into the blank field at the top of the list, or you can move the cursor onto the number in the list. Select the PhoneLst database as follows:

Type: **1**
Press F10

The following boxed message appears in the middle of the screen:

OPENING: B\PHONELST

The PC-File+ Master menu appears as shown in Figure 7-2. Read the messages near the top of the screen to verify that you have loaded the PhoneLst database. The first two message lines should look something like this:

```
B:\PHONELST - PhoneLst is my first PC-File+ database
             There are 5 records
```

Figure 7-2.

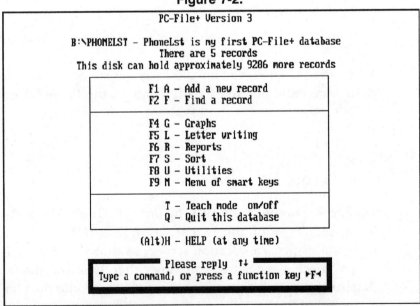

PC-File+ Master menu

The PC-File+ Utilities Menu

The PC-File+ cloning command and a number of other handy commands reside on the Utilities menu. To access the Utilities menu from the PC-File+ Master menu, do the following:

Press F8 or U

You will see the screen shown in Figure 7-3. The letters on the left side of the menu tell you which keys to press to activate selections.

Before you invoke the Clone (C) command, you should make a backup copy of the PhoneLst database. As with any computer program, it is good practice to make copies of important files, especially before you begin any operations that may alter the original files.

Figure 7-3.

```
                    PC-FILE+ UTILITIES MENU

        A.  Alter data entry screen text
        C.  Clone (change the database definition)
        D.  Duplicate records (find and list)
        E.  Export the current database
        G.  Global operations - modify and delete
        I.  Import a PC-File+ database or other file
        M.  Maintenance - Copy, Delete or Rename a PC-File+ file
        N.  Name of field, mask, constant or calc (modify)
        P.  Profile files (set up configuration)
        R.  Re-describe a file
        S.  Smart keys (modify)
        U.  Un-delete records

        Q.  Quit Utilities - Return to Master Menu

                            ┌─ Please reply ↑↓ ─┐
                            │ Enter your selection. ►Q◄ │
                            └───────────────────┘
```

PC-File+ Utilities menu

Make a Backup Copy of PhoneLst   PC-File+ can help you copy files easily. Find the Maintenance (M) command on the Utilities menu, and do the following:

    Press M

A "Please reply" portal asks you to select which type of maintenance operation you want to perform:

Copy, Delete or Rename? (C/D/R) >C<

To copy files, do the following:

    Press C or ENTER

Figure 7-4 shows the screen that appears after you tell PC-File+ you want to copy some files. The screen lists the types of files that PC-File+ can copy correctly. To copy the PhoneLst database:

    Press D or ENTER

PC-File+ asks you for the drive designation and path name of the file you want to copy. Since PhoneLst is on drive B, and there is no path name:

    Press B
    and
    press ENTER

The PC-File+ database selection screen appears as shown in Figure 7-1. You again select the PhoneLst database by either typing its name, typing its number, or moving the cursor onto the number 1. When you have selected the database:

    Press F10

Figure 7-4.

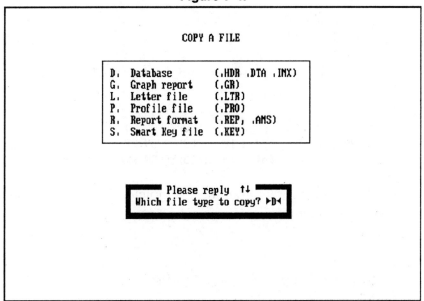

The file-type copy options

PC-File+ asks you for the drive designation and path name of where you want to store the copy. For this example, put the copy on the same disk that contains PhoneLst (drive B and no path name):

   Press B
   and
   press ENTER

Once you enter the drive and path name, PC-File+ asks you to name the copy:

```
Name of new file? >_        <
```

Type a name (up to eight characters), with no file extension, as follows:

Type:
CopyPhon
and press ENTER

PC-File+ clears the screen and displays the following messages as the files are copied:

```
B\PHONELST.HDR copied to B:\COPYPHON.HDR
B\PHONELST.DTA copied to B:\COPYPHON.DTA
B\PHONELST.INX copied to B:\COPYPHON.INX
```

When the copy operation is complete, PC-File+ redisplays the Utilities menu.

Clone PhoneLst to Make MailList

Now that you have loaded the PhoneLst files, activated the Utilities menu, and made a copy of PhoneLst called "CopyPhon," you can begin cloning PhoneLst into a new database to be called "MailList."

NOTE If you have been working straight through this chapter up to this point, you may want to take a break before cloning the PhoneLst database. The cloning process might take 20 to 30 minutes as you work with each task and learn about the PC-File+ painting and editing features.

From the Utilities menu, start the clone operation:

Press C

When you press C on the Utilities menu, PC-File+ displays a screen and a "Please reply" portal asking you which method of screen definition you want to use: "Fast" or "Paint." In Chapter 6, you used the "Fast" method to create the PhoneLst database. For this exercise, you will use the *"Paint"* method—a more flexible way to design and create PC-File+ database elements. To select the "Paint" option, do the following:

Press P

PC-File+ Editing Window When you press P on the "Fast/Paint" options screen, PC-File+ displays the screen shown in Figure 7-5, the PC-File+ editing window. The line at the top of the window tells you that you can use up to 12 letters for each field name and that you can specify data locations within the two brackets [ ].

In Figure 7-5, the second line shows an example field called "CITY," which contains 13 character positions and the data "NEW YORK."

The next line on the display shows the top border of the data creation area. In the center of the top border are the numbers 21:80. These numbers tell you that there are 21 rows and 80 columns available to edit within the bordered area.

At the bottom of the window is a list of the active keys, F3, ALT-H, and F10 that you can use as you "paint" your data entry screen. At the bottom right, within the border, are two letters and two numbers, "r:1 c:1." These letter/number combinations tell you the current row/column screen position for the cursor. In the example shown, the cursor is at row 1, column 1.

If you use the cursor (arrow) keys to move the cursor in the data creation area, the numbers next to the letters "r" and "c" change. Try it! Move the cursor all around and watch the numbers after "r" and "c" change.

Now, move the cursor back to the top left corner of the data creation area (r:1 c:1). (Your computer will beep if you try to move beyond the left corner.) Then, do the following:

Press F3

Figure 7-5.

```
┌─────────────────────────────────────────────────────────────┐
│Field names: 12 letters or less, Data locations: [ ]         │
│  Example: CITY [NEW YORK    ]          Press (Alt)H for help│
│ ┌─ Please make changes to your database ── 21:80 ─────────┐ │
│ │     Name [                              ]               │ │
│ │     Phone [             ]                               │ │
│ │                                                         │ │
│ │                                                         │ │
│ │                                                         │ │
│ │                                                         │ │
│ │                                                         │ │
│ │                                                         │ │
│ │                                                         │ │
│ │                                                         │ │
│ │                                                         │ │
│ │                                                         │ │
│ │                                                         │ │
│ │                                                         │ │
│ └─ (F3)-Menu  (Alt)H-Help  (F10)-Done ─────────── r:1 c:1 ┘ │
└─────────────────────────────────────────────────────────────┘
```

PC-File+ editing window

When you press F3, the Editor menu appears, as shown in Figure 7-6. This menu lists the editing commands available when you are using the editing window. At the bottom of the window, a message explains whichever command is highlighted. The message also shows how to invoke the command without opening the Editor menu. For example, press ↓ and move the highlight to the line that reads as follows:

(E)rase to eof

Figure 7-6.

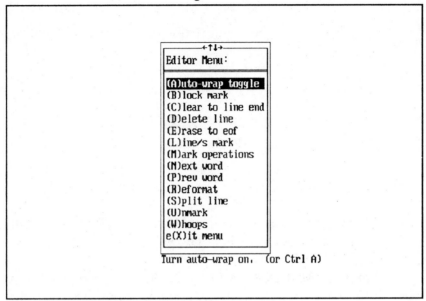

Editor menu

The message at the bottom of the menu shows:

```
Erase to end of file (or Ctrl E)
```

This message indicates that you can erase the data entry area from the cursor position to the end of file either by pressing E when the Editor menu is showing, or by pressing CTRL-E when you do not see the menu.

Since the cursor is in the top left corner of the data entry area, pressing E will clear the area for you to paint a new screen.

Press E

PC-File+ verifies that you really want to erase the entire area by asking:

```
Remainder of text will be erased.  Okay?
Press Y or N
```

To clear the screen, do the following:

Press Y

The data entry area clears, and the cursor flashes in the upper left corner, awaiting your next entry.

Paint the MailList Data Entry Screen Figure 7-7 shows a blank grid that corresponds to the appearance of the data entry screen before field names and data locations are specified. You can use this grid, or a similar grid, to lay out your data entry screens before painting them on the computer screen.

Figure 7-8 shows where the MailList data entry elements will be placed as you paint the items on the editing window. The following set of row-by-row instructions shows you how to quickly paint the MailList field names and data position markers onto the screen. You will use the TAB key to move the cursor across the screen quickly and to align items precisely. Each time you press TAB, the cursor moves to the next tab position, in this example, to columns 9, 17, 25, 33, 41, 49, 57, 65, and 73. The "r" and "c" notations (r:1 c:1), shown in parentheses after each instruction that follows, tell you where the cursor should be after you press the indicated keys.

If you have problems, simply move the cursor back to the upper left corner of the screen. Then, either press CTRL-E or bring up the Edit menu (by pressing F3) and press E to erase the screen. Then you can start over. Remember that you can also get help at

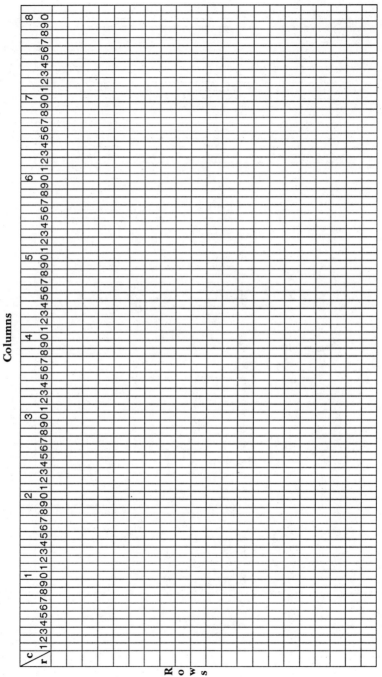

Figure 7-7. Data entry screen grid sheet

Figure 7-8.

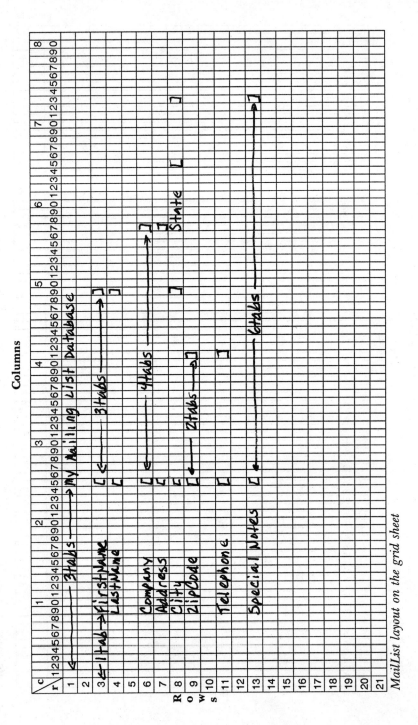

MailList layout on the grid sheet

Building a Mailing List Database **221**

Ch 7

any point by pressing ALT-H. Follow these instructions to paint the screen:

1. With the cursor in the upper left corner (r:1 c:1) of an empty screen:

   Press TAB, TAB, TAB   (r:1 c:25)
   and then type:
   My Mailing List Database   (r:1 c:49)
   and press ENTER, ENTER   (r:3 c:1)

   You can place additional text and graphics characters anywhere on the paint screen. In this case, you created a title line starting in column 25 of row 1. After you press the ENTER key twice, the cursor moves to column 1 of row 3.

2. Enter the first field designation. Include the name of the field and the two bracket characters [ ] positioned to the right of the name:

   Press TAB   (r:3 c:P9)
   Type:
   FirstName
   and press TAB, [, TAB, TAB, TAB,] (r:3 c:50)

   The first field in the MailList database is called "FirstName" and will contain the first name for each person. FirstName has a display length of 23 characters (the number of spaces between the two brackets [ ]). On the screen, your entry should look like this:

   FirstName   [   ]_

   The cursor should be in column 50 of row 3 (r:3 c:50). Once you have typed the field name and have indicated the display length, position the cursor for the next field entry and do the following:

   Press ENTER   (r:4 c:9)

Note that PC-File+ moves the cursor back to the starting position of the last field name. This feature helps you to quickly align a number of field names when you paint a screen.

3. Enter the name and display position of the second field:

   Type:
   LastName
   and press TAB,[, TAB, TAB, TAB,]   (r:4 c:50)

   If you make a typing mistake, use the cursor control keys to move the cursor to the error. Then change or reenter the incorrect or missing data. You can also type over mistakes and use the DEL and BACKSPACE keys to erase unwanted characters.

4. Position the cursor to create the third field, Company:

   Press ENTER, ENTER   (r:6 c:1)

   Since row 5 had no entries, the cursor was reset to column 1 with the last press of the ENTER key. Create the third field:

   Press TAB
   Type:
   Company
   and press TAB, TAB, [,TAB, TAB, TAB, TAB,]   (r:6 c:58)

   Press ENTER   (r:7 c:9)

   The cursor moves to the next row.

5. The fourth field will be an address line.

   Type:
   Address
   and press TAB, TAB, [,TAB, TAB, TAB, TAB,]   (r:7 c:58)

   Press ENTER   (r:8 c:9)

6. Row 8 demonstrates how the "Paint" option offers greater flexibility than the "Fast" method of screen creation. Two fields will be placed on row 8: City and State. Make sure the cursor is in column 9 of row 8, and do the following:

Type:
City
and press TAB, TAB, [,TAB, TAB, TAB,]   (r:8 c:50)

Press TAB   (r:8 c:57)

Type:
State
and press TAB, [, TAB,]   (r:8 c:74)

Press ENTER   (r:9 c:9)

In the "Paint" mode, you can position fields and display areas side by side, as long as everything fits within the editing window.

7. Position the seventh field, ZipCode, in row 9:

Type:
ZipCode
and press TAB, TAB, [, TAB, TAB,]   (r:9 c:42)

To separate the eighth field from the company/address block:

Press ENTER, ENTER   (r:11 c:1)

8. Position the telephone number in the eighth field, by doing the following:

Press TAB
Type:
Telephone
and press TAB, [,TAB, TAB,]   (r:11 c:42)

To separate the Telephone field from the last field:

Press ENTER, ENTER   (r:13 c:1)

9. The last field will contain notes about each person or place in your database:

Press TAB
Type:
Special Notes
and press TAB, [, TAB, TAB, TAB, TAB, TAB, TAB,]   (r:13 c:74)

10. Review everything that you have painted in the editing window. Figure 7-9 shows what the screen should look like. If your screen differs from that shown in Figure 7-9, correct the discrepancies before proceeding. Then, do the following:

Press F10

This completes the paint session in the editing window.

Figure 7-9.

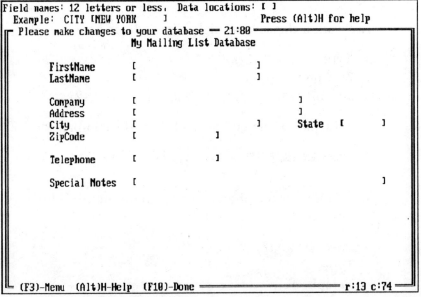

MailList layout on the editing window

Map Existing Data into the New Database When you end the paint session by pressing F10, a new screen appears with the following question on the top line:

`Which field currently contains the data?`

You will see the blinking cursor in the upper left corner within two facing arrowheads (> <) as well as a list of PhoneLst field names from your existing database. To the right of the facing arrowheads is your first field, FirstName.

During cloning operations, PC-File+ helps you map existing data into the new data fields. The program looks at the new data entry screen, pulls off the field names, and presents each field name for a possible match within the old database.

To indicate a match, and therefore a transfer of data between the two databases, either type the name or number of an existing field at the cursor position, or move the cursor onto an item in the list of field names.

For example, to transfer the data in the Name field of PhoneLst to the FirstName field of the new database, do the following:

Type either:
Name or **1** or press ↓
and then press F10

When you press F10, the field name to the right of the facing arrowheads changes to the next field, LastName.

If you do not have existing data to map into this new field name, leave the data entry area blank and do the following:

Press F10

When you press F10 without indicating an existing field name, PC-File+ simply creates a new blank field on the record in the new database.

Continue pressing F10 as the following field names appear at the top of the screen:

COMPANY
   Press F10

ADDRESS
   Press F10

CITY
   Press F10

STATE
   Press F10

ZIPCODE
   Press F10

On the last press of F10, the field name at the top of the screen becomes Telephone. Since the PhoneLst database contains telephone numbers, you can map the existing telephone numbers to the new database:

Type either:
Phone or **2** or press ↓,↓
and then press F10

After you press F10, the field name at the top changes to Notes, even though you typed **Special Notes** for the last field name. The reason PC-File+ does not include the word "Special" as part of the field name is that the program uses only the word that is next to the brackets for the field name. When PC-File+ finds a string of characters not followed by brackets [ ], the program displays the characters on the data entry screen but does not include them as part of a field name. Only the word closest to the brackets becomes

Building a Mailing List Database **227**

Ch 7

the field name. Complete the data mapping into the new database:

Press F10

When you press F10, a "Please reply" portal asks if any of the fields are window fields.

Create a Window Field   All of the fields in the PhoneLst database are regular fields. Regular fields have field lengths the same size as their display lengths on the screen. Window fields have display lengths that are shorter than the actual length of their fields. That is, a window field may contain more data than might appear on the screen.

Suppose you want to make the Notes field of the new database a window field. Respond affirmatively to the question in the "Please reply" portal:

Press Y or ENTER

When you tell PC-File+ that you have window fields by pressing Y, the screen image in Figure 7-10 appears. PC-File+ asks you to indicate window fields either by typing in a field name or number, or by moving the cursor onto the display of field names. The Notes field is field number 9. To make it a window field:

Type:
9 or **Notes**
and press F10

When you press F10, PC-File+ displays a "Please reply" portal asking you to set the actual field length for Notes. The Notes field has a display length of 47 characters.

Figure 7-10.

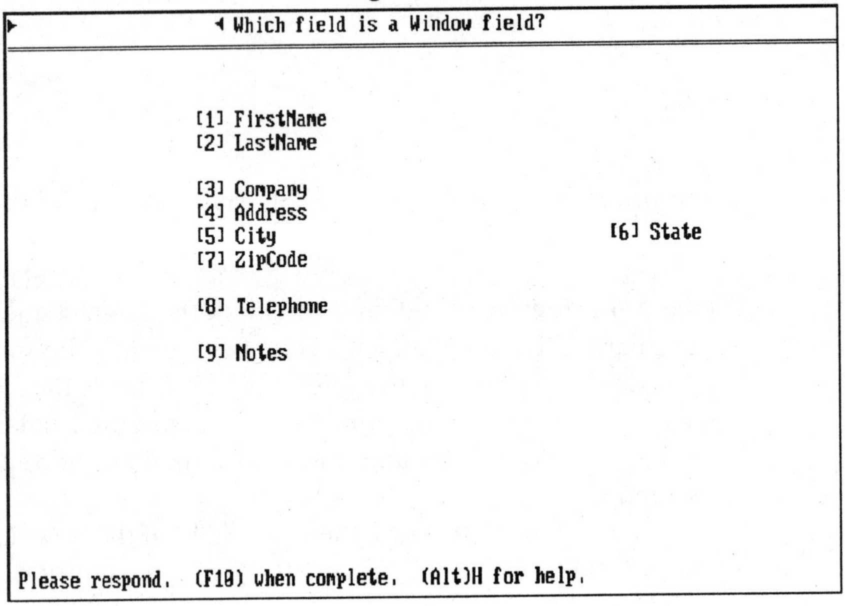

```
▶              ◀ Which field is a Window field?

                [1] FirstName
                [2] LastName

                [3] Company
                [4] Address
                [5] City                          [6] State
                [7] ZipCode

                [8] Telephone

                [9] Notes




Please respond.  (F10) when complete.  (Alt)H for help.
```

Mark the window fields

Notes   Displayed length is 47.   Enter field length >_47<

The actual length of window fields can exceed the display field length. Set the field length of Notes to 100 characters:

    Type:
    100
    and press ENTER

The screen shown in Figure 7-10 reappears. Next to the Notes field is an arrowhead and the number 1, indicating that PC-File+ marked the Notes field as the first window field.

    <1   [9] Notes

Since Notes is to be the only window field, do the following:

Press F10

This tells PC-File+ that there are no more window fields in the MailList database. When you press F10, PC-File+ displays the screen shown in Figure 7-11.

Set the Order of the Data Entry Fields   To set the *order* of the data entry fields, use the screen shown in Figure 7-11 to assign a number to each data field. The numbers tell PC-File+ how to sequence through the fields on the data entry screen when you type in data.

Figure 7-11.

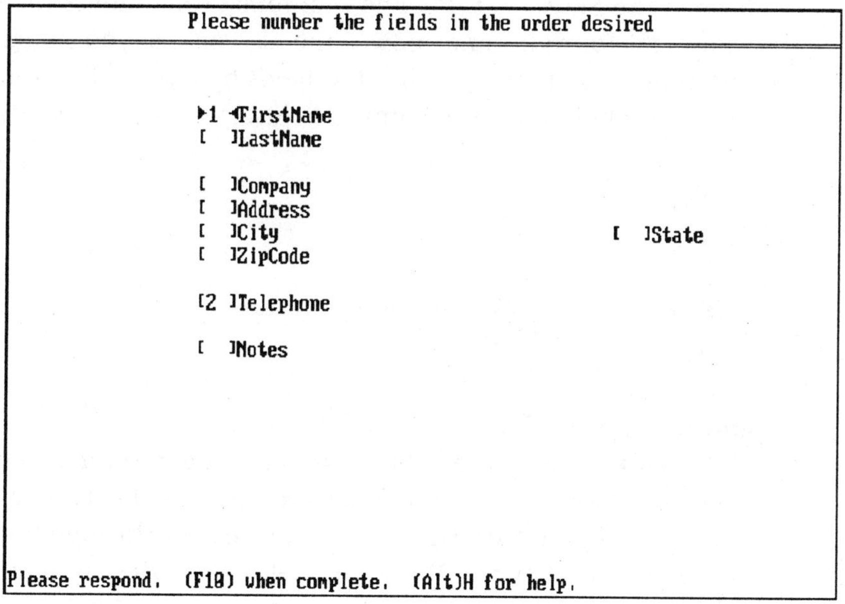

```
        Please number the fields in the order desired

           ▶1 ◀FirstName
           [  ]LastName

           [  ]Company
           [  ]Address
           [  ]City                              [  ]State
           [  ]ZipCode

           [2 ]Telephone

           [  ]Notes




Please respond.  (F10) when complete.  (Alt)H for help.
```

Set the order of the data fields

In Figure 7-11, only the fields cloned from PhoneLst have been assigned order numbers. The PhoneLst Name and Phone fields have been mapped to the FirstName and Telephone fields in the MailList database. The number 1 appears next to FirstName; the number 2 next to Telephone. Begin setting the order by typing the numbers 1 through 5 (pressing ENTER after each number), beginning with FirstName and ending with City.

Type:
1   (FirstName)
2   (LastName)
3   (Company)
4   (Address)
5   (City)

and press ENTER after each number.

After you type **5** and press ENTER, notice how the cursor jumps over to the State field. PC-File+ automatically moves the cursor from left to right and down the screen as you make field selections. Continue ordering the fields by typing the numbers 6 through 9 next to the remaining fields.

Type:
6   (State)
7   (ZipCode)
8   (Telephone)
9   (Notes)

and press ENTER after each number.

When you have entered the number **9** next to the Notes field, check to make sure that the fields are numbered correctly. If you need to change any entries, use ↑ to move back through the fields, and make the changes. When the fields are correctly numbered:

Press F10

Building a Mailing List Database **231**

Name the New Database When you press F10 after setting the data entry order, PC-File+ asks for the drive designation and path name for the new data base:

Press B
and
Press ENTER

After you press ENTER, PC-File+ asks for the name of the new database:

Type:
MailList
and press ENTER

PC-File+ prompts you for a new description for MailList. The old description for PhoneLst appears in the data entry area. Type a new description over the old one, as follows:

Type:
MailList is a clone of the PhoneLst database
and press ENTER

Clone the Records After you type the new database description and press ENTER, PC-File+ displays the following question:

Clone ALL records or SELECTED records?   (A/S) >A<

This request allows you to either selectively clone items from one database to another or to clone all the records. In this example, you want to clone all the records:

Press A or ENTER

When you press A or ENTER, record number 1 of the PhoneLst database appears on the screen along with a "Please reply" portal, as shown in Figure 7-12. The "Please reply" portal asks if you want to clone the record shown on the screen. You can respond with Y (Yes), N (No), X (clone all records), or Q (Quit cloning). To clone the first record:

　　Press Y

Pressing Y told PC-File+ to clone record number 1 of PhoneLst to the new MailList database. After performing the clone, PC-File+ displays PhoneLst's record number 2, the record for Donut Heaven. Since you want to clone all the record:

　　Press X

Figure 7-12.

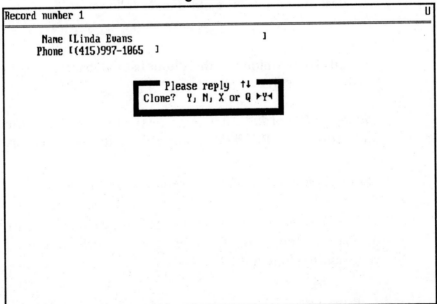

Clone the first PhoneLst record

PC-File+ stops asking questions and clones all of the remaining database records. The program displays the screen shown in Figure 7-13 when the cloning operation is complete. The "Please reply" portal confirms the completion and asks if you want to load the new database. Go ahead and load MailList:

Press Y

When you press Y, PC-File+ loads the MailList database and presents the Master menu. Check the messages at the top of the menu. You should see:

```
B:\MAILLIST - MailList is a clone of the PhoneLst database
              There are 5 records
```

Figure 7-13.

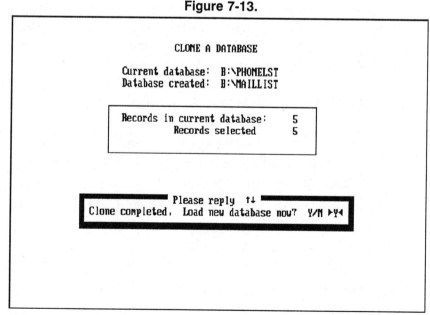

"Clone completed" messages

Congratulations! You have performed your first cloning operation on a database.

NOTE If you want to take another break at this point, you can end the session. The MailList database has been created and resides on your disk. When you restart PC-File+ later, you can reload the MailList database and continue where you left off. However, if you are curious about what the MailList database looks like after all of your cloning efforts, proceed to the next section in this chapter.

Modify Database Records

If you have *The Shareware Book* Convenience Disk, you can proceed to modify the MailList records. If you accidently mess up MailList, you can retrieve another copy from the Convenience Disk. If you do not have the Convenience Disk and your current copy of MailList (as produced in the last example session) is okay, you may want to make a backup copy. You can use either of the following two methods to make a copy:

- Use the PC-File+ Utilities menu and the Maintenance command, as described earlier in this chapter in the section, "Make a Backup Copy of PhoneLst."

- Return to the DOS A prompt and use the DOS COPY command as follows:

Type:
copy b:maillist.* b:copymail.*
and press ENTER

Building a Mailing List Database **235**
Ch 7

Once you have MailList safely copied, get back to the PC-File+ Master menu with MailList loaded and ready to go. Figure 7-14 shows the Master menu with MailList loaded.

From the Master menu, tell PC-File+ to find a record:

Press F or ENTER

Pressing F or ENTER brings up the search options menu. To search for data do the following:

Press S or ENTER

Figure 7-14.

```
                    PC-File+ Version 3

     B:\MAILLIST - MailList is a clone of the PhoneLst database
                        There are 5 records
           This disk can hold approximately 1811 more records

                    ┌─────────────────────────────────┐
                    │   F1 A - Add a new record       │
                    │   F2 F - Find a record          │
                    ├─────────────────────────────────┤
                    │   F4 G - Graphs                 │
                    │   F5 L - Letter writing         │
                    │   F6 R - Reports                │
                    │   F7 S - Sort                   │
                    │   F8 U - Utilities              │
                    │   F9 M - Menu of smart keys     │
                    ├─────────────────────────────────┤
                    │      T - Teach mode on/off      │
                    │      Q - Quit this database     │
                    └─────────────────────────────────┘

                    (Alt)H - HELP (at any time)

              ▄▄▄▄▄▄▄▄▄▄ Please reply ↑↓ ▄▄▄▄▄▄▄▄▄▄
              Type a command, or press a function key ►F◄
```

Master menu with MailList database

PC-File+ asks whether you want to make a *simple* or *complex* search. Since you want to perform a simple search, do the following:

    Press S or ENTER

Pressing S or ENTER displays the search data screen, as shown in Figure 7-15. This screen is similar to the MailList data entry screen except that asterisks are in all of the data positions. In Chapter 6, you used the PhoneLst version of the search data screen to search for selected records. In order to perform the

Figure 7-15.

```
┌─────────────────────────────────────────────────────────────────────┐
│         Please supply the search data below                       F │
├─────────────────────────────────────────────────────────────────────┤
│                    My Mailing List Database                         │
│                                                                     │
│         FirstName    ►************************◄                    │
│         LastName     [************************]                    │
│                                                                     │
│         Company      [********************************]            │
│         Address      [********************************]            │
│         City         [**********************]    State  [******]   │
│         ZipCode      [***************]                              │
│                                                                     │
│         Telephone    [***************]                              │
│                                                                     │
│         Special Notes [*****************************************]  │
│                                                                     │
│                                                                     │
│                                                                     │
│                                                                     │
│                                                                     │
│ Please respond.  (F10) when complete.  (Alt)H for help.             │
└─────────────────────────────────────────────────────────────────────┘
```

MailList search data screen

modifications to MailList, you need to retrieve all the MailList records. To retrieve all the records in a database leave the search data screen unaltered and do the following:

Press F10

Pressing F10 brings up MailList record number 1. Figure 7-16 shows this record on the screen along with the Find options menu, the boxed menu in the lower right corner of the screen with the letter "F" at the top of the box.

To activate the Find options, press the letters displayed on the left side of the menu. To modify record number 1:

Press M

The Options menu disappears and the cursor flashes in the first data position of the first field, FirstName. With the Options menu

Figure 7-16.

```
Record number 1                                                              F
            ┌─────────────────────────────────────────────────────────────────
            │            My Mailing List Database
            │
            │   FirstName    [Linda Evans           ]
            │   LastName     [                      ]
            │
            │   Company      [                              ]
            │   Address      [                              ]
            │   City         [                    ]  State [    ]
            │   ZipCode      [            ]                ┌─ F  ↑↓ ─┐
            │                                             │ D Delete │
            │   Telephone    [(415)997-1065 ]             │ M Modify │
            │                                             │ S new Search
            │   Special Notes [                           │ E End of file
            │                                             │ B Beginning
            │                                             │ N Next record
            │                                             │ P Prior record
            │                                             │ R get by Rcd#
            │                                             │ + browse down
            │                                             │ - browse up
            │                                             │ Q Quit finding
            │                                             └──────────┘
```

MailList record number 1 with Find options menu

out of the way, you can clearly see the data entry screen and the two cloned data items from the PhoneLst database.

Linda's full name appears in the FirstName field. Her telephone number occupies the Telephone field. Of course, Linda's *full* name is not her *first* name. You can correct the entry in either of the following two ways:

- Erase "Evans" from the first field and retype that word in the second field.
- Use the powerful PC-File+ editing keys to make the modifications.

If you want to learn how to use some of the PC-File+ editing keys, read the next section and follow the examples.

Introducing PC-File+ Editing Keys

You can use the PC-File+ editing keys to modify the data contained in record number 1. After placing the cursor under the letter "L" of "Linda," do the following:

Press CTRL-R, CTRL-→, F6

Pressing CTRL-→ caused the cursor to jump to the letter "E" in "Evans." Pressing F6 caused "Evans" to disappear.

When you press CTRL and either → or ← keys, the cursor moves to the beginning of either the next or the previous word, respectively. Pressing F6 erases everything from the cursor position to the end of the current line. Pressing CTRL-R reads everything from the cursor position to the end of the line into the computer's memory.

With the word "Evans" deleted from the FirstName field and the word "Linda" remaining:

Press ENTER or ↓

The cursor moves to the first data position of the LastName field. Do the following:

Press CTRL-W

Linda's full name appears in the second field! Pressing CTRL-W writes the information (that was read by CTRL-R) into a data field at the current cursor position. When you pressed CTRL-R in the first field, you read Linda's name into memory. When you pressed CTRL-W in the second field, you wrote Linda's name onto the screen.

The LastName field now contains Linda's full name. The blinking cursor should be positioned after the letter "s" of "Evans." To erase "Linda " from this field:

Press CTRL-←, and press BACKSPACE six times

When you press CTRL-←, the cursor moves to the beginning of the word "Evans." When you press the BACKSPACE key six times, all the characters preceding "Evans" are deleted. The BACKSPACE key *backspaces* over existing text, deleting one character for each keypress. The first two fields on the record now appear as follows:

```
FirstName    [Linda                    ]
LastName     >Evans                    <
```

To end the operation, do the following:

Press F10

When you press F10, PC-File+ redisplays the Find options menu. The changes you made to record number 1 have not yet been recorded. PC-File+ does not record changes in one record until you browse to another record. You can still make modifications to the current record by pressing M to reactivate the Modify option.

To look at the next record in the MailList database and record the changes to the current record, choose the "Next record" option:

Press N

PC-File+ briefly flashes a "MODIFIED" message at the top of the screen, and then displays record number 2, the Donut Heaven record. Figure 7-17 shows this record display along with the overlay of the Find options menu. The words "Donut Heaven" appear in the FirstName field.

Move the data to the Company field, as follows:

Press M
Press CTRL-R, F6, ENTER, ENTER, CTRL-W

Pressing M activates the Modify option and removes the options menu. CTRL-R reads the contents of FirstName into memory. F6 clears the FirstName field. Pressing ENTER twice positions the cursor in the Company field. CTRL-W writes the data stored in memory ("Donut Heaven") to the Company field.

When you write the data into the Company field, tell PC-File+ the modification is complete:

Press F10

PC-File+ responds by bringing back the Find options menu.

You can now modify the remaining three records. Each record has a company name in the FirstName field that needs to be

Figure 7-17.

```
Record number 2                                                         F
                       My Mailing List Database
         FirstName    [Donut Heaven         ]
         LastName     [                     ]

         Company      [                             ]
         Address      [                             ]
         City         [                     ]  State [    ]
         ZipCode      [              ]
                                                    ┌─ Q ↑↓ ──────┐
         Telephone    [(415)996-1171 ]               │ D Delete     │
                                                    │ M Modify     │
         Special Notes [                             │ S new Search │
                                                    │ E End of file│
                                                    │ B Beginning  │
                                                    │ N Next record│
                                                    │ P Prior record│
                                                    │ R get by Rcd#│
                                                    │ + browse down│
                                                    │ - browse up  │
                                                    │ Q Quit finding│
                                                    └──────────────┘
```

MailList record number 2

moved to the Company field. Use the same sequence of keystrokes to make each modification:

> Press N
> Press M
> Press CTRL-R, F6, ENTER, ENTER, CTRL-W
> Press F10

You can use the P and N keys from the Find options menu to browse the records in the database to review your edits. If you browse off the end of the database, you will see a "Please reply" portal with a "Not found" message and a request that you press ENTER. If you encounter this message, press ENTER to return to the search options menu. Then, press the default keys shown in the "Please reply" portals to return to the database records.

Using the editing keys to move and edit data has some advantages. For one thing, you are unlikely to create typing errors as you move data between fields. PC-File+ takes care of reading and writing the data; you simply control which data is accessed and where the data goes. Also, if there are more complex data edits and transfers to be made, PC-File+ has other commands to help you, described in the *PC-File+ User's Manual*.

 NOTE If you want to take a break before starting the next set of explorations, you can exit from the PC-File+ program. At this point, the MailList database records have been modified and updated with your changes. When you restart PC-File+ and reload MailList, you can easily continue from this point forward.

Fill Out the MailList Data Records

If you have stopped and restarted the PC-File+ program, load the MailList database and use the "Find a record" command on the Master menu to retrieve all the records.

Your screen should display the MailList database records, along with the Find options menu (the menu with the letter "F" at the top).

Table 7-1 contains the data to be entered for each record in the MailList database. Use the Modify option on the options menu to enter the data for each record. When you complete this data entry task, move on to the next section in this chapter, where you will learn how to use the PC-File+ report generation feature.

 NOTE If you have *The Shareware Book* Convenience Disk, you may want to enter and modify one or two data records to get the idea of how the entire data entry operation works. You are strongly

Table 7-1.

Record Number 1:

FirstName	[Linda
LastName	[Evans
Company	[AstroMeta Books Inc.
Address	[21 Star Lane
City	[Half Moon Bay
State	[CA
ZipCode	[94019
Telephone	[(415)997-1065
Special Notes	[Birthday:11/1 Likes:Chocolate, Michael Jackson, Samba Dancing, Beach Sign:Scorpio Dislikes:eggs

Record Number 2:

FirstName	[Michael
LastName	[Angel
Company	[Donut Heaven
Address	[45 Butter Way
City	[Half Moon Bay
State	[CA
ZipCode	[94019
Telephone	[(415)996-1171
Special Notes	[Best:cream filled, fruit bars Worst:coffee cakes

Record Number 3:

FirstName	[Susan B.
LastName	[Anthony
Company	[Donut Haven
Address	[One Dollar Drive
City	[Palo Alto

Data for the MailList Data Records (continued on next page)

Table 7-1.

State	[CA
ZipCode	[94301
Telephone	[(415)998-2025
Special Notes	[Best:silver slivers, golden wafers Worst:green meenies, rum cakes

Record Number 4:

FirstName	[Georgio
LastName	[Acropolis
Company	[Strawberry Pizza
Address	[77 Dough Road
City	[Sebastopol
State	[CA
ZipCode	[95472
Telephone	[(707)899-1212
Special Notes	[Best:feta, tomato, and garlic Worst:spinach and fruit Likes:Georgio loves donuts

Record Number 5:

FirstName	[Carol
LastName	[Artunian
Company	[Ultimate Pizza House
Address	[144 Verona Way
City	[Sebastopol
State	[CA
ZipCode	[95472
Telephone	[(707)898-7777
Special Notes	[Best:avocado sandwiches Worst:the pizzas Likes:Carol and Georgio are secretly married

Data for the MailList Data Records (continued)

encouraged to completely enter at least the first record (Linda Evans), so that you can get accustomed to making entries in the database and observe how the Notes field works. You can then use the prepared copy of the MailList database from the Convenience Disk to examine the PC-File+ reporting features.

Generate a PC-File+ Report

After you have entered all the data for the five MailList records (or loaded a copy of the completed MailList database), go to the Master menu. If you are on the Find options menu, press Q to get back to the Master menu. From the Master menu, do the following:

Press R

Figure 7-18 shows the screen that appears after you press R from the Master menu. The report format options screen lists the four options for defining a report format. The *page format* report prints one record per page in a format similar to the records displayed on the screen. The *row format* report prints one record on each line with the fields aligned in columns. The *free form format* lets you "paint" each section of the report. Although it provides flexibility, you have to tell PC-File+ how to lay out the report sections. The *commands format* uses the PC-File+ report command language to specify reports. To use the commands format, you have to pre-plan what you want to see printed.

You can produce reports easily and quickly with either the page or row format. Try using the row format option:

Press R or ENTER

Figure 7-18.

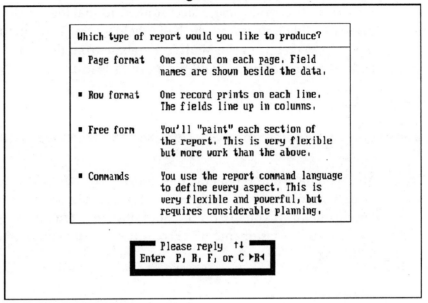

Report format options

When you press R or ENTER, PC-File+ displays a screen with a request to number the columns. The blinking cursor is positioned in the upper entry area, labeled "Record No." To print a record, type the record number in this position. As an experiment, enter the following:

Type:
1 and press ENTER
3 and press ENTER
2 and press ENTER six times
4

The result should look like the screen shown in Figure 7-19. If not, use the cursor keys and correct the entries to match those in Figure 7-19.

Figure 7-19.

```
                Number the columns to print from left to right
Record No.  [1 ]


                 FirstName [3 ]
                 LastName  [2 ]

                   Company [  ]
                   Address [  ]
                      City [  ]                          State [  ]
                   ZipCode [  ]

                 Telephone ►4 ◄

                     Notes [  ]





Please respond.  (F10) when complete.  (Alt)H for help.
```

Select fields for printing a row report

The numbers you typed instruct PC-File+ to print the record number first (1), the LastName field second (2), the FirstName field third (3), and the Telephone field last (4). The fields without numbers will not be printed.

When you have correctly entered the numbers:

press F10

After you press F10, PC-File+ asks you to enter a Title Line for the report. Enter the following:

Type:
Names and Phones from MailList
and press ENTER

PC-File+ announces that it is creating the report work file and asks if you want to save the report format. The report format specifies the report type (row), the fields to be printed (record number, LastName, FirstName, and Telephone), and the order in which to print the fields. Saving the report format allows you print the same report again without having to reenter the data. Tell PC-File+ to save the report format:

Press Y

When you press Y, PC-File+ asks you for a report description. You can enter the following description:

Type:
Names and Phones
and press ENTER

PC-File+ now asks you to name the format:

Type:
NamePhon
and press ENTER

After you enter a name for the format, the Report menu appears on the screen, as shown in Figure 7-20. For now, ignore all of the options in the menu except for the first one; "Output to Printer, Screen, Disk." You can instruct PC-File+ to print your reports to the printer, to the screen, and to a disk file, by pressing the appropriate key (P, S, or D) to set the option.

Printing small reports to the screen is often a good way to preview them. To print to the screen, do the following:

Press S, F10

Figure 7-21 shows the report you defined as it appears on the screen. Notice that the order of the fields conforms to your earlier

Figure 7-20.

```
                    REPORT MENU
   Output to Printer, Screen, Disk    P/S/D    ▶P◀
   Number of copies                   1-99     [ 1]
   Line spacing (0 = no detail lines) 0-9      [1]
   Do Subtotals?                      Y/N      [N]
   Left margin (extra spaces)         0-99     [ 0]
   Page length (in "lines")                    [ 66]
   Pause after each page?             Y/N      [N]
   Start at which page number?        1-9999 [ 1]
   Type size (Normal/Condensed)       N/C      [N]
   Remove blank lines and spaces      Y/N      [N]
   Flip~data active?                  Y/N      [Y]
   Print All or Selected records      A/S      [A]

   Press (Esc) to return to PC-File+ menu



Please respond.  (F10) when complete.  (Alt)H for help.
```

Report menu

Figure 7-21.

```
                     Names and Phones
August 13, 1989 at 4:29 p.m.                    Page   1

Recrd LastName              FirstName            Telephone
===== ======================= ======================= ================
    1 Evans                 Linda                (415)997-1865
    2 Angel                 Michael              (415)996-1171
    3 Anthony               Susan B.             (415)998-2025
    4 Acropolis             Georgio              (707)899-1212
    5 Artunian              Carol                (707)898-7777

              ▄▄▄▄▄▄▄▄ Please reply ↑↓ ▄▄▄▄▄▄▄▄
              █ Ready for Final Totals. Press (Enter) ▶ ◀ █
              ▀▀▀▀▀▀▀▀▀▀▀▀▀▀▀▀▀▀▀▀▀▀▀▀▀▀▀▀▀▀▀▀▀▀▀▀▀▀▀▀▀▀
```

A row format report

specifications. When you are ready to see the final totals for the report:

　　Press ENTER

PC-File+ displays a message telling you that five records were printed, that the fields are unsorted, and that all records were selected.
　　Pressing the requested ENTER key at this point will bring back the Master menu:

　　Press ENTER

You have saved the report format. To recall that format from the Master menu, do the following:

　　Press R

A screen appears asking you to select a report format:

　　Type:
　　1 or **NamePhon** or press ENTER
　　and then press F10

When you press F10, the Report menu reappears. Check to see if your printer is connected to your computer and ready to print. Then, with the cursor on the first entry of the Report menu screen:

　　Press P, F10

When you press F10, record number 1 appears, along with a "Please reply" portal asking if you want to output the current record. The allowed responses are Y (Yes), N (No), X (print all records), and Q (Quit). Tell PC-File+ to print all records:

　　Press X

The same report you sent to the screen, shown in Figure 7-21, will print on your printer.

If you do not get a printed version of the report, read the following section, "PC-File+ and Printers."

PC-File+ and Printers

PC-File+ automatically assumes that you are using either an IBM or an Epson, or compatible printer. If you have another type of printer, you must tell PC-File+ the type of printer you are using.

To change the PC-File+ default printer type, you need to adjust a setting in the PC-File+ *master profile file,* PCFILE.PRO, which resides on DISK ONE. The master profile file contains the system configuration commands that control the screen; the database default drive, path, and file designations; the printer assignment; and other PC-File+ program default settings.

You can also create *profile files* for individual databases. This feature allows you to customize the default settings for each database. For more information on how profile files work and interact, read Chapter 28, "Configuring System — Profiles," in the *PC-File+ User's Manual.*

To begin editing the master profile file, go to the PC-File+ Master menu and activate the Utilities menu:

Press U

One option on the PC-File+ Utilities menu is the "Profile Files (set up configuration)" command. Activate this option by doing the following:

Press P

When you press P, the screen shown in Figure 7-22 appears. Since you want to edit an existing file:

    Press E

Pressing E brings up a request for a drive designation followed by a request for a path name. Since PCFILE.PRO resides on DISK ONE in drive A with no path name, do the following:

    Press A, ENTER

The file selection screen appears, with PCFILE.PRO on the list.

    Type
    1 or **PCFILE.PRO** or press ENTER
    and press F10

Figure 7-22.

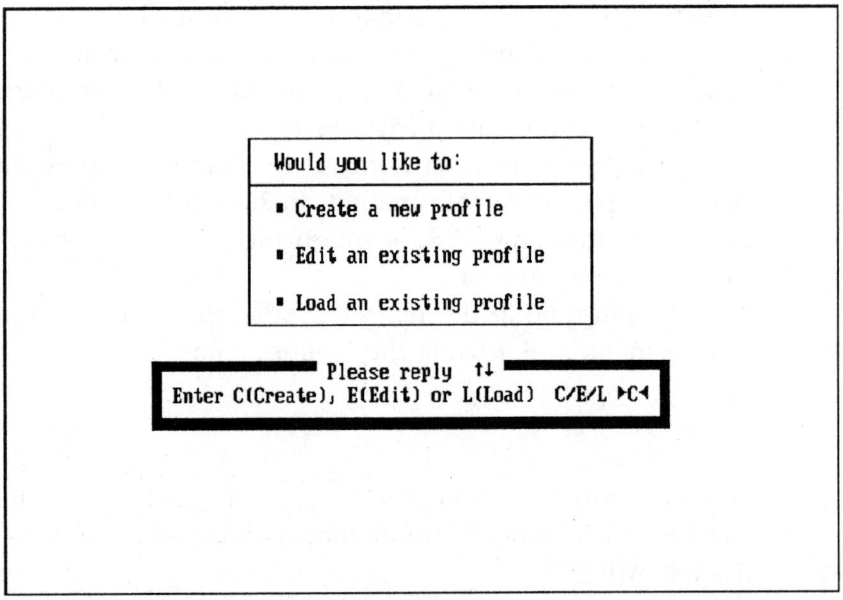

```
┌─────────────────────────────────────────────────┐
│                                                 │
│        ┌──────────────────────────────┐         │
│        │ Would you like to:           │         │
│        │                              │         │
│        │  ■ Create a new profile      │         │
│        │                              │         │
│        │  ■ Edit an existing profile  │         │
│        │                              │         │
│        │  ■ Load an existing profile  │         │
│        └──────────────────────────────┘         │
│   ┌──────────────── Please reply ↑↓ ─────────┐  │
│   │ Enter C(Create), E(Edit) or L(Load) C/E/L ►C◄│ │
│   └──────────────────────────────────────────┘  │
│                                                 │
└─────────────────────────────────────────────────┘
```

Profile options menu

Building a Mailing List Database   253
Ch 7

When you complete the file selection by pressing F10, the PC-File+ configuration screen appears, as shown in Figure 7-23. The Screen Colors are set to default arrangements of black and white. The Database Defaults are blank. All the other options are set to N (No).

To change the Printer Defaults, move the cursor to the PRINTER DEFAULTS line and do the following:

Press Y, F10

The Y tells PC-File+ that you want to define or modify the printer settings. When you press F10, the printer configuration screen appears, as shown in Figure 7-24.

Figure 7-23.

```
SCREEN COLORS:        Background (0-7) ►0◄
                      Foreground (0-15) [7 ]
    Foreground color for field names (0-15) [15]

DATABASE DEFAULTS:          Drive (A-Z) [ ]
                                   Path [                    ]
                          Database name [          ]

OPTIONS:    Case sensitive finds (Y/N) [N]
            Case sensitive sorts (Y/N) [N]
  Skip to next field when field full (Y/N) [N]
                         Fast view (Y/N) [N]
                        Fast write (Y/N) [N]
                      Expert menus (Y/N) [N]

PRINTER DEFAULTS:   Define/Modify (Y/N) [N]

MENU PASSWORDS:     Define/Modify (Y/N) [N]

KEYIN MACRO:        Define/Modify (Y/N) [N]

SNAPSHOT LABEL:     Define/Modify (Y/N) [N]

Please respond.  (F10) when complete.  (Alt)H for help.
```

PC-File+ configuration screen

Figure 7-24.

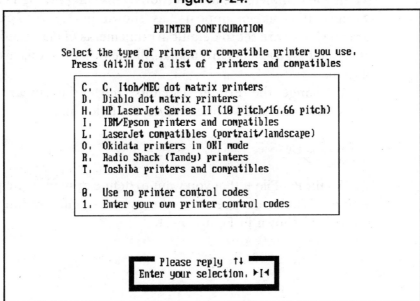

Printer configuration screen

Look down the list of printers shown on the screen. The PC-File+ default setting is I for IBM/Epson printers and compatibles. If you have a different printer, pick the letter that corresponds to your printer. If you don't see your printer listed:

Press ALT-H

A help screen will appear that gives you more information about the printers PC-File+ supports. If you still do not see your printer, you can try using one of the other printer settings, because your printer may be compatible with another printer's setting (even though you do not see your printer's name). Check the manual that came with your printer for a list of other printers compatible with your printer.

When you locate a setting that matches your printer, press that letter. PC-File+ prompts you to set the page length and port configuration. If you know that your printer already works with your computer, leave these two settings unchanged.

After you set the page and port defaults, you are asked if you want to save the profile.

Press Y or ENTER

You are then asked if it is okay to replace the existing PCFILE.PRO file:

Press Y

When you press Y, you return to the Utilities menu. Exit to the Master menu and try printing your report again, using the new printer setting.

If your printer still does not work, you can try other printer and port settings. If all else fails and you have a registered copy of PC-File+, call ButtonWare Technical Support at (206) 454-2629 for assistance.

Explore the PC-File+ Utilities

So far in this chapter, you have used three of the twelve PC-File+ utility commands: Clone, Maintenance, and "Profile files." Go to the Master menu and activate the Utilities menu.

Press U

Figure 7-25 shows the Utilities menu as it appears on the screen. The options you may not have explored so far are

A	Allows you to alter the data entry screen of the current database
D	Helps you find and list duplicate records in the current database
E	Exports the data in the current database into formats usable by other programs
G	Performs global modify and delete operations on the current database
I	Imports data into the current database from PC-File+ and other files
N	Lets you modify names of fields and other PC-File+ data elements
R	Allows you to change the description of a PC-File+ database
S	Lets you modify the PC-File+ *smart keys*. Smart keys are sets of keystrokes that you can define and assign to a single key, such as ALT-1, ALT-F1, and so on. When you assign a set of keystrokes to a smart key, the smart key "remembers" all of the keys you pressed. Later, if you press a smart key, all the keystrokes you saved are replayed in order, just as if you pressed the keys yourself at the keyboard
U	Gives you the ability to undelete a record that has been deleted

The next two sections in this chapter introduce the following two utility functions: how to perform a global modification of the MailList database, and how to undelete a record.

Figure 7-25.

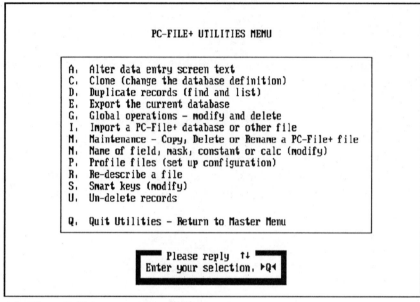

PC-File+ Utilities menu

Make Global Changes to the Database

To select the Global option from the Utilities menu:

    Press G

When you press G, the "Please reply" portal at the bottom of the screen displays the following:

Global Modify or Delete   M/D   >M<

To modify records:

    Press M or ENTER

The "Please reply" portal asks the following:

```
All records, or Selected    A/S   >S<
```

Since you want to make a global change, select all the records:

    Press A

When you press A, the replacement data screen appears, as shown in Figure 7-26. This screen is similar to the MailList data entry screen, except that it has equal signs (=) in each data position. To perform a global data substitution on all the records, replace the

Figure 7-26.

```
|              Please supply the replacement data below              |
|                                                                    |
|                        My Mailing List Database                    |
|                                                                    |
|              FirstName    ▶=======================◀                |
|              LastName     [=======================]                |
|                                                                    |
|              Company      [===============================]        |
|              Address      [===============================]        |
|              City         [=======================]  State [======]|
|              ZipCode      [================]                       |
|                                                                    |
|              Telephone    [================]                       |
|                                                                    |
|              Special Notes [==========================================]|
|                                                                    |
|                                                                    |
|                                                                    |
|                                                                    |
|Please respond.  (F10) when complete.  (Alt)H for help.             |
```

Replacement data screen

equal signs in one or more fields with data that you want to have appear on the records. In those positions where equal signs remain, PC-File+ leaves the original data unchanged.

For example, suppose you wanted to put a hyphen (-) into the current ZipCode field in the sixth data position. The MailList records already have five digits in each ZipCode field. Inserting a hyphen after the fifth digit would set up the fields to handle nine-digit zip codes.

On the replacement data screen, move the cursor down the screen to the ZipCode field. When you have the cursor on the ZipCode field, press the underline (_) character five times. (An underline is created by pressing SHIFT-HYPHEN.) Then press the hyphen character once:

Press SHIFT-HYPHEN five times
Press HYPHEN

After you press the hyphen at the sixth position, the ZipCode line looks like this:

ZipCode   _____-=========<

The underline (_) character is called the *skip over character*. When PC-File+ sees the underline on the replacement screen, it skips over that character in making a replacement. When you press five underline characters one after the other, a solid line appears in place of the first five equal signs. To make sure the hyphen is in the sixth data position, look at the line above or below ZipCode and count six equal signs. When you are sure the hyphen is in the sixth position, do the following:

Press F10

The MailList database record number 1 appears along with the following "Please reply" portal:

```
Modify?  Y,N, X(stop asking), Q(Quit)   >N<
```

Since you want to modify all the records:

> Press X

As the MailList records flash across the screen, a hyphen appears after each ZIP code number. PC-File+ stops on the last record, where the ZIP code now reads 95472-. The modification worked! Look over the records in the database to verify that each record was modified correctly. If you accidently changed the wrong character, fix the error or restore the database from a backup copy. When you finish, use the "Find a record" command on the Master menu to display record number 1.

Delete and Undelete Records

Suppose you want to delete Linda's record from the database. When the "Find a record" command displays record number 1, the Find options menu also appears on the screen. The first entry on the Options menu is Delete. To delete record number 1:

> Press D

When you press D, the Options menu disappears, and the "Please reply" portal asks:

```
OK to delete?   Y/N >N<
```

To complete the delete operation:

> Press Y

When you press Y, you will hear the disk drive start up, and the word "DELETED" will appear at the top of the screen. Record number 1 has been deleted. Notice that the options menu reappears *without* the Delete option. You cannot delete an already deleted record.

If you retrieved all the MailList records when you used the "Find a record" command, press N to display record number 2. Then, try to go back to record number 1 by pressing P. A "Not Found" message should appear, indicating that record number 1 is not there.

Go back to the Master menu and use the "Find a record" command to retrieve all the records:

Press F, ENTER, ENTER, F10

When you retrieve all the records, PC-File+ displays a new first record, record number 2. Record number 1 cannot be retrieved because PC-File+ has marked it as deleted. Record number 2 is now the first record in the database.

Suppose you change your mind and want to keep Linda's record in the database after all. No problem! PC-File+ allows you to *undelete* a record that you have deleted. Go back to the Master menu and activate the Utilities menu. With the Utilities menu showing:

Press U

When you press U, PC-File+ briefly displays a "Searching" message and then displays the deleted record number 1. At the bottom, a "Please reply" portal displays the following message:

Enter first character, / to remain deleted >/<

PC-File+ has replaced the character in position 1 of the First-Name field with a slash character:

FirstName   [/inda   ]

If you want to leave the record deleted, all you need do is press ENTER. If you want to undelete the record, enter the first character in the name "Linda," the letter "L":

Press L

When you press L, PC-File+ undeletes the record and displays a message reporting the number of records that have been undeleted. If you had more than one deleted record in the database, PC-File+ would have given you the opportunity to undelete each one.

To verify that Linda's record is back in the database, use the "Find a record" command from the Master menu and display the records in the file. Record number 1, Linda's record, will reappear as the first record in the file.

If you delete records and then exit the program, PC-File+ will still allow you to undelete records the next time you load the database.

Summary

In Chapter 7, you explored the PC-File+ Utilities menu commands. You used the cloning command to create a new database, MailList, from the PhoneLst database. You "painted" a new data entry screen for MailList and learned how to use the PC-File+ editing window. As you cloned the PhoneLst database into Mail-

List, you mapped data from selected PhoneLst fields into MailList fields.

You made your MailList Notes field a window field. You then entered data into the MailList data records using the record modify and editing features. Finally, you printed a name and telephone number report from MailList, both to the screen and to the printer, and set up a report format, NamePhon.

In addition, you explored other Utility menu features, including global modification of all records and deleting and undeleting a record.

CHAPTER

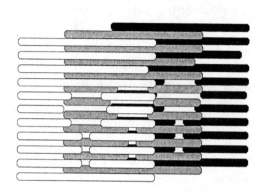

8

Form Letters and Mailing Labels

Once you have a database, such as MailList, you can use PC-File+ to create *form letters* and *mailing labels*. Form letters are printed documents that are identical except for certain variables, such as names, addresses, and, if the document is a bill, amount of money owed. You probably get form letters in the mail every day that look like the following contest entry form:

> . . . and we guarantee that you, **LINDA EVANS**,
> are one of the finalists and can win **$10,000,000**
> if you send in your entry ticket today, **LINDA** !!

Database programs are used to generate the millions of form letters, bills, notices, contest entry forms, meeting announcements, and other documents that end up in mailboxes every day.

And of course, nearly every form letter has a mailing label containing the name, address, and ZIP code of the recipient. The same database programs used to create form letters can also generate the mailing labels for the envelopes.

In this chapter, you will do the following:

- Use PC-File+ to create a form letter that pulls information out of the MailList database.
- Use a standalone PC-File+ program, PC-Label, and the data in MailList to generate mailing labels for the form letters.

Use PC-File+ to Create a Form Letter

PC-File+ has a handy letter writing feature that can be used to generate form letters as well as to write short notes.

Load the MailList database into PC-File+ either from your database disk or from *The Shareware Book* Convenience Disk. When MailList is loaded, the Master menu appears, as shown in Figure 8-1. In the middle of the menu, you see a command called "Letter writing." Activate the PC-File+ "Letter writing" command:

    Press F5 or L

If you have never before created a letter with PC-File+, you will see the following reply portal:

```
How many columns wide? (10-200) > 70<
```

Figure 8-1.

```
                    PC-File+ Version 3
     B:\MAILLIST - MailList is a clone of the PhoneLst database
                      There are 5 records
             This disk can hold approximately 1804 more records

                    ┌─────────────────────────────────┐
                    │   F1 A - Add a new record       │
                    │   F2 F - Find a record          │
                    ├─────────────────────────────────┤
                    │   F4 G - Graphs                 │
                    │   F5 L - Letter writing         │
                    │   F6 R - Reports                │
                    │   F7 S - Sort                   │
                    │   F8 U - Utilities              │
                    │   F9 M - Menu of smart keys     │
                    ├─────────────────────────────────┤
                    │   T - Teach mode  on/off        │
                    │   Q - Quit this database        │
                    └─────────────────────────────────┘
                     (Alt)H - HELP (at any time)
                    ┌──────── Please reply ↑↓ ────────┐
                    │ Type a command, or press a function key ►F◄ │
                    └─────────────────────────────────┘
```

PC-File+ Master menu

You can set the width of the letter editing window anywhere from 10 characters to 200 characters. The standard width for letters, 70 characters, shows as the default. Tell PC-File+ that you want to use the default width:

   Press ENTER

The Letter Editing Window

After you press ENTER to accept the default column width, the PC-File+ letter editing window appears, as shown in Figure 8-2. The top line of the screen displays the following message:

PRESS (F10) WHEN THE LETTER IS READY TO PRINT.

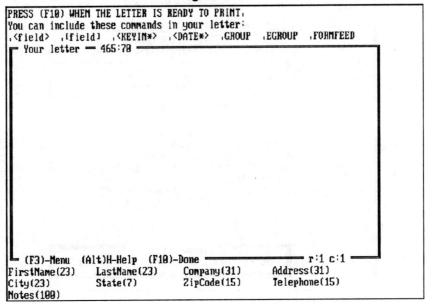

Figure 8-2.

The letter editing window

The third line lists the *mail merge commands* that you can include in the body of your letter. Mail merge commands are used to automatically insert database information into the letter and to control the letter's format. You will use these commands to build your first form letter. The mail merge commands are as follows:

.<field> .[field] .<KEYIN*> .<DATE*> .GROUP .EGROUP .FORMFEED

The first two commands can be used to automatically insert data into the letter from the database. The .<KEYIN*> command allows you to type data directly from the keyboard into the letter as the letter is printed. The .<DATE*> command inserts the current system date into the letter. The .GROUP and .EGROUP commands help you control the appearance of information on the printed letter. The .FORMFEED command tells PC-File+ to skip to a new page.

PC-File+ displays the size of the editing window in the top bordered area of your screen:

465:70

The letter editing window is 465 rows long by 70 columns wide! You can create nearly eight full pages of text with the PC-File+ letter writing feature.

Along the bottom window border, PC-File+ displays the primary active keys you use to create a letter. F3 activates the Editor menu. ALT-H displays the PC-File+ help screens appropriate to the task you are doing. Press F10 when you are finished editing and ready to print the letter.

On the right side of the bottom border, you see the row (r:) and column (c:) indicators:

r:1 c:1

The cursor sits on the first row, in the first column position. Use the arrow keys (↓, →, ←, and ↑) to move the cursor around the screen. As you move the cursor, watch how the r: and c: indicators change to indicate the cursor's current position.

Try the PGDN and PGUP keys. When you press PGDN repeatedly, the row indicator number gets larger and larger until it finally stops changing when you reach the last screen page. Continue pressing PGUP to get back to the first page. The row indicator number gets smaller and smaller until you reach the first screen page.

The bottom of the screen contains the field names and field lengths of the MailList database. This list becomes handy when you begin to place mail merge commands in your letter.

Before you begin to create your first form letter, read the following section for more details on the mail merge commands.

PC-File+ Mail Merge Commands

PC-File+ looks for mail merge commands in your letter, and replaces the commands with database information. For example, if you type .<ZipCode> in your letter, PC-File+ will replace the command with the ZIP code contained in the MailList record being processed. For Linda's and Michael's records, for example, the ZIP code is 94019. Susan's ZIP code is 94301. The records for Georgio and Carol contain 95472 in the ZipCode field.

All of the mail merge commands begin with a period. Commands that specify variables, such as field names, dates, and keyed-in messages, are enclosed in symbols (either < > or [ ]). Commands that do not involve variable information, such as group commands and form feed, begin with a period but do not use the enclosing symbols.

The tasks and functions performed by the mail merge commands are described in the following sections.

The .<field> Command Use this command to insert data from a particular field into your letter. Type the name of the field inside the < > symbols. For example, if you type .<**FirstName**>, PC-File+ will take data from the FirstName field of every record being processed and substitute the data for the mail merge command in the letter. When this command is used, all spaces, either to the right or the left of the data, are removed when the data is merged with the letter. The .<field> command allows you to insert data from the database so that it appears typed as an integral part of the letter. You can truncate this command to the first few letters of the field name, as follows:

.<First> or .<Firs> or .<Fir> or .<F>

The .[field] Command This command functions similarly to the .<field> command, except that no spaces are removed from the data during insertion. The .[field] command places the data in the amount of space allocated by the distance between the brackets [ ]. If the space between the brackets is shorter than the amount of data from the field, the data is truncated. For example, if you type .[Last] in your letter, the last names in the MailList database would be shortened to four characters as follows:

```
Evan  Ange  Anth  Acro  Artu
```

The .[field] command is useful for aligning blocks of data into neat columns.

The .<KEYIN*> Command Use this command to add a custom touch to each letter you print. When PC-File+ encounters this mail merge command, the program stops printing the letter so that you can key in a custom message. If you have several messages to insert, you can add a prompting message to each command to remind you what to type, as in the following examples:

    .<KEYIN*thanks>
    .<KEYIN*nexttime>
    .<KEYIN*last>

NOTE The word "KEYIN" must be typed in all capital letters. If you type the command in uppercase and lowercase letters, or if you misspell the word, PC-File+ will print a series of question marks (??????) wherever the unrecognizable command occurs in the letter.

The .<DATE*> Command The .<DATE*> command automatically inserts the current date when the letter is printed. The word "DATE" in the mail merge command must be in capital letters. You may want to send out a batch of letters, for example an invitation to a party, this month, and the same letters as reminders, next month. The current month's batch of letters gets this month's date. Next month's batch gets next month's date, even though the letters might be exactly the same otherwise. When PC-File+ sees this command in a letter, the program takes the current system date and inserts that date where the command occurs.

 NOTE If your computer does not have a clock-calendar, you must initialize the date when you start up your computer by using the DOS DATE command.

The .GROUP and .EGROUP Commands   You may want to print a collection of data items such as name, address, city, state, and Zip code, as a single unit. If one or more of the data items are blank, blank lines will appear between items. To solve this problem, use the .GROUP and .EGROUP commands.

Place the .GROUP command at the beginning of a collection of data; .EGROUP at the end. PC-File+ will then print the data as a group, removing all the blank lines.

The following example shows how these commands might appear in your letter:

```
.GROUP
.<First> .<Last>
.<Address>
.<City>, .<St> .<Zip>
.EGROUP
```

If any of the three data lines are empty of data, the group commands will prevent blank lines from appearing in the letter. The command words GROUP and EGROUP must be typed in capital letters to be understood by PC-File+.

The .FORMFEED Command   This mail merge command causes the printer to skip to a new page. You can type an abbreviated form of the command as follows:

```
.FF
```

You should insert the .FF command at the end of each page, including the last page, of a letter. For letters with only one page, put .FF at the end of the letter.

PC-File+ has several additional mail merge commands. The commands described in the previous section are all you need to create and print your first form letter. To find out about the other mail merge commands, refer to Chapter 17 of the *PC-File+ User's Manual,* "Using the Letter Writing Features."

Create the Form Letter

Pretend that you are the first person listed in the database, Linda Evans. Suppose you (Linda) plan to have a party next month. You want to write letters to the four food businesses contained in the MailList database to place orders for the party.

Figure 8-3 provides the rough structure of the letter you plan to print and send. The date appears at the top of the letter. The company's name and address appears below the date.

The salutation appears below the name and address block. You want each letter to begin with the first name of the person who owns the business (Dear FirstName,). After the salutation line, a paragraph announces the party date and that you want to place an order.

You plan to order a variable number of items from each vendor. The middle of the letter contains a list of these items. The next paragraph repeats the addressee's first name, tells where to make the delivery, and tells who to bill.

Finally, you want to include a special note for each person. After the special note, you have a closing salutation followed by your name, address, and telephone number. At the bottom of the letter, you put a reminder that the next letter requires a new page.

Figure 8-4 shows the same letter shown in Figure 8-3, but

Figure 8-3.

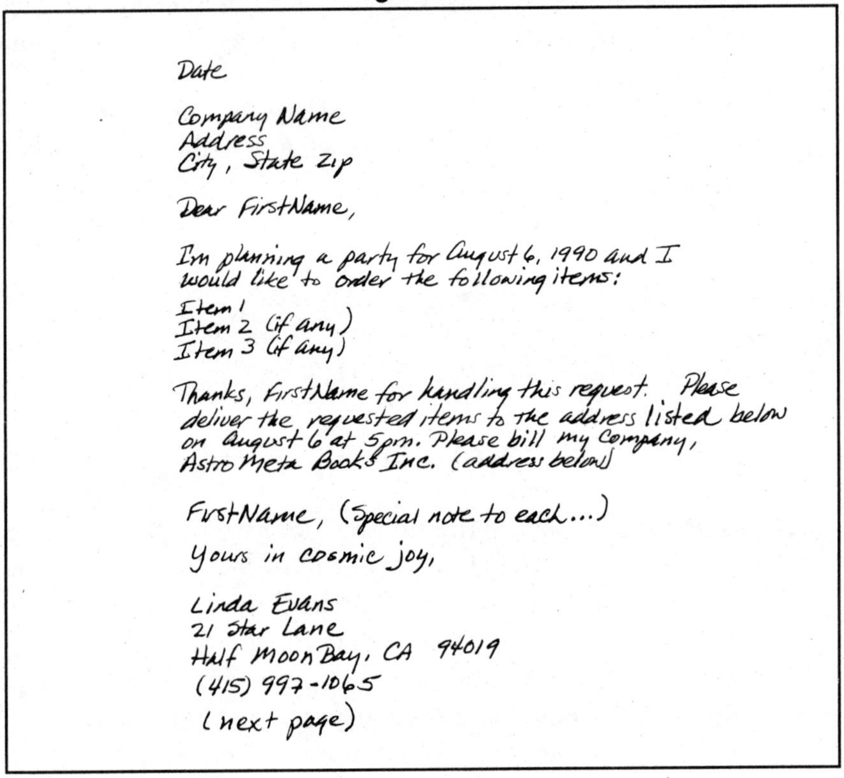

```
Date

Company Name
Address
City, State Zip

Dear FirstName,

I'm planning a party for August 6, 1990 and I
would like to order the following items:
Item 1
Item 2 (if any)
Item 3 (if any)

Thanks, FirstName for handling this request. Please
deliver the requested items to the address listed below
on August 6 at 5pm. Please bill my Company,
AstroMeta Books Inc. (address below)

FirstName, (Special note to each....)

Yours in cosmic joy,

Linda Evans
21 Star Lane
Half Moon Bay, CA 94019
(415) 997-1065
(next page)
```

The form letter outline

coded with PC-File+ mail merge commands. You can use Figure 8-4 as a guide in the creation of Linda's PC-File+ form letter.

To begin, move the cursor to the first row and column screen position (r:1 c:1), and then clear the letter editing window:

    Press CTRL-E
    or
    Press F3, E

    Press Y
    when the question box appears.   (r:1 c:1)

Figure 8-4.

```
.<DATE*>

.<Company>
.<Address>
.<City>, .<State> .<ZipCode>

Dear .<FirstName>,

I'm planning a party for August 6, 1990 and I would like to order the
following items:

.GROUP
.<KEYIN*item1>
.<KEYIN*item2>
.<KEYIN*item3>
.EGROUP

Thanks, .<FirstName> for handling this request. Please deliver the
requested items to the address listed below on August 6 at 5pm. Please
bill my company, AstroMeta Books Inc. (address below).

.<FirstName>, .<KEYIN*special>

Yours in cosmic joy,


Linda Evans
21 Star Lane
Half Moon Bay, CA 94019
(415)997-1065

.FF
```

The form letter with mail merge commands

NOTE Throughout the following screen activities, the row and column indicators (r:1 c:1) will be placed after each entry, before the instruction to press the ENTER key. Use the indicators as a guide to whether or not you typed each line correctly. The number of columns you show on each line may vary slightly from the examples, based on whether or not you use the same number of spaces between entries and whether you use the truncated or the full form of field names. The spaces between database insertion points are important; they keep the data items from being squeezed tightly together.

With the letter editing screen clear and the cursor sitting at row 1 of column 1, begin entering the data shown in Figure 8-4. Press ENTER after each single typed line and at the end of paragraphs (note that PC-File+ will wrap the paragraph text just like a regular word processing program), and move the cursor over blank lines using the cursor control keys. Enter the letter as follows:

```
Type:
.<DATE*>                                        (r:1 c:9)
(skip one line)
.<Company>                                      (r:3 c:11)
.<Address>                                      (r:4 c:11)
.<City>, .<State> .<ZipCode>                    (r:5 c:29)
(skip one line)
Dear .<FirstName>,                              (r:7 c:19)
(skip one line)
I'm planning a party for August 6, 1990
and I would like to order the following
items:                                          (r:10 c:17)
(skip one line)
.GROUP                                          (r:12 c:7)
.<KEYIN*item1>                                  (r:13 c:15)
.<KEYIN*item2>                                  (r:14 c:15)
.<KEYIN*item3>                                  (r:15 c:15)
.EGROUP                                         (r:16 c:8)
(skip one line)
Thanks, .<FirstName> for handling this
request. Please deliver the requested items
to the address listed below on August 6 at 5
pm. Please bill my company, AstroMeta
Books Inc. (address below).                     (r:20 c:62)
```

(skip one line)
.<FirstName>, .<KEYIN*special>   (r:22 c:31)
(skip one line)
Yours in cosmic joy,   (r:24 c:21)
(skip three lines)
Linda Evans   (r:28 c:12)
21 Star Lane   (r:29 c:13)
Half Moon Bay, CA 94019   (r:30 c:24)
(415)997-1065   (r:31 c:14)
(skip one line)
.FF   (r:33 c:4)

When you have typed the form letter with the embedded PC-File+ mail merge commands, review everything you entered. The letter with the mail merge commands should fill exactly two full editing windows. Figure 8-5 and Figure 8-6 show how these

Figure 8-5.

```
PRESS (F10) WHEN THE LETTER IS READY TO PRINT.
You can include these commands in your letter:
.<field>  .[field]  .<KEYIN*>  .<DATE*>  .GROUP  .EGROUP  .FORMFEED
┌─ Your letter ══ 465:70 ─────────────────────────────────┐
│ .<DATE*>                                                │
│                                                         │
│ .<Company>                                              │
│ .<Address>                                              │
│ .<City>, .<State> .<ZipCode>                            │
│                                                         │
│ Dear .<FirstName>,                                      │
│                                                         │
│ I'm planning a party for August 6, 1990 and I would like to order the
│ following items:                                        │
│                                                         │
│ .GROUP                                                  │
│ .<KEYIN*item1>                                          │
│ .<KEYIN*item2>                                          │
│ .<KEYIN*item3>                                          │
│ .EGROUP                                                 │
│                                                         │
└─ (F3)-Menu  (Alt)H-Help  (F10)-Done ─────── r:1 c:1 ────┘
FirstName(23)    LastName(23)    Company(31)    Address(31)
City(23)         State(7)        ZipCode(15)    Telephone(15)
Notes(100)
```

First half of the form letter

Figure 8-6.

```
PRESS (F10) WHEN THE LETTER IS READY TO PRINT.
You can include these commands in your letter:
.<field>  .[field]  .<KEYIN*>  .<DATE*>  .GROUP  .EGROUP  .FORMFEED
┌─ Your letter ── 465:70 ─────────────────────────────────────────┐
│                                                                  │
│Thanks, .<FirstName> for handling this request.  Please deliver the│
│requested items to the address listed below on August 6 at 5pm.   │
│Please bill my company, AstroMeta Books Inc. (address below).     │
│                                                                  │
│.<FirstName>, .<KEYIN*special>                                    │
│                                                                  │
│Yours in cosmic joy,                                              │
│                                                                  │
│                                                                  │
│Linda Evans                                                       │
│21 Star Lane                                                      │
│Half Moon Bay, CA 94019                                           │
│(415)997-1065                                                     │
│                                                                  │
│.FF                                                               │
└─ (F3)-Menu  (Alt)H-Help  (F10)-Done ──────────── r:17 c:1 ──────┘
FirstName(23)    LastName(23)    Company(31)    Address(31)
City(23)         State(7)        ZipCode(15)    Telephone(15)
Notes(100)
```

Last half of the form letter

two screens of information should appear. You can move between the two screens by pressing the PGDN and PGUP keys.

Preview the Printed Letter

When you have reviewed the form letter and made any adjustments or changes, you are ready to test the letter against the database. To test print the letter:

    Press F10

When you press F10, you see the following:

Save this letter to disk?   Y/N >Y<

Since you want to save the letter:

Press Y or ENTER

PC-File+ asks you to name the letter. Do the following:

Type:
Party
and press ENTER

When you press ENTER, you see a request to supply a description for the letter. Enter a description:

Type:
August 6 food order
and press ENTER

After you press ENTER, PC-File+ displays a message telling you that it is saving the letter. When the save operation is complete, the Report menu appears, as shown in Figure 8-7. This menu is the same menu you used in Chapter 7 to print a report from the MailList database.

Before you print your letters on paper, you may want to preview them on the screen. The first menu option controls whether the letter is printed to the printer, the screen, or the disk. To preview the letters on the screen:

Press S, F10

After you press F10, the beginnings of the letter appear, as shown in Figure 8-8. The current date (whatever date it is when you try this example) prints on the first line of the screen.

A company name and address block prints next. Since Linda's record is the first record in the database, PC-File+ inserted her company's name and address in the first letter. When you get ready to actually print the letters, you can skip her record. For this example, however, you will use Linda's record to examine the preview function.

Figure 8-7.

```
                    REPORT MENU
 Output to Printer, Screen, Disk   P/S/D   ►P◄
 Number of copies                  1-99    [ 1]
 Line spacing (0 = no detail lines) 0-9    [1]
 Do Subtotals?                      Y/N    [N]
 Left margin (extra spaces)         0-99   [ 0]
 Page length (in "lines")                  [ 66]
 Pause after each page?             Y/N    [N]
 Start at which page number?        1-9999 [   1]
 Type size (Normal/Condensed)       N/C    [N]
 Remove blank lines and spaces      Y/N    [N]
 Flip data active?                  Y/N    [Y]
 Print All or Selected records      A/S    [A]

 Press (Esc) to return to PC-File+ menu



 Please respond.  (F10) when complete.  (Alt)H for help.
```

The Report menu

Note that there is a minor problem in the address block: The ZIP code is followed by a hyphen (-). That hyphen was inserted in the database during the demonstration in Chapter 7 of the global modify feature. You will eliminate the hyphen later in this chapter.

The salutation line looks okay. PC-File+ picked up Linda's first name and inserted it into the salutation.

The opening paragraph printed up to the point where the group of .<KEYIN*> commands appeared in the letter outline. PC-File+ has detected the first .<KEYIN*> command and displays an input portal at the bottom of the screen. Remember the reminder label you put into the mail merge command .<KEYIN*item1>? The reminder label for item1 appears in the

Figure 8-8.

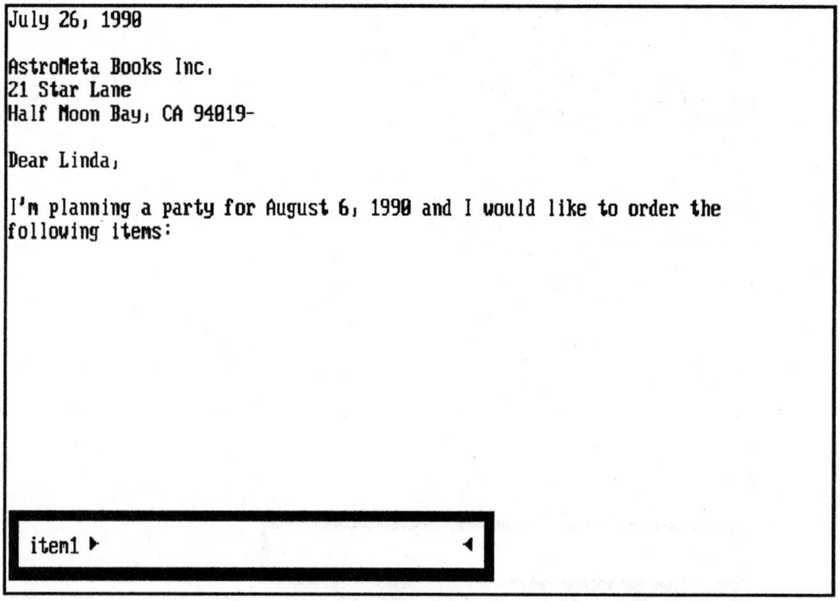

```
July 26, 1990

AstroMeta Books Inc.
21 Star Lane
Half Moon Bay, CA 94019-

Dear Linda,

I'm planning a party for August 6, 1990 and I would like to order the
following items:




                            item1 ▶                                  ◀
```

Previewing the letter

input portal so that you know which .<KEYIN*> command is being processed. Enter the following data at the "item1" prompt:

Type:
1 dozen yellow roses
and press ENTER

When you press ENTER, PC-File+ inserts the data that you typed into the letter. The screen appears as shown in Figure 8-9. The input portal at the bottom of the screen changes to the reminder prompt "item2."

Figure 8-9.

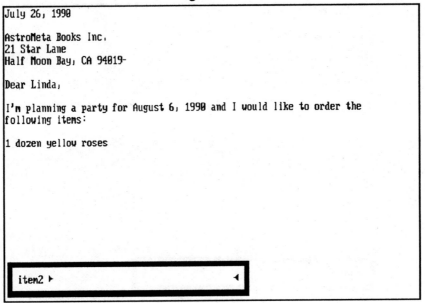

Letter after first . <KEYIN> entry*

 NOTE Because you are in preview mode, the data you enter is not being saved or recorded. The preview mode allows you to test your form letter with mail merge commands before you actually print the letters on paper.

Enter a second set of items for the party, as follows:

Type:
3 gallons ice cream
and press ENTER

When you press ENTER, "3 gallons of ice cream" appears beneath the line for "1 dozen yellow roses." The reminder prompt in the input portal changes to "item3." To test the grouping commands, do not type anything for the "item3" entry.

Press ENTER

Pressing ENTER tells PC-File+ that you do not have an item for the third .<KEYIN*> command. PC-File+ then prints the next paragraph on the screen, below the two items you entered with the first two .<KEYIN*> commands. Figure 8-10 shows the screen that appears after you press ENTER to skip the third item.

Notice how the group commands closed up the spacing between the "item2" entry and the next paragraph. Even though "item3" had no data, PC-File+ did not leave a blank line in the letter. The .GROUP and .EGROUP commands eliminate blank lines so that they are not printed.

Figure 8-10.

```
July 26, 1990

AstroMeta Books Inc.
21 Star Lane
Half Moon Bay, CA 94019-

Dear Linda,

I'm planning a party for August 6, 1990 and I would like to order the
following items:

1 dozen yellow roses
3 gallons ice cream

Thanks, Linda for handling this request.  Please deliver the
requested items to the address listed below on August 6 at 5pm.
Please bill my company, AstroMeta Books Inc. (address below).




  special ▶                                                    ◀
```

Letter after third .<KEYIN> entry*

In Figure 8-10, the input portal at the bottom of the screen is marked "special." This reminder prompts you to insert a special message for each person getting a letter. Enter a special message (to yourself in this case):

Type:
I like you.
and press ENTER

When you press ENTER, the following lines appear:

```
Linda, I like you.
Yours in cosmic joy.
```

The following reply portal also appears:

```
More...  Press (Enter) > <
```

Since the entire letter does not fit on one screen, you can view the rest of the letter by doing the following:

Press ENTER

When you press ENTER, Linda's name, address, and telephone number appear at the top of a new screen. A "Please reply" portal reading "More..." informs you that PC-File+ has more letters to process. You can browse through the rest of the letters and enter data at the prompts. Remember, you are not actually creating the letters at this point; you are merely previewing the letters before they are printed.

As you preview the letters, make notes to yourself concerning any problems that occur or changes that need to be made. The most common problems encountered in the mail merge operations include the following:

- Misspelling a mail merge command
- Not entering the command words in all capital letters
- Entering a nonexistent field name

When PC-File+ encounters one of these problems, it prints a string of question marks in the body of the letter, as follows:

???????

When you preview a form letter and see a string of question marks, you can locate the problem by looking in the letter outline at the place where the question marks appear in the letter.

Print the Letters

When you have screen previewed all the letters, the program displays a "Completed" message. Press the ENTER key to retrieve the Master menu. You can also stop the preview at any time by doing the following:

    Press ESC, ENTER, ESC

The first ESC cancels the preview mode. The ENTER takes you back to the Report menu. The last ESC returns you to the Master menu.

You want to be on the Master menu so that you can activate the "Letter writing" command and make corrections to the party letter. From the Master menu, do the following:

   Press F5 or L

This action restarts the letter writing command. PC-File+ displays a file selection screen. If the party letter is the only letter you have created, you will see the following selection list:

   [1] PARTY   August 6 food order

To select the party letter, you can either enter the number or name of the file, or move the cursor to highlight the name of the file.

   Type:
   1 or **PARTY** or press ↓
   and then press F10

When you select the party letter and press F10, PC-File+ prompts you for the column width. Choose the default setting of 70 characters as follows:

   Press ENTER

After you make the column width selection, the party letter appears on the screen. During the letter preview, you saw that the ZIP code at the top of the letter contained an extra hyphen (-) at the end. To fix that problem, change the ZIP code mail merge command from .<ZipCode> to .[ZipCo]. The form of the mail merge command with square brackets instructs PC-File+ to use only five character positions for the ZIP code. Any characters beyond the fifth position will be omitted.

Try it! Move the cursor down to the .<ZipCode> command and replace it as follows:

Type:
.[ZipCo]
and erase or space over the last two characters, "e>".

Once you make this replacement and any other corrections you need to make to your version of the letter outline, you are ready to print the letters:

Press F10

PC-File+ asks if you want to save the letter.

Press Y or ENTER

PC-File+ prompts you for the name of the letter. Since the name "PARTY" already appears in the "Please reply" portal, do the following:

Press ENTER

The "Please reply" portal asks you to verify that you want to replace the existing party letter. Since you do want to replace the letter with the current corrected version, do the following:

Press Y

The old description of the party letter appears in a "Please reply" portal. To keep the same description:

Press ENTER

When you press this last ENTER, the Report menu appears. The default setting on the first line is "P" for "Printer." Make sure your printer is connected, turned on, and ready to print. If your printer is not connected when you attempt to print your letters, PC-File+ may generate an error message, hang up until you turn on the printer, or act as if the program is printing the letters, even though nothing is coming out of the printer. What happens depends upon the kind of printer and computer system you are using.

When your printer is ready to go, check to make sure your paper is aligned so that the letters will start at the top of the page. When you are ready to print your letters:

Press F10

The screen clears and shows the first record in the MailList database, Linda's record. The "Please reply" portal at the bottom of the screen asks if you want to output the current record. Since you (Linda) do not want to send the letter to yourself:

Press N

PC-File+ skips over Linda's record and puts record number 2 on the screen, the record for Michael Angel. Make sure that your printer is connected and ready to go, and that the paper is positioned correctly. When you press the next key, the printer begins to print the letter to Michael:

Press Y

When you press Y, the date, address block, salutation, and first paragraph of Michael's letter prints on the printer. On the computer screen, an input portal appears with an "item1" reminder prompt. You can enter the first item that you want Michael to supply for the party.

Figures 8-11 through 8-14 show examples of four printed letters that Linda might have created for her party orders. You can use these example letters to guide your input entries as you explore the letter writing and printing features. You can make up your own data for each letter as well.

Figure 8-11.

July 26, 1990

Donut Heaven
45 Butter Way
Half Moon Bay, CA 94019

Dear Michael,

I'm planning a party for August 6, 1990 and I would like to order the following items:

3 dozen cream filled donuts
2 dozen fruit bars

Thanks, Michael for handling this request. Please deliver the requested items to the address listed below on August 6 at 5pm. Please bill my company, AstroMeta Books Inc. (address below).

Michael, please plan to stay for the party.

Yours in cosmic joy,

Linda Evans
21 Star Lane
Half Moon Bay, CA 94019
(415)997-1065

Michael's order

Figure 8-12.

> July 26, 1990
>
> Donut Haven
> One Dollar Drive
> Palo Alto, CA 94301
>
> Dear Susan B.,
>
> I'm planning a party for August 6, 1990 and I would like to order the following items:
>
> 1 chocolate birthday cake.
>
> Thanks, Susan B. for handling this request. Please deliver the requested items to the address listed below on August 6 at 5pm. Please bill my company, AstroMeta Books Inc. (address below). Susan B., do you have that special ice cream?
>
> Yours in cosmic joy,
>
>
> Linda Evans
> 21 Star Lane
> Half Moon Bay, CA 94019
> (415)997-1065

Susan B.'s order

Printing a letter does not save the letter on your disk. Only the letter outline and the database have been saved on your disk.

Of course, PC-File+ does have a way to actually save the entire letter including the data you entered at the .<KEYIN*> command points. On the first line of the Report menu (refer to Figure 8-7), PC-File+ offers the option to print to disk (D). As you create the letters, you can output them to a file on your data disk. Later, you can print the letters from the file. In fact, Figures 8-11 through 8-14 were created using this PC-File+ report printing feature.

Figure 8-13.

July 26, 1990

Strawberry Pizza
77 Dough Road
Sebastopol, CA 95472

Dear Georgio,

I'm planning a party for August 6, 1990 and I would like to order the following items:

3 feta,tomato,garlic pizzas
1 large plain cheese pizza

Thanks, Georgio for handling this request. Please deliver the requested items to the address listed below on August 6 at 5pm. Please bill my company, AstroMeta Books Inc. (address below).

Georgio, cut cheese pizza in small squares.

Yours in cosmic joy,

Linda Evans
21 Star Lane
Half Moon Bay, CA 94019
(415)997-1065

Georgio's order

To use the print-to-disk feature, select the D option on the Report menu. The program prompts you as follows:

`Output Filespec: >                    <`

Enter the full path name and file name of where you want to save your letters. For example, you might enter the following path and file name designation:

Type:
b:letters
and press ENTER

Figure 8-14.

July 26, 1990

Ultimate Pizza House
144 Verona Way
Sebastopol, CA 95472

Dear Carol,

I'm planning a party for August 6, 1990 and I would like to order the following items:

6 avocado sandwiches

Thanks, Carol for handling this request. Please deliver the requested items to the address listed below on August 6 at 5pm. Please bill my company, AstroMeta Books Inc. (address below). Carol, it's a surprise party for Georgio!

Yours in cosmic joy,

Linda Evans
21 Star Lane
Half Moon Bay, CA 94019
(415)997-1065

Carol's order

Once you provide the path and file name, go ahead and create the four letters as described earlier. Use Figures 8-11 through 8-14 as guides for what to type in the four letters. As you complete each letter, that letter will be written onto your database disk in the file B:LETTERS. When you exit PC-File+, you can then print B:LETTERS directly from the DOS prompt, either to your screen or to your printer. You can also load B:LETTERS into your word processor to edit the letters directly.

This concludes the sections on using the PC-File+ letter writing features. The following sections in this chapter show you how to create mailing labels for the letters you just created.

Use PC-File+ to Create Mailing Labels

To create mailing labels from a database file, such as MailList, you run one of the PC-File+ standalone programs, PC-Label. PC-Label is on DISK TWO of the set of PC-File+ disks. PC-Label is set up as a standalone program because it can create mailing labels from a variety of different data formats, including files from PC-File+, PC-File:db, PC-Calc+, ASCII data, and text data where the data are separated by commas.

Get Started with PC-Label

To use PC-Label, you will need to exit from PC-File+ and get to the A prompt. Then, take PC-File+ DISK ONE disk out of drive A and replace it with PC-File+ DISK TWO. Leave your data disk in drive B. When you have DISK TWO in drive A:

Type:
pclabel
and press ENTER

NOTE PC-Label appears in color on color monitors. If your system uses a standard color or monochrome screen, PC-Label works correctly when you type **pclabel**. If you have a graphics monitor that does not support color, you need to type the following command at the A prompt so that all the PC-Label screens can be displayed on your monitor:

Type:
pclabel /green
and press ENTER

Figure 8-15 displays the PC-Label title screen that appears when you first start the program. To go to the first working screen, press any key, as the title screen message suggests:

```
Press any key to continue ...
```

PC-Label displays the screen shown in Figure 8-16, the Main menu screen. PC-Label uses the right side of the screen to display helpful messages that tell you what to do. The menu at the lower left corner of the screen lists five options. The highlight sits on the first option, "(L)oad existing setup." The message below the menu describes the function of the highlighted option.

If you have never used PC-Label before, then you should select option D to define/modify a label setup file. To print labels from

Figure 8-15.

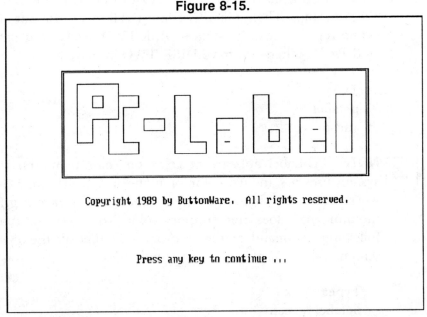

PC-Label title screen

Ch 8

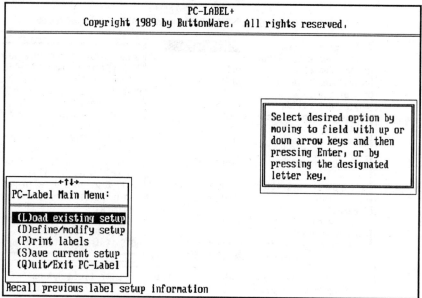

Figure 8-16.

PC-Label Main menu

a data file, PC-Label requires that you define a label setup file. To start the file definition, either move the highlight down to the D option and press ENTER, or:

Press D

When you activate the setup definition option, the PC-Label Setup Definition and Modification screen as shown in Figure 8-17 appears on the display. For the current exploration with mailing labels, you will limit your activities to only those options that help you produce a set of mailing labels from the MailList database.

Select the Label Source Type The first option on the Setup Definition and Modification screen is "Label Source type." The

Figure 8-17.

```
                        PC-LABEL+
         Copyright 1989 by ButtonWare.  All rights reserved.

Label Source type        PC-File:dB    Select data source type labels.
Label Source Location                  PC-FILE+ is standard PC-FILE+
Define Search            ALL             format with data in each record.
Output destination       LPT1          PC-File:dB is for PC-File:dB
No. of copies            1               databases.
Copies definition        By Group      PC-CALC+ assumes each label's
Compress blank lines     Yes             data is in one row.
Centering                Yes           COMMA-DELIMITED assumes data
Pause if truncation      Yes             for each label in each record.
Escape code toggle       On            ASCII-L assumes data for each
Print Escape Code        Print codes     label is on one line.
                                       ASCII-C assumes data in one
Label Sheet definition   3 1/2 x  15/16 (1 column, with empty row between.
Feed method              Continuous      groups.
Formfeed                 None            (Use this with PC-TYPE mail-
Label layout             User defined    merge output files.)
Workspace drive          A             NOTE: Enter key toggles options.

               PC-Label Setup Definition and

         ←↑↓→ - next field    --   Enter - change field option
         PgUp/PgDn - first field/last field  -  PRESS F10 or Esc when finished.
```

Label Setup Definition and Modification screen

current label source type is highlighted. PC-Label displays a help message to the right of the screen that defines the options for label source type.

To change the current label source type, press the ENTER key.

Press ENTER several times

Each time you press ENTER, a new label source type option appears within the highlight. Keep pressing ENTER until PC-File+ appears within the highlight.

This screen has two kinds of input fields. In one kind of field, you press ENTER to switch between various options, as you did for

"Label Option type." In the second kind of field, pressing ENTER activates an input portal for you to type data into a setup screen position. You will use this second kind of input field in just a moment.

Once you have set the "Label Source type" to PC-File+, move the highlight down the screen with the arrow keys. Notice that the help message on the right side of the screen changes as the highlight moves to each new line.

Set the Workspace Drive Designation Move the highlight to the option on the bottom line entitled "Workspace drive." The "Workspace drive" is initially set to A when PC-Label starts up. Change the "Workspace drive" designation to drive B:

Press ENTER
and type:
b
and press ENTER

The "Workspace drive" field is an example of the second kind of input field mentioned earlier. For the "Workspace drive" option, you press ENTER to activate an input portal. With the input portal showing, you type the new drive designation, B, and press ENTER again. On the final keystroke, the letter "B" appears on the definition screen next to "Workspace drive."

Set the Database Location Move the highlight back up the screen to the second line on the list, "Label Source Location." The information you enter here tells PC-Label where your database is located. PC-Label uses the "Label Source type" information from line one to find all your database files of that type.

Press ENTER

When you press ENTER, a small version of the edit window appears at the bottom of the screen. The word "PATH" appears to the left of the window. PC-Label wants to know the path name for your database file:

Type:
b:
and press ENTER

An informational message flashes on the screen, and a selection window appears in the lower left corner. The window contains the names of the database files on the disk in drive B. Each file name ends with the HDR extension, which PC-File+ uses to identify the files that define the database structure. Since you selected PC-File+ as the file type, PC-Label locates the PC-File+ database HDR files.

Highlight the MAILLIST.HDR file on the window and press ENTER.

The complete name of the file, b:\MAILLIST.HDR, will appear on the second option line of the Setup Definition and Modification screen.

Lay Out the Mailing Label   Move the cursor down to the "Label layout" option. The highlight rests on the current selection, "User defined." You must tell PC-Label exactly which data to extract from the database and where to place the data on the labels. To initiate the layout process, do the following:

Press ENTER

The label layout screen appears, as shown in Figure 8-18. At the top of the screen is a listing of all the field names in the MailList database, plus four items with an asterisk (*) in the first position. There are a total of 13 items listed, nine field names (numbers 1 through 9) and four command codes (numbers 10 through 13).

Figure 8-18.

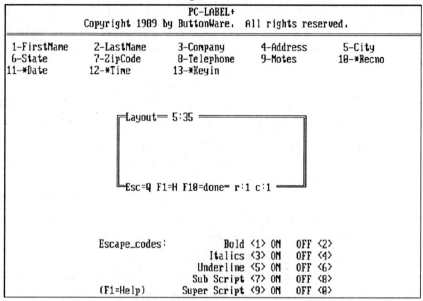

Label layout screen

In the center of the screen is a label editing window. The size of the window corresponds to the size of the actual labels to be printed. The labels in this example will have 5 rows, and each row will have 35 character positions.

A set of escape codes is listed at the bottom of the screen. *Escape codes* are special printer instructions that you can insert into your label layout to print various type styles.

The process for creating the layout of the label is similar to the way you laid out elements for the letter earlier in this chapter. Instead of entering the entire field name in the layout, however, you use only the numbers next to each name. For example, to insert the first names on the labels, you reference item 1. To insert the ZIP codes, use item 7. To insert the date on each label, use item 11.

Two symbols control the spacing of information on the labels. One symbol, the "at" sign (@), tells PC-Label to place data in a fixed column position. When you precede a field number with an @ sign, the first character of the data prints in the same column where the @ sign appears on the label.

For example, if you put @1 at label position (r:1 c:1), the letter "L" in Linda's name will print out in column 1 on the label. You can also use the @ sign to place additional text directly on the label, such as spaces, commas, periods, or small messages.

The other symbol used to control spacing is the question mark (?). Putting a question mark in front of an item number or text entry (space, comma, period, or small message) will move the item to the left until it touches either a previous data entry or the left label margin. You can use this symbol to remove excess spaces at the end of a previous data field.

Time to experiment! Lay out the mailing labels by typing the data listed below onto the layout window. If you need to clear the layout window, move the cursor to position (r:1 c:1), and do the following:

Press CTRL-E and Y

NOTE The same editing commands used in the PC-File+ editing windows also work here. For instance, F3 will bring up an Edit menu, even though the F3 key is not listed on the screen. F1 produces a help message that displays label layout examples and describes the @ and ? symbols.

With a clear label window and the cursor at position (r:1 c:1), enter the following codes and numbers. Press ENTER at the end of each line. The r: and c: notations indicate the cursor position before you press ENTER:

Type:
@1? ?2   (r:1 c:7)
               (Note the space between the question marks)
@4   (r:2 c:3)
@5?, ?6? ?7   (r:3 c:12)

Figure 8-19.

```
                              PC-LABEL+
              Copyright 1989 by ButtonWare.  All rights reserved.
  1-FirstName      2-LastName      3-Company      4-Address      5-City
  6-State          7-ZipCode       8-Telephone    9-Notes        10-*Recno
  11-*Date         12-*Time        13-*Keyin


                     ┌Layout═ 5:35 ═══════════════╕
                     │@1? ?2                      │
                     │@4                          │
                     │@5?, ?6? ?7                 │
                     │                            │
                     │                            │
                     └Esc=Q F1=H F10=done= r:3 c:12┘



            Escape_codes:            Bold <1> ON     OFF <2>
                                   Italics <3> ON     OFF <4>
                                 Underline <5> ON     OFF <6>
                                 Sub Script <7> ON     OFF <8>
                    (F1=Help)   Super Script <9> ON     OFF <0>
```

Label layout screen with label codes

When you are finished entering the label layout codes, the layout window appears as shown in Figure 8-19. Do the following:

    Press F10, F10

The first F10 tells PC-Label that you have completed the label layout process and returns you to the Setup Definition and Modification screen. The second F10 signals PC-Label that you are finished changing the setup definitions and displays the Main menu.

Now that you have defined the label setup file, use option "S" on the Main menu to save the file:

    Press S

After you press S, the small edit window appears asking for the pathname of the file to be saved. To save the setup file on drive B:

Type:
b:
and press ENTER

When you press ENTER, a file selection window displays two selection options. The highlight sits on the first option, NEW FILE.LBL:

```
New File.LBL
EXIT
```

To create a new file:

Press ENTER

An input portal prompts you to enter the new file name (with no extension):

Type:
labels
and press ENTER

An information message announces that an .LBL file was created successfully.

> **CAUTION** PC-Label will overwrite an existing label file without warning. When you enter a file name for a label file, make sure the name is either unique or represents a file you want to overwrite.

Press any key to continue. When you press a key, PC-Label puts you back on the Main menu. You are now ready to print the labels.

Print Mailing Labels

In order to print labels, you first must have created the label setup file. If you have not created the setup file, PC-Label will stop and produce an error message as the program attempts to print a set of labels.

Make sure your printer is connected, turned on, and ready to print. To initiate the printing of labels, select the "Print labels" option on the Main menu:

Press P

PC-Label asks if you want to position the labels in the printer. When you are printing on actual labels, you have the opportunity to adjust the paper so that the data prints correctly on the labels, and not on the spaces between labels. For this test run, tell PC-Label that you do not want to position the printer paper:

Press N

When you press N, PC-Label locates the first data record (Linda's record) and displays a preview of the printed version of the label. Figure 8-20 shows the PC-Label Record Selection and Output screen.

Notice that the label is centered vertically on the label screen area. Centering labels is a default option that you can change on the label Setup Definition and Modification screen.

NOTE If you did not include space characters when you entered the label layout codes, the first and last name, and also the city, state, and ZIP code, might be run together.

If you want to print this label, press Y. If you just want to review the labels, press N. If you press X, PC-Label will print all of the labels without further prompting.

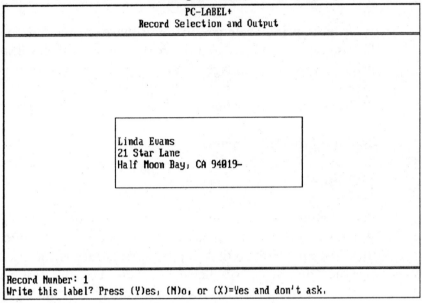

Figure 8-20.

Record selection and output screen

After you review or print the labels on your printer paper, you can print the labels onto actual mailing labels. If you have a set of standard mailing labels (3 1/2 inches by 15/16 inches, 1-up), you can insert them in your printer. The designations 1-up, 2-up, 3-up, and so forth, indicate the number of labels contained on one row of the label sheet. For this setup, you did not change the PC-Label default setting (standard size label, 1-up), so PC-Label expects to print on standard labels.

If you do not have mailing labels handy, proceed anyway and let PC-Label print the labels on the printer paper. In fact, one way to create mailing labels is to generate a mailing label master by printing the labels on paper. Then you can reproduce the labels onto mailing label sheets by using a copy machine.

Figure 8-21.

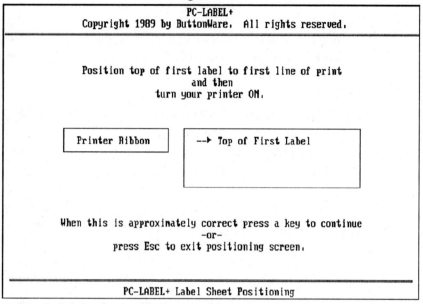

Label sheet positioning screen

From the PC-Label Main menu, select the "Print labels" option:

    Press P

When you are asked if you want to position the paper:

    Press Y

Figure 8-21 shows the PC-Label positioning screen that appears when you press Y. The screen instructs you to turn on your printer and shows you how to line up your label sheets with the printer ribbon. When you are ready to proceed:

Press any key   (except ESC)

Pressing ESC tells PC-Label to cancel the paper positioning activities. When you press any other key, a row of numbers prints across the top of your label form (or printer paper if you do not have labels).

The label alignment screen, shown in Figure 8-22, prompts you to look at the numbers printed on the first row of your label sheet. Count the numbers from the left edge of the paper to the first number printed inside the left edge of the label. For the example on the screen shown in Figure 8-22, the number would be 14. For the actual labels in your printer, the number might be different. Look at your label sheet in the printer and count the

Figure 8-22.

```
                         PC-LABEL+
            Copyright 1989 by ButtonWare.  All rights reserved.


         A row of numbers is being printed across your Top label.

         To determine how many spaces must be printed before getting to
         your label, enter the number corresponding to the first number
         printed INSIDE your label at the left edge.

                  123456789 12 |456789 123456789 1234567| 9 12..



                  In the example above, you would enter the number 14.


         Type the number at the left edge of the label and press Enter:  [ 0 ]
         (-or- press Esc to exit.)
```

Label alignment screen

spaces to the first character inside the label's left edge. (If you do not have labels in your printer, just assume that 14 spaces are needed and proceed with the example.)

Enter either **14** or the actual number of spaces you have counted:

Type:
14   (or your number)
and press ENTER

When you enter the number of spaces, PC-Label gives you a final chance to make minor adjustments to the vertical positioning of the labels. You are warned to first turn off your printer so that you do not damage the printer mechanisms. If necessary, make further adjustments. When you are ready to print:

Press N

PC-Label reminds you to turn on your printer. The program also informs you that when you press a key, PC-Label will skip to the next clean label. Remember, the alignment process printed a row of numbers across the first labels on your sheet.

Press any key

When you press a key, the printer advances to the next clean label position and displays the record selection and output screen shown in Figure 8-20. If you are printing the labels for the party letter, you can skip over record number 1, Linda's record, and print the remaining four labels.

Figure 8-23 shows the four labels as they might appear when printed.

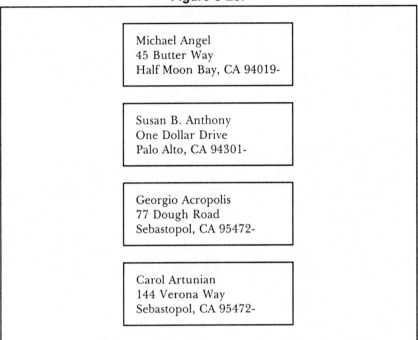

Printed labels for party letters

PC-Label's Many Labels

PC-Label can be set up to print on a variety of label formats. Figure 8-24 shows the list of label sizes available. To display this list, select the "Label Sheet definition" option on the PC-Label Setup Definition and Modification screen, which you get to by pressing D from the Main menu.

If your labels do not match any of the formats listed in Figure 8-24, you can enter the exact size of your labels by selecting the "User-defined" option at the bottom of the list.

To learn more about PC-Label and its many features, refer to Chapter 34, "Printing Mailing Labels," in the *PC-File+ User's Manual*.

Figure 8-24.

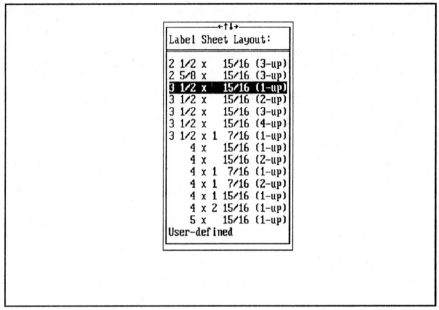

PC-Label's variety of label formats

Summary

In this chapter you explored two PC-File+ features that are used to extract data from a database:

- **Form letters**   Writing, editing, and printing
- **Mail labels**   Layout, editing, and printing

Using the PC-File+ mail merge commands, you created a form letter that retrieved data from the MailList database. You learned how to customize each letter. You previewed the letters on the screen and then printed the letters on your printer.

You used a PC-File+ standalone program, PC-Label, to specify, lay out, preview, and print a set of mailing labels from the MailList database.

These two features give you a glimpse of the kind of power and flexibility PC-File+ has to offer in the area of database management.

CHAPTER 9

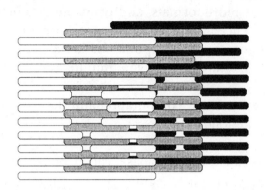

Database Calculations and Graphics

In this final chapter on PC-File+, you will explore the following two features of this powerful database management program: calculations within data fields and graphing data from a database.

PC-File+ lets you compute the contents of a data field based on information found in other data fields. You can tell PC-File+ to perform any normal arithmetic operations on fields of numbers, including addition, subtraction, multiplication, division, exponentiation (raising numbers to powers), and remaindering (dividing two numbers and sending the remainder).

PC-File+ graphs database information in a number of standard formats, including bar charts, pie charts, and line graphs. With PC-File+, you can quickly plot your data on the screen, look at the results in one or more formats, and print the graphics on your printer. The PC-File+ graphics features include a number of handy tools for doing simple computations based on plotted data—computations that might take you minutes or hours to perform by hand.

As you explore the PC-File+ computation and data graphing features, you will do the following:

- Use PC-File+ to create a new database, called BookStor.
- Learn how to use the PC-File+ field calculation features.
- Set up your computer so that you can print PC-File+ graphics.
- Set up your program disk to use the PC-File+ graphics feature.
- Use PC-File+ and the BookStor database to produce charts and graphs.

The BookStor Database

In Chapters 7 and 8, you developed the MailList database, explored the PC-File+ letter writing editor, and created mailing labels. As you worked through the examples, you used a database record containing information about Linda Evans and her company, Astro-Meta Books, Inc. As you wrote form letters and generated mailing labels, you pretended you were Linda.

Once again, suppose you are Linda and that you own Astro-Meta Books, Inc. As part of your book business, you need to keep a listing of books you sell along with some inventory information about the titles you carry. The data records might look something like those you see on the computer screens in most of today's bookstores.

Each record would contain the title of the book, the name of the author(s), the publisher's name, a few keywords related to the book's content, an International Standard Book Number (ISBN), and, how many copies of the book are on the shelf.

In addition, suppose that you also want to include the amount you paid for each book, the number of books you last ordered, the book's selling price, the total amount you paid for all the copies of the books you bought, and the total amount of money you have received from the sales of the book.

Figure 9-1 shows a rough layout of a data entry screen that contains all of these data items. You will use the data entry screen to create a new database called BookStor.

Create the BookStor Database

If you have not already done so, boot up the computer with a DOS disk. At the A prompt, insert a copy of PC-File+ DISK ONE in drive A and your formatted database disk in drive B.

Type:
pcf
and press ENTER

PC-File+ displays a title screen. At the bottom of the title screen, a "Please reply" portal requests the drive designation for the database. You will use drive B:

Press B

Figure 9-1.

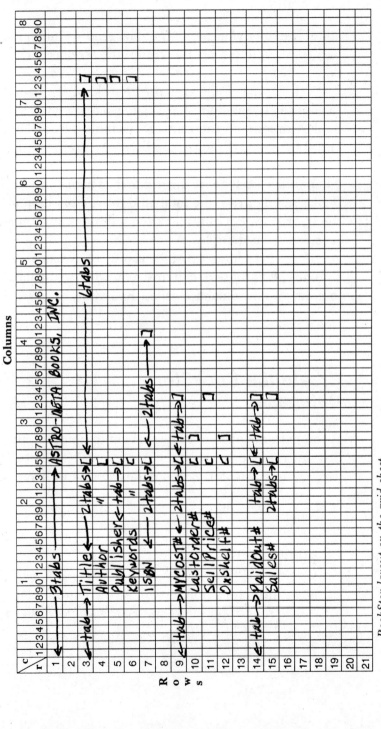

BookStor layout on the grid sheet

A new question asks for the DOS path name for the database. Since the database files on drive B require no path name:

Press ENTER

The database selection screen appears. To create a new database called BookStor, do the following:

Type:
BookStor
and press F10

NOTE If you have a copy of *The Shareware Book* Convenience Disk, you may want to load a copy of the BookStor database directly from the disk. If you load BookStor from the Convenience Disk, you can skip ahead to the section entitled "Set Up the Calculation Fields." If you do not have the Convenience Disk, or if you want to practice creating a new database, continue with the following instructions.

When you press F10, PC-File+ asks if you want to define the database. To define a new database:

Press Y or ENTER

PC-File+ now asks you which method you plan to use to define the database, "Fast" or "Paint." Since you will be using the "Paint" method:

Press P

If there are no existing database files on your database disk, the program displays the data entry editing window.
   If you have existing databases on your database disk, pressing P will display a question asking if you would like to start with a picture of an existing file. This feature comes in handy when

you wish to clone a database while making only minor changes to the data entry screen. To create the BookStor database, however, start with a fresh paint screen. Answer the question as follows:

Press N or ENTER

Paint the BookStor Screen   The data entry screen editing window appears on the display. If you remember how to paint your field messages, field names, and data locations on the data entry screen, go ahead and start painting. Figure 9-2 shows what the completed data entry screen might look like after you finish with the painting operations.

If you want some help painting the BookStor screen, use Figures 9-1 and 9-2 as guides and work through the detailed instructions that follow. If you need to erase the screen and start

Figure 9-2.

```
Field names: 12 letters or less, Data locations: [ ]
  Example: CITY [NEW YORK    ]            Press (Alt)H for help
 ┌─ Please draw your data-entry screen ── 21:80 ─────────────────┐
 │                    ASTRO-META BOOKS, Inc.                     │
 │                                                               │
 │         Title         [                                     ] │
 │         Author        [                                     ] │
 │         Publisher     [                                     ] │
 │         Keywords      [                                     ] │
 │         ISBN          [            ]                          │
 │                                                               │
 │         MyCost#       [      ]                                │
 │         LastOrder#    [ ]                                     │
 │         SellPrice#    [      ]                                │
 │         OnShelf#      [ ]                                     │
 │                                                               │
 │         PaidOut#      [   ]                                   │
 │         Sales#        [   ]                                   │
 │                                                               │
 │                                                               │
 │                                                               │
 │                                                               │
 │                                                               │
 └── (F3)-Menu  (Alt)H-Help  (F10)-Done ─────────── r:15 c:34 ──┘
```

BookStor layout on Editing window

over, simply move the cursor back to the upper left corner of the screen, and then either press CTRL-E, or press F3 to open the Edit menu and then press E. Remember, you can get help at any point by pressing ALT-H.

The row and column indicators (r:1 c:1) of the cursor location are noted at the end of each instruction line. When you are ready to paint the BookStor screen, proceed with these instructions:

1. With the cursor in the upper left corner of an empty screen (r:1 c:1):

   Press TAB, TAB, TAB   (r:1 c:25)
   and then type:
   ASTRO-META BOOKS, Inc.   (r:1 c:47)
   and press ENTER, ENTER   (r:3 c:1)

   This entry creates a title line for the data entry screen, beginning at column 25 of row 1. After you press the ENTER key twice, the cursor moves to column 1 of row 3.

2. Enter your first field designation which consists of a field name and two bracket [ ] characters that designate the field length. You will press the TAB key several times to specify the screen positions for the name and bracket characters.

   Press TAB   (r:3 c:9)
   Type:
   Title
   and press TAB, TAB, [, TAB six times,]   (r:3 c:74)

   This entry gives the name "Title" to the first field on the BookStor database. The Title field will contain the name of each book and will be 47 characters long (the number of spaces between the two bracket [ ] characters).

Once you have typed the field name and indicated the display length with the bracket characters, position the cursor for the next field entry:

Press ENTER   (r:4 c:9)

3. Enter the name and display position of the second field:

   Type:
   Author
   and press TAB, TAB, [, TAB six times,]   (r:3 c:74)

   If you make a typing mistake or press the TAB or ENTER key too many times, use the cursor controls to move the cursor to the point of error and change or reenter any incorrect or missing data.

4. Position the cursor to create the third field, Publisher:

   Press ENTER   (r:5 c:9)

   Create the third field as follows:

   Type:
   Publisher
   and press TAB, [, TAB six times,]   (r:5 c:74)

   Press ENTER   (r:6 c:9)

   Pressing ENTER moves the cursor to the next row.

5. Create the fourth field, Keywords, as follows:

   Type:
   Keywords
   and press TAB, [, TAB six times,]   (r:6 c:74)

   Press ENTER   (r:7 c:9)

6. The next field will contain the International Standard Book Number (ISBN). The ISBN is a widely accepted book identification number that can be used to identify a book uniquely. Bookstores use the ISBN to order a particular book or version of a book from a publisher. Enter the ISBN field:

Type:
ISBN
and press TAB, TAB, [, TAB, TAB,] (r:7 c:42)

Press ENTER, ENTER (r:9 c:1)

7. The next field, MyCost#, goes on row 9:

Press TAB (r:9 c:9)
and type:
MyCost#
and press TAB, TAB, [, TAB,] (r:9 c:34)

Fields that include a pound sign (#) at the end of the field name, such as MyCost#, are *numeric fields*. Numeric fields are fields that contain numbers. When PC-File+ calculates or sorts data from numeric fields, the program handles the information differently than it handles the data in regular fields. Since you will be using these fields in calculations, make sure that you include the pound sign (#) at the end of each field name.

Press ENTER (r:10 c:9)

8. The next field will contain the number of books last ordered from the publisher:

Type:
LastOrder#
and press TAB, [, SPACEBAR, SPACEBAR,] (r:10 c:29)

Press ENTER (r:11 c:9)

9. The next field will contain the selling price of the book in the store:

   Type:
   SellPrice#
   and press TAB, [, TAB,]   (r:11 c:34)

   Press ENTER   (r:12 c:9)

10. The next field will contain the number of books on the shelf:

    Type:
    OnShelf#
    and press TAB, [, SPACEBAR, SPACEBAR,]   (r:12 c:29)

    Press ENTER, ENTER   (r:14 c:1)

11. The next field, PaidOut#, goes on row 14:

    Press TAB   (r:14 c:9)
    and type:
    PaidOut#
    and press TAB, [, TAB,]   (r:14 c:34)

    Press ENTER   (r:15 c:9)

12. The last field, Sales#, goes on row 15:

    Type:
    Sales#
    and press TAB, TAB, [, TAB,]   (r:15 c:34)

13. Review the information you just painted onto the editing window. Figure 9-2 showed how the screen should appear. If your screen differs from that shown in Figure 9-2, you may want to correct the differences before proceeding. In the examples that follow, the exact location and display sizes of data fields are not very important. The most important element is that the six numeric fields are on the data entry screen and that the numeric field names end with a pound sign (#).

Database Calculations and Graphics **321**

Ch 9

When your numeric fields look like the ones shown in Figure 9-2, proceed with the next steps in the creation of the BookStor database:

Press F10

Pressing F10, completes the paint session on the editing window. A screen appears with the following question:

Are any of the fields Window Fields?

Since none of the BookStor fields are window fields:

Press N or ENTER

PC-File+ now displays a message telling you that the data items will be accessed on the data entry screen from left to right and top to bottom. The program asks if you want to change this sequence. For the explorations of calculations and graphics, you do not want to change the sequence.

Press N or ENTER

PC-File+ asks you to supply a database description. Enter the following:

Type:
database of titles, authors, etc.
and press ENTER

When you press ENTER, PC-File+ momentarily displays a message telling you that the program is creating the database. When PC-File+ completes the database creation process, a screen similar to the one shown in Figure 9-3 appears on the display. The

Figure 9-3.

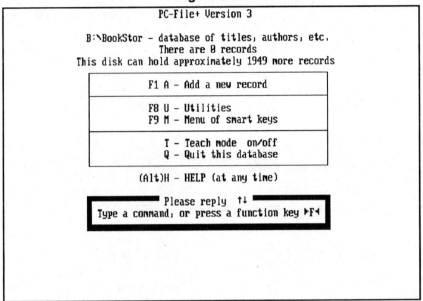

The Master menu before BookStor records get entered

screen is the shortened version of the Master menu (the menu that is displayed when a database has been created but contains no records).

 NOTE You may want to take a break before beginning the BookStor data entry tasks. If you take a break, you can exit from the PC-File+ program. At this point, the BookStor database has been created. When you restart PC-File+ and reload BookStor, you can continue from this point forward.

Enter the BookStor Data If you exited and restarted the PC-File+ program, load the BookStor database. Once BookStor is loaded, PC-File+ displays the shortened version of the Master menu. If you are using the Convenience Disk, you can skip over the BookStor data entry tasks in this section by loading a completed copy of BookStor. Then proceed to the next section, entitled "Set Up the Calculation Fields."

If you are not using the Convenience Disk, choose the "Add a new record" command:

Press F1 or A

When you press F1 or A, PC-File+ displays the blank data entry field for BookStor record number 1. Table 9-1 contains the data to be entered for five BookStor records. Refer to Table 9-1 and enter the data shown for record number 1. Do not enter any data for the last two fields, PaidOut# and Sales#. You will tell PC-File+ how to calculate those fields in the next section.

Once you have entered the data for BookStor record number 1, check your entries against the information in Table 9-1. Use the cursor control keys to move the cursor to the fields that need changes, and then make the corrections. Your entries for the regular fields need not exactly match those in Table 9-1. Data entered into the four numeric fields (MyCost#, LastOrder#, SellPrice#, and OnShelf#), however, should match the data in the table.

Once you have entered BookStor record number 1:

Press F10

PC-File+ displays an "O.K. to ADD?" message. You may respond with Y(Yes), N(No), or X(stop asking). To save record number 1 and to enter the data for the four remaining BookStor records:

Press X

Table 9-1.

Record Number 1:
Title	[Notes from Your Higher Self
Author	[Hew G. Preythur
Publisher	[Auro-Bena Publishing Co.
Keywords	[1. Meditations 2. Self 3. Guides
ISBN	[1-2345-6789-10
MyCost#	[4.50
LastOrder#	[10
SellPrice#	[7.50
OnShelf#	[5

Record Number 2:
Title	[Candid Visualizations
Author	[Shock T. Guwait
Publisher	[Karmical Press
Keywords	[1. Visualizations 2. Meditation 3. Dreams
ISBN	[0-9876-5432-10
MyCost#	[8.00
LastOrder#	[15
SellPrice#	[14.50
OnShelf#	[5

Record Number 3:
Title	[Beyond Boredom
Author	[Wat Chi Vee
Publisher	[Karmical Press
Keywords	[1. Boredom 2. Exercises 3. Stress
ISBN	[0-7777-3333-22
MyCost#	[10.75
LastOrder#	[5
SellPrice#	[17.95
OnShelf#	[3

Record Number 4:
Title	[Creative Ecology
Author	[Vasant P. K. Kapala
Publisher	[Theravadum Books Inc.
Keywords	[1. Ecology 2. Creative 3. Disasters

Data for the BookStor Database Records (continued on next page)

Table 9-1.

ISBN	[0-1111-2222-99
MyCost#	[6.75
LastOrder#	[15
SellPrice#	[11.00
OnShelf#	[7
Record Number 5:	
Title	[Kabir Meets Rumi
Author	[Rupert Blye
Publisher	[Theravadum Books Inc.
Keywords	[1. Poets 2. Mystics 3. Alcohol, effects
ISBN	[1-8888-5555-33
MyCost#	[8.75
LastOrder#	[12
SellPrice#	[15.00
OnShelf#	[6

Data for the BookStor Database Records (continued)

Enter the data for the remaining four BookStor records. When you see the blank data entry screen for record number 6:

Press F10

Pressing F10 on the blank entry screen tells PC-File+ you have completed adding new data records. The program puts you back onto an expanded version of the Master menu. You can now explore the PC-File+ calculation features.

NOTE You can exit from the PC-File+ program at this point because the BookStor data records have been saved on your database disk. When you restart PC-File+, you can reload Book-Stor and continue from this point forward.

Set Up the Calculation Fields

If you have exited and restarted the PC-File+ program, load the BookStor database. All five records should be completely filled out, except for the PaidOut# and Sales# numeric fields. When you load BookStor, PC-File+ displays the expanded version of the Master menu.

The next step is to tell PC-File+ that you want the PaidOut# and Sales# fields to be *calculated fields*. That is, you want PC-File+ to compute the values for these two fields.

The PC-File+ calculation commands can be activated from the Utilities menu. To get to the Utilities Menu from the Master menu:

Press F8 or U

The N command on the Utilities menu controls the modification of four field attributes: names, masks, constants, and calculation rules. As you know, all fields have field names established when you paint or enter names on the data entry screen.

Each field can also have an associated *edit mask*. An edit mask allows you to control the type of characters that can be typed into a field. For example, you can restrict entries in a numeric field to the characters 0 through 9, a minus sign, and a decimal point. If you type any other characters into the field, PC-File+ ignores the illegal characters and sounds a beep on the computer. The use of edit masks can help prevent data entry errors. If you want to learn more about PC-File+ edit masks, refer to Chapter 27, "Alter Field Name Mask, Const, Calc," of the *PC-File+ User's Manual*.

A field that contains identical, or nearly identical information across all records, for instance, the same ZIP code, city name, or company name, and so on, is called a *constant* value. A constant contains the exact value (name, number, symbols, characters) that you want to see on all the records. At data entry time, you can either skip over the field containing the constant or type in new values for records with different information.

Calculation rules specify the arithmetic you want PC-File+ to perform to create the data for a field. For example, suppose you want the PaidOut# field of the BookStor database to be calculated as follows:

PaidOut# = MyCost# * LastOrder#

In other words, the contents of PaidOut# is equal to the cost per copy in MyCost# multiplied by the number of copies in the LastOrder# field. The contents of PaidOut# would be the total amount of money paid for the last order of books.

To create a PC-File+ calculation rule based on the computation for the field PaidOut#, activate the N command on the Utilities menu:

Press N

Figure 9-4 shows the selection screen that PC-File+ displays. The program wants to know which field you want to modify. Since PaidOut# is field number 10:

Type:
10
and press F10

When you press F10, PC-File+ displays an information box in the center of the screen listing the current attributes for the PaidOut# field. The only current attribute displayed is the name of the field.

Figure 9-4.

```
┌─────────── ◄ Which FIELD's Name, Mask, Constant or Calcs to change ───────────┐
│                                                                                │
│                    [1] Title                                                   │
│                    [2] Author                                                  │
│                    [3] Publisher                                               │
│                    [4] Keywords                                                │
│                    [5] ISBN                                                    │
│                                                                                │
│                    [6] MyCost#                                                 │
│                    [7] LastOrder#                                              │
│                    [8] SellPrice#                                              │
│                    [9] OnShelf#                                                │
│                                                                                │
│                    [10]PaidOut#                                                │
│                    [11]Sales#                                                  │
│                                                                                │
│                                                                                │
│                                                                                │
│                                                                                │
│ Please respond.  (F10) when complete.  (Alt)H for help.                        │
└────────────────────────────────────────────────────────────────────────────────┘
```

Field attributes selection screen

Below the information box is a "Please reply" portal asking you which of the following attributes you wish to change: (N)Name, (M)Mask, K(Constant), or (C)Calcs. Since you want to enter a calculation rule for this field:

    Press C

When you press C, the "Please reply" portal requests that you enter the calculation rule:

    New calcs (a + b)   >_   <

Each calculation rule begins with a left parenthesis symbol and ends with a right parenthesis symbol. Any number of parentheses symbols may be used in the calculation rule to clarify the order of the computation. The number of left parentheses must equal the number of right parantheses for the computation to work correctly.

The following arithmetic symbols are allowed:

- `+` for addition
- `−` for subtraction
- `*` for multiplication
- `/` for division
- `^` for exponentiation (raising numbers to a power—2^3 equals 8)
- `%` for remaindering (modulo operations—5%2 equals 1)
- `.d` after the last parenthesis, where d is a number. PC-File+ truncates the value of the computation to the number of decimal places specified by d.

The following equation is one possible formulation of the calculation rule for the PaidOut# field:

(−1 * MyCost# * LastOrder#).2

The −1 multiplier at the beginning of the equation will make the PaidOut# value a negative quantity because PaidOut# is a cost to the bookstore. The .2 at the end of the rule tells PC-File+ to round off the result to two decimal places.

You can shorten any field name used in a computation rule to any set of characters that uniquely identifies the field being used. For example, all of the following PaidOut# computation rules are equivalent:

(−1 * MyCost * LastOrder).2
(−1 * MyCos * LastOrde).2
(−1 * MyC * LastO).2
(−1 * My * Last).2

Go ahead and type the following version of the PaidOut# calculation rule:

Type:
(−1 * MyCost * LastOrder).2
and press ENTER

When you press ENTER, PC-File+ removes the "Please reply" portal and information box and returns you to the field request entry screen. To verify that the PaidOut# computation rule was entered:

Type:
10
and press F10

The program displays the PaidOut# field attribute information box. Figure 9-5 shows the portion of the screen that contains your PaidOut# calculation rule. When you have reviewed your first calculation rule entry:

Press ESC

Pressing ESC returns you to the field selection screen. To create a calculation rule for Sales#, do the following:

Type:
11
and press F10

When the "Please reply" portal appears asking you which attribute to change:

Press C

Figure 9-5.

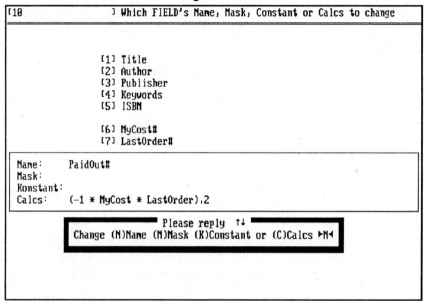

Attributes for the PaidOut# field

The "Please reply" portal prompts you to enter a calculation rule. To compute Sales# field, you need to multiply the number of books that have been sold by the selling price for each book. To compute the number of books sold, you must take the difference between the number of books ordered and the number remaining on the shelf. The equation for the computation looks like this:

$$\text{Sales\#} = (\text{LastOrder\#} - \text{OnShelf\#}) * \text{SellPrice\#}$$

The PC-File+ calculation rule that corresponds to this equation is as follows:

$$((\text{ LastOrder} - \text{OnShelf}) * \text{SellPrice}).2$$

In this rule, the extra pair of parentheses is required to preserve the order of the calculation. Arithmetic operations within a set of parentheses are performed in the following order:

- Exponentiation is always performed first.
- Multiplication, division, and remaindering are performed next and have equal priority.
- Addition and subtraction are performed last and have equal priority.

In the calculation rule for the Sales# field, the subtraction within the inner set of parentheses is performed first, and the result is multiplied by the value of SellPrice. The inner parentheses force the subtraction to be performed ahead of the multiplication. Without the inner parentheses, the product of OnShelf and SellPrice would be computed first, and the result would be subtracted from LastOrder. This form of the computation would yield an incorrect result.

Enter the computation rule for Sales# as follows:

Type:
((LastOrder − OnShelf) * SellPrice).2
and press ENTER

When you enter the rule and press ENTER, the program returns you to the field selection screen. To verify the Sales# calculation rule:

Type:
11
and press F10

Figure 9-6 displays the attribute information box for the Sales#

Figure 9-6.

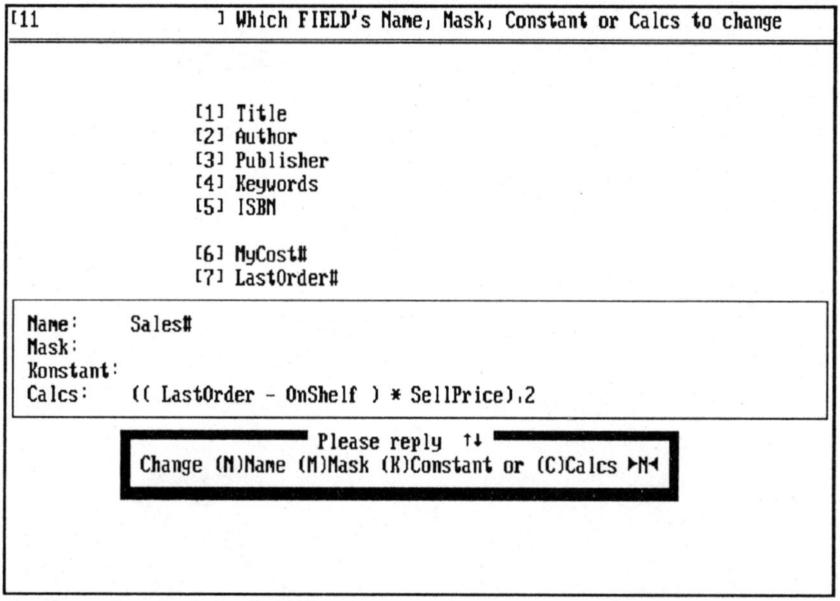

```
[11              ] Which FIELD's Name, Mask, Constant or Calcs to change

                [1] Title
                [2] Author
                [3] Publisher
                [4] Keywords
                [5] ISBN

                [6] MyCost#
                [7] LastOrder#

Name:     Sales#
Mask:
Konstant:
Calcs:    (( LastOrder - OnShelf ) * SellPrice),2

                    ┌──────── Please reply ↑↓ ────────┐
                    │ Change (N)Name (M)Mask (K)Constant or (C)Calcs ►N◄ │
                    └─────────────────────────────────┘
```

Attributes for the Sales# field

field. The box contains the name of the field and the calculation rule to be applied. If the calculation rule looks okay:

   Press ESC

When you press ESC, the program returns you to the field selection screen. You have now entered the calculation rules for the PaidOut# and Sales# fields. Since you have no other field attributes to change, you can exit to the Utilities menu as follows:

   Press F10

When you press F10, PC-File+ displays a message near the center of the screen telling you that the program is updating the BookStor database definition. The calculation rules you entered are now part of the BookStor database.

To display the Master menu from the Utilities menu:

Press Q

To find out how the calculation rules work, continue on to the next section.

Activate the Calculations

From the Master menu, use the "Find a record" command to retrieve the BookStor database records.

Press F, ENTER, ENTER, F10

PC-File+ retrieves the five BookStor records. Figure 9-7 shows BookStor record number 1 after activation of the "Find a record" command. The data you entered appears in the first nine fields. The last two fields, PaidOut# and Sales#, are empty. The Find options menu appears in the lower right corner of the screen.

You entered calculation rules for PaidOut# and Sales#, but you must activate the rules in order to obtain the results for the fields. To activate the calculation rules, first select the Modify option on the menu, and then exit back to the record:

Press M, F10

When you press M, the Options menu disappears, and the record becomes available for modification. To modify the record and activate the calculation rules, press F10. When you press F10, PC-File+ checks the record and performs any calculations needed to update calculated fields, in this case, PaidOut# and Sales#.

Figure 9-8 shows BookStor record number 1 after PC-File+

Figure 9-7.

```
Record number 1                                                              F
┌─────────────────────────────────────────────────────────────────────────────┐
│                      ASTRO-META BOOKS, Inc.                                 │
│                                                                             │
│       Title      [Notes from Your Higher Self            ]                  │
│       Author     [Hew G. Preythur                        ]                  │
│       Publisher  [Auro-Bena Publishing Co.               ]                  │
│       Keywords   [1. Meditations 2. Self 3. Guides       ]                  │
│       ISBN       [1-2345-6789-10 ]                                          │
│                                                                             │
│       MyCost#    [4.50  ]                              ┌─ F  ↑↓ ─┐          │
│       LastOrder# [10]                                  │ D Delete│          │
│       SellPrice# [7.50  ]                              │ M Modify│          │
│       OnShelf#   [5 ]                                  │ S new Search       │
│                                                        │ E End of file      │
│       PaidOut#   [      ]                              │ B Beginning        │
│       Sales#     [      ]                              │ N Next record      │
│                                                        │ P Prior record     │
│                                                        │ R get by Rcd#      │
│                                                        │ + browse down      │
│                                                        │ - browse up        │
│                                                        │ Q Quit finding     │
│                                                        └────────────────┘   │
└─────────────────────────────────────────────────────────────────────────────┘
```

BookStor record number 1

has updated the calculated fields. PaidOut# shows a value of −45.00. Sales# contains a value of 37.50. The PaidOut# value is the result of multiplying MyCost# (4.50) by LastOrder# (10) multiplied by the −1 that you put into the calculation rule.

The Sales# value is obtained by subtracting OnShelf# (5) from LastOrder# (10) and multiplying the difference by the SellPrice# (7.50). The result of this calculation is: (10−5) * 7.50, or 5 * 7.50, or 37.50. Therefore, Astro-Meta Books spent $45 on this book and received $37.50 in revenues.

 NOTE If your calculation fields did not activate or if a calculation value appeared in a field other than PaidOut# or Sales#, go back to the Utilities menu and activate the N (Name, mask, constant, or mask) command. Review the calculation formulas in the fields that did not activate. Make sure that the calculation rules

Figure 9-8.

```
Record number 1      MODIFIED                                          F
                     ASTRO-META BOOKS, Inc.

        Title       [Notes from Your Higher Self              ]
        Author      [Hew G. Preythur                          ]
        Publisher   [Auro-Bena Publishing Co.                 ]
        Keywords    [1. Meditations 2. Self 3. Guides         ]
        ISBN        [1-2345-6789-10 ]

        MyCost#     [4.50   ]                         ┌── F  ↑↓
        LastOrder#  [10]                              │ D Delete
        SellPrice#  [7.50   ]                         │ M Modify
        OnShelf#    [5  ]                             │ S new Search
                                                      │ E End of file
        PaidOut#    [-45.00 ]                         │ B Beginning
        Sales#      [37.50  ]                         │ N Next record
                                                      │ P Prior record
                                                      │ R get by Rcd#
                                                      │ + browse down
                                                      │ - browse up
                                                      │ Q Quit finding
                                                      └─────────────
```

PC-File+ updates the calculated fields

are entered correctly into the PaidOut# and Sales# fields. If you accidently placed a calculation rule in a field other than PaidOut# or Sales#, first display the rule, and then delete it by spacing over the entry and pressing the ENTER key.

To update the calculated fields on the next BookStor record, go to the next record, activate the Modify option, and exit from the Modify mode.

Press N, M, F10

The calculated fields on BookStor record number 2 should show −120.00 for PaidOut# and 145.00 for Sales#.

Call up the remaining records, and activate the calculated fields for each record. Remember, to activate the calculated fields

Table 9-2.

Record No.	PaidOut#	Sales#
1	−45.00	37.50
2	−120.00	145.00
3	−53.75	35.90
4	−101.25	88.00
5	−105.00	90.00

BookStor Calculated Field Values

for each record, choose the Modify option, and then press F10, Table 9-2 displays the calculated values for all five of the BookStor records.

You have completed an initial exploration of the PC-File+ calculation features. Based on the simple examples used in the BookStor database, you can begin to see how PC-File+ can be used to build complex databases with hundreds of embedded computational rules. The process of building a more complex, calculational database involves the same procedures used to build BookStor. PC-File+ provides exceptional power and flexibility while maintaining simple procedures and rules for creating and managing databases of any size.

In the following section, you will use the BookStor database to explore the PC-File+ graphics capabilities. You will learn how PC-File+ helps you to create charts and graphs, quickly and easily.

Let PC-File+ Graph Your Data

If you are using two floppy disks, you will need to do two things before you begin using the powerful PC-File+ charting and graphing features:

- Invoke the DOS GRAPHICS command so that you can print PC-File+ charts and graphs.
- Move the PC-File+ graphics program, PCG2.EXE, from PC-File+ DISK TWO to your database disk in drive B. You will also need to establish a DOS path between the PC-File+ main program and the graphics program.

In order to perform these tasks, you need to exit PC-File+ and go to the A prompt. When you are out of the program, remove PC-File+ DISK ONE from drive A and insert your DOS disk.

Set Up Your Printer for Graphics

With your DOS disk in Drive A, type the following DOS command:

> Type:
> **graphics**
> and press ENTER

If you are using an IBM or Epson-compatible printer, the DOS GRAPHICS command will set up your printer to print graphic screens. When you want to print a graphics screen, press SHIFT-PRTSC.

If you do not have an IBM or Epson-compatible printer, your DOS disk may have another version of GRAPHICS that works for your printer. Refer to your computer user's manual and your DOS manual for more information.

Move the Graphics Files to the Data Disk

 NOTE If you are using a hard disk drive, you can skip this section. If you copied all of the PC-File+ program and resource files from your original disks to your hard drive, the PC-File+ graphics features should function correctly.

If you are using two floppy drives, remove the DOS disk from drive A and insert a copy of PC-File+ DISK TWO into drive A. Make sure your database disk that has the BookStor database with calculational rules defined is in drive B. At the A prompt, type the following command:

Type:
copy a:pcg2.exe b:
and press ENTER

A copy of the PC-File+ graphics program, PCG2.EXE, now resides on your database disk in drive B. Remove the copy of PC-File+ DISK TWO from drive A and insert a copy of PC-File+ DISK ONE, the main program disk, into drive A. To establish a path name linkage between the PC-File+ main and graphics programs, enter the following at the A prompt:

Type:
path a:
and press ENTER

The PATH command tells DOS to look on drive A if it cannot find a requested file on the default drive. To complete the linkage and ensure that you can use the graphics program, start PC-File+ from drive B:

Type:
b: and press ENTER
pcf and press ENTER

When you type **b:** and press ENTER, the directory switches to drive B, and the B prompt appears. The second entry, the name of the PC-File+ main program, is typed at the B prompt even though, PCF, is not on the disk in drive B. The PATH command you entered earlier directs DOS to drive A to load the main program.

The PC-File+ graphics program creates a temporary file of graphics information called GRAPH.ME. Because there is not enough room on the PC-File+ program disk to store GRAPH.ME, it must be stored on your database disk. The PATH A:\ command combined with starting PC-File+ from drive B causes GRAPH.ME to be written to drive B.

 NOTE If you are using two floppy drives and have copied PCG2.EXE onto your database disk, you must (1) type the PATH A:\ command, (2) switch to drive B, and (3) start PC-File+ from the B prompt, each time you use the graphics program.

Display BookStor Charts and Graphs

If you have invoked the GRAPHICS command to set up your printer, and copied PCG2.EXE to your database disk, you are ready to begin to explore the PC-File+ chart and graphics features.

Database Calculations and Graphics **341**

Ch 9

When the PC-file+ title screen appears, load the BookStor database. If the path name and drive designation manipulations function correctly, you should see the PC-File+ Master menu. The Graphs command is the first command listed in the middle box on the menu. With the BookStor database loaded, activate the Graphs command:

Press F4 or G

When you press F4 or G, PC-File+ displays the first in a series of screens that help you specify the appearance of your graphs.

Troubleshooting If you encounter difficulties in activating the PC-File+ program or in displaying graphics on your computer screen, check the following items:

- The graphics program PCG2.EXE is on your data disk in drive B and you followed the instructions involving the DOS PATH command. Remember also that you must start PC-File+ from the B prompt in order to use the graphics program. These actions must be performed each time you start the programs.
- Your computer system is using a monitor and video card that can produce graphics. Systems that have a monochrome card cannot use the PC-File+ graphics features.
- If you have a Hercules graphics card and a monochrome monitor, run the MSHERC program *before* you start PC-File+. MSHERC is on the PC-File+ DISK TWO disk. With DISK TWO in drive A, simply type **MSHERC** at the A prompt and press ENTER.
- If you have a CGA system, the only graphics colors available are black and white. You must have an EGA or VGA system to see other colors when using the PC-File+ graphics program.

Specify the Graph Figure 9-9 shows the screen you see when you activate the Graphs command. PC-File+ wants to know how you would like to summarize the graph data—by subtotals or by totals. Select (S)ubtotals if you want to see how fields change from record to record. Select (T)otals to see how the totals for several fields compare with each other. To start, select (S)ubtotals:

Press S

After you press S, the screen shown in Figure 9-10 appears on the display. Use this screen to tell PC-File+ which fields you want to graph and the order in which you want to present the data. Using a cursor control key, move the cursor to the last field, Sales#. With the blinking cursor in the entry area next to Sales#:

Type:
1
and press F10

Figure 9-9.

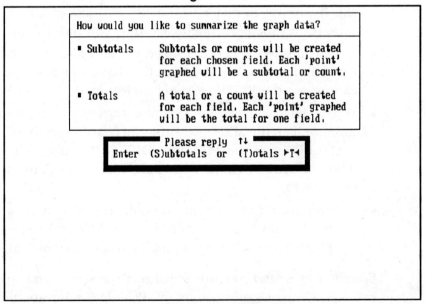

"Graphs" command summary options

Database Calculations and Graphics **343**

Ch 9

When you press F10, a "Please reply" portal appears in the middle of the screen, asking if you want to accumulate (V)alues or (C)ounts. You can instruct PC-File+ to graph either the actual values in a field or the number of times the field appears with data. For the current exploration, select Values:

Press V or ENTER

The screen clears and you are asked to enter a permanent title line. The title line will become the title of the graph. As you create various charts and graphs, you will want to alter the title line to

Figure 9-10.

```
              Number the fields to be graphed.
        Field 1 will graph at the left, then field 2, etc.


                     Title ▶  ◀
                    Author [  ]
                 Publisher [  ]
                  Keywords [  ]
                      ISBN [  ]

                   MyCost# [  ]
                 LastOrder# [  ]
                 SellPrice# [  ]
                   OnShelf# [  ]

                   PaidOut# [  ]
                    Sales# [  ]




    Please respond.  (F10) when complete.  (Alt)H for help.
```

Field graphing order screen

reflect the data being displayed. For this example, use the following:

Type:
Revenues by Title
and press ENTER

You then are asked to enter a subtitle. The subtitle line will appear beneath the title line. For this example use the following:

Type:
(Dollars)
and press ENTER

The program now asks for a label for the *dependent variable*. In general, the dependent variable is the variable that appears on the left side of a graph or chart. In this case, use the following:

Type:
$
and press ENTER

PC-File+ now asks for a label for the *independent variable*. In most PC-File+ databases, the independent variable corresponds to the database fields that are displayed across the bottom of the graph or chart. Since the field to be plotted in this example is Sales#, the label could read "Sales# by title." Enter that designation as follows:

Type:
by title
and press ENTER

When you enter the independent variable label, the screen shifts to a menu for setting the *default graph type,* as shown in Figure 9-11. The default graph type is the first type of plot or chart

Database Calculations and Graphics **345**
Ch 9

Figure 9-11.

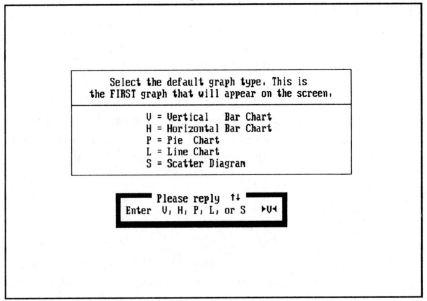

Default graph type menu

that will appear on the screen. Because you can quickly view all of the graph types after the program displays the first plot or graph, you can simply leave the default at V, for vertical bar chart:

Press ENTER

A brief message informs you that the program is creating a report work file. You are then asked if you want to save the graph format. Go ahead and save the format so that you can see how this feature works:

Press Y

You are asked to supply a graph description. For this example, enter the following:

Type:
Graphs of BookStor Sales#
and press ENTER

You are then requested to enter a file name for this graph format. This entry is restricted to eight characters. The name used for this example is RevTitle, short for "Revenues by Titles."

Type:
RevTitle
and press ENTER

The next screen that appears is the "trigger" screen. Figure 9-12 shows the trigger screen for the BookStor database. You have already told PC-File+ that you are plotting subtotals for Sales#. You can also *trigger* the accumulation of Sales# subtotals by any other field on the record—that is, ask PC-File+ to calculate Sales# subtotals as a function of any field. For example, you could trigger off of author names to tell how well any particular author might be selling. You could trigger off of publishers to show how well an entire book line might be doing.

You have named this graph "Revenues by Title." To trigger the plotting of Sales# from the first field, Title, do the following:

Type:
1
and press F10

PC-File+ asks you whether to graph all of the records or selected records. For this case, you indicate you want to graph all the records, as follows:

Press A or ENTER

Record number 1 from the BookStor database appears on the screen. You are given a set of options for controlling which records will be used in the graphing operation. Since you want to plot all of the records:

Press X

A report status message appears on the screen while the computer graphs the records. When the process is complete, PC-File+ displays the vertical bar chart shown in Figure 9-13.

How to Read the Chart The bar chart shown in Figure 9-13 displays the heading, "Revenues by Title," in large letters at the top of the screen. Under the heading is the subtitle, "(Dollars)."

Figure 9-12.

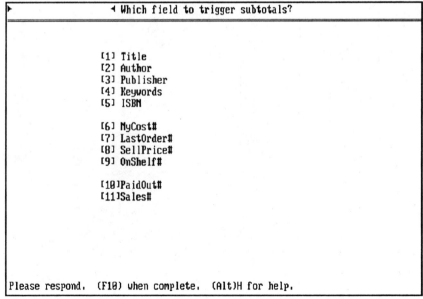

The trigger screen

On the left side of the chart, a set of numbers from 0 to 150 in increments of 25 is labeled with a dollar sign ($). "Sales#," the name of the field being plotted, and the label "by title" are displayed across the bottom.

A legend indicating what each item on the chart represents is located to the right of the chart. Because you set the subtotals to trigger off the Title field, that field name appears above the legend. Each legend item corresponds to one of the vertical bars in the center of the chart.

The first legend item is for the book with the title *Notes from Your Higher Self*. Because there is limited screen space, PC-File+ truncates the legend entry to "NOTES FROM Y."

The first legend entry also corresponds to the leftmost vertical bar on the chart. The chart indicates that the revenues for the book *Notes from Your Higher Self* are about halfway between $25 and $50. The actual value in the database is $37.50.

Figure 9-13.

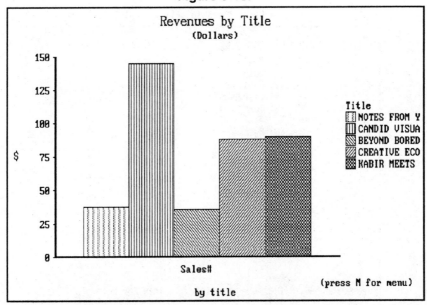

Vertical bar chart

The second legend entry is for *Candid Visualizations*. That book's revenues, according to the second bar on the left side of the chart, are nearly $150. The actual Sales# value for this title is $145. In this fashion, each of the legend entries corresponds to a specific book and a specific bar on the chart.

When reading graphs and charts, you are looking for trends and general impressions that might lead you to take specific actions. You usually do not look at graphics for detailed information, such as the exact revenues for a particular book.

For example, as the bookstore owner, you might look at the chart shown in Figure 9-13 and ask the following questions:

- Why are the sales on the first and third book low relative to other book sales?

- Book two is selling well. Should more be ordered soon?

- Does the author of the second book have other titles you can order?

- The last two books are from the same publisher. Does that publisher carry other titles you can order?

As you can see, looking at data in graphical form can help you assimilate information in ways that cannot be done easily by reading at tables of numbers. Using graphs and charts forces your brain to consider "the big picture."

In the lower right corner of the vertical bar chart screen, you see the following message:

(press M for menu)

When a chart or graph is displayed, pressing the letter M will cause the Graphics menu to toggle on and off the screen. Right now, the menu is off. Pressing M will toggle the menu onto the screen.

The Graphics Menu   With the Revenues by Title vertical bar chart on the screen, do the following:

   Press M

PC-File+ displays the two lines of the Graphics menu across the bottom of the screen. You will see either the CGA and monochrome version or the EGA/VGA version of the Graphics menu.
   The CGA/monochrome version displays the following:

```
GENERAL: (O)utput (M)enu   (Q)uit (L)ine (P)ie (H)bar (V)bar (S)catter
    BAR:          (T)-log (G)rid (X)chg c(U)m (A)vg  ov(E)rlap
```

The EGA/VGA version displays the following:

```
GENERAL: (O)utput (C)olor (M)enu (Q)uit (P)ie (L)ine (H)bar (V)bar (S)catter
    BAR:          (T)-log (G)rid (X)chg c(U)m (A)vg  ov(E)rlap
```

The EGA/VGA Graphics menu has an additional item, (C)olor, that allows you to adjust the colors of the graphics display. The EGA/VGA menu presents the option (P)ie before the option (L)ine, where the CGA monochrome menu shows (L)ine first followed by (P)ie.
   In the examples that follow, only the CGA/monochrome menu will be used. All of the commands on this menu can be activated by pressing the keys that match the letters in the sets of parentheses. The menu lines do not have to be visible for you to use the command keys.
   The GENERAL menu line remains the same no matter which graph is being displayed. From the GENERAL line, you can activate (O)utput to print a graphic with your printer. (M)enu toggles the menu lines on and off the screen. (Q)uit exits the PC-File+ graphics program and returns to the PC-File+ main program.

The remaining five options on the GENERAL line allow you to select the type of graphic you want displayed: (L)ine graph, (P)ie chart, (H)bar for horizontal bar chart, (V)bar for vertical bar chart, or (S)catter plot. You will explore these five options in the section that follows.

The second menu line, marked BAR, changes as you activate the menu commands. In the current example, PC-File+ displays a vertical bar chart. The BAR line indicates that a bar chart is being displayed, and therefore, the options on the BAR line relate to bar charts. As you explore the various types of charts that PC-File+ produces, you will also explore the menu options on the second menu line.

In the following explorations, remember that you can remove the menu lines by pressing the M key. As you become familiar with the Graphics menu options, you will not need to see the menu lines to activate a command; you can simply press the key for the command you want to use.

Line Graphs   To produce a line graph from the data, select the (L)ine command:

Press L

PC-File+ instantly displays the data in line graph format, as shown in Figure 9-14 (the menu lines have been toggled off so you can see the bottom of the graph.) On the vertical bar chart shown in Figure 9-13, the individual titles are coded by shadings to the bars on the chart. A line graph represents the data as points. Lines are constructed from point to point to form the graph. The line graph and the vertical bar chart both contain the same information. The information is simply displayed in different formats.

PC-File+ writes the first three letters of each book title across the bottom of the graph to indicate which point corresponds to which book. NOT stands for the book in record number 1, *Notes from Your Higher Self.* CAN represents *Candid Visualizations.* KAB, the last entry, is from BookStor record number 5, *Kabir Meets Rumi.*

When you press M to toggle the menu, note that the second menu line has changed. The line is now marked "LINE," for line graph, and the options are appropriate for line graphs.

```
GENERAL: (O)utput (M)enu  (Q)uit (L)ine (P)ie (H)bar (V)bar (S)catter
   LINE:         (T)-log (G)rid (X)chg c(U)m (A)vg  (F)it (0-9)-Smoothed Avg
```

The ov(E)rlap option for bar charts has disappeared and two new options for line graphs are shown: (F)it and (0-9)-Smoothed Avg. These two options deal with analyzing the plotted data for trends and patterns. They are most often used with data that varies over time, such as sales revenues for a book over several months or several years.

Figure 9-14.

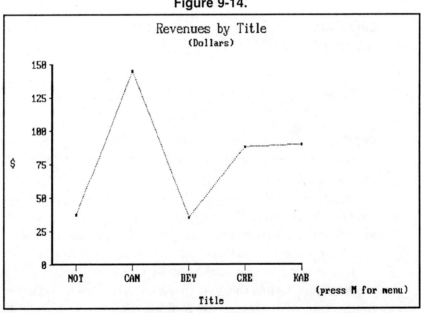

Line graph

Pie Charts   The next type of graph is a pie chart. To create a PC-File+ pie chart graphic:

   Press P

The very first time you select the (P)ie option, PC-File+ automatically displays the *aspect ratio screen*. The aspect ratio screen allows you to use the arrow keys to adjust the default length and height of pie charts. Subsequent selections of the (P)ie option do not automatically call up the aspect ratio screen; you must select the (A)spect option from the PIE line to change the pie chart shape. For this example, simply exit the aspect ratio screen as follows:

   Press Q

After you press P for pie chart and Q to quit the aspect ratio screen, PC-File+ displays your database data in the form of pie chart, as shown in Figure 9-15. This graphic is the PC-File+ standard way of displaying pie chart information.

The pie chart format provides an entirely new way to look at your company data. Instead of gross dollar amounts, as displayed in the bar chart and the line graph, the pie chart displays revenues as percentages. You can quickly see that *Candid Visualizations* constitutes 37% of your total revenues. *Creative Ecology* and *Kabir Meets Rumi* each provide a little over 20% of your revenues. Each of the two remaining books represents 9% of revenues.

As with the other commands, the use of the (P)ie command changes the second menu line.

```
GENERAL: (O)utput (M)enu  (Q)uit (L)ine (P)ie (H)bar (V)bar (S)catter
    PIE: (A)spect (W)edge (D)isp (X)chg
```

(A)spect controls how round or oval-shaped you want your pie chart to be on the screen. The (A)spect command is easy to use, and you may want to explore it on your own.

Figure 9-15.

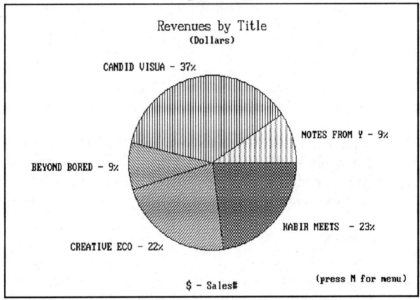

Standard pie chart

 NOTE Changes you make to the shape of pie charts are recorded and used on future pie chart displays. If you use the (A)spect command to change the shape of the pie chart shown in Figure 9-15, the pie charts shown in the examples that follow will also be changed to your new aspect setting.

(W)edge lets you detach one or more sections of your pie chart. This feature is handy when you are making presentations and want to emphasize one part of a pie chart for discussion. The (W)edge feature is both fun and easy to use. You can explore it on your own. If you use the (W)edge command to alter the pie chart shown in Figure 9-15, the same alterations will appear in all of the pie chart examples.

The (D)isp command switches the pie chart display to one of

Figure 9-16.

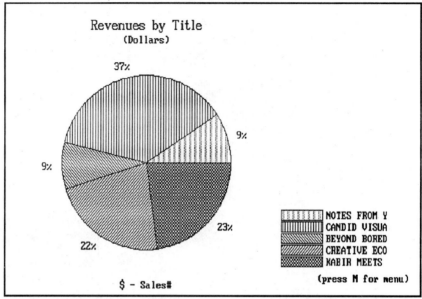

Pie chart display option 1

three formats. The first format is the standard display shown in Figure 9-15. To change the pie chart format to that shown in Figure 9-16:

Press D

When you press D this first time, PC-File+ rearranges the display so that only the percentages appear next to the pie. The book titles are pulled back into a legend block in the lower right corner of the screen. This pie chart format might come in handy should you want to use the (W)edge option to detach a couple of the parts of the pie while keeping the area around the pie uncluttered. Figure 9-17 shows a version of the pie chart with two wedges detached for emphasis.

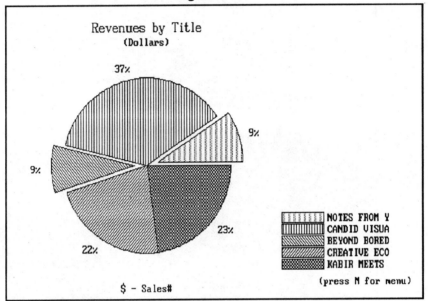

Pie chart display option 1 (wedges detached)

To display the final pie chart format:

Press D

In this version of the pie chart, all the data around the pie has been pulled back to the legend block in the lower right corner, as shown in Figure 9-18. Use this pie chart format when you want to emphasize a single part of the chart. You can alter the pie chart by doing the following:

Press W, S, D, Q

Figure 9-18.

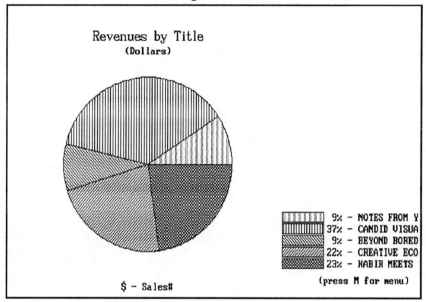

Pie chart display option 2

The W keypress activates the (W)edge command. The (S)kip command skips over the first wedge. The (D)etach command detaches the second wedge. Finally, the (Q)uit command quits the (W)edge command. The result on your screen should be similar to the pie chart shown in Figure 9-19.

PC-File+ provides easy-to-use, powerful graphics capabilities with only a few keystrokes.

Bar Charts PC-File+ displays bar charts in two formats: vertical and horizontal. The PC-File+ graphic shown in Figure 9-13 is a vertical bar chart. To view the same chart in a horizontal format:

Press H

Figure 9-19.

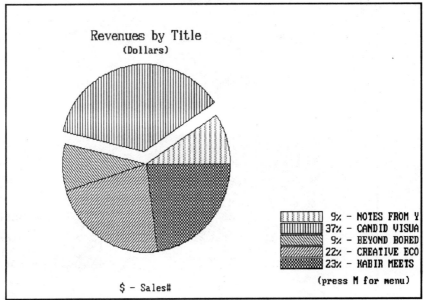

Pie chart display option 2 (wedge detached)

The resultant chart looks like the vertical chart rotated clockwise. The bars go across, rather than up the screen. PC-File+ rearranges the labels to reflect the new orientation for the graphic.

Scatter Diagrams A *scatter diagram* is a line graph without the lines. In a scatter diagram, only the data points are plotted. To see the BookStor data as a scatter diagram:

   Press S

The graph looks exactly like the line graph shown in Figure 9-14, but without the lines. If you alternately press L and S, PC-File+ will flip back and forth between the line graph and scatter diagram formats, and you can see the correspondence between the two graphs.

Averages and Other Arithmetic PC-File+ can perform several easy and complex arithmetic tasks with graphed and plotted data. To explore one of these PC-File+ arithmetic features, first display the vertical bar chart for the Sales# data:

    Press V

Suppose you are looking at the bar chart and would like to know the average sales figure for the displayed records. Of course, you could look back at your actual data, add up the five Sales# values, and divide the total by five to figure the average revenues.

PC-File+ has an easy way to get a quick approximation for the average. All you have to do is the following:

    Press A

When you press A with the vertical bar chart for the Sales# data on the screen, you see a horizontal line appear across the bars as shown in Figure 9-20. The line represents the average of the five displayed values. According to the bar chart, the average for the revenues figures is about $80.

The (A)vg graphics command works on any chart type, except the pie chart. Try it yourself. Switch around to the different type of graphics that PC-File+ can produce, and press A for each type. Since the data for the graphs are the same, the average for each graph should be the same, about $80.

After you finish exploring the PC-File+ (A)vg command, bring back the vertical bar chart:

    Press V

Suppose you wanted to know the total revenues for all the books being displayed. Again, no problem for PC-File+. To get the total

Figure 9-20.

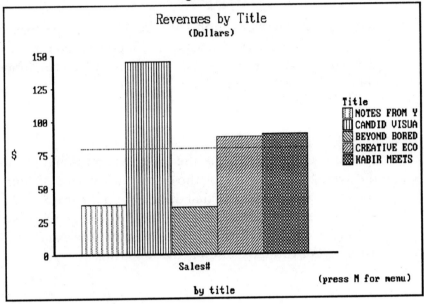

Average revenues

revenues, activate the c(U)m command. The c(U)m command tells PC-File+ to accumulate, or form, the cumulative total of the displayed data. Activate the command as follows:

Press U

When you press U, the bar chart shown in Figure 9-21 appears on the screen. The chart indicates that the total revenues is about $400! Notice that you still can see the individual contribution of each title to the total. The first book (bottom layer of the bar) produced less than $50. The third book (the middle layer of the bar) also produced $50 or less. The second book (second layer from the bottom) produced over $100. The two books at the top of the chart generated less than $100 each.

Figure 9-21.

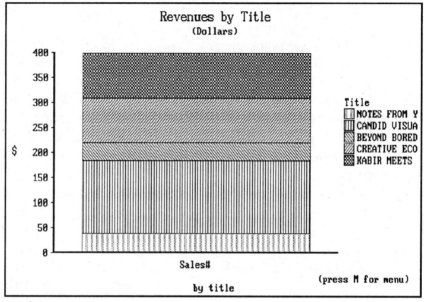

Total revenues

This section concludes a preliminary investigation of the PC-File+ graphics capabilities. As you have seen, PC-File+ allows you to quickly and easily produce sophisticated and informative graphics from your database records. In following set of explorations, you will create graphics based on more than one field in your BookStor database.

Exit the Graphics Program

To create more graphics based on different data, you must leave the graphics program and return to the PC-File+ main program. To do that:

Press Q

You should see a brief display of the ButtonWare copyright notice, the PC-File+ title screen, and a message telling you that PC-File+ is loading the BookStor database. Since you loaded the PC-File+ graphics program from the Master menu, PC-File+ automatically returns you to the Master menu when you exit the graphics command area.

If you encounter difficulties exiting to the Master menu, you may still have a problem with the location of the PCG2.EXE graphics program (it should be on your data disk in drive B), the path name linkage between programs (you need to set the DOS PATH command to PATH A:\), or the startup drive for using graphics (it must be drive B). Refer to the section entitled "Move the Graphics Files to the Data Disk" in this chapter for information on how to set up the graphics program and path name linkages.

When you are back to the PC-File+ Master menu, you can proceed with the final explorations dealing with PC-File+.

NOTE   If you want to take a break before starting the next section, you can exit from the PC-File+ program. At this point, all of the BookStor data records and the RevTitle graphic format file are saved on your database disk. When you return, set the path name to PATH A:\, switch to the drive B directory, and start PC-File+ from drive B.

Charting Two Fields of Data

In this section, you will tell PC-File+ to plot data from two BookStor database fields onto one graph. Placing data from two fields on the same graph or chart can help you make comparisons and observations.

If you took a break and turned off your computer, you will need to perform the following steps:

1. Boot your system with the DOS disk in drive A.

2. At the A prompt, set up your system to print graphics:

   Type:
   graphics
   and press ENTER

3. Remove the DOS disk from drive A. Insert a copy of PC-File+ DISK ONE in drive A and your data disk containing PCG2.EXE in drive B.

   Type:
   path a: (and press ENTER)
   b: (and press ENTER)
   pcf   (and press ENTER)

4. Load the BookStor database from drive B.

When you have loaded BookStor, and PC-File+ displays the Master menu, then activate the Graphics command as follows:

Press G

You will see a selection screen that lists the RevTitle graph format. If you select RevTitle, you reproduce all of the graphics you viewed previously dealing with revenues by title. However, for this example you want to create a new graph format:

Press F10

PC-File+ wants to know whether you would like to summarize the graph data by subtotals or by totals. Select (S)ubtotals:

Press S

After you press S, a screen asks you to number the data fields to be graphed. Using a cursor control key, move the cursor to the PaidOut# field. With the blinking cursor in the entry area next to PaidOut#, do the following:

Type:
1
and press ENTER

When you type **1** and press ENTER, the cursor moves down to the input area next to Sales#. Tell PC-File+ that you want Sales# to be the second field to be graphed:

Type:
2
and press F10

When you press F10, a "Please reply" portal appears in the middle of the screen asking if you want to accumulate (V)alues or (C)ounts. Since you want to accumulate values:

Press V or ENTER

The screen clears, and you are asked to enter a permanent title line. For this example, use the following:

Type:
Costs and Revenues
and press ENTER

You then are asked to enter a subtitle. For this example use the following:

Type:
(by title)
and press ENTER

Database Calculations and Graphics **365**

Ch 9

The program now asks for a label for the dependent variable. Enter the label as follows:

Type:
$
and press ENTER

PC-File+ asks you for a label for the independent variable. For this example, leave this label line blank:

Press ENTER

When you enter the blank label, the screen shifts to a menu screen for setting the default graph type. Leave the default at "V" for vertical bar graphs:

Press V or ENTER

A message appears briefly, telling you that the program is creating a report work file. You are then asked if you want to save the graph format. Save the format so you can come back to this set of graphs at a later time:

Press Y

You are asked to supply a graph description. For this example, enter the description as follows:

Type:
Graphs of BookStor PaidOut# and Sales#
and press ENTER

When you see the request to enter a name for this graph format:

Type:
CostRevs
and press ENTER

The next screen that appears is the trigger screen. As in the previous example, you want to trigger off of the first field, Title:

Type:
1
and press F10

PC-File+ now displays a question asking you if you want to include all of the records, or selected records. For this example, you want to graph all the records:

Press A or ENTER

Record number 1 from the BookStor database appears on the screen, along with a set of options that control which records are to be plotted. Since you want to plot all of the records:

Press X

A status report message appears on the screen, while the computer plots the records. When the process is complete, PC-File+ displays a vertical bar chart as shown in Figure 9-22. Part of this bar chart is similar to the one produced earlier for Revenues by Titles. The upper right side of the chart, above the label Sales#, is the same as the bar chart Revenues by Title shown in Figure 9-13. The values for PaidOut# are displayed as negative dollars, or costs, on the lower left side of the display.

This is where the graphic power of PC-File+ can be used to good advantage. The information displayed in Figure 9-22 is interesting, but difficult to assimilate. The costs for the first title appear on the far left of the screen. The revenues for that same title appear near the middle of the screen. A visual comparison can be attempted, but it is difficult to scan back and forth across the chart.

PC-File+ allows you to change the type of graphic format with one keypress. Try changing to the horizontal format and see if that format is easier to read than the vertical chart.

Press H

Better in some ways! Figure 9-23 shows the improvement gained

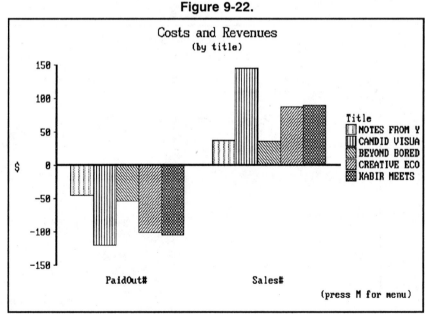

Vertical bar chart of costs and revenues

by using the horizontal bar chart. However, the items to be compared are still separated from the numbers along the dollar axis.

What would the data look like if plotted instead of charted? To change the format to a line graph, do the following:

Press L

Much better! Figure 9-24 shows the line graph produced for the plot of costs and revenues. The bottom line plots the PaidOut# data. The top line plots the Sales# data. Each data point of costs and revenues is aligned over the first three letters of the corresponding book title.

The first book, NOT (*Notes from Your Higher Self*), shows costs of nearly $50 and revenues of nearly $50. The next book, CAN

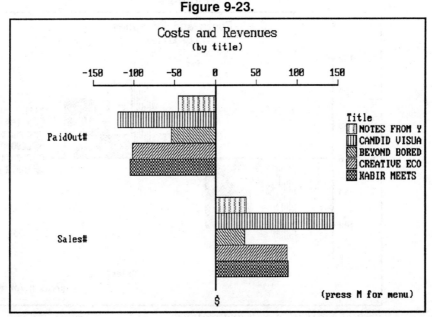

Horizontal bar chart of costs and revenues

(Candid Visualizations), shows costs of over $100 dollars and revenues of nearly $150. This form of the graphical data provides a better way to make comparisons than the bar charts.

PC-File+ has one other feature, the (X)chg command, that lets you move graphical data components around on the screen. The result often produces surprising and informative ways to display the same data items. Go back to the vertical bar chart format:

Press V

When you have the vertical bar chart of costs and revenues on the screen, activate the (X)chg command:

Press X

Figure 9-24.

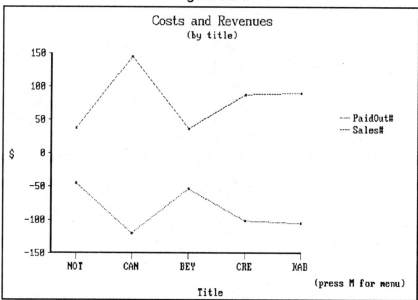

Line Graph of costs and revenues

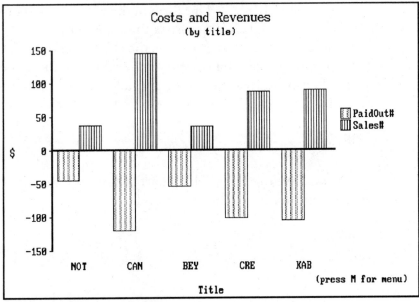

Figure 9-25.

Vertical bar chart after "(X)chg"

A message appears briefly near the bottom of the screen, telling you that PC-File+ is creating a file called GRAPH.ME2. Then, the chart shown in Figure 9-25 appears on your screen.

Amazing! The field and title parameters have been exchanged. The fields are now in the legend block area on the upper right side of the screen. The bar codings now represent the two fields, PaidOut# and Sales#. The title designations appear across the bottom of the screen. The cost and revenue bars for each book are displayed side by side.

Try one last experiment. Convert the exchanged version of the bar chart to a horizontal format:

Press H

The chart shown in Figure 9-26 appears on your screen. This may

Figure 9-26.

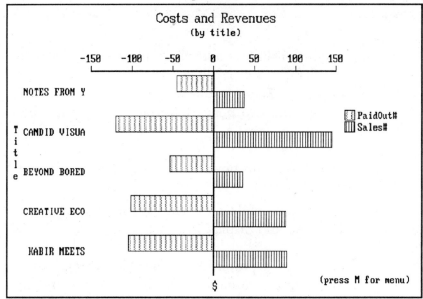

Horizontal bar chart after (X)chg

be the best of the two exchanged versions of the chart. The horizontal format displays more letters for each book title.

Using what you have learned about the PC-File+ graphics capabilities, try plotting other data from the BookStor database. Make plots of how much you paid to each publisher (hint: plot the PaidOut# field with the Publisher field as the trigger). Plot the revenues by publisher. Make charts or graphs of the number of books ordered versus the books still on the shelf. Even though the BookStor database is quite small, the variety and number of charts and graphs you can produce is astounding.

Summary

This section concludes both your explorations of PC-File+ calculation and graphics capabilities and your general introduction to many of the PC-File+ features.

The following two points have been made with the explorations in this chapter:

- PC-File+ contains powerful, flexible, easy-to-use graphics features.

- You need powerful features in a graphics program to help you understand and display your data in meaningful ways.

PC-File+, as a powerful and flexible database management program, contains numerous other commands and capabilities that could only be covered in a larger book. Based on what you have learned and discovered within these chapters, you are encouraged to go ahead and explore more of PC-File+ on your own.

You will find helpful reference material about PC-File+ listed in Appendix G, H, and I at the end of this book. In addition, you can refer to the *PC-File+ User's Manual* for more information. The manual comes with every registered copy of PC-File+. Remember, if you are a registered PC-File+ owner, you have unlimited access to ButtonWare technical support.

PART III

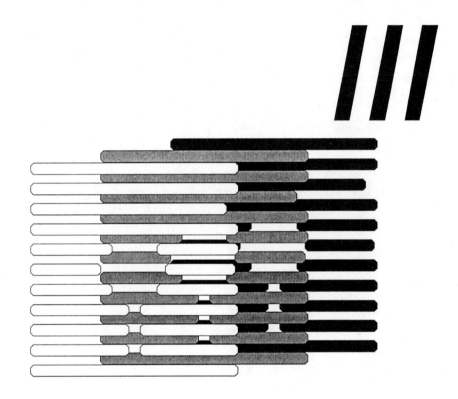

PC-Calc+

CHAPTER

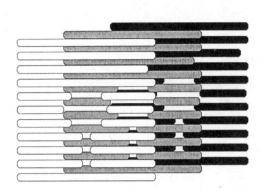

PC-Calc+:
Getting Started

Part III of this book introduces you to PC-Calc+, a sophisticated and versatile *electronic spreadsheet* software package. An electronic spreadsheet program can perform dozens, and even hundreds, of numeric calculations directly on your computer screen. The computations can be as simple and personal as keeping records of your home expenses, or as complex as developing mathematical models that help you run your business. And when the computations are complete, the PC-Calc+ spreadsheet program can print out the results in neatly formatted tables and graphics.

Electronic spreadsheet programs such as PC-Calc+ have revolutionized the way individuals and businesses deal with financial calculations, statistical data, and engineering computations. With

PC-Calc+, you can develop electronic spreadsheets for many different applications, including the following:

- Budgets
- Personal finances
- Forecasts and models
- Statistical reports and analyses
- Accounting reports and summaries
- Engineering studies
- Small business systems

In this chapter, you will learn the fundamentals of using the PC-Calc+ electronic spreadsheet program. In particular, you will create, edit, print, and save a small PC-Calc+ electronic spreadsheet while learning a few electronic spreadsheet introductory terms and concepts.

Before you begin your electronic spreadsheet explorations, check your package of PC-Calc+ materials and disks. Go through the next few sections, verify that PC-Calc+ will run on your computer system, make backup copies of your original PC-Calc+ disks, and install PC-Calc+, using the program's installation procedures.

PC-Calc+: The Package

PC-Calc+ version 2 is published by ButtonWare, Inc., P.O. Box 96058, Bellevue, Washington 98009. If you purchased a licensed copy of PC-Calc+, you received a typeset copy of the *PC-Calc+ User's Guide*, informational flyers that describe version 2 changes, features, and capabilities, and the disks that contain the PC-Calc+ programs and auxiliary files.

All of the PC-Calc+ programs and auxiliary files come on either a disk set of two 5 1/4-inch disks or a single 3 1/2-inch disk.

If a friend gave you a copy of the PC-Calc+ programs and auxiliary files, ButtonWare assumes that you are evaluating the program. Under the shareware agreement that accompanies any usage of PC-Calc+, after a reasonable evaluation period, you must either discontinue using the program or purchase a licensed copy.

One major advantage to purchasing your own copy of PC-Calc+ is that you receive the printed *PC-Calc+ User's Guide,* which is over 330 pages long. Otherwise, the *PC-Calc+ User's Guide* is only available in electronic form from computer clubs, user groups, bulletin boards, and approved shareware disk vendors. If you locate an electronic version of the *PC-Calc+ User's Guide,* plan to expend a lot of time, ribbon ink, and paper printing your own non-typeset, unbound version of the document.

A second advantage to purchasing a licensed copy of PC-Calc+ is that you receive the *current* version of the product. Shareware products are updated and improved regularly. You want to use only the latest version of PC-Calc+. For example, PC-Calc+ version 2 contains many new features and improvements which are not found in earlier versions of PC-Calc.

When you purchase a licensed copy of PC-Calc+, you also get a third advantage: one year of technical support and access to the ButtonWare bulletin board to help you resolve technical questions about PC-Calc+. So, if you have an evaluation copy of PC-Calc+ and believe you have a need for the program, go ahead and license a copy and support the shareware revolution.

Back Up Your PC-Calc+ Disks

PC-Calc+ requires at least 320K of memory in order to operate correctly. In addition, PC-Calc+ requires a system with either one floppy disk drive and a hard disk drive or two 720K disk drives.

It also requires an 80-column display (monochrome, graphics, CGA, EGA, or VGA) and DOS 2.0 (or a later version). To print reports or graphs, you will also need a printer. PC-Calc+ supports any printer that does not use PostScript.

 NOTE If you do not have a hard disk drive and plan to install PC-Calc+ on two 720K disks, please look at the READ.ME file first for both installation instructions and potential program limitations. In this part of the book, the user is assumed to have a hard disk drive when using the program. It is also assumed during program installation that the user has one floppy drive (either 5 1/4-inch or 3 1/2-inch). The examples in this book may occasionally exceed the disk space on a system using two 720K disks.

PC-Calc+ comes on either two 5 1/4-inch disks or one 3 1/2-inch disk. If you have not already done so, back up your PC-Calc+ disks. To make backup copies of the original PC-Calc+ disk sets, you can do the following:

- Follow the instructions in the *PC-Calc+ User's Guide*.
- Boot up your computer with a DOS disk and, when the DOS prompt appears, proceed with the following, step-by-step procedures appropriate for your set of disks.

Back Up the 5 1/4-inch Disk Set

If you have a 3 1/2-inch disk, please skip to the next section, "Back Up the 3 1/2-inch Disk."

The PC-Calc+ 5 1/4-inch disk set consists of two disks, labeled DISK ONE and DISK TWO. The files on your set of distribution disks have been compressed to fit on these two disks. You must run the PC-Calc+ installation procedure to extract the compressed files before you can actually use the PC-Calc+ programs and auxiliary files. The files contained on the disks are as follows:

DISK ONE (PC-Calc+ installation and file extraction programs)

INSTALL.EXE	The PC-Calc+ installation program that controls the installation process
PKUNZIP.EXE	The PC-Calc+ file extraction utility. This program extracts the compressed files from the files PCCP.ZIP and PCCU.ZIP
PCCP.ZIP	Contains the compressed main program files

DISK TWO (PC-Calc+ auxiliary program and resource disk)

READ.ME	An informational file about shareware programs, PC-Calc+ installation procedures, undocumented features, and command reference listing
VENDOR.DOC	Information for disk shareware disk dealers/distributors
PCCU.ZIP	The set of compressed PC-Calc+ utility programs and resource files

To back up this disk set, you will need two blank (either formatted or unformatted) disks. With the DOS prompt showing, do the following:

Type:
diskcopy a: a:
and press ENTER

You will be prompted to insert a source disk in drive A. Insert PC-Calc+ DISK ONE in drive A (source disk). When you have DISK ONE inserted in drive A:

Press ENTER

When the light on drive A turns off, you will see a message asking you to insert the target disk in drive A. Remove PC-Calc+ DISK ONE, and insert a blank disk (target disk) in drive A.

As the copy operation proceeds, you may receive an instruction to reinsert the source disk followed by an instruction to reinsert the target disk. Follow the on-screen instructions, inserting the source and target disks as many times as needed. When the copy operation is complete, remove the target disk from drive A and label it as a backup copy of PC-Calc+ DISK ONE.

On the screen, you will see a prompt asking if you want to copy another disk. Since you want to copy PC-Calc+ DISK TWO, do the following:

Press Y

Once again, you will be prompted to insert a source disk in drive A. Insert PC-Calc+ DISK TWO in drive A (source disk). When you have DISK TWO in drive A:

Press ENTER

When the light on drive A turns off, you will see a message asking you to insert the target disk in drive A. Remove PC-Calc+ DISK TWO and insert a blank disk (target disk) in drive A.

As the copy operation proceeds, you may receive an instruction to reinsert the source disk, followed by an instruction to reinsert the target disk. Follow the on-screen instructions, inserting the source and target disks as many times as needed. When the copy operations complete, remove the target disk from drive A and label it as a backup copy of PC-Calc+ DISK TWO.

On the screen, you will see a prompt asking if you want to copy another disk. Since you do not, answer as follows:

Press N

The disk copying operation terminates. You have made copies of both of the original PC-Calc+ 5 1/4-inch disks. Put the originals in a safe place and use the copies to install PC-Calc+. To start the installation of PC-Calc+, skip over the next section on backing up the 3 1/2-inch disk and proceed to the section titled, "Install PC-Calc+."

Back Up the 3 1/2-inch Disk

If you have 5 1/4-inch disks, please skip this section. If you need to make copies of your 5 1/4-inch disk set, refer to the previous section, "Back Up the 5 1/4-inch Disk Set."

The PC-Calc+ 3 1/2-inch disk is labeled DISK ONE. The files on this distribution disk have been compressed to fit on a single disk. You must run the PC-Calc+ installation procedure to extract the compressed files before you can actually use the PC-Calc+ programs and auxiliary files. The disk contains the following files:

DISK ONE (PC-Calc+ installation and file extraction programs)

INSTALL.EXE	The PC-Calc+ installation program that controls the installation process
PKUNZIP.EXE	The PC-Calc+ file extraction utility that extracts the compressed files from the files PCCP.ZIP and PCCU.ZIP

PCCP.ZIP	Contains the compressed main program files
READ.ME	An informational file about shareware programs, PC-Calc+ installation procedures, undocumented features, and command reference listing
VENDOR.DOC	Information for disk shareware disk dealers/distributors
PCCU.ZIP	The set of compressed PC-Calc+ utility programs and resource files

To back up this disk, you will need one blank (formatted or unformatted) disk. With the DOS prompt showing, do the following:

Type:
diskcopy a: a:
and press ENTER

You will be prompted to insert a source disk in drive A. Insert PC-Calc+ DISK ONE in drive A (source disk). When you have DISK ONE inserted in drive A:

Press ENTER

When the light on drive A turns off, you will see a message asking you to insert the target disk in drive A. Remove PC-Calc+ DISK ONE and insert a blank disk (target disk) in drive A.

As the copy operation proceeds, you may receive an instruction to reinsert the source disk, followed by an instruction to reinsert the target disk. Follow the on-screen instructions, inserting the source and target disks as many times as needed. When the copy operation is complete, remove the target disk from drive A and label it as a backup copy of PC-Calc+ DISK ONE.

On the screen, you will see a prompt asking if you want to copy another disk. Since you do not, answer as follows:

Press N

The disk copying operation terminates. You have made a copy of the original PC-Calc+ 3 1/2-inch disk. Put the original disk in a safe place and use the copy to install PC-Calc+.

Install PC-Calc+

 NOTE PC-Calc+ can be installed either on a hard disk drive or on two 720K disks. To install the programs and auxiliary files on two 720K disks, use the INST.BAT file that comes only on the 3 1/2-inch PC-Calc+ distribution disk. If you do not have a hard disk drive and want to install PC-Calc+ on two 720K disks, look at the READ.ME file first for both installation instructions and potential program limitations. In this book, the user is assumed to have a hard disk drive when using the program. One floppy drive (either 5 1/4-inch or 3 1/2-inch) is required for installation purposes only. The examples in this book may occasionally exceed the disk space on a system where PC-Calc+ is installed on two 720K disks.

To install PC-Calc+, you must use the installation program, INSTALL.EXE. Many of PC-Calc+ programs and auxiliary files have been compressed on the distribution disks. Part of the installation procedure involves the extraction of the compressed files.

You will need 1 megabyte of hard disk drive space to store the extracted files for PC-Calc+. Before starting the installation procedure, verify that your hard drive has enough free space to accommodate the 1 megabyte of PC-Calc+ files. (Issue either a DOS DIR or CHKDSK command while on your hard drive directory and look at the resulting messages that are produced. If you use DIR, the "bytes free" message must show more than 1 megabyte. If you use CHKDSK, the "bytes available on disk"

Figure 10-1.

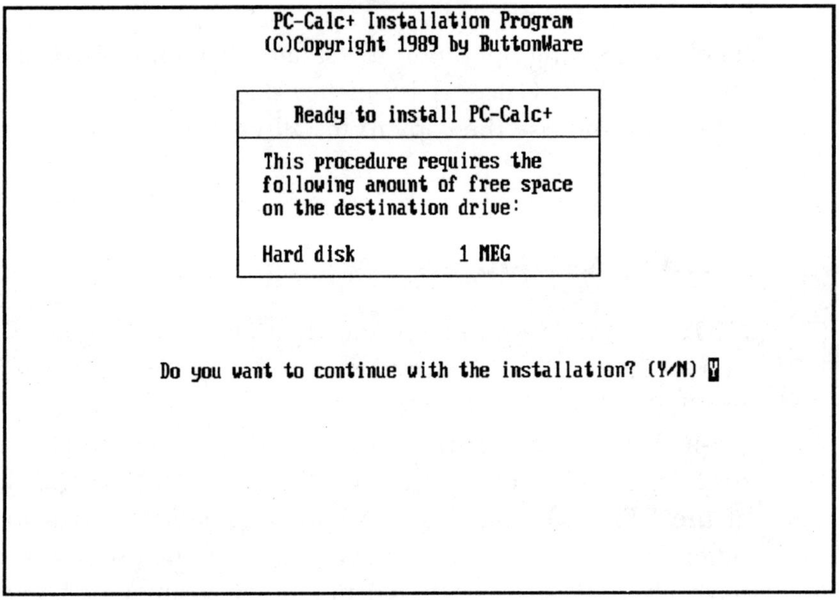

```
PC-Calc+ Installation Program
(C)Copyright 1989 by ButtonWare

    ┌─────────────────────────────────┐
    │    Ready to install PC-Calc+    │
    ├─────────────────────────────────┤
    │ This procedure requires the     │
    │ following amount of free space  │
    │ on the destination drive:       │
    │                                 │
    │ Hard disk            1 MEG      │
    └─────────────────────────────────┘



    Do you want to continue with the installation? (Y/N) Y
```

PC-Calc+ installation program title screen

message must be over 1 megabyte.) When you have established that your hard drive can hold all of the PC-Calc+ files, follow these steps to install PC-Calc+:

1. Make sure the DOS prompt is the one you expect to see when you are logged onto your hard drive. For example, if your hard drive is assigned to drive C, you should see the C prompt.

2. Make sure you are at the root directory by doing the following:

   Type:
   cd
   and press ENTER

3. Insert a copy of PC-Calc+ DISK ONE in drive A. When a copy of DISK ONE is in drive A:

Type:
a:install
and press ENTER

4. Disk drive A activates, and the installation program title screen appears, as shown in Figure 10-1. The message in the boxed area reminds you that 1 megabyte of free space will be needed for the installation procedure. If you do not want to continue with the installation procedure, you can press N and ENTER, CTRL-BREAK, or ESC. To continue with the installation of PC-Calc+:

Press ENTER

5. The screen changes to the one shown in Figure 10-2. The program prompts you for the source drive designation (A, B).

Figure 10-2.

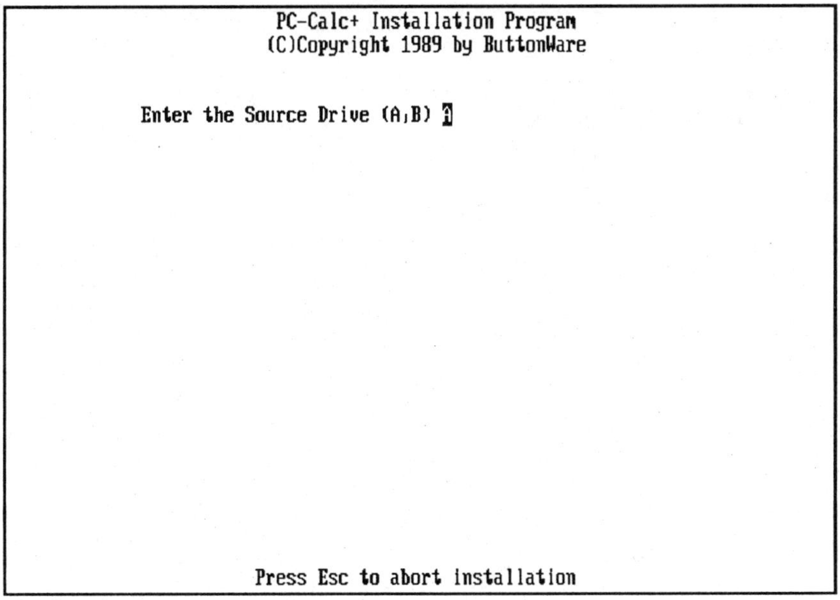

```
              PC-Calc+ Installation Program
               (C)Copyright 1989 by ButtonWare


    Enter the Source Drive (A,B) ▌












                 Press Esc to abort installation
```

Source drive installation prompt

Since DISK ONE is in drive A, and the default entry on the screen is A, do the following:

Press ENTER

6. The program prompts you to identify the destination drive, as shown in Figure 10-3. The default destination is drive C. If your destination drive is different, enter the letter that corresponds to your destination drive (A, B, C, D, E, F). After you you have set the destination drive designation:

Press ENTER

Figure 10-3.

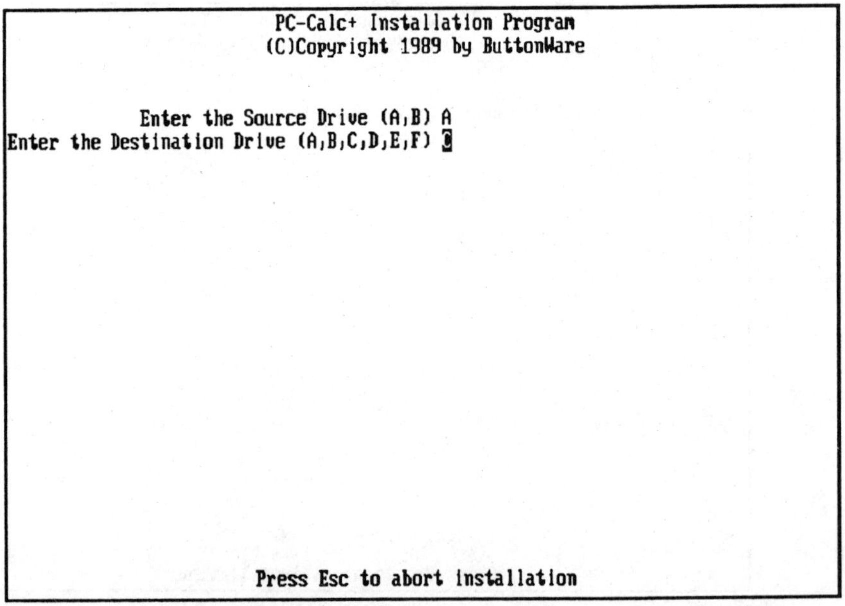

```
                    PC-Calc+ Installation Program
                    (C)Copyright 1989 by ButtonWare


              Enter the Source Drive (A,B) A
     Enter the Destination Drive (A,B,C,D,E,F) C













                    Press Esc to abort installation
```

Destination drive installation prompt

7. The program asks for the destination directory. The default is \PCCALC as is displayed on the screen shown in Figure 10-4. If you want to install PC-Calc+ in another directory, enter the directory name in place of \PCCALC. When you have entered the directory name:

Press ENTER

8. If the directory name you entered in step 7 does not exist, the installation program displays the message shown in Figure 10-5. (If your directory already exists, you will not see this screen.) The program asks if you want to create the directory. If you are installing PC-Calc+ for the first time, you do want to create the directory:

Press Y

Figure 10-4.

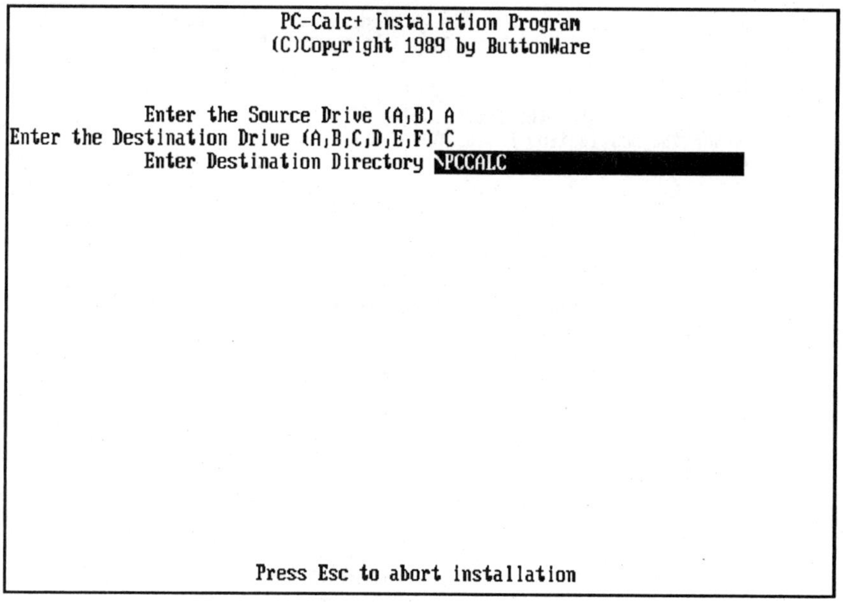

```
                    PC-Calc+ Installation Program
                    (C)Copyright 1989 by ButtonWare


             Enter the Source Drive (A,B) A
     Enter the Destination Drive (A,B,C,D,E,F) C
             Enter Destination Directory \PCCALC









                    Press Esc to abort installation
```

Destination directory installation prompt

9. A brief message from the installation program tells you that the program is extracting the files. Then, you see a couple of screens from the PKUNZIP file extraction program that unpacks, unshrinks, and expands the compressed PC-Calc+ files. PKUNZIP lists each file as it extracts it from PCCP.ZIP and PCCU.ZIP.

If you are installing PC-Calc+ from 5 1/4-inch disks, you will see the following message during the extraction process:

```
Put the "DISK TWO" in drive A
Press a key to continue...
```

When you see this message, remove DISK ONE from drive A and insert DISK TWO. Then, do the following:

Press any key

Figure 10-5.

```
            PC-Calc+ Installation Program
              (C)Copyright 1989 by ButtonWare


             Enter the Source Drive (A,B) A
   Enter the Destination Drive (A,B,C,D,E,F) C
           Enter Destination Directory \PCCALC
                       ←↑↓→
              ┌─────────────────────────────┐
              │ Question:                   │
              ├─────────────────────────────┤
              │ Directory does not exist. May I create it? │
              │ Press Y or N                │
              └─────────────────────────────┘




                  Press Esc to abort installation
```

Installation request to create directory

If you are installing PC-Calc+ from a 3 1/2-inch disk, you will not see any messages about DISK TWO.

10. When the extraction process is complete, the installation program asks you if you want to move the major EXE programs to another directory on your path, as shown in Figure 10-6. For now, move all of the PC-Calc+ files into the directory you named in step 7:

Press N

A reminder message tells you to add your destination drive and directory name (for instance, C:\PCCALC) to your DOS path. To continue with the installation:

Press any key

Figure 10-6.

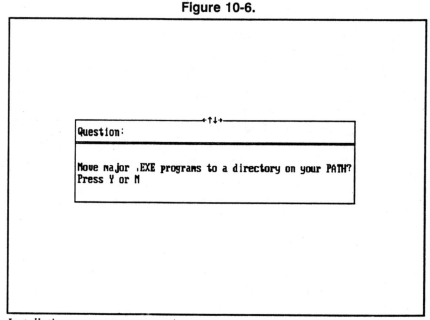

Installation request to move major programs

11. The next question you see is shown in Figure 10-7. The installation program wants to know if the display should be in (C)olor or (B)lack and white. PC-Calc+ supports monochrome, graphics, CGA, EGA, and VGA monitors. If you have a color monitor of any type, press C. If your system can only display black and white, press B.

12. The installation program asks if you want it to inspect and update your CONFIG.SYS file, as shown in Figure 10-8.

    PC-Calc+ works best if your CONFIG.SYS file contains a FILES=20 entry. To tell the installation program to automatically update your CONFIG.SYS file, do the following:

    Press Y

    When you press Y, you see the message:

    ```
    Which disk do you boot your computer from?
    ```

    Enter a drive designation (A, B, C, D, E, F) and press ENTER. The installation program inspects and updates your CONFIG.SYS file. If you have no CONFIG.SYS file on the designated drive, the installation program creates one for you.

13. The final installation screen is shown in Figure 10-9. The program wants to know if you want to print the READ.ME file. You can choose to print the file to the (S)creen, to the (P)rinter, or (N)owhere. If you press S, the file will be printed to your screen one page at a time. If you want to print the file to your printer, first make sure your printer is connected, turned on, and ready to go, and then press P. If you choose not to print the file, press N for Nowhere.

14. At the end of the installation process, you see the following message:

    ```
    End of PC-Calc+ installation.
    ```

Figure 10-7.

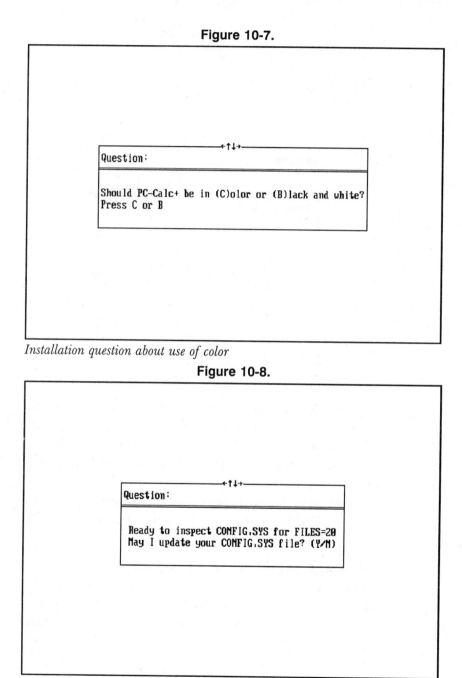

Installation question about use of color

Figure 10-8.

Installation request to inspect CONFIG.SYS

Figure 10-9.

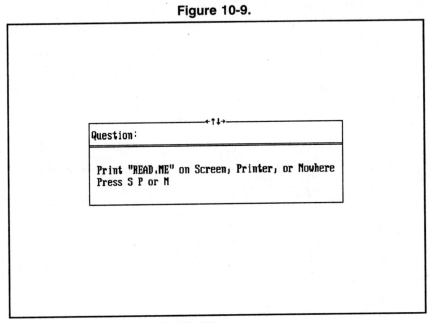

Installation request to print READ.ME

Below the message you see the DOS prompt, and if the full path name is displayed, the directory into which you put the PC-Calc+ files (for instance, C:\PCCALC>). At the end of the installation procedure, the program leaves you in the PC-Calc+ directory.

The installation process creates a number of files within the \PCCALC directory. The following is a list of key PC-Calc+ files:

/PCCALC Directory (or the directory you used)

PCC.EXE	The PC-Calc+ main program
PCG2.EXE	The PC-Calc+ graphics program
P90.EXE	A program that prints spreadsheets sideways
PCC.HLP	The PC-Calc+ help message file

PCCALC.PRO	The PC-Calc+ profile or configuration file
COLOR.PRO	Optional profile for using a color monitor
MSHERC.COM	A command file for systems with monochrome monitors and Hercules graphics cards
CONVERT.EXE	A program that converts previous versions of PC-Calc+ files to PC-Calc+ version 2 format
READ.ME	An informational file about shareware programs, PC-Calc+ installation procedures, undocumented features, and command reference listing
FILES	Detailed listing of PC-Calc+ files and PC-Calc+ file conventions
*.PRN	Printer control files
*.PCC	Spreadsheet files. PC-Calc+ comes with two example spreadsheets, LOAN.PCC and TUTORIAL.PCC

For a detailed listing of the files used by PC-Calc+, look at the file called FILES in the PC-Calc+ directory. You are now ready to start PC-Calc+.

Start PC-Calc+

If you have not already done so, install the PC-Calc+ files from a copy of your distribution disks, as detailed in the previous section. You cannot run PC-Calc+ directly from a copy of your distribution disks, because all the files on the disks are compressed.

In the examples that follow, it is assumed that all of the PC-Calc+ files have been installed in the default directory \PCCALC on drive C. If you have installed the files in another directory or on another drive, substitute your drive and directory for the ones shown in the examples.

If you are not already on the C drive and in the PC-Calc+ directory, do the following:

Type:
c:
and press ENTER   (to move to the hard drive)

Type:
cd \pccalc   (to change to the PC-Calc+ directory)
and press ENTER

When you are in the PC-Calc+ directory, you are ready to start PC-Calc+, as follows:

Type:
pcc
and press ENTER

PC-Calc+ displays the startup screen shown in Figure 10-10. You can think of this screen as your window into an extensive electronic worksheet which extends out to the right and down through the floor. On the screen, you see only eight columns labeled across the top with the letters A through H. However, the PC-Calc+ worksheet extends to the right for 256 columns! Twenty-one rows labeled down the left side with the numbers 1 through 21, are displayed on the screen. Although they are not all displayed on the screen, PC-Calc+ has 8000 rows! If the electronic worksheet were an actual piece of paper, it would extend to the right about 30 feet and down through the floor about 400 feet.

Figure 10-10.

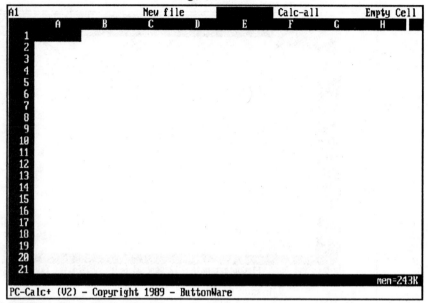

PC-Calc+ startup screen

Fortunately, you do not have to see all of the worksheet at once. And, as you will soon learn, if you need to see a part of the worksheet beyond the screen you can "fly" your window to that location. You will also learn that you can "fold up" the worksheet, so that data in column 256 appears next to the data in the first column, or data in row 8000 is displayed right under the data in the first row.

The PC-Calc+ Screen

To start your "flying" lessons, you need to learn a few terms and concepts which deal with your window into the worksheet. Do the following to make all of the window's controls appear:

Press ESC

Figure 10-11.

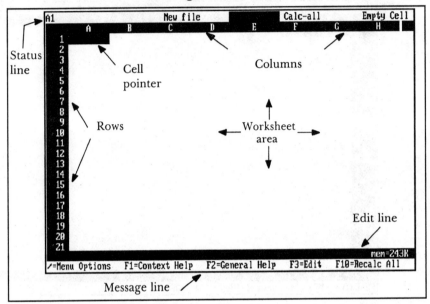

PC-Calc+ startup screen with message line

When you press ESC, the PC-Calc+ copyright notice at the bottom of the startup screen changes to the *message line.* Figure 10-11 shows the PC-Calc+ startup screen with the message line displayed. The message line usually displays a list of function keys you can use to get additional help or information. PC-Calc+ also uses the message line to display program and error messages.

Directly above the message line, on the right side of the highlighted border, you see a message displaying the amount of *free memory.* Free memory represents the amount of memory available to hold your spreadsheet data. For a new spreadsheet running on a computer with 640K of memory, the free memory number will be over 200K, or 200,000 bytes. The number on your screen may differ slightly from the number in the message of Figure 10-11, which shows the following:

mem=243K

The part of the window that contains the free memory message, that is the bottom highlighted bar that spans the screen, is called the *edit line*. When you enter and modify data on your PC-Calc+ worksheet, you will often use the edit line. The large blank area of the bar, beginning at the left side of the screen, is used to display the data you type and modify.

The large blank area above the edit line is called the *worksheet area*. Your data (text, numbers, and calculation results) will appear on the worksheet area. The worksheet area is divided up into *cells*. Each cell corresponds to a row and column intersection point in the worksheet area. For example, the worksheet area currently displayed is eight columns wide (designated by the letters A through H along the top of the worksheet area) and 21 rows down the screen (designated by the numbers 1 through 21 along the left edge of the worksheet area). Your window currently shows a total of 168 worksheet cells (8 columns multiplied by 21 rows).

To locate a cell, use the *cell pointer*. The cell pointer is the highlighted rectangle that currently sits in cell A1, which is the cell in the upper left corner of the worksheet. You can move the cell pointer with the arrow keys. Press the → key once:

Press →   (one time)

Did the cell pointer move to cell B1? You can tell which cell the cell pointer is on by looking at the *status line* at the top of the screen. The leftmost part of the status line always displays the current location of the cell pointer. If you pressed the → key once, the status line should display "B1" in the upper left corner of your screen.

The status line also indicates that you are working with a new file. If you were working with a previously saved spreadsheet, the new file message would be replaced with the name of your current spreadsheet.

On the far right side of the status line, PC-Calc+ displays either the current cell type (in this case, "Empty Cell") or the name of any menu you have activated.

The status line has a number of other indicators and message areas. You will learn more about the status line and its messages as you build your electronic spreadsheets.

For now, try "flying" around the worksheet, using the arrow keys (←, ↑, →, ↓). If you press the → key and hold it down for about a minute (depending on your computer's speed), you will hit the right edge of the worksheet, labeled column IV. PC-Calc+ begins labeling the columns with the letters A through Z. The program labels the column following column Z as AA, and then proceeds to label the next 25 columns with the letters AB through AZ. Next, columns are labeled BA through BZ, CA through CZ, and so on, until the final column, IV, is displayed. If you press and hold the ↓ key for a long time, you will eventually get to the bottom of the worksheet, row 8000.

PC-Calc+ has faster ways to move about the worksheet. The next section discusses the PC-Calc+ help features, which include help screens that explain better and faster ways to move the cell pointer around the screen.

Get Help Anytime and Anywhere

PC-Calc+ provides both a general help feature and *context sensitive* help messages. Context sensitive help messages provide specific help information about the task that you are currently performing.

To view the PC-Calc+ general help screens:

Press F2

 NOTE If your copy of PC-Calc+ does not contain the help message file, PC-Calc+ simply "beeps" when you ask for help, to indicate that the help function keys are not active. All distribution copies of PC-Calc+ disks include the help message file.

When you press F2 to activate the PC-Calc+ general help screens, the first general help screen appears, as shown in Figure 10-12. The cell and screen movement screen details how to control the movement of the cell pointer for cells, by screens, and across the entire spreadsheet. You have already explored the use of the arrow keys to move between cells. Those controls are listed at the top of the screen shown in Figure 10-12.

The screen movement controls that are located in the middle of the display shown in Figure 10-12 allow you to move the cell pointer by entire spreadsheet screens. You can move the entire screen to the left and right, and up and down. Also, you can use the screen controls to quickly move the cell pointer to the corner cells and the center cell of the current screen.

The last set of controls, as shown at the bottom of Figure 10-12, allows you to move across the entire spreadsheet. With these

Figure 10-12.

```
                       CELL AND SCREEN MOVEMENT
       CELL
             Up / Down arrow - up / down one row in current column
         Left / Right arrow - left / right one column in current row
                      Enter - direction of Smart Cursor

       SCREEN
                PgUp / PgDn - scroll one screen up / down
                      - / + - scroll one screen left / right (numeric keypad)
                       Home - left column / top row of screen then file
                        End - right column / bottom row of screen then file
              AltUp / AltDown - first / last row on screen , current column
          AltLeft / AltRight - first / last column on screen, current row
            AltHome / AltEnd - upper left / lower left cell on screen
            AltPgUp / AltPgDn - upper right / lower right cell on screen
                       Alt5 - (Number pad) center cell on screen

       SPREADSHEET
            CtrlUp / CtrlDown - first / last active row, current column
          CtrlLeft / CtrlRight - first / last active column, current row
            CtrlHome / CtrlEnd - upper left / lower left cell in spreadsheet
          CtrlPgUp / CtrlPgDn - upper right / lower right cell in spreadsheet
                       Ctrl5 - (Number pad) center cell in spreadsheet
                                              Press PgUp, PgDn, or Esc
```

First PC-Calc+ general help screen

controls, you can move to the spreadsheet's last active row or column, to the lower left or right cell, and to the very center cell.

You might like to keep a record handy of these movement controls as you explore PC-Calc+. If your printer is connected, turned on, and ready to print, print a copy of this screen to your printer:

Press SHIFT-PRTSC

REMEMBER You can display this general help screen at any time by pressing F2.

The PC-Calc+ general help feature has a number of other help screens. To see the next general help screen:

Press PGDN

Figure 10-13 shows the second general help screen, which deals with moving the cursor on the edit line. Here again, you might like to print this screen for future reference:

Press SHIFT-PRTSC

PC-Calc+ has a total of 15 general help screens. The remaining 13 screens detail the many PC-Calc+ functions, operators, and special commands. Go ahead and browse through the rest of these general help screens by pressing PGDN (and PGUP). When you finish browsing, go back to the worksheet screen:

Press ESC

When you return to the worksheet screen, examine the PC-Calc+ context help feature. You can activate that feature at any time by pressing the F1 key.

Press F1

Figure 10-14 shows you the context sensitive help message when the cell pointer sits on a worksheet cell and no menus are active. The help message tells you that you have the following three options: you can enter or modify the cell data, you can move the cell pointer, or you can press the slash (/) character to activate the Main menu. The PC-Calc+ context help messages tell you what options you have, based on the task you are performing and the current state of the PC-Calc+ program.

The top of the help message box contains four arrows, one for each of the four directions: left (←), up (↑), down (↓), and right (→).

Press ↑

Figure 10-13.

```
                    CURSOR MOVEMENT ON EDIT LINE

    Left / Right arrow - left / right one character
    Tab / Shift Tab    - left / right five characters

              Home - first character on Edit Line
               End - one position right of last character

               Ins - toggle insert mode
               Del - delete current character
              Bksp - delete character to the left
                F6 - delete data from cursor to end of Edit Line

             Enter - accept entry, return to Worksheet Area and move
                     cell pointer in direction of Smart Cursor

    CtrlLeft / CtrlRight - accept contents as with Enter and
    CtrlUp   / CtrlDown    move to next field in indicated
    Up       / Down        direction

               Esc - return to Worksheet Area without saving entry

                                       ══════ Press PgUp, PgDn, or Esc ══════
```

Second PC-Calc+ general help screen

When you press ↑, the help message box moves up the screen. Move the message box around the screen with the arrow keys. If the message box covers up the cell on which you are working, you can use the arrow keys to relocate the box to another part of the screen.

To make a context sensitive help message disappear, you can press any key.

Press any key

Quit PC-Calc+

When you return to the PC-Calc+ worksheet screen, use the slash key (/) to bring up the PC-Calc+ Main menu.

Figure 10-14.

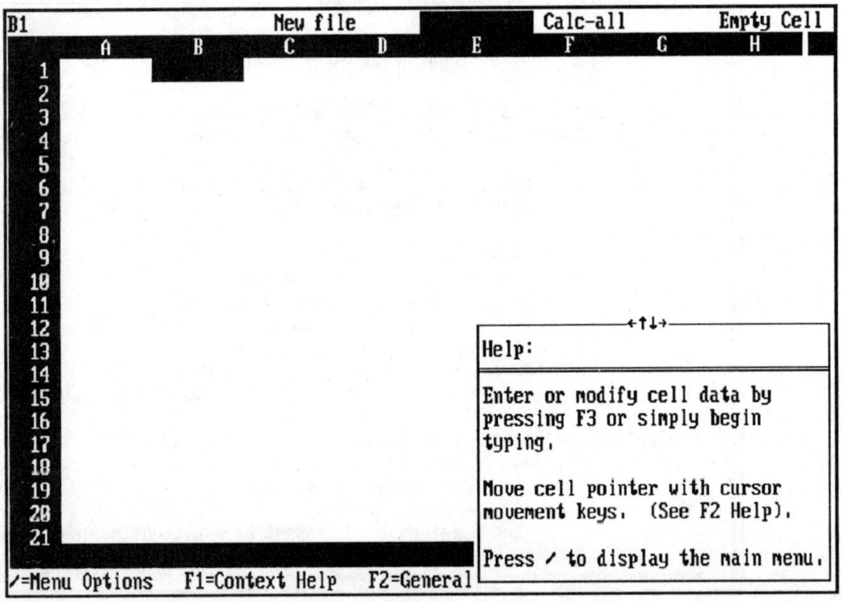

PC-Calc+ context sensitive help message

Press /

When you press /, the Main menu appears on the left side of the worksheet screen, as shown in Figure 10-15. To select an option, move the highlight up and down the options list by using the ↑ and ↓ keys. Each time you press one of the arrow keys to move the highlight, the message across the bottom of the screen tells you about the option that is highlighted.

Here you have another opportunity to explore the PC-Calc+ context help feature. The help features, both context sensitive and general, are always available. To see the context help message for the Main menu:

Press F1

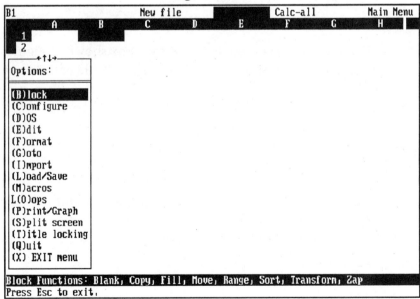

Figure 10-15.

PC-Calc+ Main menu

Figure 10-16.

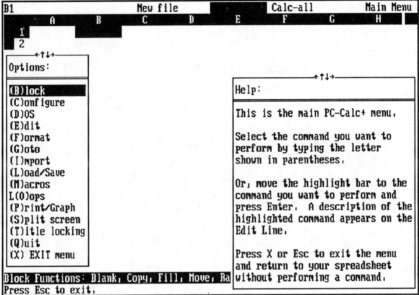

PC-Calc+ context help about the Main menu

PC-Calc+ brings up the help message box shown in Figure 10-16. The help message box, located on the right side of the screen, tells you how to make selections on the PC-Calc+ Main menu. To remove the context help message, press any key.

> Press any key

You will explore the PC-Calc+ Main menu as you build your electronic spreadsheets. For now, you want to quit PC-Calc+. To do so, you can either move the highlight down to the (Q)uit option and press ENTER, or you can simply press the letter Q, as follows:

> Press Q

When you press Q (or highlight (Q)uit and press ENTER), a list of Quit options appears, as shown in Figure 10-17. The highlight

Figure 10-17.

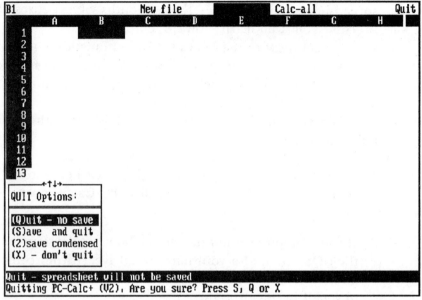

Quit options

rests on the first option, which quits PC-Calc+ and does not save the spreadsheet. Since you do not want to save this empty spreadsheet, do the following:

    Press Q

When you press Q this second time, PC-Calc+ stops, and you are returned to the DOS prompt. You are now ready to use PC-Calc+ to build a simple electronic spreadsheet.

Getting to Know PC-Calc+ in 30 Minutes

The following exploration introduces you to the basic PC-Calc+ features required to create, print, and save a small electronic spreadsheet. The example involves the creation of a simple spreadsheet that calculates three months of expenses. In the process, you will learn how to enter data into a PC-Calc+ spreadsheet, how to tell PC-Calc+ to automatically add a set of values, how to save and print the spreadsheet, and how to alter cell entries on an electronic spreadsheet. You can expect to spend about 30 minutes on the entire exploration.

To create your first electronic spreadsheet with PC-Calc+, follow these steps:

1. Make sure you have gone through the earlier sections of this chapter and that you have installed PC-Calc+ on your hard disk.

2. If your computer is not turned on, boot your system and go to the DOS prompt for your hard disk drive. (If your computer is already on and you are already in the PC-Calc+ directory, go to step 4 in this procedure.)

3. When you see the drive designation for your hard disk drive (the C drive on most systems), go into the directory where the PC-Calc+ files are stored. In this book, the directory is assumed to be \PCCALC.

    Type:
    cd \pccalc
    and press ENTER

4. When you are in the PC-Calc+ directory, start up PC-Calc+.

    Type:
    pcc
    and press ENTER

5. A blank PC-Calc+ worksheet screen appears. At the bottom of the screen is the product's version number (V2) and a copyright notice.

On this screen, you are going to enter labels, data values representing three months of travel expenses, and a formula for adding the three expense numbers together to form a total. Figure 10-18 shows what the EXPENSES spreadsheet looks like after you have entered all of the labels, data, and the formula. Use this figure as a guide as you enter the information into the spreadsheet.

 REMEMBER Use the arrow keys to position the cell pointer (the highlighted rectangle that moves from cell-to-cell). In all the following instructions, you are told exactly where to put the cell pointer and what to type when the cell pointer is at the desired position. If you make a mistake, use the arrow keys to go back to the cell with the error and either type the correct entry and press ENTER to record the new entry (in the case of spelling mistakes or

Figure 10-18.

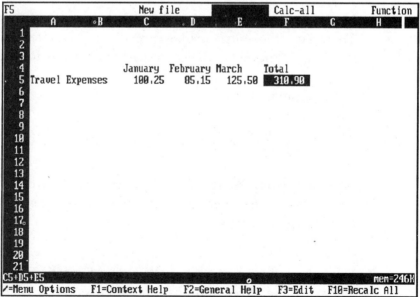

The Expenses spreadsheet

wrong values), or empty the cell by pressing DEL until the current entry disappears, and then press ENTER. The first data entry example will demonstrate how to make a correction.

6. Move the cell pointer to the cell location A5 (column A, row 5) and type the label "Travl Expenses" (intentionally misspelled). If the cell pointer is on cell A1, move it to cell location A5 by pressing ↓ four times. If the cell pointer starts on cell B1, press ↑ four times and then press ← once.

   At cell location A5
   Type:
   Travl Expenses
   and press ENTER

NOTE When you type, the characters do not appear in cell A5 immediately. They appear in the edit line at the bottom of the screen. The characters are put into cell A5 when you press ENTER.

PC-Calc+ accepts the misspelled label when you press ENTER. To correct the entry, make sure the cell pointer is at cell location A5 and enter the correct label name, as follows:

At cell location A5
Type:
Travel Expenses
and press ENTER

PC-Calc+ removes the old label and replaces it with your latest entry. Most spreadsheet cell corrections involve nothing more than retyping a new entry, as you just did for "Travel Expenses."

7. Move the cell pointer to the following cell locations, enter the labels for the three months, and then enter a label called "Total."

At cell location C4
Type:
January
and press ENTER

At cell location D4
Type:
February
and press ENTER

At cell location E4
Type:
March
and press ENTER

At cell location F4
Type:
Total
and press ENTER

When you complete these four label entries, look back and verify that your entries match the ones shown in Figure 10-18. If you need to make a correction, move the cell pointer to the cell needing correction and retype the label.

8. Enter the following three expense values at the indicated cell locations:

At cell location C5
Type:
100.25
and press ENTER

At cell location D5
Type:
85.15
and press ENTER

At cell location E5
Type:
125.50
and press ENTER

Again, verify that your data values have been entered correctly by looking back at Figure 10-18. If you need to make corrections, move the cell pointer to the cell needing correction and retype the number.

9. The last entry you make to complete this version of the spreadsheet will be a formula that adds together the three expense values and places the total in the cell F5 under the column label "Total." Go to cell F5 and type the indicated formula.

At cell location F5
Type:
c5+d5+e5
and press ENTER

When you enter the formula and press ENTER, the number 310.90 appears at the F5 cell location. If your cell pointer is on cell F5, look at the left side of the edit line. You should see this version of the formula you typed: C5+D5+E5.

An electronic spreadsheet differs from a sheet of paper in that each cell on the electronic sheet "remembers" the formula that gets typed at each cell location. The spreadsheet then displays the result of any formula on the screen as a data value.

This ability to "remember" formulas has an interesting side effect: if you change a data value that a formula uses, the spreadsheet automatically updates the worksheet to reflect the data value change.

10. Change the March data value to 9000.00 and see what happens.

   At cell location E5
   Type:
   9000.00
   and press ENTER

   When you enter the new value for March, the total value in F5 automatically changes to 9185.40. To recompute your original expense total, insert 125.50 back into cell location E5.

   At cell location E5
   Type:
   125.50
   and press ENTER

   When you reenter the original March expense number, the total automatically gets recomputed, and you see 310.90 in cell location F5.

11. When your spreadsheet looks like the one shown in Figure 10-18, try printing the spreadsheet on your printer. To use a printer with PC-Calc+, make sure your printer is hooked up, turned on, and ready to print. When your printer is ready, open the PC-Calc+ Main menu:

   Press /

Figure 10-19.

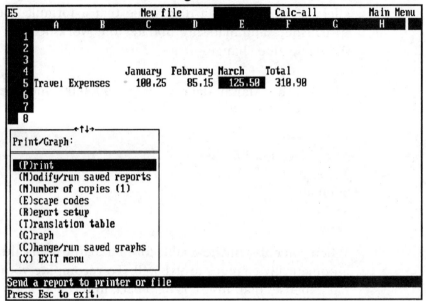

The Print/Graph option list

The Main menu appears on the left side of the worksheet screen. Select the (P)rint/Graph option:

Press P

The Print/Graph option list appears as shown in Figure 10-19. Select the (P)rint option, as follows:

Press P or ENTER

The Reports option list appears, as shown in Figure 10-20. Since your entire spreadsheet fits on one screen, you can select the first option, (S)creen. This option will print the spreadsheet that is displayed on your screen.

Press S or ENTER

Figure 10-20.

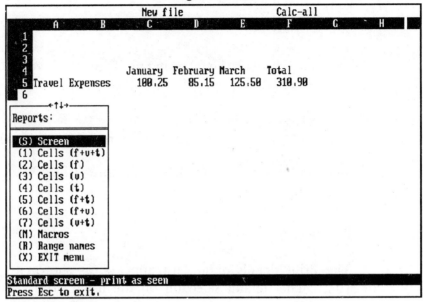

The Reports option list

PC-Calc+ displays the following message in the edit line that says:

```
Enter destination (blank=LPT1)  LPT1
Press Esc to exit.
```

If your printer is connected and ready to print:

Press ENTER

A prompt in the edit line asks you to supply a title for the report. Enter a title, as follows:

Type:
Expense Report
and press ENTER

PC-Calc+ displays the following message asking you to define the area to be printed:

```
Enter source def: B5:E8   ALL
Or press F8 to define target screen area.  (Esc=cancel)
```

Since you want to print the entire spreadsheet, choose the default option, ALL:

Press ENTER

The Print details option list appears, as shown in Figure 10-21. The default selection on the list is "(P)roceed with print." Since you want to proceed, do the following:

Press P or ENTER

A final question from PC-Calc+ asks you if you want to save the print definition information in a table, as follows:

```
Save definition information in table?
Press Y or N
```

For now, do not save the information for this initial spreadsheet:

Press N

A message appears in the edit line area telling you how much of the report remains to be printed, and that you can abort printing by pressing ESC. The report prints on your printer. At

Figure 10-21.

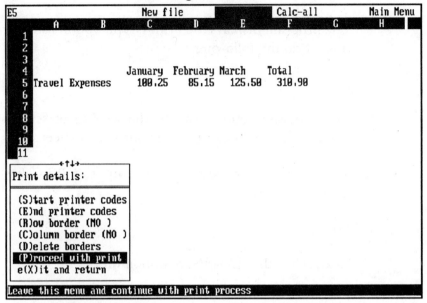

The Print details option list

the top of the report, the current system date and time are printed, followed by the report title, Expense Report. A dashed line prints below the title. The two lines from your spreadsheet print below the dashed line. At the bottom of the page, PC-Calc+ prints another dashed line and the legend, "Page 1 of 1."

 NOTE If your spreadsheet did not print or printed incorrectly, do not become concerned. In the next chapter, you will learn how to install a PC-Calc+ printer driver that works with your brand of printer. Simply go back to the worksheet screen (press ESC as many times as needed) and proceed to step 12, in which you learn to save your spreadsheet to your disk.

PC-Calc+ displays a "Printing completed" message on the screen and asks you to press a key to continue:

Press any key

The program displays the Print/Graph option list. To remove this list do the following:

Press ESC

The program returns you to the worksheet screen. From here, you can proceed to save your spreadsheet.

12. To save your spreadsheet, open up the PC-Calc+ Main menu:

Press /

Next, select the (L)oad/Save option on the list:

Press L

The Load/Save option list appears. Select the second option on the list, "(S)ave spreadsheet":

Press S

A PATH request appears above the edit line area at the bottom of the screen. Since you are already in the /PCCALC directory, you can press ENTER to have the file stored in the current directory:

Press ENTER

PC-Calc+ displays a file selection box in the center of the screen with the names New_File, LOAN, and TUTORIAL, as shown in Figure 10-22. The highlight rests on the New_ File entry in the box. Since you want to save your spreadsheet into a new file:

Press ENTER

A message appears at the bottom of the screen asking you to name the file. The program wants only the file name with no extension.

Type:
Expense
and press ENTER

An informational message briefly appears telling you that the program is saving the file.
 Congratulations! You have created, edited, printed, and saved your first spreadsheet.

Figure 10-22.

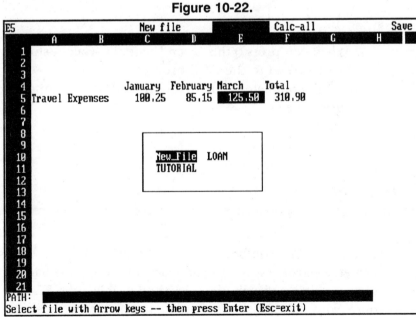

The file selection box

13. After you save your spreadsheet, use the slash key (/) to bring up the PC-Calc+ Main menu.

Press /

To quit PC-Calc+, either move the highlight down to the (Q)uit option and press ENTER, or simply press the letter Q, as follows:

Press Q

When you press Q, the list of Quit options appears. The highlight rests on the first option which quits PC-Calc+ and does not save the spreadsheet. Since you have already saved this spreadsheet, do the following:

Press Q

When you press Q this second time, PC-Calc+ stops and you are returned to the DOS prompt.

This completes your first tour of PC-Calc+ and electronic spreadsheets.

Summary

In this chapter, you began an exploration of PC-Calc+, a sophisticated electronic spreadsheet program. You made backup copies of your original distribution disks and installed the PC-Calc+ files onto your hard disk drive. You learned how to start up the PC-Calc+ program, to move the cell pointer around the screen, to use the PC-Calc+ general help and context help features, and to exit from the PC-Calc+ program.

You then created a PC-Calc+ spreadsheet called Expenses. You entered labels, data, and a formula into cells on the worksheet, explored how PC-Calc+ performs calculations, and printed and saved the finished spreadsheet.

CHAPTER 11

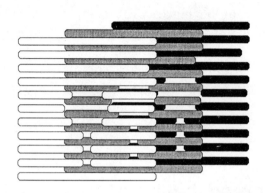

Building a Spreadsheet

In this chapter you will build a simple three-month budget using the PC-Calc+ spreadsheet program. The goal is not to teach you how to do budgets, but to show you how PC-Calc+ can assist you in building an electronic spreadsheet of moderate complexity. Along the way, you will learn quite a bit about PC-Calc+ *commands* and *functions*.

In Chapter 10, you got an introduction to some of the PC-Calc+ commands when you used the main menu to print and save your first spreadsheet, EXPENSES. Each PC-Calc+ command lets you perform a task related to building, editing, printing, saving, and manipulating information on a spreadsheet. In this chapter, you will use several new PC-Calc+ commands to build a three-month budget spreadsheet.

PC-Calc+ functions provide you with dozens of ready-made formulas. Instead of your having to write complex formulas to perform specific calculations, PC-Calc+ functions automatically perform computations and give you answers.

To begin your exploration of PC-Calc+ commands and functions, you will learn the commands that help you load and zap spreadsheets ("zapping" will be defined shortly).

Load and Zap a Spreadsheet

If you have not already done so, boot up your computer and go to the directory for your hard disk drive. When you see the DOS prompt for your hard disk directory (drive C on most computers), go to the PC-Calc+ directory (\PCCALC), and then activate the PC-Calc+ program:

Type:
cd \pccalc   (and press ENTER)
pcc   (and press ENTER)

PC-Calc+ immediately displays a blank worksheet screen with a copyright notice at the bottom and the words "New File" in the status line at the top of the screen.

To load an existing spreadsheet file, you activate the PC-Calc+ Main menu by pressing the slash (/) character. Open the PC-Calc+ Main menu as follows:

Press /

The Main menu appears as a list of options on the left side of the screen. To select an option, you can perform one of the following actions:

- Press the letter of the option you want that appears inside the set of parentheses. For example, to choose the (L)oad/Save option, you would press the letter L.
- Move the highlight using the ↑ and ↓ arrow keys to the desired option, and then press ENTER.

To load an existing spreadsheet, choose the (L)oad/Save option:

Press L

When you press L from the Main menu, PC-Calc+ displays the Load/Save option list on the left side of the screen. The highlight in this menu sits on the first option, (L)oad spreadsheet. Since you want to load an existing spreadsheet, do the following:

Press L or ENTER

When you press either L or ENTER, the Load/Save option list disappears, and the program displays a "PATH" prompt at the bottom of the screen. The prompt is for you to enter the path name for your spreadsheets. Since all your spreadsheets are in the current directory, press ENTER to tell PC-Calc+ to look for spreadsheets in the current directory:

Press ENTER

When you press ENTER at the "PATH" request, PC-Calc+ displays a file selection box on top of the the worksheet screen, as shown in Figure 11-1. The highlight is on the spreadsheet named EXPENSES, which is the spreadsheet you created in Chapter 10.

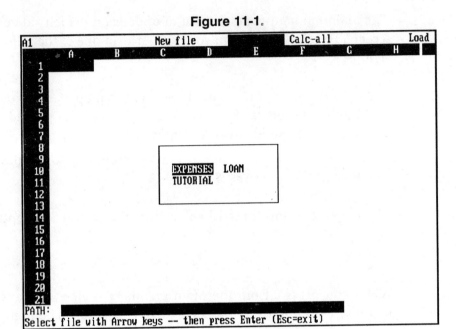

Figure 11-1.

File selection box

 NOTE If you did not create the EXPENSES spreadsheet in Chapter 10, you can use a copy of the EXPENSES spreadsheet contained on *The Shareware Book* Convenience Disk. The Convenience Disk, which you purchase separately, contains a number of key files that correspond to the activities in this book. Using a copy of a file from the Convenience Disk ensures that your screen examples match what appears in the book. If you do not have the Convenience Disk, you can still proceed with the examples in this chapter. Simply choose another spreadsheet, either LOAN or TUTORIAL, for this section on loading and zapping spreadsheets.

The highlight can be moved from EXPENSES to another name by using the arrow keys. Go ahead and move the highlight to the other names, LOAN and TUTORIAL. Then, move the highlight back to EXPENSES and do the following:

Press ENTER

PC-Calc+ loads the EXPENSES spreadsheet and displays the screen shown in Figure 11-2. Note that PC-Calc+ loads the spreadsheet to exactly the same state that it was in when it was saved in the last chapter. The cell pointer was at cell location E5 when the spreadsheet was saved in Chapter 10, and it remains at position E5 in the current screen.

You have now used the Main menu command, (L)oad/Save, to load a spreadsheet.

Figure 11-2.

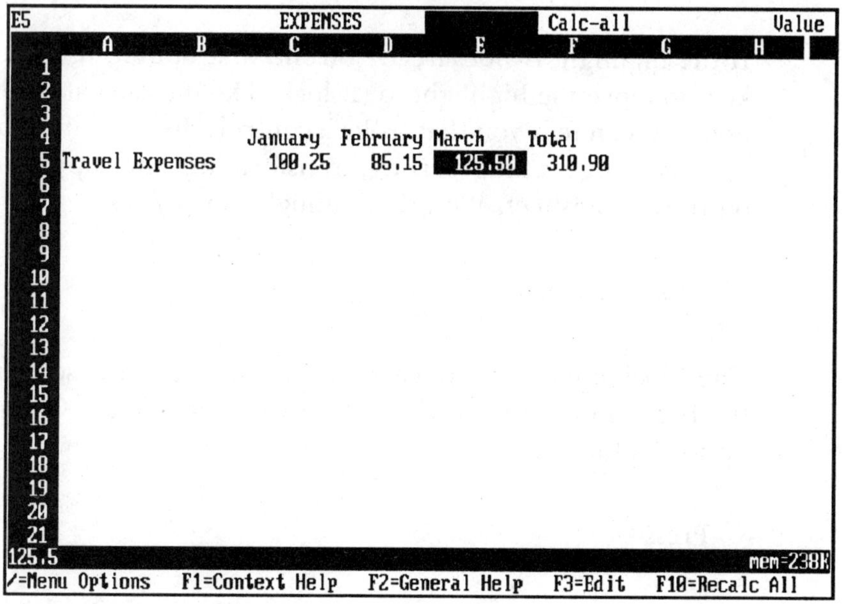

EXPENSES spreadsheet

Zapping a spreadsheet is a convenient way to clear all of the spreadsheet's cells and return them to default format settings (text left justified; numbers right justified). As you will see, a cell can be formatted in many different ways. If you simply clear, or *blank*, the information in a cell, the cell will retain its format settings. To empty all cells and reset default format settings, you need to zap the spreadsheet.

NOTE Zapping the current spreadsheet and saving the "zapped" version under a new file name is one way to create a new spreadsheet.

To zap the EXPENSES spreadsheet, first bring up the PC-Calc+ Main menu:

Press /

If the highlight is not already on the first option, use the arrow keys to move the highlight to (B)lock. The message at the bottom of the screen tells you that (B)lock controls the blanking, copying, moving, range setting, sorting, transforming, and zapping of cells on the spreadsheet. With the highlight on (B)lock:

Press ENTER or B

The Block option list appears on the left side of the screen. Near the bottom of the list is the option you want, (Z)ap. Choose that option as follows:

Press Z

PC-Calc+ displays the following prompt at the bottom of the screen asking you to enter the block definition:

```
Enter block definition.  Example: B5:E8 E5
Or press F8 to define target in screen area.  (Esc=cancel)
```

PC-Calc+ wants to know which cells to zap. You can enter a range of cells such as the B5:E8 range shown in the message example. Entering B5:E8 would clear all of the cells in a block, starting at B5 and ending in E8. All cells in columns B, C, D, and E and rows 5, 6, 7, and 8 would be zapped. Since the cell pointer is now on cell E5, that cell location appears in the input area of the prompt message. You could enter a range definition that uses or overwrites the current location of the cell pointer.

Another way to define the block to be zapped is to press F8 and follow the instructions to mark a block by moving the cell pointer around the screen. You will get a chance to use this method later in this chapter.

Since you want to zap the entire spreadsheet, simply type **all** in the range definition area:

Type:
all
and press ENTER

When you type **all** and press ENTER, PC-Calc+ automatically highlights all of the active cells in the spreadsheet (no matter how many there are or where they are located). The program then displays a confirmation question as shown in Figure 11-3. Since you do want to zap the current spreadsheet:

Press Y

PC-Calc+ follows your instructions and zaps the EXPENSES spreadsheet. Figure 11-4 shows the zapped EXPENSES spreadsheet, with the cell pointer sitting at position E5.

Figure 11-3.

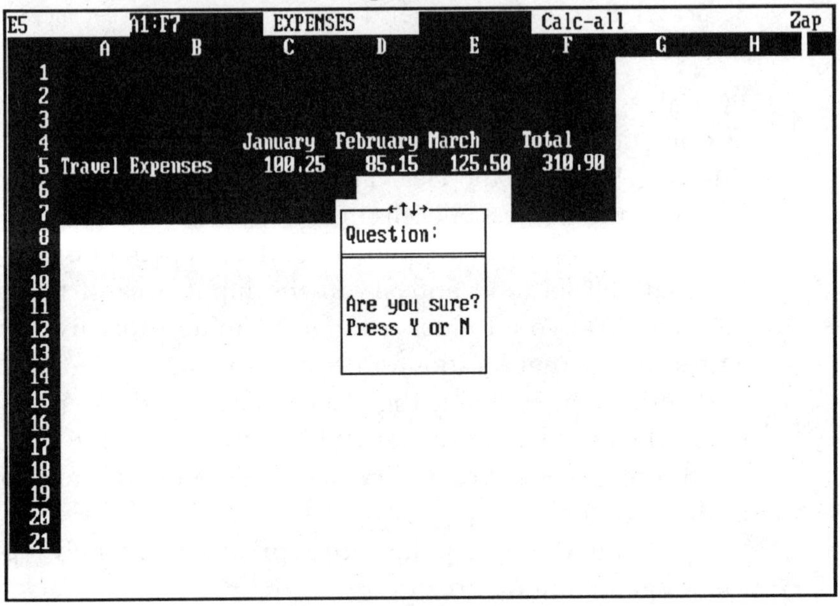

[Screenshot: PC-Calc+ spreadsheet showing cell E5, range A1:F7, titled EXPENSES, with Calc-all and Zap options. Row 4 shows column headers January, February, March, Total. Row 5 shows "Travel Expenses 100.25 85.15 125.50 310.90". A dialog box displays "Question: Are you sure? Press Y or N"]

PC-Calc+ ready to zap EXPENSES spreadsheet

 CAUTION This spreadsheet is still labeled EXPENSES. If you inadvertently save this spreadsheet over the old EXPENSES spreadsheet, you would end up with only the zapped version of the spreadsheet in the EXPENSES file. The program saves the contents of the new spreadsheet, changes included, over the contents of the file you originally selected. PC-Calc+ does not automatically create a backup copy of the file being overwritten.

Since you are about to create a new spreadsheet which deals with budgets, save the zapped EXPENSES spreadsheet under a new name BUDGET, by doing the following:

Press /	(to call up the Main menu)
Press L	(to select the (L)oad/Save option)
Press S	(to select the (S)ave spreadsheet option)
Press ENTER	(to accept the current path designation)

Figure 11-4.

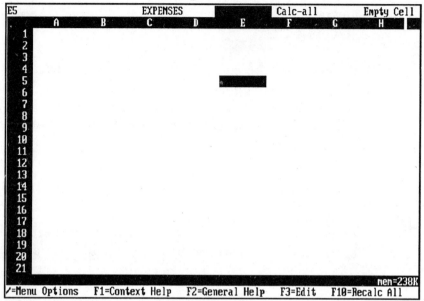

EXPENSES *spreadsheet after being zapped*

When you press ENTER at the end of this sequence, the file selection box appears, as shown in Figure 11-5. The highlight is on the name EXPENSES.

Use the ← arrow key to move the highlight onto "New_File." Then, do the following:

Press ENTER

The following prompt message at the bottom of the screen asks you for a new file name:

```
Enter new filename (NO EXTENSION):
Press Esc to exit.
```

Enter the file name, with no extension, for your new spreadsheet:

Type:
budget
and press ENTER

PC-Calc+ saves the empty spreadsheet under the name BUDGET, and partially updates the file name area in the status line. Since the name EXPENSES was a bit longer than BUDGET, there is a trailing "ES" at the end of BUDGET. To eliminate the "ES," you must load BUDGET again:

Press /   (to call up the Main menu)
Press L   (to select the (L)oad/Save option)
Press L   (to select the (L) Load spreadsheet option)
Press ENTER   (to accept the current path designation)

Figure 11-5.

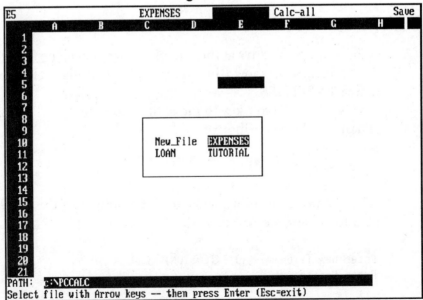

File selection box

When you press ENTER at the end of this sequence, the file selection box appears with the highlight on BUDGET. (If the highlight is not on BUDGET, use the arrow keys to move the highlight onto BUDGET.) With the highlight on BUDGET:

Press ENTER

The screen again looks like the screen shown in Figure 11-5, except that the name area on the status line displays BUDGET instead of "budgetES."

NOTE You may want to take a break now and then as you go through your explorations of the PC-Calc+ program. For example, this point in the chapter is a good place to take a rest. Since the empty BUDGET file has been saved to your hard disk, you can exit PC-Calc+, turn off your computer, and begin the next section at your convenience.

Build the Budget Spreadsheet

If you took a break and turned off your computer, you need to boot your system, start PC-Calc+, and load the empty BUDGET spreadsheet. When you see the DOS prompt and you are logged on the hard disk directory:

Type:
cd \pccalc and press ENTER
pcc budget and press ENTER

If you restart PC-Calc+ in this manner, it automatically loads BUDGET when you type the spreadsheet name after the name of the PC-Calc+ program (**pcc**). PC-Calc+ will automatically load a spreadsheet at startup if you include the spreadsheet name. If the spreadsheet is in another directory, you must include the path name (for instance B:\MYFILE).

Suppose that you plan to start your own consulting business. You want to rent a small office, stock it with supplies, get a telephone, prepare brochures about your services, and plan a few marketing trips. To get an idea of how much all these activities might cost, you decide to build a planning budget. You want to use the planning budget to help you understand the likely new business startup costs. Later, you will want to use the same budget to help you track your actual-versus-budgeted expenses.

Figure 11-6 shows the BUDGET spreadsheet in completed form. Use Figure 11-6 as a guide when you input the various data items, labels, and formulas to build your version of BUDGET. The

Figure 11-6.

```
C9                    BUDGET                     Calc-all              Value
       A       B       C       D       E       F       G       H
 1
 2                           Budget: Three-Month Period
 3                                  (Dollars)
 4
 5
 6                   January                February           March
 7                   Budget   Actual        Budget   Actual    Budget   Actual
 8                   -------  -------       -------  -------   -------  -------
 9 Office Rent       500.00                 500.00             500.00
10 Office Supplies   300.00                 100.00             50.00
11 Computer Supplies 50.00                  50.00              50.00
12 Telephone         150.00                 75.00              75.00
13 Utilties          100.00                 50.00              50.00
14 Printing          250.00
15 Marketing         150.00                 150.00             75.00
16 Travel            200.00                 200.00             400.00
17 Misc.             200.00                 100.00             100.00
18                   -------                -------            -------
19 Totals            1900.00                1225.00            1300.00
20
21
500                                                                  mem=233K
/=Menu Options    F1=Context Help   F2=General Help   F3=Edit   F10=Recalc All
```

Completed BUDGET spreadsheet

set of instructions that follow show you how to build BUDGET step by step. In many steps, you are introduced to new PC-Calc+ commands and functions which facilitate your job of building BUDGET.

Create Titles and Column Headings

Starting with the empty BUDGET worksheet screen, begin by typing a couple of title lines at the top of the screen. Move the cell pointer to cell location D2 and do the following:

> At cell location D2, type:
> **Budget: Three-Month Period**
> and press ENTER

Then, move the cell pointer to cell location E3 and enter the following subtitle:

> At cell location E3, type:
> **(Dollars)**
> and press ENTER

Move the cell pointer to cell location C6, where you will enter the names for the three months covered by this budget. First, activate the PC-Calc+ Smart feature, which configures the spreadsheet to make data entry tasks easier. As you press the following keys, you will activate the Main menu, the (C)onfiguration option, and the PC-Calc+ Smart feature which controls the automatic movement of the cell pointer. After you activate the (S)mart option, you will tell PC-Calc+ that you want the cell pointer to automatically move to the (R)ight. Perform the following sequence of keypresses:

Press /   (to bring up the Main menu)
Press C   (to choose (C)onfigure option)
Press S   (to choose (S)mart option)
Press R   (to choose (R)ight option)
Press X   (to exit the Configure options list)
Press N   (at the question of saving configuration to disk)

You will see how the Smart feature works in just a moment as you enter the names of the months. Do the following:

At cell location C6, type:
January
and press ENTER

Figure 11-7.

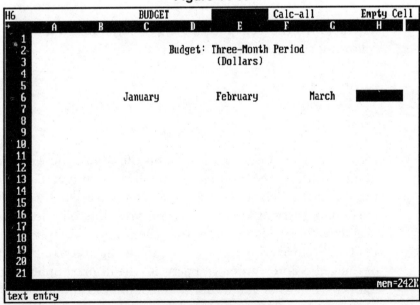

BUDGET spreadsheet after month names are entered

When you press ENTER, the cell pointer jumps one cell to the right, to cell location D6. Previously, each time you pressed ENTER, the cell pointer stayed at the same cell location. The PC-Calc+ Smart feature allows you to control the movement of the cell pointer after you make each cell entry. This feature saves you time when you enter data along an entire row or down an entire column. PC-Calc+ lets you know that the Smart feature is active and set to move to the right by displaying a right-pointing arrow below the letter "D" of the current cell pointer location (D6) in the left corner of the screen.

The next month name goes into cell location E6. You can move the cell pointer to cell location E6 either by pressing → or by pressing ENTER, because the Smart feature is set to move the cell pointer to the right.

Press ENTER

With the cell pointer on E6, enter the names of the following two months:

Starting at cell location E6, type:
February (and press ENTER twice)
March (and press ENTER)

Figure 11-7 shows what your screen should look like after you type **March** and press ENTER. The cell pointer is in cell location H6. If you need to make corrections, use the arrow keys to move to each cell that needs adjustment and enter the correct data.

Move the cell pointer to cell location C7. You want to enter three pairs of labels marked "Budget" and "Actual," as follows:

Starting at cell location C7, type:
Budget (and press ENTER)
Actual (and press ENTER)
Budget (and press ENTER)

Actual	(and press ENTER)
Budget	(and press ENTER)
Actual	(and press ENTER)

The Smart feature helps you by moving the cell pointer one cell to the right each time you press ENTER. With the last press of ENTER, the cell pointer moves to cell location I7, and the entire worksheet moves one column to the left. Column A disappears from the left edge of the screen, and column I appears on the right. The cell pointer remains at the right edge of the worksheet area. The cell pointer did not actually move—the spreadsheet did! Figure 11-8 shows your screen with the spreadsheet shifted to the left one column.

PC-Calc+ was just trying to help you out in case you planned

Figure 11-8.

```
I7                    BUDGET              Calc-all          Empty Cell
      B       C         D         E         F       G       H       I
  1
  2                       Budget: Three-Month Period
  3                               (Dollars)
  4
  5
  6           January             February          March
  7           Budget    Actual    Budget   Actual   Budget   Actual
  8
  9
 10
 11
 12
 13
 14
 15
 16
 17
 18
 19
 20
 21                                                              mem=242K
 /=Menu Options    F1=Context Help   F2=General Help   F3=Edit   F10=Recalc All
```

BUDGET spreadsheet shifted one column to the left

Building a Spreadsheet **437**
Ch 11

to fill more cells to the right of column H. The next entry you want to make is in a visible cell location, C8.

Use the Copy Command Move the cell pointer to cell location C8. Then, enter the first set of hyphens (-------) under the first Budget column.

> At cell location C8, type:
> -------   (seven hyphens)
> and press ENTER

After you make this entry, the cell pointer moves to the right to location D8. You could go ahead and manually type the next five sets of hyphens under each of the remaining columns. Or, you can let PC-Calc+ do the typing for you, by using the PC-Calc+ copy feature to fill in the next five columns with the information from cell C8. To begin the copy operation, do the following:

> Press /   (to activate the Main menu)
> Press B   (to choose the (B)lock option)
> Press C   (to choose the (C)opy option)

When you choose the (C)opy option, PC-Calc+ displays the following prompt at the bottom of the screen:

```
Enter source def: B5:E8  D8
Or press F8 to define target in screen area.  (Esc=cancel)
```

The prompt wants you to define the *source* cell, or cells, to be copied. The default in the input area is set to D8, because that is where the cell pointer currently sits. Since you want to copy from the source cell C8, do the following:

> Type:
> **c8**
> and press ENTER

When you type **c8** and press ENTER, the prompt message changes to the following:

```
Enter target def: B5:E8  D8
Or press F8 to define target in screen area.  (Esc=cancel)
```

You are being asked to identify the *target* cell, or cells, in which to copy the data from cell C8. Since you want the C8 information to be copied to the cells D8 through H8, type **d8:h8** into the input area next to the prompt, as follows:

> Type:
> **d8:h8**
> and press ENTER

When you press ENTER, the screen flashes, and the copied hyphens appear under the remaining five columns! You only had to push a few keys. PC-Calc+ did all the work.

With the cell pointer at cell location D8, copy the hyphens to the cell range C18:H18 as well by doing the following:

> Press /   (to activate the Main menu)
> Press B   (to choose the (B)lock option)
> Press C   (to choose the (C)opy option)
> Press ENTER   (to accept D8 as "source" cell)
>
> Type:
> **c18:h18**   (Target range where hyphens will go)
> and press ENTER

When you press ENTER, the screen flashes and six sets of hyphens appear in columns C18 through H18. The cell pointer remains at cell location D8. Your screen should look like the screen shown in Figure 11-9.

Figure 11-9.

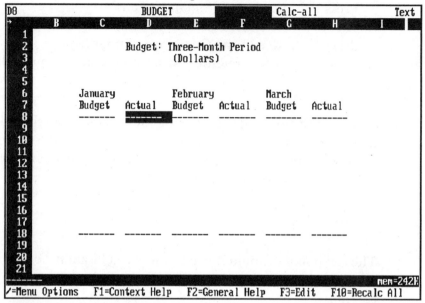

BUDGET spreadsheet with dashes in place

Create the Budget Category Labels

You are ready to enter the budget categories into column A. First, move the cell pointer to the left until column A reappears:

   Press ←, ←, ←

The cell pointer should now be at location A8. Since you are about to enter an entire column of labels, change the Smart feature to automatically move the cell pointer down the screen, by doing the following:

   Press / (to bring up the Main menu)
   Press C (to choose (C)onfigure option)

Press S   (to choose (S)mart option)
Press D   (to choose (D)own option)
Press X   (to exit the Configure options list)
Press N   (at the question of saving configuration to disk)

Look at the upper left corner of the screen. You should see a downward-pointing arrow under the letter "A" of the current cell pointer location (A8). The PC-Calc+ Smart feature is ready to go. Verify the change you made to the Smart feature:

Press ENTER

The cell pointer should move down to cell location A9. Beginning at cell location A9, go ahead and enter the budget categories for column A:

Starting at cell location A9, type:
Office Rent   (and press ENTER)
Office Supplies   (and press ENTER)
Computer Supplies   (and press ENTER)
Telephone   (and press ENTER)
Utilities   (and press ENTER)
Printing   (and press ENTER)
Marketing   (and press ENTER)
Travel   (and press ENTER)
Misc.   (and press ENTER twice)
Totals   (and press ENTER)

When you finish entering the column labels, the cell pointer will be in cell location A20. Figure 11-10 shows what your screen should look like now. If you need to correct anything, use the arrow keys to move to any cell that requires a correction, and retype the entry.

Figure 11-10.

```
A20                  BUDGET                Calc-all          Empty Cell
↓      A      B      C      D      E      F      G      H
 1
 2                         Budget: Three-Month Period
 3                                 (Dollars)
 4
 5
 6                  January         February        March
 7                  Budget  Actual  Budget  Actual  Budget  Actual
 8                  ------- ------- ------- ------- ------- -------
 9 Office Rent
10 Office Supplies
11 Computer Supplies
12 Telephone
13 Utilities
14 Printing
15 Marketing
16 Travel
17 Misc.
18                  ------- ------- ------- ------- ------- -------
19 Totals
20
21
                                                              mem=239K
/=Menu Options    F1=Context Help    F2=General Help    F3=Edit    F10=Recalc All
```

BUDGET spreadsheet with budget categories

After you make any needed corrections, you may want to save what you have typed. It is good practice to occasionally stop and save your partially finished spreadsheet.

    Press /   (to call up the Main menu)
    Press L   (to select the (L)oad/Save option)
    Press S   (to select the (S)ave spreadsheet option)
    Press ENTER   (to accept the current path designation)

When you press ENTER at the end of this sequence, the file selection box appears with the highlight on the name BUDGET. (If the highlight is not on BUDGET, use the arrow keys to move the highlight to BUDGET.) With the highlight on BUDGET:

    Press ENTER

You have completed entering all of the labels for the BUDGET spreadsheet. In the next section, you will begin to enter the initial column of data.

NOTE   You may want to take another break before continuing to build the BUDGET spreadsheet. The partially completed BUDGET file has been saved to your hard disk. You can exit PC-Calc+, turn off your computer, and come back to the next section, after your break. If you do leave PC-Calc+ and turn off your computer, when you return and restart your computer, remember to start PC-Calc+ by typing **pcc budget** from within the \PCCALC directory.

Enter January Data

Suppose you have made preliminary estimates for each of the budget categories for the month of January. In most cases, you have assigned a fixed dollar amount to each budget item. For example, you believe that office rent will be $500 and that you will have to spend $300 to buy office supplies. You think you will need $50 worth of computer supplies. Your telephone will cost $75 to install, plus $75 for the first month's charges, for a total of $150. You expect to pay a $50 fee to have the utilities turned on and $50 for a month's usage, a total of $100. The printer gave you an estimate of $250 for your stationery and brochures. January marketing costs will be $150, and you will spend another $200 on travel. Since January is your first month, you have budgeted $200 for miscellaneous expenses.

To enter these initial budget figures, move the cell pointer to location C9. Cell C9 represents the Office Rent budget item for January. With the cell pointer on C9, proceed to enter the entire column of data for January. Remember to press ENTER after you type each entry. When you press ENTER, you record each entry, and the cell pointer moves down to the next cell location.

Starting at cell location C9, type:

500	(Office Rent)
300	(Office Supplies)
50	(Computer Supplies)
75+75	(Telephone; installation + first month)
50+50	(Utilities; fee + first month)
250	(Printing)
150	(Marketing)
200	(Travel)
200	(Misc.)

When you type the last value and press ENTER, the cell pointer moves to location C18, which is filled with hyphens (-------). Figure 11-11 shows the screen with the January data correctly entered.

Figure 11-11.

```
C18                BUDGET                      Calc-all           Text
      A      B      C       D       E       F       G      H
 1
 2                        Budget: Three-Month Period
 3                                (Dollars)
 4
 5
 6                   January         February        March
 7                   Budget  Actual  Budget  Actual  Budget  Actual
 8                   ------- ------- ------- ------- ------- -------
 9 Office Rent        500.00
10 Office Supplies    300.00
11 Computer Supplies   50.00
12 Telephone          150.00
13 Utilities          100.00
14 Printing           250.00
15 Marketing          150.00
16 Travel             200.00
17 Misc.              200.00
18                   -------  ------- ------- ------- ------- -------
19 Totals
20
21
                                                              mem=239K
/=Menu Options    F1=Context Help   F2=General Help   F3=Edit   F10=Recalc All
```

BUDGET spreadsheet with January data

Notice that when you typed **75+75** and **50+50** for January Telephone and Utilities, respectively, PC-Calc+ accepted those two entries as formulas, and calculated the results shown in the two cell locations (C12 and C13). If you move the cell pointer back up to January Utilities (C13), the edit line will display "50+50." If you move up to January Telephone, the edit line shows "75+75."

You may want to save BUDGET before you fill in the February column. If you need a reminder, refer to the end of the section "Create the Budget Category Labels."

Compute February Data

Move the cell pointer to location E9, the beginning of the February Budget column. In this column, you are going to use PC-Calc+ formulas to generate all of the February data values. In each cell, you will enter a formula which references the data or formulas you already typed in the January column.

Cross-referencing the data across cells highlights the major difference between using an electronic spreadsheet and performing paper and pencil calculations. Referencing the January entries in the February column, will cause the February entries to automatically change whenever you change the January entries. This powerful feature of electronic spreadsheets allows you to ask "what if" questions and get immediate answers. For example, what if the office rent is $600 instead of $500? What if the office supplies are $200 instead of $300?

To see how this feature works, enter the following formulas for the February budget items. Remember to press ENTER after you type each formula. Beside each formula is a brief explanation for the formula being used. (When you get to February Printing, there are no budgeted expenses. Just press ENTER.)

Starting at cell location E9, type:
    c9   (Office Rent: same as January)

  c10∗1/3 (Office Supplies: 1/3 of January; Jan. was startup)
  c11 (Computer Supplies: same as January)
  c12-75 (Telephone: January minus installation)
  c13-50 (Utilities: January minus fee)
  Press ENTER (No printing)
  c15 (Marketing: same as January)
  c16 (Travel: same as January)
  c17∗1/2 (Misc.: 1/2 of January; Jan. was startup)

When you type the last formula and press ENTER, the cell pointer moves to location E18, which contains hyphens. The entire February Budget column should be filled with numbers, as shown on the screen in Figure 11-12. Check the numbers in your February column against the numbers shown in Figure 11-12. If you notice differences, move the cell pointer to the cells where the

Figure 11-12.

```
E18                    BUDGET                 Calc-all              Text
↓      A         B         C        D         E        F        G        H
 1
 2                              Budget: Three-Month Period
 3                                       (Dollars)
 4
 5
 6                            January            February           March
 7                            Budget   Actual    Budget   Actual    Budget   Actual
 8                            ------   ------    ------   ------    ------   ------
 9 Office Rent                500.00             500.00
10 Office Supplies            300.00             100.00
11 Computer Supplies           50.00              50.00
12 Telephone                  150.00              75.00
13 Utilities                  100.00              50.00
14 Printing                   250.00
15 Marketing                  150.00             150.00
16 Travel                     200.00             200.00
17 Misc.                      200.00             100.00
18                            ------   ------    ------   ------    ------   ------
19 Totals
20
21
                                                                       mem=237K
/=Menu Options    F1=Context Help    F2=General Help    F3=Edit    F10=Recalc All
```

BUDGET spreadsheet with February data

differences appear. Check the display in the edit line to ensure that you entered the correct formulas. If the formulas need correction, retype them and verify that the resultant calculated values match those shown in Figure 11-12.

When your screen matches the one shown in Figure 11-12, save your BUDGET spreadsheet before going on to the next step.

Copy February Formulas into the March Column

Move the cell pointer to G9, the first budget item in the March Budget column. For this column, you are going to use another PC-Calc+ feature, the Copy command.

Most of your March formula entries will be the same as the February entries, (that is, then will relate to January's values). If you set up your spreadsheet in this way, changing a January value will automatically change the values in both February and March. To duplicate February's formulas in the March column, you activate the PC-Calc+ Copy command:

With the cell pointer at location G9:
    Press /   (to activate the Main menu)
    Press B   (to choose the (B)lock option)
    Press C   (to choose the (C)opy option)

Type:
e9:e17   (Source range to be copied)
and press ENTER

Press ENTER   (Accept G9 as target cell)

When you select G9 as the target cell, a "Relative or Fixed" option list appears on the left side of the screen. Figure 11-13 shows the screen with the option list covering a portion of the worksheet area. The "(K)eep as defined" option is highlighted.

PC-Calc+ assumes that all cell references within a formula are *relative* references. That is, when PC-Calc+ copies or moves a formula to another cell location, the program automatically adjusts all cell references to fit the new location.

For example, if cell B2 contained the formula B1*100, and if that formula were moved to cell C6, then PC-Calc+ would automatically change the formula to C5*100 (unless you instructed the program otherwise). Note that the cell reference B1 in the original formula becomes C5 in the new formula. PC-Calc+ adjusts the cell reference by first determining the relationship between the original cell reference (B1) to the original cell location

Figure 11-13.

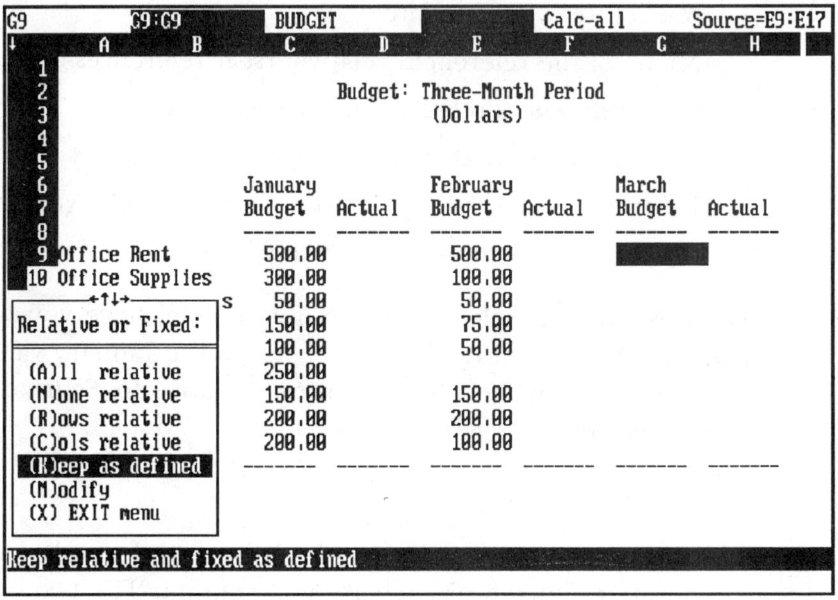

"Relative or Fixed" option list

(B2). In this case, the relationship is that the column location (B) is the same as the column reference (B), and the row location (1) is one row previous to the row reference (2). Therefore, cell reference B1 located in cell B2 becomes cell reference C5 when moved to location C6.

PC-Calc+ also recognizes *fixed* references. A fixed reference is one that stays the same regardless of where the formula is moved or copied. (You can also specify that just the row or the column is fixed while the remaining coordinate reference is relative.) To mark a cell reference as fixed, insert the number symbol (#) after the coordinate you want to be fixed. For example, "B#1#" fixes both the column and row components of cell reference B1 when used in a formula.

The "Relative or Fixed" option list shown in Figure 11-13 provides the following options for defining cell references in formulas:

- (A)ll cell references relative
- (N)one of the references relative; treat references as fixed
- (R)ow references relative; adjust rows only
- (C)olumn references relative; adjust columns only
- (K)eep references as they are defined; leave relative/fixed as is
- (M)odify each formula individually as it is copied

For this exercise, select option N for (N)one, since you want to keep the March cell references related to the January values. (If you wanted to make March's entries relative to February, you would choose either (A)ll or (K)eep.)

Press N

When you press N, PC-Calc+ copies February's formulas, without modification, into the March Budget column. The two columns should show the exact same values.

Edit March Formulas

After you copy the formulas from February to March, the cell pointer remains at location G9. Next, begin to edit a couple of the formulas as follows:

    With the cell pointer at cell location G9:
    Press ENTER   (to move to G10)
    Press F3   (to activate the edit mode)

When you press ENTER at G9, the cell pointer moves down to location G10. The formula for G10 (C10*1/3) appears in the edit line area. When you press F3, PC-Calc+ activates the edit mode. The edit cursor blinks under the first character of the formula in the edit line area.

Suppose you thought that by March, you would need 1/6 of the supplies you bought in January. You can proceed to edit the formula accordingly:

    Press → six times   (to put cursor under the 3)
    Type:
    6
    and press ENTER

When you press ENTER, the formula contained at location G10 changes to C10*1/6, the value at G10 changes to 50, and the cell pointer moves to G11.

Suppose you want to change the formula at G15 to C15*1/2. Move the cell pointer to G15 and do the following.

    At cell location G15:
    Press F3
    Press → three times   (to put cursor to right of 5)

Type:
*1/2
and press ENTER

The cell pointer moves to G16, and the value at G15 changes to 75.

Assume that you know you will be taking an extra flight to a conference in March. The cost for that flight will be $200 in addition to the regular monthly flight allocation. Edit the March Travel value to reflect the extra $200.

At cell location G16:
Press F3
Press → three times   (to put cursor to right of 6)
Type:
+200
and press ENTER

The cell pointer moves to G17, and the value at G16 changes to 400. Look at Figure 11-14 and check that your March budget numbers match the ones in the figure. Again, if you see variations, review the formulas in the March Budget column, especially the formulas you just edited. Make any necessary adjustments or corrections.

When you are satisfied that your spreadsheet looks like the one in Figure 11-14, save the BUDGET spreadsheet. Finally, you will conclude the building process by using a PC-Calc+ function to total up your budget numbers.

Add Up Each Month's Expenses

The final step in building the BUDGET spreadsheet involves creating a formula for the Totals for each month. Move the cell

Figure 11-14.

```
G17                     BUDGET                  Calc-all          Function
      A        B        C         D        E        F        G         H
 1
 2                          Budget: Three-Month Period
 3                                 (Dollars)
 4
 5
 6                     January           February           March
 7                     Budget   Actual   Budget   Actual   Budget   Actual
 8                     -------  -------  -------  -------  -------  -------
 9 Office Rent         500.00            500.00            500.00
10 Office Supplies     300.00            100.00             50.00
11 Computer Supplies    50.00             50.00             50.00
12 Telephone           150.00             75.00             75.00
13 Utilities           100.00             50.00             50.00
14 Printing            250.00
15 Marketing           150.00            150.00             75.00
16 Travel              200.00            200.00            400.00
17 Misc.               200.00            100.00            100.00
18                     -------  -------  -------  -------  -------  -------
19 Totals
20
21
C17*1/2                                                            mem=237K
/=Menu Options    F1=Context Help    F2=General Help    F3=Edit    F10=Recalc All
```

BUDGET spreadsheet with March data

pointer to location C19, the cell that will hold the total for the January Budget numbers.

One way to create a total for the January Budget column of numbers would be to type the following formula into cell C19:

Type:
c9+c10+c11+c12+c13+c14+c15+c16+c17

However, PC-Calc+ provides an easier way to specify this calculation—the SUM function. SUM is one of the many PC-Calc+ functions that automatically performs computations without your having to type long and involved formulas. To use SUM to add up the January Budget numbers, do the following:

At location C19, type:
sum(c9:c17)
and press ENTER

When you type **SUM**, a left parenthesis, the range definition for the January Budget numbers (C9:C17), a right parenthesis, and then press ENTER, PC-Calc+ quickly does the rest. SUM adds up all the numbers from C9 through C17 and places the answer, 1900, into cell C19.

You can use the PC-Calc+ Copy command to enter the Totals formula for February and March. Do not move the cell pointer. Just follow these instructions to copy C19 to February:

Press /   (to activate the Main menu)
Press B   (to choose the (B)lock option)
Press C   (to choose the (C)opy option)

Type:
c19   (Source range to be copied)
and press ENTER

Type:
e19   (Target range into which C19 gets copied)
and press ENTER

When you enter the target range and press ENTER, the "Relative or Fixed" option list appears. The highlight is on the "(K)eep as defined" option. Select that option to keep the relative cell references as they are defined:

Press ENTER or K

When you press ENTER, PC-Calc+ copies the formula in cell C19 to cell E19. At the same time, PC-Calc+ adjusts the formula to match its new location. The formula in cell E19 now reads:

SUM(E9:E17)

The total under the February Budget column is 1225. Repeat the same steps (used to copy January to February) to copy February (C19) to March (G19).

    Press /   (to activate the Main menu)
    Press B   (to choose the (B)lock option)
    Press C   (to choose the (C)opy option)

    Type:
    c19   (Source range to be copied)
    and press ENTER

    Type:
    g19   (Target range into which C19 gets copied)
    and press ENTER
    Press ENTER or K   (to choose (K)eep option)

When you press ENTER, PC-Calc+ copies the formula in cell C19 to cell G19. PC-Calc+ also adjusts the formula to match its new location, G19, as follows:

SUM(G9:G17)

The total for March Budget is 1300. Figure 11-15 shows the completed BUDGET spreadsheet. If your spreadsheet looks the same as the one in Figure 11-15, save your file. If you need to make adjustments or corrections first, do so, and then save your BUDGET spreadsheet.

 NOTE You might like to take a break now that you have completed building and saving the BUDGET spreadsheet. After a short break, you may want to spend a little time playing with your finished version of BUDGET. In the process of building BUDGET, you were introduced to a number of spreadsheet concepts as well as many PC-Calc+ features, commands, and functions.

Figure 11-15.

```
C20                  BUDGET                    Calc-all           Empty Cell
↓     A         B        C        D        E        F        G        H
 1
 2                             Budget: Three-Month Period
 3                                     (Dollars)
 4
 5
 6                       January              February            March
 7                       Budget    Actual    Budget   Actual     Budget   Actual
 8                       -------   -------   -------  -------    -------  -------
 9   Office Rent         500.00              500.00              500.00
10   Office Supplies     300.00              100.00               50.00
11   Computer Supplies    50.00               50.00               50.00
12   Telephone           150.00               75.00               75.00
13   Utilities           100.00               50.00               50.00
14   Printing            250.00
15   Marketing           150.00              150.00               75.00
16   Travel              200.00              200.00              400.00
17   Misc.               200.00              100.00              100.00
18                       -------   -------   -------  -------    -------  -------
19   Totals             1900.00             1225.00             1300.00
20
21
                                                                        mem=237K
/=Menu Options   F1=Context Help   F2=General Help   F3=Edit   F10=Recalc All
```

Completed BUDGET spreadsheet

You might like to let what you have experienced settle in a bit before you charge ahead to the next section of this chapter. If you leave PC-Calc+ and turn off your computer, remember to start PC-Calc+ by typing **pcc budget** from within the \PCCALC directory when you return.

Look at the Spreadsheet Formulas

 NOTE If you did not create a BUDGET spreadsheet in the previous section, you can use a copy of the completed BUDGET spreadsheet from *The Shareware Book* Convenience Disk. The Convenience Disk, which you purchase separately, contains a number of key files that correspond to the activities in this book.

If you do not have the Convenience Disk, and if you want to try the next set of examples on your computer, you must go back and create BUDGET as outlined in the previous section.

After you finish building even a small spreadsheet like BUDGET, you may forget which cells contain data and which contain formulas. Of course, you could move the cell pointer around to each cell and make notes of what is stored there. PC-Calc+ has a handy feature which provides you an easy way to find out what is in each cell. To use this feature, do the following:

    Press /   (to call up the Main menu)
    Press F   (to select the (F)ormat option)
    Press F   (to select the (F)ormulas option)

When you activate the (F)ormulas option of the (F)ormat command, the BUDGET spreadsheet screen changes to that shown in Figure 11-16. PC-Calc+ displays the formulas instead of the numerical results of the formulas. Labels are shown as text entries with a double quote mark (") in front of each label. *Constants* (numeric values that were input into a cell from the keyboard) are displayed as numbers. For example, almost all of the values in column C, January Budget, are constants. Cells C12 and C13, Telephone and Utilities, are formulas made up of two constants. All of the entries in the February and March Budget columns are formulas. All of the formulas in these two columns contain cell references to the January Budget column.

To obtain a record of how your spreadsheet is constructed, you can print the spreadsheet as it is currently set to display formulas.

To restore the spreadsheet to its normal state where it shows the numerical results of the formulas, you press the same sequence of keys:

    Press /   (to call up the Main menu)
    Press F   (to select the (F)ormat option)
    Press F   (to select the (F)ormulas option)

Figure 11-16.

```
C20                    BUDGET                Calc-all              Empty Cell
     A         B         C         D         E         F         G         H
 1
 2                              "Budget: Three-Month Period
 3                                     "(Dollars)
 4
 5
 6                     "January            "February           "March
 7                     "Budget  "Actual    "Budget  "Actual    "Budget  "Actual
 8                     "_____ "_____   "_____ "_____   "_____ "_____
 9  "Office Rent       500.00              C9                  C9
10  "Office Supplies   300.00              C10*1/3             C10*1/6
11  "Computer Supplies  50.00              C11                 C11
12  "Telephone         75+75               C12-75              C12-75
13  "Utilities         50+50               C13-50              C13-50
14  "Printing          250.00
15  "Marketing         150.00              C15                 C15*1/2
16  "Travel            200.00              C16                 C16+200
17  "Misc.             200.00              C17*1/2             C17*1/2
18                     "_____ "_____   "_____ "_____   "_____ "_____
19  "Totals            SUM(C9:C17)         SUM(E9:E17)         SUM(G9:G17)
20
21                                                                   mem=237K
/=Menu Options    F1=Context Help    F2=General Help    F3=Edit    F10=Recalc All
```

(F)ormulas option active

BUDGET once again displays the three columns of numbers, with the results of the formulas calculated at each of the cell locations.

Use a Spreadsheet for "What If" Questions

As mentioned previously in this chapter, one reason to use an electronic spreadsheet and its formulas is that you can ask "what if" questions. Some "what if" questions have obvious answers and require almost no thinking—much less the use of a spreadsheet. For example, the question posed earlier of "what if the rent is $600 instead of $500?" has an obvious answer: Each month's budget goes up by $100.

However, the electronic spreadsheet still has an advantage, over manual calculations even in this simple and obvious case. Because of the way the information is linked across columns, if you change the January Office Rent figure, the entire spreadsheet gets updated automatically. Try it, by doing the following:

At cell location C9, type:
600
and press ENTER

Almost instantly, your screen changes to the one shown in Figure 11-17. The new Office Rent figure appears across all three columns. The totals for each column are automatically updated.

 NOTE The linkages in this spreadsheet are relatively simple. In more complex spreadsheets, what may seem like a simple "what

Figure 11-17.

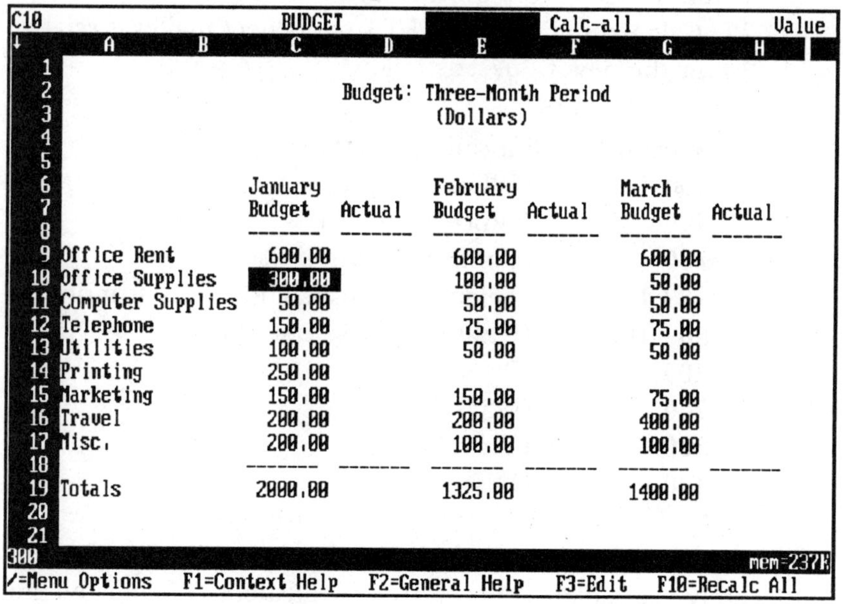

"What if" Office Rent is $600?

if" question may not have an obvious answer. One data item might depend on another data item which in turn depends on a third, and a fourth, and so on. Making what seems like a small change to one item might cause ripple effects all through the spreadsheet.

While many single changes to the BUDGET spreadsheet have obvious results, you also can use the power of the spreadsheet to ask more complex questions. These might be questions that you normally would not ask because of the tedious work involved. For example, suppose you wanted to ask "what if all of the budgeted figures are too low?" What if the rent is $600, office supplies are $400, computer supplies $100, telephone $100/month instead of $75, utilities $100/month instead of $50, printing $400, marketing starts off at $200, travel is $300, and miscellaneous is $400? This kind of "what if" question is often called a *worst case scenario*. To calculate the answer to this question—even with the simple three-month budget—is not easy. Using paper and pencil, you could not do it very quickly and you might make mistakes. Using PC-Calc+ and the BUDGET spreadsheet makes it relatively easy. Enter the new values, as follows:

Starting at cell location C9, type:
600	(Office Rent)
400	(Office Supplies)
100	(Computer Supplies)
75+100	(Telephone; installation + first month)
50+100	(Utilities; fee + first month)
400	(Printing)
200	(Marketing)
300	(Travel)
400	(Misc.)

As you type each new value and press ENTER, PC-Calc+ immediately recalculates the entire spreadsheet. When you finish with the last entry, the spreadsheet reflects all of your changes.

Figure 11-18 shows your worst case scenario. A quick comparison of Figure 11-15 with Figure 11-18 allows you to assess the possible risk involved if your original estimates actually varied as much as those shown in Figure 11-18. However, you do not need to calculate the variance in your head. PC-Calc+ has a "Quick Calc" feature for cases just like this. Do the following:

Press F9
Type:
sum(c19:g19) − 1900 − 1225 − 1300
and press ENTER

The SUM function adds up the three totals on the currently displayed spreadsheet. The three negative values come from the

Figure 11-18.

C18		BUDGET			Calc-all		Text
	A	B	C	D	E	F	G	H

				Budget: Three-Month Period			
				(Dollars)			
			January		February		March	
			Budget	Actual	Budget	Actual	Budget	Actual
			-------	-------	-------	-------	-------	-------
9	Office Rent		600.00		600.00		600.00	
10	Office Supplies		400.00		133.33		66.67	
11	Computer Supplies		100.00		100.00		100.00	
12	Telephone		175.00		100.00		100.00	
13	Utilities		150.00		100.00		100.00	
14	Printing		400.00					
15	Marketing		200.00		200.00		100.00	
16	Travel		300.00		300.00		500.00	
17	Misc.		400.00		200.00		200.00	
18			-------	-------	-------	-------	-------	-------
19	Totals		2725.00		1733.33		1766.67	
20								
21								

mem=237K

/=Menu Options   F1=Context Help   F2=General Help   F3=Edit   F10=Recalc All

Worst case scenario

BUDGET spreadsheet shown in Figure 11-15. PC-Calc+ displays the result of the "Quick Calc" formula in the center of the screen—1800. The worst case scenario results in a three-month budget increase of $1800, or about $600 per month. As the decision maker, you can use this information to decide if you could sustain this kind of increase.

The box in the center of the screen asks if you want to save the "Quick Calc" result. If you answer (Y)es, the result is saved at the current cell pointer location. In this example, the result would be saved at location C20. To not save the result, answer by either selecting (N)o or pressing ESC.

    Press N or ESC

This concludes the section on using a spreadsheet to answer "what if" questions and concludes this chapter on building the BUDGET spreadsheet. If you want to save the current altered version of BUDGET under another name, such as WORSTCAS, go ahead and save it. Otherwise, try not to accidently save this version of the spreadsheet onto the file BUDGET when you exit PC-Calc+. The way to exit PC-Calc+ without saving these changes is to do the following:

    Press /   (to call up the Main menu)
    Press Q   (to select the (Q)uit option)
    Press Q   (to select the (Q)uit - no save option)
    Press Y   (to confirm that you want to quit and not save)

Summary

In this chapter, you learned how to load and zap a spreadsheet. You discovered that zapping an existing spreadsheet and saving the zapped version under a new name gives you a new spreadsheet.

You loaded and zapped the EXPENSES spreadsheet and saved the zapped version under the name BUDGET. You built a finished version of BUDGET using a combination of PC-Calc+ commands, formulas, and the SUM function. You used a number of PC-Calc+ features and commands, including Copy, Smart, and the Relative and Fixed cell reference options.

You learned how to view a spreadsheet with either numeric values or formulas displayed in the cells. Finally, you used BUDGET to explore the connection between electronic spreadsheets and getting quick, efficient, and accurate answers to "what if" questions. In the process, you discovered the PC-Calc+ Quick Calc feature.

CHAPTER

Going Camping with a Spreadsheet

People devise thousands of unique applications for electronic spreadsheets in the areas of personal, business, and educational computing. One of the more interesting applications involves a project called "Problem-Solver's Backpack," designed by Bob Albrecht, one of the authors of this book. This project is ideal for an electronic spreadsheet because you must take into account several factors when arriving at the final cost of the items you decide to take with you on a special camping trip.

Problem-Solver's Backpack asks you to put together a list of what you need. You can take anything you want, with the following two constraints: the total weight of what you plan to take must fall between 50 and 60 pounds, and the cost of all the items you take cannot be more than $2,000. The solutions to Problem-Solver's Backpack vary according to who puts the list together. There are no "correct answers" because of the many tradeoffs involved. As you create the list of camping items needed for the project, you will learn more about PC-Calc+, including how to build a spreadsheet that extends beyond the size of the window, how to format cells and resize columns, how to use the PC-Calc+ Copy command to prevent unnecessary typing, how to use PC-Calc+ formulas to perform accurate data conversions, and how to get PC-Calc+ to add up entire blocks of data with a few simple formulas.

To prepare you for this exercise, Figure 12-1 provides some of the background and guidelines for Problem-Solver's Backpack.

For the classroom projects, the students are given copies of either the Recreational Equipment, Inc. (REI) catalog or the CAMPMOR catalog. The only restriction imposed is that everything must come from one catalog to simplify the verification process. For each item selected, the students write down the catalog page number, the item number or code, the description of the item, the quantity of each item, the item's price, and the item's weight in pounds and ounces (the way the weights appear in the catalogs).

In one Problem-Solver's Backpack summer project, the students were encouraged to share their "funwork" (previously called homework) with their parents. Using the REI catalog, a nine year-old, Shannon, came up with her solution to the Problem-Solver's Backpack scenario as shown in Figure 12-2. Remember, no one solution is correct. Each solution reflects the individual adventurer's own preferences and ideas. With a little help from her parents and their home computer, Shannon computed the total price and total weight for each item, and then

Figure 12-1.

During the past few years, Bob Albrecht has been introducing a classroom learning project called "Problem-Solver's Backpack." The project has been used with teams of 3rd-6th graders at several schools during *situational lessons*. Teams of children are presented with a task that calls upon a number of problem-solving skills. For example, the Problem-Solver's Backpack scenario requires that the children use skills in math, science, geography, survival, orienteering, climatology, and comparative shopping, to name but a few. The Problem-Solver's Backpack scenario runs like this:

A Year in 30,000 B.C.

Pretend that you have invented a time machine. Your time machine can go backward into the past but not forward into the future. Also, for some unknown reason, your time machine cannot go into the recent past. It only goes into the far distant past.

You are interested in acquiring some firsthand information about how things were in 30,000 B.C. You plan to send yourself back to the year 30,000 B.C., plus or minus a few thousand years.

Imagine that you are about 20 years old. You will be gone for one year. You will explore and come back to report on the state of affairs in prehistoric North America at about 30,000 B.C. At that time, the weather was cold and the glaciers were much farther south. Summers were nice and not too hot. Winters were very cold.

Problem-Solver's Backpack (continued on next page)

Figure 12-1.

> You will soon leave on your time travel journey. Your time machine will transport you and a limited amount of equipment (50 to 60 pounds) back into prehistory. Because you spent so much money developing your time machine, you only have $2,000 to buy the equipment you wish to carry. You will have to survive for one year on what you take with you.

Problem-Solver's Backpack (continued)

computed the total cost and total weight of all the items put together.

Using the data in Figure 12-2, you can follow in Shannon's footsteps and use PC-Calc+ to build a spreadsheet to list the selected items and perform the required calculations.

Building the Backpack Spreadsheet

NOTE As you build the BACKPACK spreadsheet, you will be introduced to several new PC-Calc+ features, shortcuts, and commands. You are encouraged to go ahead and build BACKPACK using the step-by-step instructions that follow. If you want to skip over the final details of entering all of the data and formulas contained in Figure 12-2, you can load a copy of the completed BACKPACK spreadsheet from *The Shareware Book* Convenience Disk. If you do not have the Convenience Disk, you are strongly urged to create the full BACKPACK spreadsheet. The completed spreadsheet is used in both this chapter and in Chapter 13 to demonstrate various PC-Calc+ capabilities.

Figure 12-2.

```
                    Problem Solver's Backpack
                           30,000 B.C.

Page    Item #     Description      Qty    Price   Tot Price  Item-    Weight  Tot Weight
                                                              pounds   ounces  pounds
   3    G472-007   Rope             200    $0.15                         0.25
   5    G114-009   Boots              1   $79.95               2         7.00
   9    G240-098   Socks              4    $3.00                         3.00
  16    G105-100   Tennis shoes       1   $18.95               1         8.00
  21    G292-037   Shorts             2   $14.95                         4.50
  21    G299-002   Tank top           2    $8.95                         3.50
  22    G299-207   T-shirt            3    $9.95                         4.00
  24    G211-001   Turtle T-shirt     3   $11.45                         6.00
  24    G196-021   Pants              3   $20.50                         8.00
  26    G231-066   Underwear-top      2   $13.95                         5.00
  26    G234-034   Underwear-bottoms  2   $13.95                         4.50
  28    G141-018   Jacket             1  $189.95               2        15.00
  30    G239-052   Gloves             1    $7.95                         2.00
  30    G239-022   Mittens            1   $19.95                         3.00
  39    G238-155   Hat (screen)       1    $3.95                         1.00
  39    G238-139   Wool hat           1    $5.95                         2.00
  40    G332-057   Backpack           1  $299.95               7        11.00
  47    G409-131   Goggles            1   $11.95                         1.50
  50    G407-026   Toothbrush         1    $3.95                         2.00
  52    G353-051   Tent               1  $189.95               6        14.00
  59    G407-019   Matches            1    $0.95                         4.00
  71    G493-028   Fishing pole       1   $29.95               1         7.50
  62    G401-025   Cup                1    $2.95                         3.00
  62    G401-081   Utensils           1    $1.95                         2.00
  62    G401-026   Pots and pans      1   $17.95               1        13.00
  78    G407-046   First aid kit      1   $44.95               1         6.00
  78    G373-009   Sleeping bag       1  $199.95               2
  86    G404-028   Compass            1   $29.95                         3.00
  88    G402-147   Water bag          1    $4.95                         3.50
  88    G402-145   Shower             1   $12.95                        12.00
  88    G402-052   Water bottle       1    $2.75                         3.50
  89    G407-075   Water purifier     1  $167.95               1         7.00
  90    G403-019   Pocket knife       1   $22.95                         4.00
  90    G403-112   Knife              1   $27.95                         4.75
  90    G404-013   Saw                1   $12.95               1         1.00
  90    G404-019   Replacement blade  2    $3.75                         3.50
  95    G473-068   Hammer             1   $19.95               1         2.50
  95    G407-011   Survival matches   1    $2.95                         2.00
  20    G579-472   Harmonica          1   $15.95                        11.50
  20    G579-425   Juggling balls     1    $9.95                        14.50
  23    G408-094   Watch              1   $33.95                         0.50
  73    G495-154   Kite               1   $19.95                         4.50
  81    G374-041   Mattress           1   $34.95               1         1.00
  81    G407-106   Blanket            1    $9.50                        12.00
  49    G408-077   Binoculars         1  $109.95               1         5.00
  73    G491-049   Raft               1   $49.95               6         6.00
```

Raw BACKPACK data

If you turned off your computer, you need to boot your system and start PC-Calc+. When you see the DOS prompt and are on the hard disk directory:

Type:
cd \pccalc   (and press ENTER)
pcc   (and press ENTER)

PC-Calc+ starts up and displays a blank spreadsheet. To build the BACKPACK spreadsheet, perform the step-by-step instructions that follow.

To begin, enter the BACKPACK spreadsheet title lines:

At cell location D1, type:
Problem-Solver's Backpack
and press ENTER

At cell location E2, type:
30,000 B.C.
and press ENTER

To enter the column headings for BACKPACK, first set the PC-Calc+ Smart feature so that the cell pointer moves to the right each time you press ENTER:

Press /   (to bring up the Main menu)
Press C   (to choose (C)onfigure option)
Press S   (to choose (S)mart option)
Press R   (to choose (R)ight option)
Press X   (to exit the Configure options list)
Press N   (at the question of saving configuration to disk)

If you answer with (Y)es to the last question, the change you made to the configuration setting the Smart feature would be recorded permanently in the PC-Calc+ configuration file, PCCALC.PRO. For this exercise, there is no need to record the setting change. Go ahead and enter the column headings:

At cell locations A4 through I4, type:
Page #   (and press ENTER)
Item #   (and press ENTER)
Description (and press ENTER)
Qty   (and press ENTER)
Price   (and press ENTER)
Tot Price   (and press ENTER)
Item-   (and press ENTER)
Weight   (and press ENTER)
Tot Weight   (and press ENTER)

After you enter the last column label, "Tot Weight," the screen looks like the one shown in Figure 12-3. Notice how the information in cell C4 seems to have been truncated. If you move the cell pointer back to cell C4, you will see that all the characters of the label are still in the cell. The cell is simply not wide enough to display all of its contents on the screen. You will change the width of column C after you enter the next row of headings.

Enter three subheadings for the last three columns:

At cell locations G5 through I5, type:
pounds   (and press ENTER)
ounces   (and press ENTER)
pounds   (and press ENTER)

After the last entry, the cell pointer is in location J5. The spreadsheet columns A and B have moved off the left side of the screen. Move the cell pointer back to the beginning of row 4, cell location A4. You can move the cell pointer with the ← key. You also can use the PC-Calc+ (G)oto command:

Press / (to bring up the Main menu)
Press G (to choose (G)oto command)
At the prompt, type:
a4
and press ENTER

When you type **a4** and press ENTER, the cell pointer instantly moves to cell location A4. You can use the PC-Calc+ (G)oto command to fly immediately to any row, column, cell, or range. When you build large spreadsheets, the (G)oto command can save you time in moving about the worksheet.

Format Titles and Column Headings

With the cell pointer at the beginning of row 4, adjust the format of each cell in row 4. The standard format is text

Figure 12-3.

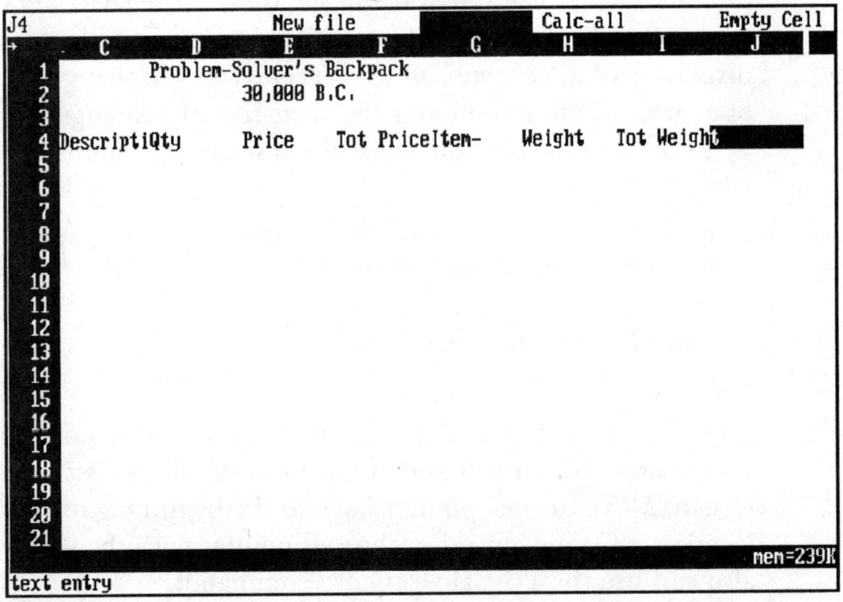

```
J4                       New file            Calc-all          Empty Cell
      C        D        E        F        G        H        I        J
 1             Problem-Solver's Backpack
 2                      30,000 B.C.
 3
 4  DescriptiQty        Price    Tot PriceItem-   Weight   Tot Weight
 5
 6
 7
 8
 9
10
11
12
13
14
15
16
17
18
19
20
21
                                                                   mem=239K
text entry
```

BACKPACK with row 4 column headings

left-justified and numbers right-justified. Do the following to display all the labels in row 4 in the center of their cells (center-justified):

    Press /   (to bring up the Main menu)
    Press F   (to choose (F)ormat option)
    Press C   (to choose (C)ells option)
    Press S   (to choose "(S)elect area" option)

The Format Area options list lets you define the area to which you will be applying the format changes. The "(S)elect area" option allows you to choose the specific area to format. When you press S, a prompt appears at the bottom of the screen asking you to enter the definition for the area. Select all of row 4, as follows:

    Press F6   (to clear the default entry, A4, from the input area)
    Type:
    4
    and press ENTER

Pressing ENTER highlights row 4, and the Cell Definition options list appears. This list controls many of the format options for spreadsheet cells. You will explore several of the Cell Definition features as you continue to build BACKPACK. For now, you want to change the justification of the cells in row 4. To the right of the (J)ustification option, the letter "S" indicates that the selected cells in row 4 currently have the standard setting: text left-justified. To change the (J)ustification option setting:

    Press J   (to choose (J)ustification option)
    Press C   (to choose (C)enter option)

When you press C, the screen flashes and the Cell Definition options list reappears. Note that the letter "C" now appears next to the (J)ustification option. The cells in row 4 have been center-justified. To exit from the Format options list:

Press X, X

Figure 12-4 shows the BACKPACK worksheet after row 4 has been center-justified. The centered labels are spread out and do not "bump" into each other. Before you applied center justification, cells C4 and D4 looked like this: "DescriptiQty." Now, there are spaces between the end of the label in cell C4 and the beginning of the label in cell D4. However, C4 still is not wide enough. You can easily fix that with another PC-Calc+ Format option. Move the cell pointer to C4 and do the following:

Press /   (to bring up the Main menu)
Press F   (to choose (F)ormat option)
Press W   (to choose (W)idth option)

Figure 12-4.

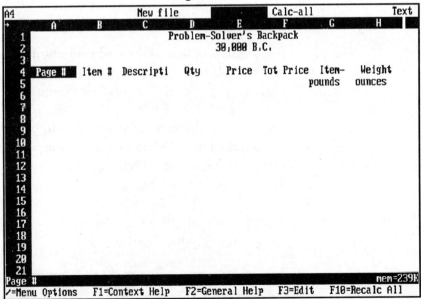

BACKPACK after center-justification of row 4

When you press W, PC-Calc+ displays a prompt at the bottom of the screen. The prompt asks you for the names of the columns you want to alter. If the cell pointer is on cell C4, the default will be set to "C," for column C. If the cell pointer is on another column, the default will be set to that column's name. To ensure that you are changing column C:

Press C and press ENTER

When you press ENTER, the prompt at the bottom of the screen changes to a request for the new column width. The current column is displayed in the input area. Column C is now 9 characters wide. Make the width of column C 18 characters wide:

Type:
18
and press ENTER

When you press ENTER, the screen changes to the one shown in Figure 12-5. The entire contents of cell C4 appears on the screen. The label is no longer truncated. PC-Calc+ widened the cells in column C to 18 characters and moved the columns beyond column C to the right, which caused column H to move out of view.

Make one more format change to the next row, row 5, and then save the spreadsheet. The three subheadings on row 5 might be aligned with the headings in row 4, if they were fully right-justified. Tell PC-Calc+ to right-justify row 5:

Press /   (to bring up the Main menu)
Press F   (to choose (F)ormat option)
Press C   (to choose (C)ells option)
Press S   (to choose "(S)elect area" option)

Press F6   (to clear the default entry from the input area)
Type:
5   (to select all of row 5)
and press ENTER

Press J   (to choose (J)ustification option)
Press R   (to choose (R)ight option)
Press X, X   (to exit the Format options list)

Notice that you did not have to place the cell pointer in any particular place to make the format changes. Your cell pointer might still be back on cell C4. PC-Calc+ allows you to alter cell formats anywhere on the spreadsheet. All you have to do is tell PC-Calc+ which cells to reformat and what new formats to use.

Figure 12-5.

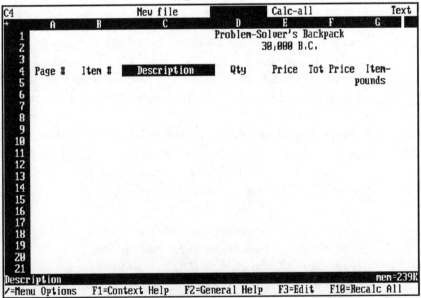

BACKPACK with column C widened

Go ahead and save your spreadsheet under the name BACKPACK:

Press /	(to bring up the Main menu)
Press L	(to choose (L)oad/Save option)
Press S	(to choose (S) Save spreadsheet option)
Press ENTER	(to select default path)
Press ENTER	(to select "New_File")

Type:
backpack
and press ENTER

BACKPACK has now been saved. You can either take a break or go on to the next step where you will begin to enter the data for the BACKPACK spreadsheet. If you take a break and shut down your computer, you should restart PC-Calc+ by typing **pcc backpack** to automatically reload the BACKPACK spreadsheet.

Enter the BACKPACK Data

An easy way to type most of the BACKPACK data is to set the Smart feature to move the cell pointer down the screen so that you can type the data by columns. However, before setting the Smart feature, go ahead and enter a complete row of data. Typing a complete row of data will let you see how each data entry looks on the screen, how you might like to reformat some columns to better display the data, and how to handle a few PC-Calc+ data entry activities that can cause problems. Type the first row of data that appears in Figure 12-2, in the designated columns:

At cell location A6, type:
3
and press ENTER

Next, enter the item number for the first item. The item number is the code in the camping catalog that is used to order the selected item.

> At cell location B6, type:
> **G472−007**
> and press ENTER

There seems to be a problem! When you pressed ENTER, a minus seven (−7.00) appeared in cell B6. PC-Calc+ accepted your *label* as a *formula,* because G472 is a valid cell location identifier. To PC-Calc+, the label looks like a formula that says: take the contents of cell G472 (which is zero) and subtract (−) seven (007). The result is −7.00.

To tell PC-Calc+ that you are entering a label and not a formula, you must type a quotation mark (") in front of the label entry:

> At cell location B6, type:
> **"G472−007**
> and press ENTER

Cell B6 should now contain G472−007 instead of −7.00. All of the entries in column B will have to be made with a leading quotation mark.

Type the description, the quantity, and the price for the first item on the list:

> At cell locations C6 through E6, type:
> **Rope**   (and press ENTER)
> **200**   (and press ENTER)
> **0.15**   (and press ENTER)

The rope weighs 1/4 ounce, or .25, per foot. Put this last entry into the ounces column of Item-Weight:

At cell location H6, type:
0.25
and press ENTER

Since each unit of rope weighs less than one pound, no entry is needed in cell G6. The values in cells F6 and I6 will be computed with a formula once all the data have been entered.

Format the Data Cells Move the cell pointer back to cell A6. Notice that the entries for the Page # column in Figure 12-2 are integers. The numbers have no decimal points or trailing zeros. You can tell PC-Calc+ to format all the numbers in column A as integers.

Press /	(to bring up the Main menu)
Press F	(to choose (F)ormat option)
Press C	(to choose (C)ells option)
Press S	(to choose "(S)elect area" option)
Press F6	(to clear the default entry from the input area)

Type:
a   (to select all of column A)
and press ENTER

Press D	(to choose (D)ecimals option)
Press N	(to choose "(N)umber of places")

Type:
0   (to select no decimals)
and press ENTER

Press X, X   (to exit the Format options list)

After you complete this sequence of command selections and data entries, the number in column A appears as the integer 3 instead of the decimal value 3.00.

To make your entries match those in Figure 12-2, you should apply this same format sequence to columns D and G. Go back through the same format sequence that was presented for column A. When you get to the point where you designate the area to be formatted, enter **d** the first time and **g** the second time. When you apply the format change to column D, the 200.00 will change to 200, with no decimal point or trailing zeros. When you apply the format to column G, nothing will change on the screen. However, when you later type data into column G, the numbers will be integers. There does not have to be data in the cells in order for you to format the cells.

When you have reformatted columns D and G, go on to the next step.

Move the cell pointer to column E, the Price column. In Figure 12-2 each item in column E is preceded by a dollar sign ($). The PC-Calc+ Format command can be used to automatically insert a dollar sign in front of spreadsheet values. To format column E with leading dollar signs:

Press /	(to bring up the Main menu)
Press F	(to choose (F)ormat option)
Press C	(to choose (C)ells option)
Press S	(to choose "(S)elect area" option)
Press F6	(to clear the default entry from the input area)

Type:
e   (to select all of column E)
and press ENTER

Press M   (to choose "(M)ask display" option)

When you select the "(M)ask display" option, the Display Masks options list appears on the left side of the screen. Most of the options on this list are *toggles*. When you select an option, that item changes to its opposite state. For example, if the option is off, then selecting it turns it on. If the option is on, selecting it turns it off. The option that controls dollar signs is the (M)onetary command, and its current state is off.

    Press M   (to toggle (M)onetary to "on")

When you press M, the word "off," located to the left of the (M)onetary command changes to a dollar sign ($). A dollar sign also appears in front of the Price column entry for Rope ($0.15). As you can see, PC-Calc+ lets you control a number of other display masks with the "(M)ask display" command. You will use more of these options as you continue to build BACKPACK. For now, exit from the Format command by pressing X three times:

    Press X, X, X   (to exit the Format options list)

Column F, which contains the total price for each item, will also display money figures. Follow the sequence just described to tell PC-Calc+ to place dollar signs in front of the data values in column F, except type **f** instead of **e** to identify the area to be formatted. Since column F has no current data values, nothing on the screen will change. Later, when you enter formulas to calculate the Tot Price column, the results in column F will have dollar signs.

NOTE As you made format changes to columns A, D, E, F, and G, the labels in rows 1 through 5 remained unaffected. PC-Calc+ knows the difference between cells with text entries and cells with data entries. The two types of entries can have completely separate formats, and PC-Calc+ displays each type according to its appropriate format specification.

Before going on to the next steps, save BACKPACK to preserve all of the format changes you have made.

Enter Data into Column A Move the cell pointer to A7. As mentioned earlier, the easiest way to input most of the BACKPACK data is by column. Now that you have set the formats for the columns, you can change the PC-Calc+ Smart feature to move the cell pointer down the screen. Then you can begin entering data for column A.

Press /	(to bring up the Main menu)
Press C	(to choose (C)onfigure option)
Press S	(to choose (S)mart option)
Press D	(to choose (D)own option)
Press X	(to exit the Configure options list)
Press N	(at the question of saving configuration to disk)

With the Smart feature set to move the cell pointer down the screen, turn back to Figure 12-2 and input the remaining values for column A. Although the list of numbers appears lengthy, you will be surprised at how fast you complete the entry task. The PC-Calc+ Smart feature makes the job go quickly. Because of the format change you made to this column, the entries should display as integers with no decimal point or trailing zeros.

The last entry for column A should be typed in row 51. If your first entry is in cell A6 and your last entry is *not* in cell A51, you probably skipped a page number somewhere. Figure 12-6 demonstrates the problem of a skipped number. The screen in

Figure 12-6 is missing the second entry, page number "5." All of the page numbers from A7 through A50 (off the screen) are correct, but in the wrong cells.

To get PC-Calc+ to help you move the numbers to their correct positions, use the (B)lock command:

Press /   (to bring up the Main menu)
Press B   (to choose (B)lock option)
Press M   (to choose (M)ove option)

Press F6   (to clear the default entry from the input area)

Type:
a7:a50   (to select all the entries to be moved)
and press ENTER

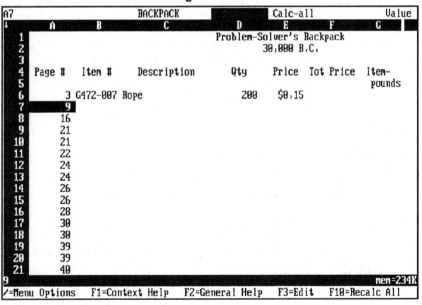

Figure 12-6.

Page # column with missing data item

The selected cells are highlighted, and the prompt at the bottom of the screen asks for the "cell or upper-left corner of the target." To move all of the highlighted entries down one cell, starting at cell A8:

Press F6   (to clear the default entry from the input area)

Type:
a8   (to select where the entries will be moved)
and press ENTER

When the target area is selected and ENTER is pressed, PC-Calc+ displays a message at the bottom of the screen warning that existing data is about to be overwritten. The program wants you to confirm that the overwrite is to take place.

Press Y

When Y is pressed, all of the highlighted entries move one position down the screen and cell A7 is left empty. You can enter the missing value, 5, into cell A7. When that value is in place, the correct page numbers now appear in cells A6 through A51.

When you have entered the column A data, stop and save BACKPACK, especially if you have not done so recently.

NOTE You may want to take a break before you finish building the BACKPACK spreadsheet. The partially completed BACK-PACK file is saved to your hard disk. You can exit PC-Calc+, turn off your computer, and return to the next step later, after a break. If you do leave PC-Calc+ and turn off your computer, remember to restart PC-Calc+ by typing **pcc backpack** from within the \PCCALC directory.

Enter Data into Column B   If you stopped PC-Calc+, turned off your computer, and took a break, reboot the computer and restart PC-Calc+ from the \PCCALC directory. You can automatically bring up the BACKPACK spreadsheet by typing **pcc backpack** at the system prompt from within the \PCCALC directory.

 NOTE If you do not have a partially completed version of BACKPACK, you can retrieve a copy from *The Shareware Book* Convenience Disk. The Convenience Disk, which you purchase separately, contains a number of key files which correspond to the activities in this book. If you do not have the Convenience Disk, and if you want to try the rest of this section on your computer, you must go back and create BACKPACK as outlined previously in this section. The Convenience Disk also contains a file with the data already entered for column B on the BACKPACK spreadsheet. You can use this file if you want to skip over this step in the process of building BACKPACK.

The text data in column B is not critical to having the calculations come out correctly. Use your own judgement and input as many or as few of the column B entries as you feel like doing. You are encouraged to input data at least through cell B30, the item number for "Pots and pans."

To enter the data for Column B, the Item # column, all you need to remember is to insert a quotation mark (") in front of each text entry, so that PC-Calc+ will not think your item numbers are formulas. For example, to input the second item number:

At cell location B7, type:
"G114−009
and press ENTER

If you complete the entries for column B, they should extend down through B51. If you end up with too many or too few entries, look back at the suggestions on using the PC-Calc+ Block/Move command to correct errors.

Enter Data into Column C The comments about the text entries for column B also apply to those for column C. The entries are not critical to calculations. You can enter as many or as few as you wish. You are encouraged to input entries at least through cell C30, "Pots and pans." If you have the Convenience Disk, you can load the copy of BACKPACK that has the text entries for column C already in place.

If you enter all of the BACKPACK data, you will get a feel for the amount of time and effort involved in creating a large spreadsheet. You should be pleasantly surprised at how quickly you can enter data using the PC-Calc+ Smart feature.

PC-Calc+ also has an Import feature that allows you to import data from a variety of files created by other shareware products. For example, the data in Figure 12-2 could have been created in your word processor and then imported into PC-Calc+. Conversely, PC-Calc+ allows you to output your spreadsheets into files that can be used by other shareware programs, including your favorite shareware word processor. Figure 12-2 was created in this reverse manner. The data entries were first entered into PC-Calc+, then output into a file, and then word processed into the figure format.

Enter Data into Column D The entries in column D, Qty (quantity), are critical to the calculations that will be made. The number of entries required is not as large as it looks.

At cell locations D7 through D17, type:
1   (and press ENTER)
4   (and press ENTER)
1   (and press ENTER)
2   (and press ENTER)
2   (and prcss ENTER)
3   (and press ENTER)
3   (and press ENTER)
3   (and press ENTER)

2	(and press ENTER)
2	(and press ENTER)
1	(and press ENTER)

Since you previously made a format change to this column instructing PC-Calc+ to use zero decimal places, the displayed values will be integers.

When you finish the data entry for D17, look down through the rest of the entries on Figure 12-2. Except for the two (2) at "Replacement blade," all of the remaining entries are one (1). Use the PC-Calc+ Block command to fill the cells from D18 through D51 with the number one. Then, go back and correct the entry at "Replacement blade."

Press /	(to bring up the Main menu)
Press B	(to choose (B)lock option)
Press F	(to choose (F)ill option)
Press F6	(to clear the default entry from the input area)

Type:
d18:d51   (to select the entry to be filled)
and press ENTER

When you designate which cells to be filled, those cells are highlighted. The program prompts you for the value with which you wish to fill the cells. The PC-Calc+ Fill feature can place the same value into each cell, as required in this case. You can also direct the program to start with a value, and then increment the value based on row and column positions, if, for example, you wanted 1.01 in the first cell, 1.02 in the second cell, 1.03 in the third cell, and so forth.

Type:
1   (to set the Fill value)
and press ENTER

When you press ENTER, PC-Calc+ instantly fills cells D18 through D51. Next, correct the entry for "Replacement blade" at cell D41.

At cell location D41, type:
2
and press ENTER

Save the BACKPACK spreadsheet before you continue with the next step of entering data in the Price column.

Enter Data into Column E   Even though most of the price entries in Figure 12-2 end with 95 cents, there is no reasonable shortcut to directly entering the values. Shannon, in putting together her list of items, could have rounded up each item to the nearest dollar. However, as you will soon see, each nickel she saved let her keep needed items on the list without exceeding the budget of $2,000. In fact, to Shannon, pennies became important.

Go ahead and enter the Price column figures, starting at cell E7 for "Boots" and ending at cell E51 with "Raft." If you get to the end of the list and notice that you have too few or too many entries, check column E against Figure 12-2 and correct the mistakes. The entries in column E will affect the totals that will be calculated.

Enter Data into Columns G and H   It is time to type the final two columns of values, Item-Weight pounds and ounces, columns G and H. If you attempt to type the values for pounds, you may discover that you have difficulty keeping pound entries aligned with the corresponding items on the left side of the screen. Here is an opportunity to use another PC-Calc+ feature, "Title locking," to *fold* your electronic spreadsheet and make the alignment task easier. First, move the cell pointer anywhere in column D. Then, do the following:

With the cell pointer in column D:
Press /   (to bring up the Main menu)
Press T   (to choose "(T)itle locking" option)
Press C   (to choose (C)olumn option)

When you press C to lock the column titles to the left of the cell pointer, PC-Calc+ highlights all of columns A, B, and C. The highlighted columns are now *locked* and will not move as you scroll off the right side of the screen.

Press → six times

The first three times you press →, the cell pointer moves toward the right screen edge. The next three times you press →, the program seems to slide, or fold, columns D, E, and F under the highlighted edge of column C. Figure 12-7 shows what the screen looks like with locked titles in columns A, B, and C. The right half of the worksheet area has been scrolled so that column G is displayed next to column C.

With the titles locked in this way, you can easily input the values for pounds and ounces. Go ahead and enter the remaining two columns of values. Here again, these values are important to the final calculations about to be performed.

When you finish the data entry tasks for columns G and H, unlock the titles as follows:

Press /   (to bring up the Main menu)
Press T   (to choose "(T)itle locking" option)
Press U   (to choose (U)nlock option)

When you press U, the locked, highlighted titles are unlocked, and the highlighted area over columns A, B, and C disappears. The BACKPACK data entry task is now complete.

Save BACKPACK before you proceed to the next step in which you will print this version of BACKPACK on your printer.

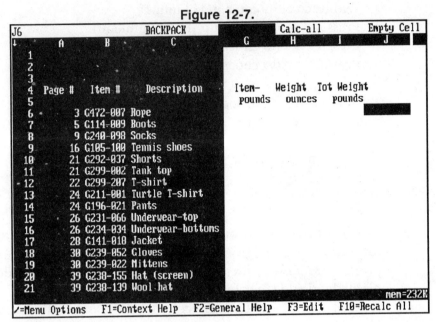

Figure 12-7.

BACKPACK with titles locked

Print BACKPACK

Once you have a spreadsheet that goes off the screen to the side and to the bottom, it is difficult to keep track of what you have typed. A solution is to print the spreadsheet and use that printed copy for verification work. To print a PC-Calc+ spreadsheet the size of BACKPACK, you need to do two things: set your printer to a compressed printing format and alter the program's configuration so that PC-Calc+ prints more than the standard number of characters across the page.

Setting a printer to a compressed printing format can be accomplished on most printers by setting a switch on the printer itself. Usually, using compressed printing means that the printer can print 132 or more characters across a normal 8 1/2- by 11-inch page. After you change the switch setting, do the following to change the PC-Calc+ printer configuration settings:

Press /	(to bring up the Main menu)
Press C	(to choose (C)onfigure option)
Press P	(to choose "(P)rinter setup" option)
Press R	(to choose "(R)eport setup" option)
Press P	(to choose "(P)age layout" option)

Figure 12-8 shows the screen that appears when you choose the "(P)age layout" option. You want to change the fourth option on

Figure 12-8.

```
┌─────────────────────────────────┐                    Print Defaults
│   Page Layout and Destination   │   The page layout should be set
│                                 │   assuming 10 characters per inch
├─────────────────────┬───────────┤   across the page and 6 lines per
│  Variable           │  Value    │   inch down the page.
├─────────────────────┼───────────┤
│ Lines per page      │ 66        │   To send output to printer, specify
│ Lines in header     │ 6         │   LPT1, LPT2, etc.  To send output
│ Lines in footer     │ 4         │   to a file, enter complete filespec.
│ Columns per page    │ 80        │
│ Columns - left margin│ 5        │   Enter 99 in columns/page or lines/
│ Columns - right margin│ 0       │   page if no limit in that direction.
│ Spacing (1, 2 or 3) │ 1         │
│ Target output location│ LPT1    │
├─────────────────────┴───────────┤
│ Use ↑↓←→ to move highlight.     │
│ Press / to exit                 │
└─────────────────────────────────┘
```

Page layout and destination screen

the list, "Columns per page." The current setting is 80 columns per page, which is not wide enough to print BACKPACK. You need to set the "Columns per page" option to 132.

Move the highlight down to the "Columns per page" option and do the following:

Type:
132
and press ENTER

To exit from this screen, press the slash character (/). When you press slash (/), PC-Calc+ displays an Exit menu option.

Press X

The program then redisplays the Print Format options list. To exit from the Configuration command:

Press X, X, X

On entering the final X, a question box appears in the middle of the screen asking you if you want to save this new configuration. In this case, you want to save the configuration, because you may need to print additional versions of BACKPACK as you proceed.

Press Y

When you press Y, the program prompts you for the path name of the PC-Calc+ configuration file. Since you are already in the \PCCALC directory:

Press ENTER

A file name list appears in the center of the screen, containing two entries: New_File and PCCALC. Move the highlight onto the name PCCALC. When the highlight is on PCCALC:

Press ENTER

With the program's configuration changed and with your printer hooked up, turned on, and set to compressed mode, activate the PC-Calc+ Print command:

Press /	(to bring up the Main menu)
Press P	(to choose (P)rint/Graph option)
Press P	(to choose (P)rint option)
Press S	(to choose (S)creen option)

The program prompts you for the destination of the printed report. The default is LPT1, which is the most common output port for printers. If your printer is attached to another communications port, enter the name of the port in place of LPT1. You can also use this option to print the report to a file, by supplying a file name. Press ENTER to tell PC-Calc+ where you want to send the report:

Press ENTER

The program prompts you for a title, which will be centered above the body of the printed spreadsheet. Enter the following title:

Type:
BACKPACK Data Table
and press ENTER

Another prompt appears asking you for the source definition of the cells to be printed. The default is set to ALL. Choosing ALL will cause PC-Calc+ to print all of the active, that is, non-empty, cells.

Press ENTER

The Print Details options list appears. The most commonly used option, "(P)roceed with print" is highlighted.

Press P

When you press P, a question box appears asking you if you want to save the definition information in a table. For now, select the (N)o option. You will learn about PC-Calc+ tables in Chapter 13.

Press N

When you press N, if all goes well, BACKPACK will print on your printer. A message at the bottom of the screen tells you what percentage of BACKPACK remains to be printed. For extremely large reports, including reports that got too large by mistake, this indicator helps you gauge how many pages will be printed. For example, if one page prints and you still have 99% to go, you may want to reconsider printing the report.

When PC-Calc+ finishes printing your report, an information box appears in the middle of the screen asking you to press any key to continue. When you press a key, the Print/Graph options list reappears. To get back to the worksheet screen:

Press X

Figure 12-9 displays the printed BACKPACK report as it has been generated up to this point. The report with compressed characters should fit on a single 8 1/2- by 11-inch piece of paper. (On

Figure 12-9.

```
Tuesday September 5,1990                                                  19:48:08
                            BACKPACK Data Table
--------------------------------------------------------------------------------
                           Problem Solver's Backpack
                                  30,000 B.C.

  Page    Item #     Description    Qty    Price    Tot Price  Item- Weight  Tot Weight
                                                               pounds ounces pounds
    3   G472-007   Rope             200    $0.15                        0.25
    5   G114-009   Boots              1   $79.95                 2      7.00
    9   G240-098   Socks              4    $3.00                        3.00
   16   G105-100   Tennis shoes       1   $18.95                 1      8.00
   21   G292-037   Shorts             2   $14.95                        4.50
   21   G299-002   Tank top           2    $8.95                        3.50
   22   G299-207   T-shirt            3    $9.95                        4.00
   24   G211-001   Turtle T-shirt     3   $11.45                        6.00
   24   G196-021   Pants              3   $20.50                        8.00
   26   G231-066   Underwear-top      2   $13.95                        5.00
   26   G234-034   Underwear-bottoms  2   $13.95                        4.50
   28   G141-018   Jacket             1  $189.95                 2     15.00
   30   G239-052   Gloves             1    $7.95                        2.00
   30   G239-022   Mittens            1   $19.95                        3.00
   39   G238-155   Hat (screen)       1    $3.95                        1.00
   39   G238-139   Wool hat           1    $5.95                        2.00
   40   G332-057   Backpack           1  $299.95                 7     11.00
   47   G409-131   Goggles            1   $11.95                        1.50
   50   G407-026   Toothbrush         1    $3.95                        2.00
   52   G353-051   Tent               1  $189.95                 6     14.00
   59   G407-019   Matches            1    $0.95                        4.00
   71   G493-028   Fishing pole       1   $29.95                 1      7.50
   62   G401-025   Cup                1    $2.95                        3.00
   62   G401-081   Utensils           1    $1.95                        2.00
   62   G401-026   Pots and pans      1   $17.95                 1     13.00
   78   G407-046   First aid kit      1   $44.95                 1      6.00
   78   G373-009   Sleeping bag       1  $199.95                 2
   86   G404-028   Compass            1   $29.95                        3.00
   88   G402-147   Water bag          1    $4.95                        3.50
   88   G402-145   Shower             1   $12.95                       12.00
   88   G402-052   Water bottle       1    $2.75                        3.50
   89   G407-075   Water purifier     1  $167.95                 1      7.00
   90   G403-019   Pocket knife       1   $22.95                        4.00
   90   G403-112   Knife              1   $27.95                        4.75
   90   G404-013   Saw                1   $12.95                 1      1.00
   90   G404-019   Replacement blade  2    $3.75                        3.50
   95   G473-068   Hammer             1   $19.95                 1      2.50
   95   G407-011   Survival matches   1    $2.95                        2.00
   20   G579-472   Harmonica          1   $15.95                       11.50
   20   G579-425   Juggling balls     1    $9.95                       14.50
   23   G408-094   Watch              1   $33.95                        0.50
   73   G495-154   Kite               1   $19.95                        4.50
   81   G374-041   Mattress           1   $34.95                 1      1.00
   81   G407-106   Blanket            1    $9.50                       12.00
   49   G408-077   Binoculars         1  $109.95                 1      5.00
   73   G491-049   Raft               1   $49.95                 6      6.00
```

The printed BACKPACK spreadsheet

your printer, you might get a second blank page.) PC-Calc+ inserts header information from the system time and date functions, the title you typed for the report, and dashed lines at the top and bottom. Below the bottom dashed line is a page count. Check the printed version of your BACKPACK spreadsheet against the one shown in Figure 12-9 to ensure that you have entered the BACKPACK data correctly.

If you have problems getting PC-Calc+ to print your spreadsheet, first try the following:

Press /   (to bring up the Main menu)
Press L   (to choose (L)oad/Save option)
Press P   (to choose (P) "Load print codes")

When you select the P option, the program prompts you for the path name of the printer files. You are already on the \PCCALC directory, and the printer files were placed into \PCCALC during the installation process.

Press ENTER

After you press ENTER, a file name selection list appears in the middle of the screen. The list contains the names of several printers. If you see your printer listed, move the highlight to that name. If you do not see your printer listed, check your printer manual to see if one of the listed printers matches your printer's operations. If you have no printer manual handy, try using a printer name that you think will work. When you have selected a printer name:

Press ENTER

With a specific printer selected, try printing BACKPACK again. If you still encounter difficulties, and you are a registered PC-Calc+ owner, call ButtonWare Technical Support, which is listed in the front of your *PC-Calc+ User's Manual*.

Install the Price Formulas

You have now completed the task of entering the BACKPACK data. The next few steps show you how to install the formulas that tell PC-Calc+ what calculations you want done. Figure 12-10 shows Shannon's camping list with all the data and calculations complete. Refer to Figure 12-10 as you proceed to install your own calculation formulas into the BACKPACK spreadsheet.

To begin, move the cell pointer to F6, the first cell in Tot Price, column F. The formula for computing the total price at any cell location is the following:

Quantity * Price

The following is the specific formula for total price at cell F6:

D6*E6

Go ahead and type the total price formula into cell F6:

At cell location F6, type:
d6*e6
and press ENTER

Figure 12-10.

```
                    Problem Solver's Backpack
                          30,000 B.C.

Page  Item #     Description         Qty    Price   Tot Price  Item-    Weight   Tot Weight
                                                               pounds   ounces   pounds
  3   G472-007   Rope                200   $0.15     $30.00              0.25     3.13
  5   G114-009   Boots                 1  $79.95     $79.95       2      7.00     2.44
  9   G240-098   Socks                 4   $3.00     $12.00              3.00     0.75
 16   G105-100   Tennis shoes          1  $18.95     $18.95       1      8.00     1.50
 21   G292-037   Shorts                2  $14.95     $29.90              4.50     0.56
 21   G299-002   Tank top              2   $8.95     $17.90              3.50     0.44
 22   G299-207   T-shirt               3   $9.95     $29.85              4.00     0.75
 24   G211-001   Turtle T-shirt        3  $11.45     $34.35              6.00     1.13
 24   G196-021   Pants                 3  $20.50     $61.50              8.00     1.50
 26   G231-066   Underwear-top         2  $13.95     $27.90              5.00     0.63
 26   G234-034   Underwear-bottoms     2  $13.95     $27.90              4.50     0.56
 28   G141-018   Jacket                1 $189.95    $189.95       2     15.00     2.94
 30   G239-052   Gloves                1   $7.95      $7.95              2.00     0.13
 30   G239-022   Mittens               1  $19.95     $19.95              3.00     0.19
 39   G238-155   Hat (screen)          1   $3.95      $3.95              1.00     0.06
 39   G238-139   Wool hat              1   $5.95      $5.95              2.00     0.13
 40   G332-057   Backpack              1 $299.95    $299.95       7     11.00     7.69
 47   G409-131   Goggles               1  $11.95     $11.95              1.50     0.09
 50   G407-026   Toothbrush            1   $3.95      $3.95              2.00     0.13
 52   G353-051   Tent                  1 $189.95    $189.95       6     14.00     6.88
 59   G407-019   Matches               1   $0.95      $0.95              4.00     0.25
 71   G493-028   Fishing pole          1  $29.95     $29.95       1      7.50     1.47
 62   G401-025   Cup                   1   $2.95      $2.95              3.00     0.19
 62   G401-081   Utensils              1   $1.95      $1.95              2.00     0.13
 62   G401-026   Pots and pans         1  $17.95     $17.95       1     13.00     1.81
 78   G407-046   First aid kit         1  $44.95     $44.95       1      6.00     1.38
 78   G373-009   Sleeping bag          1 $199.95    $199.95       2               2.00
 86   G404-028   Compass               1  $29.95     $29.95              3.00     0.19
 88   G402-147   Water bag             1   $4.95      $4.95              3.50     0.22
 88   G402-145   Shower                1  $12.95     $12.95             12.00     0.75
 88   G402-052   Water bottle          1   $2.75      $2.75              3.50     0.22
 89   G407-075   Water purifier        1 $167.95    $167.95       1      7.00     1.44
 90   G403-019   Pocket knife          1  $22.95     $22.95              4.00     0.25
 90   G403-112   Knife                 1  $27.95     $27.95              4.75     0.30
 90   G404-013   Saw                   1  $12.95     $12.95       1      1.00     1.06
 90   G404-019   Replacement blade     2   $3.75      $7.50              3.50     0.44
 95   G473-068   Hammer                1  $19.95     $19.95       1      2.50     1.16
 95   G407-011   Survival matches      1   $2.95      $2.95              2.00     0.13
 20   G579-472   Harmonica             1  $15.95     $15.95             11.50     0.72
 20   G579-425   Juggling balls        1   $9.95      $9.95             14.50     0.91
 23   G408-094   Watch                 1  $33.95     $33.95              0.50     0.03
 73   G495-154   Kite                  1  $19.95     $19.95              4.50     0.28
 81   G374-041   Mattress              1  $34.95     $34.95       1      1.00     1.06
 81   G407-106   Blanket               1   $9.50      $9.50             12.00     0.75
 49   G408-077   Binoculars            1 $109.95    $109.95       1      5.00     1.31
 73   G491-049   Raft                  1  $49.95     $49.95       6      6.00     6.38
                                                   $1999.35                      56.39
```

Complete BACKPACK data

When you type this formula and press ENTER, the value $30.00 should automatically appear in cell F6. The leading dollar sign is the result of your previously selecting the Monetary format option.

You do not need to type formulas in all the other cells in column F, because PC-Calc+ can do it for you! You can use the PC-Calc+ Block command to copy the F6 formula into cells F7 through F51, and let PC-Calc+ do the work of changing the cell references to match the new cell locations. Ready? Go!

Press /   (to bring up the Main menu)
Press B   (to choose (B)lock option)
Press C   (to choose (C)opy option on Block options list)
Press F6   (to clear the default entry in the input area)

Type:
f6   (to select the formula to be copied)
and press ENTER

Press F6   (to clear the default entry in the input area)

Type:
f7:f51   (to select the cells to receive a copy of F6)
and press ENTER

Press K   (to select (K)eep as defined option)

In a flash, PC-Calc+ fills cells F7 through F51 with altered copies of the formula from cell F6. The entire column is filled with calculated values with dollar signs.

Scroll down to F51 and verify that the formulas were copied correctly. To scroll to F51, you can either use the arrow keys, or, if you want to fly a bit faster, use the PGDN key. Then use the PGUP key to fly back up to the top of the spreadsheet.

Install the Weight Formulas

After you verify that the results in column F are correct, move the cell pointer to I6. In column I, you want to compute the total weight of every item in pounds. In several cases, Shannon has selected more than one of each item. Also, within the computation, you must account for part of the weight being in pounds and part in ounces. The general formula for the calculation looks like this:

Quantity * (pounds + ounces/16)

The weight of each set of items on the list is obtained by multiplying the quantity of items selected by the sum of the pounds plus the ounces, converted to pounds, for each item. To convert ounces to pounds, you divide the ounces by 16, since 1 pound is equal to 16 ounces.

The corresponding formula for cell I6, including specific cell notations, is the following:

D6 * (G6 + H6/16)

First, type the total weight formula into cell I6:

At cell location I6, type:
d6*(g6*h6/16)
and press ENTER

When you type the formula and press ENTER, the value 3.13 appears in cell I6. Is this correct? It is not easy to perform the calculation without a computer, but here goes! Each foot of rope weighs 1/4 ounce, and Shannon wants 200 feet. Since the value in cell G6 is zero, the result in I6 can be formulated as any of the following:

200 * (0 + 0.25/16)
200 * 0.25/16
50/16
3.125

When rounded up and displayed with two decimal places, 3.125 becomes 3.13!

Next, use the PC-Calc+ Block command to copy the I6 formula into cells I7 through I51, just as you did for the Tot Price column.

Press /	(to bring up the Main menu)
Press B	(to choose (B)lock option)
Press C	(to choose (C)opy option on Block options list)
Press F6	(to clear the default entry in the input area)

Type:
i6   (to select the formula to be copied)
and press ENTER

Press F6   (to clear the default entry in the input area)
Type:
i7:i51   (to select the cells to receive a copy of F6)
and press ENTER

Press K   (to select (K)eep as defined option)

PC-Calc+ fills the designated cells with altered copies of the I6 formula. In a blink of your eye, the cells in column I fill up with the total weight for each item.

Create Summary Totals

Look over the spreadsheet to see if there are any problems. If there are no problems, add the following two final touches to BACKPACK, which will let you know if you and Shannon are using the same data.

Move the cell pointer to anywhere in row 6. With the cell pointer in row 6, lock the row titles:

With the cell pointer in row 6:
Press /   (to bring up the Main menu)
Press T   (to choose "(T)itle locking" option)
Press R   (to choose (R)ow option)

Figure 12-11 shows BACKPACK with the top five title rows locked. The five rows are highlighted by PC-Calc+. Use a combination of the arrow keys and the PGDN key to move the cell pointer to cell location F52. The screen should appear somewhat like the one shown in Figure 12-12. With the row titles locked, you can scroll down the spreadsheet while keeping the column titles in view.

Figure 12-11.

I6		BACKPACK			Calc-all		Function
	C	D	E	F	G	H	I
1		Problem-Solver's Backpack					
2			30,000 B.C.				
3							
4		Description	Qty	Price	Tot Price	Item-	Weight	Tot Weigh
5						pounds	ounces	pounds
6	Rope	200	$0.15	$30.00		0.25	3.13
7	Boots	1	$79.95	$79.95	2	7.00	2.44
8	Socks	4	$3.00	$12.00		3.00	0.75
9	Tennis shoes	1	$18.95	$18.95	1	8.00	1.50
10	Shorts	2	$14.95	$29.90		4.50	0.56
11	Tank top	2	$8.95	$17.90		3.50	0.44
12	T-shirt	3	$9.95	$29.85		4.00	0.75
13	Turtle T-shirt	3	$11.45	$34.35		6.00	1.13
14	Pants	3	$20.50	$61.50		8.00	1.50
15	Underwear-top	2	$13.95	$27.90		5.00	0.63
16	Underwear-bottoms	2	$13.95	$27.90		4.50	0.56
17	Jacket	1	$109.95	$109.95	2	15.00	2.94
18	Gloves	1	$7.95	$7.95		2.00	0.13
19	Mittens	1	$19.95	$19.95		3.00	0.19
20	Hat (screen)	1	$3.95	$3.95		1.00	0.06
21	Wool hat	1	$5.95	$5.95		2.00	0.13

D6*(G6+H6/16)   mem=223K
/=Menu Options   F1=Context Help   F2=General Help   F3=Edit   F10=Recalc All

BACKPACK with row titles locked

Figure 12-12.

F52		BACKPACK			Calc-all		Empty Cell
	C	D	E	F	G	H	I
1		Problem-Solver's Backpack					
2		30,000 B.C.					
3							
4	Description	Qty	Price	Tot Price	Item–	Weight	Tot Weight
5					pounds	ounces	pounds
39	Knife	1	$27.95	$27.95		4.75	0.30
40	Saw	1	$12.95	$12.95	1	1.00	1.06
41	Replacement blade	2	$3.75	$7.50		3.50	0.44
42	Hammer	1	$19.95	$19.95	1	2.50	1.16
43	Survival matches	1	$2.95	$2.95		2.00	0.13
44	Harmonica	1	$15.95	$15.95		11.50	0.72
45	Juggling balls	1	$9.95	$9.95		14.50	0.91
46	Watch	1	$33.95	$33.95		0.50	0.03
47	Kite	1	$19.95	$19.95		4.50	0.28
48	Mattress	1	$34.95	$34.95	1	1.00	1.06
49	Blanket	1	$9.50	$9.50		12.00	0.75
50	Binoculars	1	$109.95	$109.95	1	5.00	1.31
51	Raft	1	$49.95	$49.95	6	6.00	6.38
52							
53							
54							

mem=223K

/=Menu Options   F1=Context Help   F2=General Help   F3=Edit   F10=Recalc All

Cell pointer at cell F52 and row titles locked

With the cell pointer on cell F52, enter a formula that adds up the Tot Price column. This result is an important measure in the Problem-Solver's Backpack project, because the price of all the items should not be over $2,000. To sum the Tot Price column, use the PC-Calc+ SUM function:

At cell location F52, type:
sum(f6:f51)
and press ENTER

PC-Calc+ hesitates for a moment after you press ENTER. A message flashes near the center of the screen telling you that the program is calculating. In a moment, the value $1999.95 appears. Good work, Shannon! If your value matches Shannon's, good work on your part as well!

If your spreadsheet has a different number in F52, then either the data values in columns D and E are not the same as Shannon's, or there is a problem with the formula you used in F6. Before trying to check what happened, go ahead and enter the following formula in cell location I52:

At cell location I52, type:
sum(i6:i51)
and press ENTER

Did you get 56.39 pounds for the total weight of all of Shannon's items? If you obtained the same result, but you had a problem with total cost, what does that tell you? The quantity data column is correct. Therefore, any total price problem has to be in either column E or F. Of course, if both the total price and the total weight do not match with Shannon's numbers, then you might have problems with both columns D and E.

Before you go on to the final step in building the BACKPACK spreadsheet, unlock the row titles and save the BACKPACK spreadsheet, even if you did not get the same numbers shown in the figures. Later, if you want to chase down the differences between your version of BACKPACK and Shannon's answers, then you can print out a copy of BACKPACK with all the data and formulas and compare your printout with the information in Figure 12-10.

Reformat the Price Summary Total

To add a final touch to BACKPACK, move the cell pointer to cell F52. The number in cell F52 is not in the conventional format for dollar amounts. There is no comma in front of the hundreds dollar position. To be fully acceptable to financial and accounting people, the format for this value should be $1,999.95. To insert the needed comma, use the Format command:

With the cell pointer on cell location F52:
Press /   (to bring up the Main menu)
Press F   (to choose (F)ormat option)
Press C   (to choose (C)ells option)
Press S   (to choose "(S)elect area" option)
Press ENTER   (to accept default entry: F52)
Press M   (to choose "(M)ask display" option)
Press D   (to toggle (D)elimiters to "on")
Press X, X, X   (to exit the Format options list)

When you press D to toggle the Delimiters feature to "on," PC-Calc+ inserts a comma into the value displayed in F52. Cell F52 now has been set for the following two Mask display options: dollar sign, or (M)onetary, and commas, or (D)elimiters.

Look at what happened to cell F52. Instead of showing a neatly delimited value of $1,999.95, the cell is filled with asterisks (********).

When PC-Calc+ cannot fit all of the characters of a calculated data value into a cell, the program fills the cell with asterisks. The asterisks let you know that the cell is not wide enough to show all of the data. There are several ways to fix the current problem. You could reformat F52 as a comma delimited, integer dollar value with decimal point. Or, you could widen column F by one or two characters, using the same procedure you used to widen column C earlier in this chapter. You might even think of some other solutions.

For this exercise, reformat F52 as an integer. Later, you can experiment on your own with other ways of fixing a cell overflow problem.

With the cell pointer at cell location F52:

Press /	(to bring up the Main menu)
Press F	(to choose (F)ormat option)
Press C	(to choose (C)ells option)
Press S	(to choose "(S)elect area" option)
Press ENTER	(to accept default entry: F52)
Press D	(to choose (D)ecimals option)
Press N	(to select "(N)umber of places")

Type:
0	(to set number of decimals to zero = none)

and press ENTER

Press X, X	(to exit the Format options list)

When you complete this sequence of commands, the F52 cell displays $1,999 instead of a row of asterisks.

If you wish, you can save BACKPACK to include this latest change to cell F52. You will use the completed form of BACKPACK in Chapter 13 to explore additional PC-Calc+ features, functions, and capabilities.

Summary

In Chapter 12, you were introduced to the Problem-Solver's Backpack project, an innovative electronic spreadsheet application. In building the BACKPACK spreadsheet, you used the PC-Calc+ Format command to set the column headings in place, to widen a column, and to automatically insert dollar signs and commas into calculated data values.

You entered different types of data into the BACKPACK spreadsheet. As you entered data, you used the PC-Calc+ Smart feature to assist you with moving the cell pointer to adjacent cell locations. The Smart feature helped to facilitate the data entry tasks.

You told PC-Calc+ how to distinguish between text entries and formulas, by putting a quotation mark in front of some BACKPACK data items. You used the PC-Calc+ Block/Fill commands to speed up a data entry task. You learned how to use the PC-Calc+ "Title locking" command to help you align data entries.

You explored the PC-Calc+ Print command and the Configuration commands that control printer output. Finally, you quickly entered nearly 100 formulas into BACKPACK cells by using the PC-Calc+ Block/Copy commands.

CHAPTER

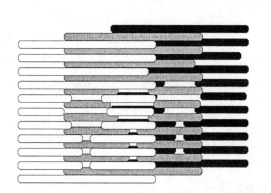

Importing, Graphing, and Other Features

In the previous chapters, you have used PC-Calc+ to build a small spreadsheet called BUDGET and a larger, more complex spreadsheet called BACKPACK.

In this chapter, you will use BUDGET and BACKPACK to continue your explorations of PC-Calc+ features and functions. In particular, you will use BACKPACK to:

- Examine the PC-Calc+ "Split screen" command, which allows you to open two windows onto the same spreadsheet. The "Split screen" command lets you quickly and easily compare two parts of a large spreadsheet. Using "Split screen" you can make changes in one part of a spreadsheet and watch the effects of the change in another part.

- Try the PC-Calc+ Block/Sort command, which lets you instantly sort entire spreadsheets by multiple columns and rows.
- Explore the PC-Calc+ Table feature, which lets you record a series of commands and data entries into a table which you can recall and use later.
- Examine the PC-Calc+ Import command. Using Import, you will move entire columns of results from BUDGET into a new spreadsheet, just by pressing a few keys.
- Experiment with the PC-Calc+ Graph command to generate graphics directly from the data imported from the BUDGET spreadsheet.

Back Up the BACKPACK File

In the next few sections, you will be working with the version of the BACKPACK spreadsheet developed in Chapter 12. You can use either a copy of BACKPACK that you created in Chapter 12 or a copy from *The Shareware Book* Convenience Disk. The Convenience Disk, which you purchase separately, contains a number of key files which correspond to the activities in this book. If you do not have the Convenience Disk or a completed version of BACKPACK, and if you want to try the next series of example sessions on your computer, you must go back and create BACKPACK as outlined in Chapter 12.

CAUTION Since nearly all of the subsequent examples involve alterations to BACKPACK, *make a backup copy* of the file before you begin your explorations. One way to make a backup copy of the file is to use the DOS COPY command and copy BACKPACK.PCC to a file with a different name, for example, BPACK. (The extension of the file to be copied must be included because DOS will not otherwise recognize the file name.) At the DOS prompt, and from within the \PCCALC directory, do the following:

Type:
copy backpack.pcc bpack
and press ENTER

When you type this DOS command sequence, a backup copy of BACKPACK.PCC is saved in the file called BPACK. If you need to restore BACKPACK.PCC to its original state, then all you would need to do is the following:

Type:
copy bpack backpack.pcc
and press ENTER

Another way to make a backup copy of BACKPACK is to load the file into PC-Calc+. When the file is loaded, use the PC-Calc+ Load/Save command to save the file under a new name.

In any case, make sure that you back up BACKPACK before you proceed.

Use the "Split Screen" Command

If you turned off your computer, you need to boot your system again and start PC-Calc+. When you see the DOS prompt on the hard disk directory, do the following:

Type:
cd \pccalc   (and press ENTER)
pcc backpack   (and press ENTER)

PC-Calc+ starts up and displays the BACKPACK spreadsheet. To make sure your screen corresponds to the figures you are about to see in this book, move the cell pointer to cell A1, at the upper left corner of the spreadsheet. You can either move the cell pointer with the arrow keys, or you can use the PC-Calc+ (G)oto command as follows:

Press /   (to bring up the Main menu)
Press G   (to choose (G)oto option)

At the prompt, type:
a1
and press ENTER

Split the Screen Horizontally

With the cell pointer at cell location A1, your screen should look like the one shown in Figure 13-1. Move the cell pointer down the screen to cell location A12 (column A, row 12). The cell pointer at cell A12 highlights the page number 22 entry, under the "Page #" column, for three T-shirts.

With the cell pointer at A12, activate the PC-Calc+ "Split screen" command:

Press /   (to bring up the Main menu)
Press S   (to choose "(S)plit screen" option)
Press H   (to choose (H)orizontal option)

Figure 13-1.

```
A1                    BACKPACK              Calc-all          Empty Cell
        A       B        C            D          E        F         G
   1                            Problem-Solver's Backpack
   2                                  30,000 B.C.
   3
   4   Page #  Item #   Description       Qty      Price   Tot Price   Item-
   5                                                                   pounds
   6          3 G472-007 Rope              200     $0.15    $30.00
   7          5 G114-009 Boots             1       $79.95   $79.95     2
   8          9 G240-090 Socks             4       $3.00    $12.00
   9         16 G105-100 Tennis shoes      1       $18.95   $18.95     1
  10         21 G292-037 Shorts            2       $14.95   $29.90
  11         21 G299-002 Tank top          2       $8.95    $17.90
  12         22 G299-207 T-shirt           3       $9.95    $29.85
  13         24 G211-001 Turtle T-shirt    3       $11.45   $34.35
  14         24 G196-021 Pants             3       $20.50   $61.50
  15         26 G231-066 Underwear-top     2       $13.95   $27.90
  16         26 G234-034 Underwear-bottoms 2       $13.95   $27.90
  17         28 G141-010 Jacket            1       $189.95  $189.95    2
  18         30 G239-052 Gloves            1       $7.95    $7.95
  19         30 G239-022 Mittens           1       $19.95   $19.95
  20         39 G238-155 Hat (screen)      1       $3.95    $3.95
  21         39 G238-139 Wool hat          1       $5.95    $5.95
                                                                mem=223K
/=Menu Options     F1=Context Help   F2=General Help   F3=Edit   F10=Recalc All
```

BACKPACK with cell pointer at A1

When you press H, your screen displays two horizontal windows, as shown in Figure 13-2. The cell pointer is at position A12 in the bottom window. When you split a spreadsheet screen, PC-Calc+ performs the following actions:

- Creates a second window at the current cell pointer location. A new horizontal window appears on the lower part of the screen. If you choose the "Vertical split" option, a new vertical window appears on the right side of the screen.
- Makes the newly opened window the active window.
- Positions the cell that was highlighted when the split was made in the upper left corner of the new window.
- Places the cell pointer in the upper left corner of the new window.

Figure 13-2.

```
A12                    BACKPACK              Calc-all              Value
      A       B         C           D          E        F         G
 1                            Problem-Solver's Backpack
 2                                   30,000 B.C.
 3
 4   Page #  Item #   Description    Qty      Price   Tot Price  Item-
 5                                                                pounds
 6        3  G472-007 Rope           200      $0.15    $30.00
 7        5  G114-009 Boots           1      $79.95    $79.95      2
 8        9  G240-098 Socks           4       $3.00    $12.00
 9       16  G105-100 Tennis shoes    1      $18.95    $18.95      1
10       21  G292-037 Shorts          2      $14.95    $29.90
      A       B         C           D          E        F         G
12       22  G299-207 T-shirt         3       $9.95    $29.85
13       24  G211-001 Turtle T-shirt  3      $11.45    $34.35
14       24  G196-021 Pants           3      $20.50    $61.50
15       26  G231-066 Underwear-top   2      $13.95    $27.90
16       26  G234-034 Underwear-bottoms 2    $13.95    $27.90
17       28  G141-018 Jacket          1     $189.95   $189.95      2
18       30  G239-052 Gloves          1       $7.95    $7.95
19       30  G239-022 Mittens         1      $19.95   $19.95
20       39  G238-155 Hat (screen)    1       $3.95    $3.95
21       39  G238-139 Wool hat        1       $5.95    $5.95
22                                                               mem=223K
Ctrl T toggles split screen synchronization On and Off
```

BACKPACK split into two horizontal windows

With the screen horizontally split, use the arrow keys to fly around in the lower window. You should discover that, as you scroll through the bottom window, the upper window display does not move. The lower window can display the bottom of the BACKPACK spreadsheet, while the upper window shows the title and column headings at the beginning of the BACKPACK spreadsheet.

What can you do with the "Split screen" feature other than scroll around the new window? One thing you can do is to switch control back and forth between the two windows. The shortcut method for moving the cell pointer to the other window is the following:

Press CTRL-S

Each time you press CTRL-S, the cell pointer jumps to the other window. Try it. Press CTRL-S several times and watch where the cell pointer goes. The window that contains the cell pointer becomes the active window. When you move the cell pointer in the active window, the other window display remains unchanged. You can also activate this command by opening up the Main menu, selecting the "Split screen" option, and then selecting the (S)witch option on the Split Screen options list. Using CTRL-S is a much faster way to accomplish the same task.

Using the arrow keys and CTRL-S, adjust the two windows on your display so that they match the screen shown in Figure 13-3. The upper window shows cell A1 in the upper left corner of the screen. This part of the screen appears as it did before the screen was split.

The spreadsheet in the lower window has been scrolled so that the bottom of columns C through I appears on the screen.

Figure 13-3.

D6		BACKPACK		Calc-all		Value
A	B	C	D	E	F	G
1				Problem-Solver's Backpack		
2				30,000 B.C.		
3						
4	Page #	Item #	Description	Qty	Price	Tot Price	Item-
5							pounds
6		3 G472-007	Rope	200	$0.15	$30.00	
7		5 G114-009	Boots	1	$79.95	$79.95	2
8		9 G240-090	Socks	4	$3.00	$12.00	
9		16 G105-100	Tennis shoes	1	$18.95	$18.95	1
10		21 G292-037	Shorts	2	$14.95	$29.90	

	C	D	E	F	G	H	I
45	Juggling balls	1	$9.95	$9.95		14.50	0.91
46	Watch	1	$33.95	$33.95		0.50	0.03
47	Kite	1	$19.95	$19.95		4.50	0.28
48	Mattress	1	$34.95	$34.95	1	1.00	1.06
49	Blanket	1	$9.50	$9.50		12.00	0.75
50	Binoculars	1	$109.95	$109.95	1	5.00	1.31
51	Raft	1	$49.95	$49.95	6	6.00	6.38
52				$1,999			56.39
53							
54							

200   mem=223K
/=Menu Options   F1=Context Help   F2=General Help   F3=Edit   F10=Recalc All

BACKPACK windows aligned for experiment

Columns A and B are not visible in the lower window display. More importantly, the two cells that contain total dollars and total weight, F52 and I52, are both displayed on the screen in the lower window. Adjust your lower window (using the arrow keys), so that you can see both F52 and I52 clearly.

When you have both F52 and I52 displayed in the lower window, press CTRL-S to move the cell pointer to the upper window, and then move the pointer to cell location D6.

With the cell pointer at D6 in the upper display, imagine for a moment that you are Shannon, the student who developed the raw data for BACKPACK. Shannon notices that she has not yet exceeded her dollar and weight budgets for the trip to 30,000 B.C. Her total dollars amount to less than $2,000, and her total weight for all the BACKPACK items is well under the 60 pound limit.

Shannon knows that rope is low priced and does not weigh much on a per foot basis. She decides that she wants to squeeze in another 20 feet of rope. But what does an extra 20 feet of rope do to the dollar and weight totals? The answer is easy to compute with an electronic spreadsheet. First, turn off the PC-Calc+ Smart feature, so that the cell pointer does not automatically move when you enter data. Then, do the following:

Press /	(to bring up the Main menu)
Press C	(to choose (C)onfigure option)
Press S	(to choose (S)mart option)
Press O	(to choose (O)ff option)
Press X	(to exit the Configure options list)
Press N	(at prompt asking if you want to save configuration)

With the Smart feature turned off and the cell pointer at D6 in the upper window, watch what happens when you enter a value of 220 for the amount of rope to be carried:

At cell location D6 in the upper window, type:
220
and press ENTER

PC-Calc+ displays a message telling you that it is recalculating the data. When the calculation is complete, look at the two new values at F6 and I6 in the lower window. F6 now shows $2,002 instead of $1,999. Cell I6 contains 56.70 instead of 56.39. The total weight remains within limits; the total dollar amount is slightly over budget.

What about trying 210 feet of rope? Clearly weight will not be a problem. The only issues are cost and keeping the total dollars at or below $2,000. Try entering 210 feet of rope:

At cell location D6 in the upper window, type:
210
and press ENTER

Again, PC-Calc+ displays the "recalculating data" message. At the end of the recalculation, F6 shows $2,001. Shannon is only one dollar over budget now. She just has to drop another five feet of rope. Try entering 205 feet of rope at D6:

At cell location D6 in the upper window, type:
205
and press ENTER

F6, the total dollar amount, now shows exactly $2,000! That extra five feet of rope might really come in handy in 30,000 B.C.

To unsplit the screen, activate the PC-Calc+ "Split screen" command and choose the (U)nsplit option from the Split Screen options list:

Press /   (to bring up the Main menu)

Press S   (to choose "(S)plit screen" option)
Press U   (to choose (U)nsplit option)

When you press U, the display returns to the single window mode. The cell pointer is positioned at the last location of the *inactive* window, which, in this case, was the lower part of the BACKPACK spreadsheet.

Split the Screen Vertically

Before you begin to split the screen vertically, move the cell pointer back to cell location A1:

Press /   (to bring up the Main menu)
Press G   (to choose (G)oto option)

At the prompt, type:
a1
and press ENTER

With the cell pointer at location A1, move the cell pointer to cell location E1 (column E, row 1). Column E contains the prices for each of the items on the list.
    With the cell pointer at E1, activate the PC-Calc+ "Split screen" command:

Press /   (to bring up the Main menu)
Press S   (to choose "(S)plit screen" option)
Press V   (to choose (V)ertical option)

When you press V, the screen displays two vertical windows, as shown in Figure 13-4. The cell pointer is at position E1 in the newly opened window. Notice the following message at the bottom of the screen:

```
Ctrl T toggles split screen synchronization On and Off
```

You will be using CTRL-T after you scroll the righthand window to a new position. Press → six times to scroll the righthand window, until the entire screen looks like the screen shown in Figure 13-5. Notice that only columns I, J, and K appear on the right side of

Figure 13-4.

E1		BACKPACK		Calc-all		Empty Cell
	A	B	C	E	F	G
1				1 olver's Backpack		
2				2 30,000 B.C.		
3				3		
4	Page #	Item #	Description	4 Price	Tot Price	Item-
5				5		pounds
6	3	G472-007	Rope	6 $0.15	$30.75	
7	5	G114-009	Boots	7 $79.95	$79.95	2
8	9	G240-098	Socks	8 $3.00	$12.00	
9	16	G105-100	Tennis shoes	9 $18.95	$18.95	1
10	21	G292-037	Shorts	10 $14.95	$29.90	
11	21	G299-002	Tank top	11 $8.95	$17.90	
12	22	G299-207	T-shirt	12 $9.95	$29.85	
13	24	G211-001	Turtle T-shirt	13 $11.45	$34.35	
14	24	G196-021	Pants	14 $20.50	$61.50	
15	26	G231-066	Underwear-top	15 $13.95	$27.90	
16	26	G234-034	Underwear-bottoms	16 $13.95	$27.90	
17	28	G141-018	Jacket	17 $109.95	$109.95	2
18	30	G239-052	Gloves	18 $7.95	$7.95	
19	30	G239-022	Mittens	19 $19.95	$19.95	
20	39	G238-155	Hat (screen)	20 $3.95	$3.95	
21	39	G238-139	Wool hat	21 $5.95	$5.95	

```
                                                              mem=223K
Ctrl T toggles split screen synchronization On and Off
```

BACKPACK *split into two vertical windows*

Figure 13-5.

```
K1                    BACKPACK              Calc-all            Empty Cell
     A       B        C                       I         J         K
  1                                      1
  2                                      2
  3                                      3
  4  Page #  Item #   Description        4  Tot Weight
  5                                      5  pounds
  6      3   G472-007 Rope               6  3.20
  7      5   G114-009 Boots              7  2.44
  8      9   G240-098 Socks              8  0.75
  9     16   G105-100 Tennis shoes       9  1.50
 10     21   G292-037 Shorts            10  0.56
 11     21   G299-002 Tank top          11  0.44
 12     22   G299-207 T-shirt           12  0.75
 13     24   G211-001 Turtle T-shirt    13  1.13
 14     24   G196-021 Pants             14  1.50
 15     26   G231-066 Underwear-top     15  0.63
 16     26   G234-034 Underwear-bottoms 16  0.56
 17     28   G141-018 Jacket            17  2.94
 18     30   G239-052 Gloves            18  0.13
 19     30   G239-022 Mittens           19  0.19
 20     39   G238-155 Hat (screen)      20  0.06
 21     39   G238-139 Wool hat          21  0.13
                                                              mem=223K
Ctrl T toggles split screen synchronization On and Off
```

Righthand window scrolled to show only columns I, J, and K

the screen shown in Figure 13-5. When you scroll the righthand window, the left side of the screen stays fixed on columns A, B, and C.

Use Split Screen Synchronization

With your screen adjusted to look like one in Figure 13-5, scroll down the righthand window:

Press PGDN

Importing, Graphing, and Other Features **519**

Ch 13

When you press PGDN, the data in the total weight column moves off the top of the screen, as shown in Figure 13-6. The labels and information in the inactive window on the left no longer correspond to the data in the active window on the right.

In some cases, you may want both windows to scroll in *synchronization*. That is, when you scroll cells in one window, you want the cells in the other window to move also.

Position the righthand window back to its starting position:

Press PGUP

With the two windows aligned as shown in Figure 13-5 (so that row numbers down the sides of each window are identical), activate the PC-Calc+ Synchronization feature:

Figure 13-6.

```
K22                    BACKPACK             Calc-all        Empty Cell
         A        B           C                   I      J      K
 1                                       22      7.69
 2                                       23      0.09
 3                                       24      0.13
 4    Page #    Item #    Description    25      6.00
 5                                       26      0.25
 6              3 G472-007 Rope          27      1.47
 7              5 G114-009 Boots         28      0.19
 8              9 G240-098 Socks         29      0.13
 9             16 G105-100 Tennis shoes  30      1.81
10             21 G292-037 Shorts        31      1.38
11             21 G299-002 Tank top      32      2.00
12             22 G299-207 T-shirt       33      0.19
13             24 G211-001 Turtle T-shirt 34     0.22
14             24 G196-021 Pants         35      0.75
15             26 G231-066 Underwear-top 36      0.22
16             26 G234-034 Underwear-bottoms 37  1.44
17             28 G141-010 Jacket        38      0.25
18             30 G239-052 Gloves        39      0.30
19             30 G239-022 Mittens       40      1.06
20             39 G238-155 Hat (screen)  41      0.44
21             39 G238-139 Wool hat      42      1.16
                                                              mem=223K
Ctrl T toggles split screen synchronization On and Off
```

Righthand window scrolled down

Press CTRL-T

When you press CTRL-T, the word "Synch" appears in the status line at the top of the screen, next to the name of the spreadsheet. The two windows are now in "synch" with each other. When you move cells in one window, the cells in the other window move also. Try it:

Press PGDN

This time when you press PGDN, both windows move the data up and off the top of the screen. Both windows display the data for the same rows, 22 through 42. If you press PGDN again, the windows will scroll to the bottom of the spreadsheet, and you will see rows 43 through 63.

Press PGDN

What happens if you switch to the inactive window? Use CTRL-S to try switching between windows:

Press CTRL-S

When you switch to the inactive window, the cell pointer jumps to the window on the left. Press ↑ to start scrolling back toward the top of the spreadsheet. As you hold down ↑, the cells in both windows move together down the screen.

The PC-Calc+ Synchronization feature also works when the cells are not perfectly aligned by row or column. For example, you might want to compare two sets of values that are in completely different locations (such as A1:A20 with D31:D40). To make such a comparison, first, split the screen, so that you can align the cells to be compared (a vertical split in this situation). Then, align the cells by scrolling the cells in one of the windows to match the cells in the other window. When the cells in the two windows are aligned, then activate the synchronization feature (CTRL-T). Then, when you scroll the cells in either of the windows, the cells in the other window move correspondingly, and you can make comparisons.

If you wish, go ahead and experiment with both splitting the screen and using the Synchronization feature. When you finish your experiments, unsplit the screen as follows:

Press /   (to bring up the Main menu)
Press S   (to choose "(S)plit screen" option)
Press U   (to choose (U)nsplit option)

The next section shows you how to use the PC-Calc+ Sort command. Before using the Sort command, unsplit the screen (if you have not already done so) and move the cell pointer to cell location A1.

Sort Data on the Spreadsheet

When you scroll down column A, the Page # column of the BACKPACK spreadsheet, the numbers remain in ascending order until you get near the bottom of the column. After the entry for "survival matches" at page 95, all of the remaining page numbers are out of order. Figure 13-7 shows the data entries at the bottom of column A, with page numbers out of order. The cell pointer is at location A43.

PC-Calc+ can sort the contents of the cells in BACKPACK, so that all page numbers in column A are in order. To activate the PC-Calc+ Block/Sort command:

Press /   (to bring up the Main menu)
Press B   (to choose (B)lock option)
Press S   (to choose (S)ort option)

At this point, PC-Calc+ prompts you for the "block definition" to be sorted. The prompt appears at the bottom of the screen on the edit line. Since you want to sort the entries in column A, you might think that all you have to do is tell PC-Calc+ to sort column A. However, if PC-Calc+ sorts and rearranges column A without also rearranging the data in columns B through I, the page numbers may no longer correspond to the item information in columns B through I.

You must tell PC-Calc+ to sort the numbers in column A and rearrange the data in columns B through I, so that all the data

Figure 13-7.

```
A43                         BACKPACK            Calc-all            Value
       A      B        C              D      E        F          G
 39    90 G403-112 Knife              1    $27.95   $27.95
 40    90 G404-013 Saw                1    $12.95   $12.95        1
 41    90 G404-019 Replacement blade  2    $3.75    $7.50
 42    95 C473-068 Hammer             1    $19.95   $19.95        1
 43    95 G407-011 Survival matches   1    $2.95    $2.95
 44    20 G579-472 Harmonica          1    $15.95   $15.95
 45    20 G579-425 Juggling balls     1    $9.95    $9.95
 46    23 G400-094 Watch              1    $33.95   $33.95
 47    73 G495-154 Kite               1    $19.95   $19.95
 48    81 G374-041 Mattress           1    $34.95   $34.95        1
 49    81 G407-106 Blanket            1    $9.50    $9.50
 50    49 G400-077 Binoculars         1    $109.95  $109.95       1
 51    73 G491-049 Raft               1    $49.95   $49.95        6
 52                                                 $2,000
 53
 54
 55
 56
 57
 58
 59
95                                                          mem=223K
/=Menu Options   F1=Context Help   F2=General Help   F3=Edit   F10=Recalc All
```

BACKPACK *with page numbers out of order in column A*

stays with the new arrangement of page numbers. You must give PC-Calc+ the entire set of cells that will be affected by the sort. In this case, the block of cells involved in the sort will begin at A6 and end at I51. A1 is the upper left corner of the block of cells. I51 is the lower right corner of the block.

>Press F6   (to clear the default entry from the input area)
>Type:
>**a6:i51**
>and press ENTER

When you enter the block definition for the sort and press ENTER, the cells in that block are highlighted on your screen. At the bottom of the screen, PC-Calc+ displays a prompt asking you for the rows or columns to be sorted. Since you want to sort column A, you only have to type the letter for column A at the prompt:

>Type:
>**a**
>and press ENTER

When you select column A and press ENTER, a question box appears in the middle of the screen. The program wants to know if you want the sort to be ascending or descending. An *ascending sort* will rearrange the page numbers in the order of smallest to largest, with the smallest page number in location A6 and the largest in location A51. A *descending sort* will do the reverse, put the largest page number into A6 and the smallest page number into A51. Tell PC-Calc+ that you want to sort the data into ascending order:

>Press A

When you press A, the program first displays a message asking you to wait for the sort to finish, and then displays a message telling you that the program is "recalculating." Then, the last message disappears, and the screen flashes as the display gets refreshed.

With column A sorted, your screen should look like the one shown in Figure 13-8. The page 95 entry for survival matches is now at cell location A50. The page number entries are all in order; the out-of-order page numbers have been moved to different cell locations. Scroll up column A. You will find all of the page numbers now in ascending order. Page number 3 is at the top of the list; page number 95 is at the bottom.

When PC-Calc+ sorted the data in column A and rearranged all of the entries in columns B through I, the program moved both data and formulas. The cell references of the formulas that were moved were updated to match the formulas' new location. Quite a feat! PC-Calc+ had to update most of the formulas in columns F and I during the sort operation.

To verify that the update was performed correctly and that the sort did not create unexpected problems, look at cells F52 and I52. The two results should be the same as before the sort: $2000 and 56.47.

Figure 13-8.

A43		BACKPACK		Calc-all		Value
A	B	C	D	E	F	G
39	81 G407-106	Blanket	1	$9.50	$9.50	
40	81 G374-041	Mattress	1	$34.95	$34.95	1
41	86 G404-028	Compass	1	$29.95	$29.95	
42	88 G402-052	Water bottle	1	$2.75	$2.75	
43	88 G402-145	Shower	1	$12.95	$12.95	
44	88 G402-147	Water bag	1	$4.95	$4.95	
45	89 G407-075	Water purifier	1	$167.95	$167.95	1
46	90 G404-019	Replacement blade	2	$3.75	$7.50	
47	90 G404-013	Saw	1	$12.95	$12.95	1
48	90 G403-112	Knife	1	$27.95	$27.95	
49	90 G403-019	Pocket knife	1	$22.95	$22.95	
50	95 G407-011	Survival matches	1	$2.95	$2.95	
51	95 G473-068	Hammer	1	$19.95	$19.95	1
52					$2,000	
53						
54						
55						
56						
57						
58						
59						

```
88                                                        mem=223K
/=Menu Options   F1=Context Help  F2=General Help  F3=Edit  F10=Recalc All
```

BACKPACK with column A sorted

Figure 13-9.

B10		BACKPACK		Calc-all		Text
	A	B	C	D	E	F	G
1				Problem-Solver's Backpack		
2				30,000 B.C.		
3						
4	Page #	Item #	Description	Qty	Price	Tot Price	Item-
5							pounds
6	3	G472-007	Rope	205	$0.15	$30.75	
7	5	G114-009	Boots	1	$79.95	$79.95	2
8	9	G240-098	Socks	4	$3.00	$12.00	
9	16	G105-100	Tennis shoes	1	$10.95	$10.95	1
10	20	G579-472	Harmonica	1	$15.95	$15.95	
11	20	G579-425	Juggling balls	1	$9.95	$9.95	
12	21	G292-037	Shorts	2	$14.95	$29.90	
13	21	G299-002	Tank top	2	$8.95	$17.90	
14	22	G299-207	T-shirt	3	$9.95	$29.85	
15	23	G400-094	Watch	1	$33.95	$33.95	
16	24	G196-021	Pants	3	$20.50	$61.50	
17	24	G211-001	Turtle T-shirt	3	$11.45	$34.35	
18	26	G234-034	Underwear-bottoms	2	$13.95	$27.90	
19	26	G231-066	Underwear-top	2	$13.95	$27.90	
20	28	G141-010	Jacket	1	$109.95	$109.95	2
21	30	G239-822	Mittens	1	$19.95	$19.95	

"G579-472   mem=223K
/=Menu Options   F1=Context Help   F2=General Help   F3=Edit   F10=Recalc All

BACKPACK with column A sorted and column B unsorted

Move the cell pointer up the screen until you see the topmost entries in column A. The page numbers in column A are arranged in ascending order. What about the entries in column B? In Figure 13-9, the cell pointer is at location B10. The item number at B10 and the item number at B11 are slightly out of order. Both item numbers start off with G579, but the three digits after the dash (-) show B10 with 472 and B11 with 425.

A similar inversion of numbers occurs in cells B18 and B19. Cell B18 starts off with G234, and B19 starts off with G231. To have PC-Calc+ sort both the page numbers and the item numbers in ascending order, do the following:

Press /	(to bring up the Main menu)
Press B	(to choose (B)lock option)
Press S	(to choose (S)ort option)

Press F6 (to clear the default entry from the input area)

Type:
a6:i51 (block definition for sort)
and press ENTER

After you enter the block definition, PC-Calc+ displays a prompt at the bottom of the screen asking you for the rows or columns to be sorted. Since column A is already sorted, you might think that all you have to do is tell PC-Calc+ to sort column B. Try it!

Type:
b
and press ENTER

When you tell PC-Calc+ to sort column B, the program displays the question box that asks you to set the sort order. Direct PC-Calc+ to sort the data into ascending order:

Press A

When you press A, PC-Calc+ quickly sorts and rearranges BACK-PACK so that column B is in ascending order. Figure 13-10 displays the results of this sort operation. Column B is definitely sorted, but column A is now out of order. To sort column B without unsorting column A, you have to tell PC-Calc+ to sort both columns at the same time. Also, you have to tell the program which of the two sorts is more important. Do you want cells to be sorted first by page numbers and then by item number, or the reverse?

Since PC-Calc+ performs sort operations so easily and quickly, you need only repeat the commands, and the program does the real work.

Importing, Graphing, and Other Features   **527**

Ch 13

Press /   (to bring up the Main menu)
Press B   (to choose (B)lock option)
Press S   (to choose (S)ort option)
Press F6   (to clear the default entry from the input area)

Type:
a6:i51   (block definition for sort)
and press ENTER

If you want to sort first by column A (page numbers), and then by column B (item numbers), then type the letters for the two columns, separated by a comma:

Type:
a, b
and press ENTER

Figure 13-10.

```
B10                    BACKPACK              Calc-all                Text
        A         B           C         D         E         F         G
  1                             Problem-Solver's Backpack
  2                                  30,000 B.C.
  3
  4    Page #    Item #    Description   Qty     Price   Tot Price  Item-
  5                                                                 pounds
  6            16 G105-100 Tennis shoes    1    $18.95    $18.95      1
  7             5 G114-009 Boots           1    $79.95    $79.95      2
  8            20 G141-010 Jacket          1   $109.95   $109.95      2
  9            24 G196-021 Pants           3    $20.50    $61.50
 10            24 G211-001 Turtle T-shirt  3    $11.45    $34.35
 11            26 G231-066 Underwear-top   2    $13.95    $27.90
 12            26 G234-034 Underwear-bottoms 2  $13.95    $27.90
 13            39 G238-139 Wool hat        1     $5.95     $5.95
 14            39 G238-155 Hat (screen)    1     $3.95     $3.95
 15            30 G239-022 Mittens         1    $19.95    $19.95
 16            30 G239-052 Gloves          1     $7.95     $7.95
 17             9 G240-098 Socks           4     $3.00    $12.00
 18            21 G292-037 Shorts          2    $14.95    $29.90
 19            21 G299-002 Tank top        2     $8.95    $17.90
 20            22 G299-207 T-shirt         3     $9.95    $29.85
 21            40 G332-057 Backpack        1   $299.95   $299.95      7
"G211-001                                                         mem=223K
/=Menu Options    F1=Context Help   F2=General Help   F3=Edit   F10=Recalc All
```

BACKPACK with column B sorted and column A unsorted

This entry directs PC-Calc+ to first sort column A and then sort column B. Since you have specified two columns to be sorted, you will see two question boxes asking you to set the sorting order. You can control the order of sort for each row and column being sorted; the order can be different for each. In this case, tell PC-Calc+ to sort both columns in ascending order:

Press A, A

When you press the second A, PC-Calc+ sorts and rearranges BACKPACK once again. Figure 13-11 displays the results of this final sort operation. Both columns A and B are now sorted. The primary sort was made to column A to put all the entries in order by page number. Then, a secondary sort was made to put the item

Figure 13-11.

```
B10                     BACKPACK              Calc-all                Text
↓      A       B        C               D       E        F          G
  1                              Problem-Solver's Backpack
  2                                     30,000 B.C.
  3
  4   Page #  Item #   Description     Qty     Price    Tot Price  Item-
  5                                                                pounds
  6         3 G472-007 Rope            205     $0.15    $30.75
  7         5 G114-009 Boots             1    $79.95    $79.95       2
  8         9 G240-098 Socks             4     $3.00    $12.00
  9        16 G105-100 Tennis shoes      1    $18.95    $18.95       1
 10        20 G579-425 Juggling balls    1     $9.95     $9.95
 11        20 G579-472 Harmonica         1    $15.95    $15.95
 12        21 G292-037 Shorts            2    $14.95    $29.90
 13        21 G299-002 Tank top          2     $8.95    $17.90
 14        22 G299-207 T-shirt           3     $9.95    $29.85
 15        23 G400-094 Watch             1    $33.95    $33.95
 16        24 G196-021 Pants             3    $20.50    $61.50
 17        24 G211-001 Turtle T-shirt    3    $11.45    $34.35
 18        26 G231-066 Underwear-top     2    $13.95    $27.90
 19        26 G234-034 Underwear-bottoms 2    $13.95    $27.90
 20        28 G141-018 Jacket            1   $109.95   $109.95       2
 21        30 G239-022 Mittens           1    $19.95    $19.95
"G579-425                                                         mem=223K
/=Menu Options   F1=Context Help   F2=General Help   F3=Edit   F10=Recalc All
```

BACKPACK with columns A and B sorted

numbers in order for each set of page numbers. The item numbers at B10 and B11 are now in order, as are the item numbers at B18 and B19.

If you wish, you can save this version of BACKPACK. If you have made a backup copy of BACKPACK, you can save the final sorted version as BACKPACK. If you have not made a backup copy of BACKPACK, save this version under a new file (New_File) name.

Print the Spreadsheet and Use Tables

With the final version of BACKPACK loaded into PC-Calc+ (a version with both columns A and B sorted as shown in Figure 13-11), you can print BACKPACK to your printer. (In Chapter 12, you altered the printer and report configurations in order to print the BACKPACK spreadsheet on a single 8 1/2- by 11-inch piece of paper. You then saved the altered configuration to your configuration file, PCCALC.PRO.) To print the current version of BACKPACK, make sure your printer is connected, turned on, and ready to go. Then activate the following options:

Press /   (to bring up the Main menu)
Press P   (to choose (P)rint/Graph option)
Press P   (to choose (P)rint option)
Press S   (to choose (S)creen option)

The program prompts you for the destination of the printed report. The default is LPT1, which is the most common output port for printers. If your printer is attached to a different communications port, enter the name of the port in place of LPT1. When the correct destination port is entered, do the following:

Press ENTER

The program prompts you for a title which will be centered above the body of the printed spreadsheet. Enter the following title:

Type:
Final BACKPACK Data Table
and press ENTER

Another prompt appears asking for the source definition of the cells to be printed. The default is set to ALL. Choosing ALL will cause PC-Calc+ to print all of the active (non-empty) cells:

Press ENTER

The Print Details options list appears. The most commonly used option, "(P)roceed with print," is highlighted.

Press P

When you press P, a question box appears asking you if you want to save the definition information in a table. For this example, select (Y)es. Later you will examine the table that PC-Calc+ creates.

Press Y

When you press Y, BACKPACK prints on your printer. A message at the bottom of the screen tells you how much remains to be printed, expressed as a percentage. When PC-Calc+ completes the printing of your report, an information box appears in the middle of the screen asking you to press any key to continue. When you press a key, the Print/Graph options list reappears. To return to the worksheet screen:

Importing, Graphing, and Other Features **531**
Ch 13

Press X

Figure 13-12 displays the BACKPACK report that you printed to your printer. The report in Figure 13-12 shows the new amount of rope being carried to 30,000 B.C., 205 feet.

Suppose that you want to print a version of this spreadsheet (with the sorted page and item numbers), but with the original quantity of rope, 200 feet. Move the cell pointer to D6 and enter the original quantity of rope:

At cell location D6, type:
200
and press ENTER

PC-Calc+ automatically updates the spreadsheet totals to reflect the amount of rope being carried. After the program recalculates the new totals, activate the PC-Calc+ Print command:

Press /   (to bring up the Main menu)
Press P   (to choose (P)rint/Graph option)

When the Print/Graph options list appears, choose the "(M)odify/run saved reports" option instead of the (P)rint option:

Press M   (to choose "(M)odify/run saved reports" option)

When you choose the "(M)odify/run saved reports" option, PC-Calc+ displays the Reports table shown in Figure 13-13. The table displays a line of data across the screen which is a summary of the selections and entries you made when you printed BACKPACK. You can quickly print reports from this table without having to reenter the printer setup data. You can also change the data in the table to create new forms of the same report. When you save the printer setup data for each new report you create, that collection of data becomes a new line in the Reports table.

Figure 13-12.

```
Saturday September 9, 1990                                          12:03:26
                              Final BACKPACK Data Table
-----------------------------------------------------------------------------
                          Problem-Solver's Backpack
                                30,000 B.C.

 Page #   Item #     Description       Qty    Price  Tot Price  Item-   Weight  Tot Weight
                                                                pounds  ounces  pounds
    3   G472-007   Rope               205    $0.15    $30.75             0.25     3.20
    5   G114-009   Boots                1   $79.95    $79.95      2      7.00     2.44
    9   G240-098   Socks                4    $3.00    $12.00             3.00     0.75
   16   G105-100   Tennis shoes         1   $18.95    $18.95      1      8.00     1.50
   20   G579-425   Juggling balls       1    $9.95     $9.95            14.50     0.91
   20   G579-472   Harmonica            1   $15.95    $15.95            11.50     0.72
   21   G292-037   Shorts               2   $14.95    $29.90             4.50     0.56
   21   G299-002   Tank top             2    $8.95    $17.90             3.50     0.44
   22   G299-207   T-shirt              3    $9.95    $29.85             4.00     0.75
   23   G408-094   Watch                1   $33.95    $33.95             0.50     0.03
   24   G196-021   Pants                3   $20.50    $61.50             8.00     1.50
   24   G211-001   Turtle T-shirt       3   $11.45    $34.35             6.00     1.13
   26   G231-066   Underwear-top        2   $13.95    $27.90             5.00     0.63
   26   G234-034   Underwear-bottoms    2   $13.95    $27.90             4.50     0.56
   28   G141-018   Jacket               1  $189.95   $189.95      2     15.00     2.94
   30   G239-022   Mittens              1   $19.95    $19.95             3.00     0.19
   30   G239-052   Gloves               1    $7.95     $7.95             2.00     0.13
   39   G238-139   Wool hat             1    $5.95     $5.95             2.00     0.13
   39   G238-155   Hat (screen)         1    $3.95     $3.95             1.00     0.06
   40   G332-057   Backpack             1  $299.95   $299.95      7     11.00     7.69
   47   G409-131   Goggles              1   $11.95    $11.95             1.50     0.09
   49   G408-077   Binoculars           1  $109.95   $109.95      1      5.00     1.31
   50   G407-026   Toothbrush           1    $3.95     $3.95             2.00     0.13
   52   G353-051   Tent                 1  $189.95   $189.95      6     14.00     6.88
   59   G407-019   Matches              1    $0.95     $0.95             4.00     0.25
   62   G401-025   Cup                  1    $2.95     $2.95             3.00     0.19
   62   G401-026   Pots and pans        1   $17.95    $17.95      1     13.00     1.81
   62   G401-081   Utensils             1    $1.95     $1.95             2.00     0.13
   71   G493-028   Fishing pole         1   $29.95    $29.95      1      7.50     1.47
   73   G491-049   Raft                 1   $49.95    $49.95      6      6.00     6.38
   73   G495-154   Kite                 1   $19.95    $19.95             4.50     0.28
   78   G373-009   Sleeping bag         1  $199.95   $199.95      2               2.00
   78   G407-046   First aid kit        1   $44.95    $44.95      1      6.00     1.38
   81   G374-041   Mattress             1   $34.95    $34.95      1      1.00     1.06
   81   G407-106   Blanket              1    $9.50     $9.50            12.00     0.75
   86   G404-028   Compass              1   $29.95    $29.95             3.00     0.19
   88   G402-052   Water bottle         1    $2.75     $2.75             3.50     0.22
   88   G402-145   Shower               1   $12.95    $12.95            12.00     0.75
   88   G402-147   Water bag            1    $4.95     $4.95             3.50     0.22
   89   G407-075   Water purifier       1  $167.95   $167.95      1      7.00     1.44
   90   G403-019   Pocket knife         1   $22.95    $22.95             4.00     0.25
   90   G403-112   Knife                1   $27.95    $27.95             4.75     0.30
   90   G404-013   Saw                  1   $12.95    $12.95      1      1.00     1.06
   90   G404-019   Replacement blade    2    $3.75     $7.50             3.50     0.44
   95   G407-011   Survival matches     1    $2.95     $2.95             2.00     0.13
   95   G473-068   Hammer               1   $19.95    $19.95      1      2.50     1.16
                                                     $2,000                      56.47
-----------------------------------------------------------------------------
```

Final BACKPACK Data Table

Importing, Graphing, and Other Features **533**

Ch 13

Figure 13-13.

```
                                                              Print Table
┌────────────────────────────────────────────────────────────────────────┐
│                       PC-Calc+ REPORTS TABLE                           │
├─────────┬──────────┬─────┬────────┬─────────┬─────────┬────────┬───────┤
│ ⏎Type   │  Title   │⏎Act │ Source │Brdr rows│Brdr cols│⏎Beg Pr │⏎End Pr│
├─────────┼──────────┼─────┼────────┼─────────┼─────────┼────────┼───────┤
│ Screen  │Final BACK│  A  │  ALL   │         │         │        │       │
└─────────┴──────────┴─────┴────────┴─────────┴─────────┴────────┴───────┘
                      A=Active
                      I=Inactive

  Use ↑↓←→ to move highlight. (⏎ Press Enter to toggle data.)
  Press / for line options and to exit
```

PC-Calc+ Reports table

Entries in the columns marked with the ENTER symbol (the symbol ⏎ that appears on the ENTER key on most keyboards) are selections you made from option lists. The highlight, currently in the column labeled "Type," shows the Screen option. The Screen option is one option in a list of Type options which determine the kind of cell information that gets printed (results, formulas, and text). You can cycle through the options on the list by pressing the ENTER key. Press the ENTER key and watch the options change in the Type column. If you press ENTER 10 times, the Screen option reappears. Most of the other options deal with printing cell values (v), cell formulas (f), and cell text (t) entries. The list of Type options is the same list that you saw when you printed BACK-PACK at the beginning of this section (by activating the Main menu, choosing the Print/Graph option, and then selecting the Print option from the Print/Graph options list).

Entries in the other columns are either items that you typed or items that you selected as defaults. Use the arrow keys to move the highlight to the entry in the Title column. Then, press the following key:

Press F3   (to activate the Edit mode)

The entry under the Title column is "Final BACK," the first few characters of the title you typed earlier in this section. When you place the highlight in the Title column and press F3 (to activate editing), the complete title entry appears on the edit line at the bottom of the screen. You can use the edit line to edit the title of the report. When editing is complete, return the highlight to the entry on the table by pressing either ESC (to cancel and make no changes) or ENTER (to record any modifications). In this case, return to the table without changing the report title:

Press ESC

The column labeled "Act" has two options: A=Active and I=Inactive. When set to A, the report is made active. If set to I, the report is made inactive. If you have several reports and issue a "Print all" command, then only the reports that are marked active will print.

For the BACKPACK report, the Source column is set to ALL, indicating that you printed all of the active cells in your earlier report. To change the range to be printed, you would position the highlight on ALL and press F3 to edit the entry.

The "Brdr rows" and "Brdr cols" columns contain the row(s) and column(s) designation(s) of the row(s) or column(s) you want printed on the borders of your report. Any row(s) that you list are printed at the the top of the report. Any column(s) that you list are printed down the left side of the report. The current entries are blank, indicating you want no row(s) or column(s) on the report borders.

The "Beg Pr" and "End Pr" columns contain the beginning and ending printer codes that you want sent to the printer. Your current report shows no printer codes. If you move the highlight to one of these two columns and press ENTER, PC-Calc+ will display an options list of allowed printer attributes.

If you want to view the list of attributes now, then position the highlight in either one of the two columns and press ENTER. The attribute list is a set of printer codes that control the horizontal (characters per inch, or CPI) spacing of the printout, the vertical (lines per inch, or LPI) spacing, and the "near letter quality," or NLQ, features on a printer. If, for example, you have been unable to print a compressed listing of BACKPACK on a single sheet of paper, you may need to experiment with sending printer codes to your printer. Try sending a "Beg Pr" code of 17 CPI and an "End Pr" code of either 10 CPI or 12 CPI. The "End Pr" code will reset your printer to its normal character sizing.

If you have successfully printed BACKPACK on a single sheet of paper, then leave the "Beg Pr" and "End Pr" columns blank. To activate printing from the Reports table, press the slash (/) key to display the Table Options list:

Press /

The Table Options list includes printing (A)ll the active reports, (E)xecuting the current report line in the table, and several editing commands that let you edit lines in the table: (C)opy, (D)elete, (I)nsert, and (M)ove. You can use the edit commands to construct new reports by copying a current report line and editing the columns in the new line to give you a new report. For now, verify that the PC-Calc+ Report Table can be used to print your BACKPACK report:

Press A or E

Since you have only one active report, choosing the A option gives the same result as using the E option. When you press A (or E),

PC-Calc+ asks you for the report destination. You can accept the current default (LPT1 or whatever port you have entered for your printer):

Press ENTER

PC-Calc+ proceeds to print your report from the Reports table. A message on the screen display shows the percentage remaining to be printed. When printing is complete, a message is displayed to press any key to continue. Press a key to return to the Print/Graph options list. To exit this options list, choose the e(X)it option:

Press X

If you changed none of the settings in the Reports table, then your latest printout will closely match the report in Figure 13-12. The time at the top of your latest printout will be different. The totals will also be different, because you changed the quantity of rope back to 200 feet.

 NOTE You may want to take a break before learning how to use PC-Calc+ to import and graph your spreadsheet data. You may even want to exit PC-Calc+ at this point and turn off your computer. The next two sections use the BUDGET spreadsheet, developed in Chapter 11, to explore the PC-Calc+ importing and graphics features and commands.

Import Spreadsheet Data

If you turned off your computer, then you need to boot your system and start PC-Calc+. When you see the DOS prompt and you are on the hard disk root directory:

Type:
cd \pccalc   (and press ENTER)
pcc budget   (and press ENTER)

PC-Calc+ starts up and displays the BUDGET spreadsheet. (If you did not turn off your computer, go ahead and load BUDGET using the PC-Calc+ Load/Save command.)

When you have loaded BUDGET, compare your screen with the screen shown in Figure 13-14 to make sure that you are using the same version of BUDGET as used in the book. All of the examples in this chapter correspond to the version of BUDGET saved back in Chapter 11. If your version of BUDGET is different than the one shown in Figure 13-14, you can either alter your

Figure 13-14.

	January Budget	Actual	February Budget	Actual	March Budget	Actual
Office Rent	500.00		500.00		500.00	
Office Supplies	300.00		100.00		50.00	
Computer Supplies	50.00		50.00		50.00	
Telephone	150.00		75.00		75.00	
Utilities	100.00		50.00		50.00	
Printing	250.00					
Marketing	150.00		150.00		75.00	
Travel	200.00		200.00		400.00	
Misc.	200.00		100.00		100.00	
Totals	1900.00		1225.00		1300.00	

The BUDGET spreadsheet

version or load a copy of BUDGET from *The Shareware Book Convenience Disk*.

To alter your version, all you have to do is change the cells in your spreadsheet to match the ones shown in Figure 13-14. You do not have to worry about formulas; just type the correct numbers directly into the cells. When your version of BUDGET matches the one in Figure 13-14, save your version of BUDGET.

Once you have saved BUDGET, save the file again under a new name, BUDGRAPH, as follows:

Press /	(to bring up the Main menu)
Press L	(to choose (L)oad/Save option)
Press S	(to choose (S)ave spreadsheet option)
Press ENTER	(to accept the default entry for path request)

When the File Selection options list appears in the middle of the screen, move the highlight to the "New_File" selection and:

Press ENTER

At the new filename prompt, type:
budgraph
and press ENTER

When you save BUDGET as BUDGRAPH, the filename on the status line at the top of the PC-Calc+ worksheet area changes to "budgraph."

You will alter the BUDGRAPH spreadsheet by using a combination of PC-Calc+ commands which clear the spreadsheet, import data, and delete unwanted cells. First, clear the BUDGRAPH spreadsheet by zapping all of the cells:

Press /	(to bring up the Main menu)
Press B	(to choose (B)lock option)

Press Z   (to choose (Z)ap option on Block options list)

At the block definition prompt, type:
all
and press ENTER

Press Y   (at the "Are you sure?" question)

When you complete this sequence of PC-Calc+ commands, BUDGRAPH should contain only a set of empty cells. Now, you are ready to import some selected data:

Press /   (to bring up the Main menu)
Press I   (to choose (I)mport option)

When you press I for (I)mport, PC-Calc+ displays the Import options list. The list indicates that you can import from a variety of sources, including PC-Calc+, PC-File:dB, PC-File+, PC-Type, ASCII files, and MailMerge files. You can move data into PC-Calc+ from files created by any of the programs listed. Importing data from other files is a handy way to move data around without retyping anything. When you import data from another source, you can be sure that every imported value is the same as the value in the original file. To demonstrate how the PC-Calc+ import feature works, you will import data from BUDGET, which is a PC-Calc+ file. Begin the import as follows:

Press C   (to select PC-Calc+ option)
Press ENTER   (to accept the default path entry at the prompt)

PC-Calc+ displays a file selection list in the center of the screen. Move the highlight to BUDGET and do the following:

Press ENTER

At the prompt to enter the range of data to be imported,

Type:
a6:g17   (selects column labels, row labels, and all data)
and press ENTER

At the prompt to enter the cell of upper left corner of target:
Press F6   (to clear the default entry)
Type:
a1   (imports data to upper left corner of worksheet)
and press ENTER

PC-Calc+ displays a question in the center of the screen. The program wants to know if you want to import formulas and text as well as cell values. If you respond with (N)o, then you will only get cell values. If you respond with (Y)es, then you will get everything in all the designated cells. In this case, you want everything:

Press Y

When you press Y, you see a question asking if you want to save the import specifications (definition information) in a table. If you plan to use this set of import specifications many times, then you would respond with (Y)es. Since you are only going to import the BUDGET data this one time, tell PC-Calc+ that you do not want to save the information in a table:

Press N

When you press N, a copy of the imported cells from BUDGET appear in the upper left corner of the BUDGRAPH worksheet area. The Import options list appears on top of the worksheet. To remove the Import options list:

Press X

Figure 13-15 shows what BUDGRAPH looks like after the import operation is complete. PC-Calc+ picked up the entire middle section of BUDGET (formulas, data, and text) and moved those cells into the upper left corner of BUDGRAPH.

Before you save BUDGRAPH, use the PC-Calc+ Format/Delete command to remove columns D and F, which are empty of data:

Press /	(to bring up the Main menu)
Press F	(to choose (F)ormat option)
Press D	(to choose (D)elete option)

At the prompt to enter row(s) and/or column(s), type:
d, f
and press ENTER

Figure 13-15.

		January		February		March
		Budget	Actual	Budget	Actual	Budget
Office Rent		500.00		500.00		500.00
Office Supplies		300.00		100.00		50.00
Computer Supplies		50.00		50.00		50.00
Telephone		150.00		75.00		75.00
Utilities		100.00		50.00		50.00
Printing		250.00				
Marketing		150.00		150.00		75.00
Travel		200.00		200.00		400.00
Misc.		200.00		100.00		100.00

BUDGET data imported into BUDGRAPH

PC-Calc+ displays a question box in the middle of the screen asking you to verify the deletion:

Press Y

When you press Y, the two columns labeled "Actual" disappear, as shown in Figure 13-16. BUDGRAPH is ready for you to use the PC-Calc+ Graph commands.

 NOTE Save BUDGRAPH before you proceed to the next section, in which you will learn to graph the data in the BUDGRAPH spreadsheet.

Figure 13-16.

```
C19                    budgraph              Calc-all         Empty Cell
       A       B        C        D        E       F       G        H
 1                   January  February  March
 2                   Budget   Budget    Budget
 3                   -------  --------  ------
 4  Office Rent       500.00   500.00   500.00
 5  Office Supplies   300.00   100.00    50.00
 6  Computer Supplies  50.00    50.00    50.00
 7  Telephone         150.00    75.00    75.00
 8  Utilities         100.00    50.00    50.00
 9  Printing          250.00
10  Marketing         150.00   150.00    75.00
11  Travel            200.00   200.00   400.00
12  Misc.             200.00   100.00   100.00
13
14
15
16
17
18
19
20
21
                                                             mem=234K
/=Menu Options    F1=Context Help    F2=General Help    F3=Edit    F10=Recalc All
```

BUDGRAPH ready for Graph commands

Graph Spreadsheet Data

If you encounter difficulties in displaying graphics on your computer screen or in printing your graphic images, then check the following items:

- The graphics program PCG2.EXE must be in the same directory as the PC-Calc+ program (normally the \PCCALC directory). If your PCG2.EXE program file is in another directory, then you must put a copy of that file in the \PCCALC directory (or the directory you are using for PC-Calc+), before you try using the Graph command.
- Your computer system must have a monitor and video card that can produce graphics. PC-Calc+ works with a wide variety of CGA, EGA, and VGA display adapters and monitors. Systems that have only a monochrome card cannot use the PC-Calc+ graphics features unless that card is Hercules-compatible.
- If you have a Hercules graphics card and a monochrome monitor, then run the MSHERC program *before* you start up PC-Calc+. Go into the \PCCALC directory and, at the DOS prompt, type **msherc** and press ENTER. Then, restart PC-Calc+ and load the BUDGRAPH file.
- If you have a CGA system, the only graphic colors available are black and white. You must have an EGA or VGA system to see other colors when using the PC-Calc+ graphics program.
- To print graphics on your printer, your printer must be compatible with one of the following pieces of equipment: EPSON (FX or MX) dot matrix, IBM dot matrix, Okidata dot matrix, or HP Laserjet.

Before you try to print a PC-Calc+ graphic, you must invoke the DOS GRAPHICS command:

At the DOS prompt, type:
graphics
and press ENTER

If you are using a printer supported by PC-Calc+, the DOS GRAPHICS command sets up your printer to print graphic screens. When you want to print a graphics screen, you press SHIFT-PRTSC. The DOS GRAPHICS program and your printer will do the rest.

If you do not have an IBM- or EPSON-compatible printer, then check your DOS disk for a version of GRAPHICS that works for your type of printer. Refer to your computer user's manuals and your DOS manual for more information.

If you had to exit PC-Calc+ in order to set up your graphics card or printer, start PC-Calc+ again and load the BUDGRAPH spreadsheet.

Activate the Graph Command

With BUDGRAPH loaded, do the following to activate the PC-Calc+ Graph command:

  Press /   (to bring up the Main menu)
  Press P   (to choose (P)rint/Graph option)
  Press G   (to choose (G)raph option)

The program first asks you to define the area to be graphed. To begin, tell PC-Calc+ to graph the January expense data in column C:

Press F6 (to clear the default input entry)
Type:
c4:c12 (only the numbers in column C)
and press ENTER

When you tell PC-Calc+ which data to graph, the program asks you to supply a label which describes what is being graphed. In this case, you are plotting dollar amounts of expenses:

Type:
Expenses in Dollars
and press ENTER

PC-Calc+ now asks you for the row number of the labels that identify the column(s) of data to be graphed. Since row 1 contains the labels for the January, February, and March columns:

Type:
1
and press ENTER

When you identify the row that contains the column identifiers, PC-Calc+ asks for the column that contains the row labels for the data. Column A contains that set of labels.

Type:
a
and press ENTER

A prompt asks for the *row category,* that is, the type of items being plotted. A good category name for all the row items would be Expenses:

Type:
Expenses
and press ENTER

Next, two separate prompts ask for a graph title and subtitle:

Type:
January Budget Figures   (at the prompt for TITLE)
and press ENTER

Type:
(Dollars)   (at the subTITLE prompt)
and press ENTER

A list of graph type options appears in the bottom left corner of the screen. The Graph Title options list shows you the different kinds of graphs that can be produced with PC-Calc+. The option you pick on this list becomes the default graphic display that PC-Calc+ uses to display your first graphic screen. Once PC-Calc+ displays the initial graphic, you will be able to switch between all of the other graphic formats with the touch of a key. For now, select the (V)ertical Bar graph format:

Press V

When you press V, PC-Calc+ asks if you want to save this definition in a table similar to the tables produced for a printed report. Go ahead and save the information:

Press Y

When you press Y, first the screen clears, and then you see PCG2.EXE appear in the upper left corner. After just a moment, PC-Calc+ displays the vertical bar chart shown in Figure 13-17.

How to Read the Chart

The bar chart in Figure 13-17 displays the heading "January Budget Figures" in large letters at the top of the screen. Under the heading is the subtitle "(Dollars)."

On the left side of the chart, you see a set of numbers (0 to 500) going up the screen, labeled with a vertical label, "Expenses in Dollars." Across the bottom, you see the name of the spreadsheet column that is being plotted, January.

On the middle right side of the chart, PC-Calc+ displays a legend to indicate what each item on the chart represents. Each legend item corresponds to one of the vertical bar chart towers in the center of the display.

The first legend item in the Expenses category is "Office Rent." The second legend item is "Office Suppl." Because of limited screen space, PC-Calc+ truncates the legend entries at the right edge of the screen.

Figure 13-17.

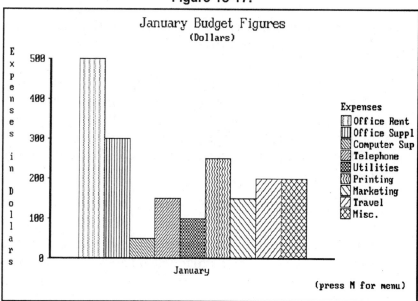

Vertical bar chart for January

The first legend entry corresponds to the leftmost vertical bar on the chart. The chart indicates that the office rent expense for January is $500, the exact value from the BUDGRAPH spreadsheet.

The second legend entry is for "Office Suppl." According to the second bar on the left side of the chart, that expense is $300. In this fashion, each of the legend entries match up with a specific January expense item on the chart.

When looking at graphs or charts made from a database, you often do not look for detailed information, such as the exact expenses for a particular month. You may look for trends and general impressions that might lead you to take specific actions.

For example, as the creator of this budget, you might look at the chart in Figure 13-17 and ask questions such as:

- Is it realistic to think that computer supplies will be the smallest monthly expense?
- Will office expenses actually be the second largest item after rent?
- What would this chart look like if all the data values in the spreadsheet were sorted into ascending order?

As you can see, putting data into graphical form can help you to assimilate information in ways that you cannot easily do by looking at tables of numbers. Using graphs and charts forces your brain to consider "the big picture."

In the bottom right corner of the screen, you see the following message:

(press M for menu)

When charts and graphs are displayed, pressing the letter M causes the Graphics menu to toggle on and off the screen. Since in the current screen the menu is off, pressing M will toggle the menu onto the screen.

The Graphics Menu

With the vertical bar chart "January Budget Figures" on the screen:

    Press M

When you press M, PC-Calc+ displays two Graphics menu lines across the bottom of the screen. You will see either the CGA/monochrome version or the EGA/VGA version of the menu display.

    The CGA/monochrome version looks like this:

```
GENERAL: (O)utput (M)enu  (Q)uit (L)ine (P)ie (H)bar (V)bar (S)catter
    BAR:          (T)-log (G)rid (X)chg c(U)m (A)vg  ov(E)rlap
```

The EGA/VGA version looks like this:

```
GENERAL: (O)utput (C)olor (M)enu (Q)uit  (P)ie  (L)ine (H)bar (V)bar (S)catter
    BAR:          (T)-log (G)rid (X)chg c(U)m (A)vg  ov(E)rlap
```

The EGA/VGA menu has the additional menu item (C)olor, which lets you adjust the colors of the graphic displays. Also, the EGA/VGA menu presents the option (P)ie before the option (L)ine. The CGA/monochrome menu shows (L)ine first, followed by (P)ie.

    In this chapter, only the EGA/VGA version of the Graphics menu will be used in examples. All of the commands on this menu can be activated by pressing the keys that match the letters in the sets of parentheses. The menu lines do not have to be visible for you to use the command keys.

    The GENERAL line of the menu remains the same, no matter which graph is being displayed. From the GENERAL line, you can activate (O)utput to print a graphic onto your printer. Choosing (C)olor brings up the color selection screen, where you can adjust the colors of PC-Calc+ to your system. Choosing (M)enu toggles the menu lines off the screen. (Q)uit causes you to exit from the PC-Calc+ graphics program and return to the PC-Calc+ main program.

The next five options on the GENERAL line let you select the type of graphic you want displayed: (P)ie charts, (L)ine graph, (H)bar for horizontal bar charts, (V)bar for vertical bar charts, and (S)catter plots. You will explore these last five options in just a moment.

The second menu line, marked BAR, changes as you activate the menu commands. In the current screen, PC-Calc+ displays a vertical bar chart. The presence of the BAR line indicates that a bar chart is being displayed. The options on the BAR line relate to bar charts. As you explore the various types of charts that PC-Calc+ produces, you will also explore the menu options on the second menu line.

In all of the following explorations, remember that you can remove the menu lines by pressing the M key. Also, as you get familiar with the graphics menu options, you will not need to see the menu lines to activate a command, because you only need to press the key for the command you want to use.

Line Graphs Figure 13-18 shows the PC-Calc+ graphic you get when you ask for a line graph of the data. The menu lines have been toggled off, so that you can see the bottom of the graph. To produce this graph, choose the (L)ine command:

    Press L

PC-Calc+ instantly displays the data in the line graph format! On the vertical bar chart (Figure 13-17), the individual titles were coded to the bars on the chart by shadings. A line graph represents the data only as points. Lines are constructed from point to point to form the graph. The line graph and the vertical bar chart both contain the same information. The information is simply displayed in different formats.

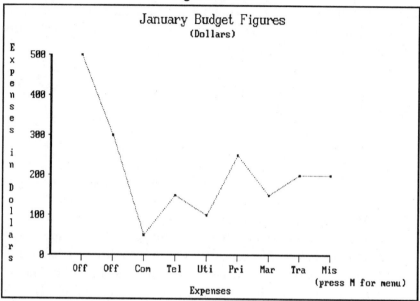

Line graph for January

PC-Calc+ writes the first few letters of each expense item across the bottom of the graph to indicate which point corresponds to which expense. In Figure 13-17, the first vertical indicator labeled "Off" is for Office Rent. The second vertical indicator labeled "Off" is for Office Supplies. As you can see, this form of the display is difficult to decipher because of the truncated labels.

When you press M to toggle the menu, you see that the second menu line has changed. The line is now marked LINE, for line graph, and the options are slightly different, as shown here:

```
GENERAL:  (O)utput (C)olor (M)enu (Q)uit (P)ie (L)ine (H)bar (V)bar (S)catter
   LINE:           (T)-log (G)rid (X)chg c(U)m (A)vg  (F)it  (0-9)-Smoothed Avg
```

The ov(E)rlap option for bar charts has disappeared, and two new options for line graphs are shown: (F)it and "(0-9)-Smoothed

Avg." These two options deal with analyzing the plotted data for trends and patterns. In general, these options are most often used with data that varies over time, for example, expenses across several months or years.

Pie Charts   The next type of graph is a pie chart. To see the PC-Calc+ pie chart graphic:

   Press P

The first time you use the PC-Calc+ graphics features and press P, the program automatically brings up the aspect ratio screen. After the first automatic display, the program will display the aspect ratio screen only when you select the (A)spect menu item. The aspect ratio screen allows you to adjust the shape of the pie charts that are produced. You can press the arrow keys to make the sample pie shape shrink and grow in height and width. For now, if you see the aspect ratio screen, simply exit that screen:

   Press Q

When you press P (or Q if the aspect ratio screen is on the screen), PC-Calc+ displays your data in the form of pie chart. Figure 13-19 shows how the pie chart screen looks, with the menu removed. This graphic is the PC-Calc+ standard way of displaying pie chart information.

The pie chart offers you an entirely new way to look at data. Instead of gross dollar amounts, as in the bar chart and the line graph, the pie chart displays expenses as percentages. You can quickly see that office rent constitutes 26% of your total expenses. January office supplies represent 16% of that month's budget. Printing is 13% and travel and miscellaneous expenses are each 11%. Each of the other expense items are under 10% each.

As with the other graphics commands, using the (P)ie command changes the second menu line:

Importing, Graphing, and Other Features **553**
Ch 13

```
GENERAL: (O)utput (C)olor (M)enu (Q)uit (P)ie (L)ine (H)bar (V)bar (S)catter
PIE: (A)spect (W)edge (D)isp (X)chg
```

(A)spect controls how round or oval shaped the pie chart will be. The (A)spect command is easy to use, and you may want to explore it on your own. Changes you make to the shape of pie charts get recorded and are used on future pie chart displays. If you use the (A)spect command to change the shape of the pie chart shown in Figure 13-19, the next three pie charts (Figures 13-20, 13-21, and 13-22) will also be changed to your new Aspect setting.

(W)edge lets you detach one or more sections of your pie chart. This feature is handy when you are making presentations and you want to emphasize one part of a pie chart for discussion. The (W)edge feature is both fun and easy to use. You can explore it on

Figure 13-19.

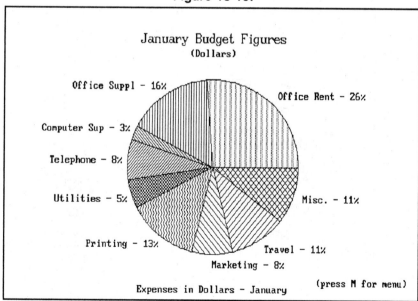

Pie chart for January

your own. Again, if you use the (W)edge command to alter the pie chart shown in Figure 13-19, you will see the same alterations appear in the pie charts shown in Figures 13-20, 13-21, and 13-22.

Each time you press D to activate the (D)isp command, PC-Calc+ switches the pie chart display to one of three formats. The first format is the standard display shown in Figure 13-19. To see the pie chart that is shown in Figure 13-20:

Press D

When you press D, PC-Calc+ rearranges the display so that only the percentages appear next to the pie. The expense labels are pulled back into a legend block on the right corner of the screen. This pie chart format might come in handy should you want to use the (W)edge option to detach a couple of the parts of the pie while keeping the area around the pie uncluttered.

Figure 13-20.

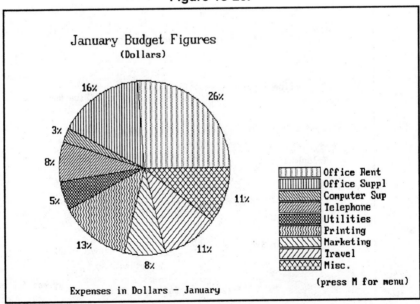

Pie chart for January: Display option 2

Figure 13-21.

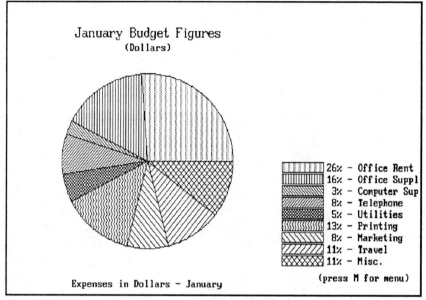

Pie chart for January: Display option 3

To see the final form of the pie chart display:

Press D

When you press D, you see the pie chart shown in Figure 13-21. In this version of the pie chart, all the data around the pie has been pulled back to the legend block in the right corner. This pie chart format might be used when you want to emphasize and talk about a single part of the chart. Alter the pie chart as follows:

Press W, D, Q

When you press this sequence of keys, you first activate the (W)edge command. Then, you (D)etach the first wedge. Finally, you (Q)uit the (W)edge command. The result on your screen should look like the pie chart shown in Figure 13-22.

Figure 13-22.

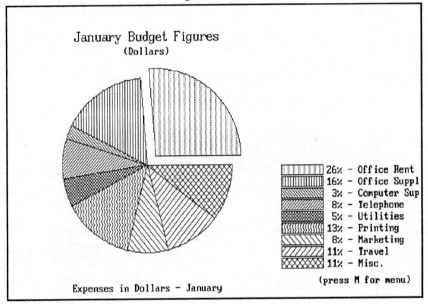

Pie chart for January with wedge detached

PC-Calc+ gives you easy-to-use powerful graphics capabilities with only a few keystrokes.

Bar Charts   PC-Calc+ displays bar charts in two formats: vertical and horizontal. The first PC-Calc+ graphic you saw was a vertical bar chart of the data from the BUDGRAPH spreadsheet. To see the same chart in a horizontal format:

Press H

The resultant chart is the vertical bar chart rotated clockwise to a horizontal orientation. The bars go across rather than up the screen. PC-Calc+ has rearranged the labels to reflect the new orientation for the graphic.

Importing, Graphing, and Other Features

Scatter Diagrams A *scatter diagram* is a line graph without the lines. In a scatter diagram, only the data points get plotted. To see the January expense data as a scatter diagram:

   Press S

The scatter diagram looks exactly like the line graph displayed earlier, but without the lines. If you alternately press L and S, PC-Calc+ will flip back and forth between the line graph and scatter diagram formats, and you can see the correspondence.

Averages and Other Arithmetic PC-Calc+ can perform simple and complex arithmetic tasks with graphed and plotted data. To explore one of these PC-Calc+ arithmetic features, display the vertical bar chart for the January expenses data:

   Press V

Suppose you are looking at the bar chart and would like to know what the average expenses are for the month. Of course, you could look back at your actual data, locate the total, $1,900, and divide by nine, for the nine expense categories. The result would be the average expenses.

   PC-Calc+ provides an easy way to calculate the average expenses, with one keypress:

   Press A

When you press A with at the vertical bar chart for the January expenses on the screen, a horizontal line appears across the bars, as shown in Figure 13-23. The line represents the average value for the nine displayed values. According to PC-Calc+, the average for the expense figures is about $210. The actual value is $1,900 divided by 9, or $211.11.

Figure 13-23.

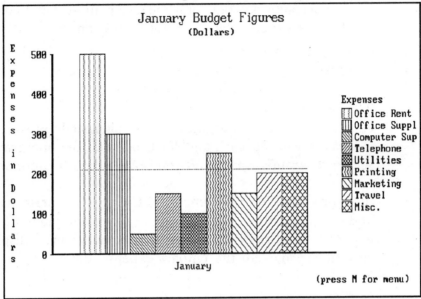

Average of January expenses

The (A)vg graphics command works on any chart type except pie charts. Experiment with the (A)vg command by switching around to the different types of graphics that PC-Calc+ can produce and pressing A. Since the data for the graphs are all the same, the average for each graph should be the same, about $210.

After you finish exploring the PC-Calc+ (A)vg command, bring back the vertical bar chart:

Press V

Suppose you want to express the total of the January expense categories as a graphic. You know that the total is $1,900, but how would you display that result? To get the total January expenses, you would activate the c(U)m command. The c(U)m command tells PC-Calc+ to accumulate, or form, the cumulative total of all the displayed data. Do the following:

Press U

When you press U, the cumulative bar chart shown in Figure 13-24 appears on the screen. PC-Calc+ automatically scaled the numbers on the left side by 1000 and put a note to that effect (Scaled by: 1000) at the bottom of the screen. The top of the chart indicates that the total revenue is about 1.9 times 1000, or $1,900. Notice that you still can see the relative contribution of each expense item to the total. The first item, "Office Rent" (bottom of the bar on the chart), represents $500 (.5 times 1000). The second item, "Office suppl," contributed about $300 to the monthly total.

This section concludes the preliminary investigation of the PC-Calc+ graphics capabilities. As you have seen, PC-Calc+ lets you quickly and easily produce sophisticated and informative

Figure 13-24.

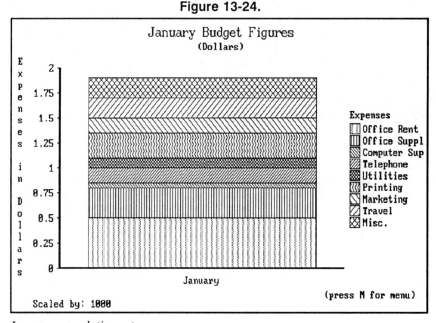

January cumulative expenses

graphics from your spreadsheet data. In the following section, you will create graphics based on more than one column of the BUDGRAPH spreadsheet.

Leave the Graphics Program

To create additional graphics based on different data, you must leave the graphics program and return to the PC-Calc+ main program:

    Press Q

When you press Q, the screen clears, and you see the ButtonWare copyright notice. Then the BUDGRAPH spreadsheet reappears along with the Print/Graph options list. PC-Calc+ returned you to the exact place from which you began your first exploration of PC-Calc+ graphics.

Graph Multiple Columns

To graph two columns of BUDGRAPH data, you can make use of the table that PC-Calc+ created when you activated the first set of graphs and charts. The Print/Graph options list contains an option called "(C)hange/run saved graphs." Select that option:

    Press C   (to select "(C)hange/run saved graphs" option)

When you press C, PC-Calc+ displays the Graph Data table shown in Figure 13-25. This table works exactly like the Reports table

Importing, Graphing, and Other Features

Figure 13-25.

									Graph Table
PC-Calc+ GRAPH DATA TABLE									
Title	Sub-tit	Col-Cat	Row-Cat	Data-df	Data-loc	HD-C	HD-R	⏎Type	⏎X-VAR
January	(Dollar	A1		Expense	Expense	C4:C12	A	1	V-BAR	X-VAL

Use ↑↓←→ to move highlight. (⏎ Press Enter to toggle data.)
Press / for line options and to exit

PC-Calc+ Graph Data Table

you used in printing the BACKPACK spreadsheet earlier in this chapter. Most of the items in the Graph Data table are data entries you made when you first used the Graph command. Therefore, you can change those items by editing the original values.

Suppose you wished to graph the first two month's of the BUDGRAPH data together. You could go back and use the Graph command and reenter all the necessary data. An easier way to accomplish the same task is to use the PC-Calc+ Graph Data table and create a new graph specification. With the Graph Data table displayed as shown in Figure 13-25, here is how to do that task:

    Press /   (to activate the Table options list)
    Press C   (to select "(C)opy line" option)

When you press C, the current graph specification (the only row in the table) begins to blink. If there were more entries in the table, the blinking would follow your movements as you moved to different lines. At the bottom of the screen, PC-Calc+ tells you to move to a line, and then press either CTRL-A or CTRL-B. CTRL-A places a copy of the selected line above the blinking line. CTRL-B places a copy of the selected line below the blinking line. CTRL-X cancels the copy operation.

Insert a copy of the selected line (in this case the only line) below the blinking line:

Press CTRL-B

The table now contains two copies of the graph specification for the January expenses. Move the highlight down to the second line and to the word "January" in the Title column. Then, do the following:

Press F3

When you press F3, the edit line at the bottom of the screen displays the title for the previous graphics, "January Budget Figures." Change the title as follows:

Type:
Jan/Feb Budget Figures
and press ENTER

When you press ENTER, the entry on the second line under Title becomes "Jan/Feb." Next, move the highlight to the second entry, C4:C12, of the "Data-loc" column. Then, do the following:

Importing, Graphing, and Other Features **563**

Ch 13

    Press F3   (to activate the Edit mode)

    Type:
    c4:d12   (to select January and February data)
    and press ENTER

You are ready to ask PC-Calc+ to display the new set of graphics. Bring up the Table Options list and execute the current Graph Data table line:

    Press /   (to activate the Table options list)
    Press E   (to select (E)xecute option)

PC-Calc+ displays a question box asking if you want to change any of your responses. Since you do not need to make any changes:

    Press N

After you press N, PC-Calc+ loads the graphics program and displays your first January/February plot: a vertical bar chart of expenses for the two months. Figure 13-26 shows what this bar chart looks like on your screen.

    Do you notice anything different about this chart when compared to the chart for January alone? The legends are interchanged. On the January chart (Figure 13-17), the label at the bottom of the chart is the word "January," and the legends on the right side of the screen are labeled "Expenses." On the January/February chart the label at the bottom of the screen is "Expenses," the individual expense labels appear in truncated form across the bottom of the chart, and the legend on the right side of the screen lists "January" and "February."

Figure 13-26.

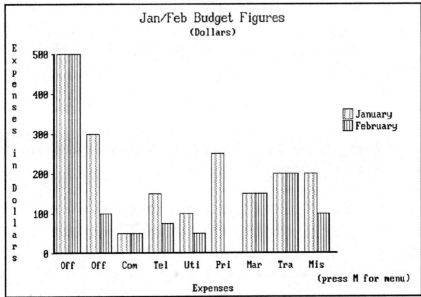

Vertical bar chart of Jan/Feb data

Despite these temporary rearrangements, the chart itself is useful. Expense items for the two months appear side by side on the chart making comparisons easy. At a glance, you can see that the first item, office rent (the first "Off"), is the same for both months. Office supplies (the second "Off") shows a $200 difference. Printing (Pri) has no February expense.

What if you wanted to compare this chart with the chart shown in Figure 13-17, while maintaining the same general format? First, activate the PC-Calc+ graphics menu:

Press M

When you press M, the Graphics menu appears, as shown below:

```
GENERAL: (O)utput (C)olor (M)enu (Q)uit (P)ie (L)ine (H)bar (V)bar (S)catter
    BAR:         (T)-log (G)rid (X)chg c(U)m (A)vg  ov(E)rlap
```

Try the (X)chg command on the second menu line:

Press X

When you press X, PC-Calc+ exchanges the labels and legends on the bar chart. The chart now looks like the one shown in Figure 13-27. The format of this chart is similar to the chart in Figure 13-17—the data for each month appears in a separate cluster.

Try creating a pie chart with two months of data:

Press P

The pie chart for January appears when you press P. Where is the February data? If you examine the Graphics menu, you will see a

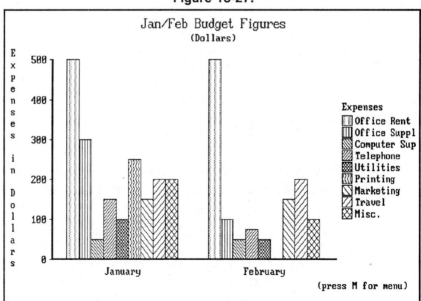

Figure 13-27.

Vertical bar chart of Jan/Feb after the (X)chg command

couple of new options, which appeared because there is now additional data. Bring up the menu:

Press M

The Graphics menu now looks like this:

```
GENERAL: (O)utput (C)olor (M)enu (Q)uit (P)ie (L)ine (H)bar (V)bar (S)catter
    PIE: (A)spect (W)edge (D)isp (X)chg (1-2) #pies  (N)ext group
```

One new option is "(N)ext group." The "(N)ext group" option will bring up the February pie chart:

Press N

When you press N, the pie chart for February is displayed. What if you want to look at both pie charts at the same time? You can use the "(1-2) #pies" option to display two pie charts at a time:

Press 2

Figure 13-28 shows the two pie charts as they appear on one screen. To go back to a single pie chart display, press 1.

Go ahead and experiment with all of the PC-Calc+ commands on the Graphics menu. Create a line graph with the January/February data. Exchange the legends on that graph by using the (X)chg command. Try the (A)verage command, the c(U)mulative command, and all the other commands. When you are ready to go back to the PC-Calc+ main program, use the (Q)uit command.

Figure 13-28.

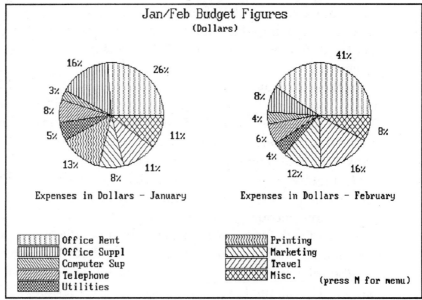

Jan/Feb data as two pie charts

Summary

In this final chapter of *The Shareware Book,* you learned how to split the PC-Calc+ spreadsheet screen and use the two windows to perform a variety of spreadsheet tasks. You also experimented with the powerful PC-Calc+ Sort command. You used the Sort command to rearrange entire blocks of spreadsheet data.

You learned how to use the PC-Calc+ table features which "remember" the sets of commands and data entries that you type. The PC-Calc+ table features display your typed sequences of commands and data in neatly organized tables. You used the tabular displays to store report and graphics specifications. You also used the tables to edit the saved data and to create new specifications based on the saved information.

You explored the PC-Calc+ Import command, which allowed you to move selected data from one spreadsheet to another. You then used the imported data to generate a variety of charts, graphs, and plots, using the PC-Calc+ sophisticated graphics capabilities.

In these last four chapters, you have been introduced to the major features of PC-Calc+, an electronic spreadsheet package that lets you take control of the calculational powers of the personal computer. No attempt has been made to cover all of the many PC-Calc+ commands, functions, and resources. To do so would require a much larger book. However, based on what you have learned and discovered within these chapters on PC-Calc+, you are now encouraged to explore PC-Calc+ on your own.

To assist with future explorations, the appendixes at the end of this book list additional reference material about PC-Calc+. You can also refer to the *PC-Calc+ User's Manual* for additional information. The manual is included with every registered copy of PC-Calc+. Remember, if you are a registered PC-Calc+ owner, you also have unlimited access to the ButtonWare technical support system.

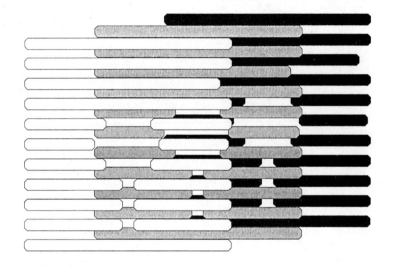

Appendixes

PART IV

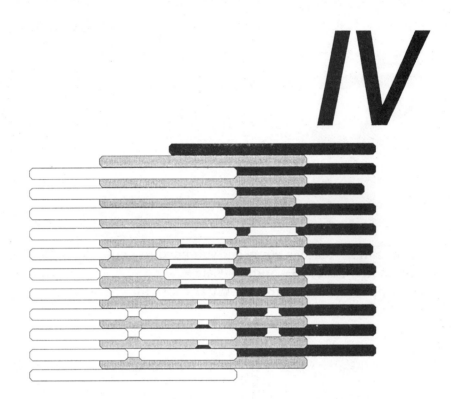

General Information for PC Users

Appendix A teaches you what you need to know about DOS to use PC-Write, PC-File+, and PC-Calc+.

Appendix B is a table of ASCII codes for characters.

APPENDIX

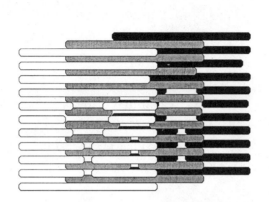

DOS Essentials

This appendix provides an introduction to DOS, the computer's Disk Operating System. Computer programs (software) are usually supplied on disks. In order to use disk software, you must first load DOS into your computer. In this appendix, you will learn a little bit about DOS, enough to enable you to use PC-Write, PC-File+, and PC-Calc+. In particular, you will learn:

- How to load DOS into the computer
- How to set the date and time
- How to use the DOS CLS command to clear the screen
- How to use the DOS DIR command to display a directory of all files on a disk
- How to use the DOS FORMAT command to format a disk
- How to use the DOS DISKCOPY command to copy everything on a disk to another disk
- How to use the DOS COPY command to copy a file
- How to use the DOS DEL command to delete a file

In this appendix, and throughout the book, the term DOS is used to mean either Microsoft MS-DOS or IBM PC-DOS. For a thorough introduction to DOS, try the book *DOS Made Easy*, by Herbert Schildt (Berkeley, Calif.: Osborne McGraw-Hill, 1988).

Starting DOS

DOS is the master program that you use to control your computer. You first load DOS, and then you type DOS *commands* to tell the computer what you want it to do. You can type a command whenever you see the DOS prompt (>) and the blinking cursor (_) on the screen. The prompt is preceded by a disk drive letter.

Types of Systems

If you have a hard disk system, DOS is probably resident on your hard disk. A hard disk is usually designated drive C. Therefore, you can type a DOS command whenever you see the DOS C prompt (C>) and the blinking cursor, as shown here:

```
C>_
```

If you have a floppy disk system (no hard disk), then you will load DOS from disk drive A. Therefore, you can type a DOS command whenever you see a DOS A prompt (A>) and the blinking cursor, as follows:

```
A>_
```

An easy system for a beginner to use is a computer such as the Tandy 1000SL or 1000TL, in which the essential parts of DOS are in read-only memory (ROM). Since DOS is built in to the system, it is always there. You do not have to install it on a hard disk or load it from a floppy disk. On these computers, you can type a DOS command whenever you see the DOS C prompt and the blinking cursor, as shown here:

```
C>_
```

Other computers that have the essential parts of DOS in ROM include the Toshiba T1000 laptop computer and the Headstart Explorer. This seems to be a trend for computers designed for home or school use, where ease of use is especially important. In the future, you can expect to see more computers featuring DOS in ROM.

Load DOS from Disk Drive A

In this section, it is assumed that you have a system with one or two floppy disk drives, but no hard disk. The main disk drive is designated drive A. You will load DOS from a disk in drive A. The information shown here is for a Tandy 1000TX using MS-DOS version 3.20. If you are using a different system, then the procedures are the same, but the information shown on your screen may be somewhat different.

Insert the DOS disk in drive A, and turn on your computer. You will soon see information on the screen similar to the following:

```
Microsoft MS-DOS Version 3.20
(C)Copyright Microsoft Corp 1981, 1986
Tandy version 03.20.21
Licensed to Tandy Corp.
All rights reserved.

Current date is Tue  1-01-1980
Enter new date (mm-dd-yy): _
```

Of course, if your computer is equipped with an automatic clock and calendar, then you will not see the request to enter a new date. If you see the request for a new date, go ahead and enter it. Type the number of the month (1 to 12), a hyphen (-), the day of the month (1 to 31), a hyphen (-), and the last two digits of the year. Here is an example:

```
Enter new date (mm-dd-yy): 1-1-90
```

After typing the date, press the ENTER key. If your computer does not have an automatic clock, then you will see the following (or a similar) message:

```
Current time is  0:07:38.57
Enter new time: _
```

Since the computer uses a 24-hour clock, you should enter the time by typing the hour (0 to 23), a colon (:), the minutes (0 to 59), and, if you wish, another colon (:) followed by the seconds (0 to 59). For example:

```
Enter new time: 13:30
```

The time shown here (13:30) is 1:30 P.M. Remember, the computer uses a 24-hour clock, so add 12 to the number of hours at or after 1:00 P.M.

After typing the time, press the ENTER key. You will next see the disk drive designation (A), the prompt (>), and the blinking cursor, as shown here:

```
A>_
```

The screen on your computer should now be similar to the screen shown in Figure A-1. Of course, the date and time will be the date and time that you entered; other information on the screen may also differ. If your computer has an automatic clock and calendar, you are not prompted to enter the date and time. The appearance of your screen will be similar to the one shown in Figure A-2.

The screens shown in Figures A-1 and A-2 are two possible versions of the DOS opening screen. Note the DOS A prompt (A>) and the blinking cursor (_). This is the DOS *command line*. At the DOS command line, you can type a valid DOS command and press the ENTER key. DOS will immediately execute your command. In this appendix, you will learn how to use the following DOS commands: CLS, DIR, FORMAT, DISKCOPY, COPY, and DEL.

Load DOS on a Hard Disk System

A hard disk system typically has a hard disk drive designated drive C, a floppy disk drive designated drive A, and perhaps a second floppy drive designated drive B. DOS resides on the hard disk.

Figure A-1.

```
BIOS ROM version 01.03.00
Compatibility Software
Copyright (C) 1984,1985,1986,1987
Phoenix Software Associates Ltd.
and Tandy Corporation.
All rights reserved.

Microsoft MS-DOS Version 3.20
(C)Copyright Microsoft Corp 1981, 1986
Tandy version 03.20.21
Licensed to Tandy Corp.
All rights reserved.

Current date is Tue 1-01-1980
Enter new date (mm-dd-yy): 1-1-90
Current time is 0:07:38.57
Enter new time: 13:30

Microsoft(R) MS-DOS(R) Version 3.20
         (C)Copyright Microsoft Corp 1981-1986

A>_
```

Tandy 1000TX screen after loading DOS

When you turn on your computer, it will first try to load DOS from drive A. If there is no disk in drive A, then it will then try to load DOS from drive C, the hard disk drive. Therefore, to run DOS from your hard disk, first make sure that there is no disk in drive A, and then turn on your computer. The computer will check drive A, find no DOS disk, and then load DOS from drive C, the hard disk drive.

In loading DOS from your hard disk, proceed as described in loading DOS from drive A. If your computer does not have an automatic clock and calendar, you will be prompted to set the date

DOS Essentials **579**

Appendix A

Figure A-2.

```
BIOS ROM version 01.04.02
Compatibility Software
Copyright (C) 1984,1985,1986,1987,1988
Phoenix Software Associates Ltd.
and Tandy Corporation.
All rights reserved.

Microsoft MS-DOS Version 3.30
(C)Copyright Microsoft Corp 1981-1987
Tandy Version 03.30.20
Licensed to Tandy Corp.
All rights reserved.


A>_
```

After loading DOS on a system with an automatic clock and calendar

and time. Simply follow the directions on the screen. When DOS is loaded, you will see the DOS C prompt and blinking cursor, as shown here:

C>_

The Default Drive

If you load DOS from disk drive A and see the DOS A prompt, then you know that disk drive A is the *default drive*. Unless you designate another drive when you give certain DOS commands, DOS will look to drive A.

If you load DOS from the hard disk (drive C) and see the DOS C prompt, then you know that disk drive C is the default drive. Unless you designate another drive when you give certain DOS commands, DOS will look to drive C.

After DOS is loaded from either drive A or drive C, you can change the default drive. Of course, you can only change the default drive to a drive that exists on your computer. For example, suppose your computer is a system with two floppy drives, but no hard drive. You have loaded DOS from drive A and see the DOS A prompt and cursor, as shown here:

A>_

Drive A is the default drive. Change the default drive to drive B, as follows:

Type:
b:
and press ENTER

The DOS A prompt will change to a DOS B prompt. The screen will appear as shown here:

A>B:
B>_

Drive B is now the default drive. To change back to drive A as the default drive, simply type **a:** and press ENTER. You will again see the DOS A prompt and cursor (A>_).

DOS Commands

Recent versions of DOS have more than 60 commands. Some commands have several variations. Fortunately, you can start with only a few commands and use DOS quite effectively. In this section, you will learn how to use the following DOS commands: CLS, DIR, FORMAT, DISKCOPY, COPY, and DEL.

In describing DOS commands, it is assumed that the default drive is drive A. You type a command at the DOS A prompt. If you are working out of your hard disk, then substitute the DOS C prompt wherever you see the A prompt.

Before you begin, try entering a nonexistent DOS command. At the A prompt (or C prompt), do the following:

Type:
SING
and press ENTER

After a brief pause, DOS replies with the message "Bad command or file name." It then displays the A prompt and blinking cursor, and waits for your next command. The screen looks like this:

```
A>SING
Bad command or file name

A>_
```

DOS cannot sing, but it can do many other useful things. If you misspell a command word or type a word that DOS does not understand, then you will see an error message. That's okay, just try again.

The CLS Command

The CLS command clears the screen, leaving only the A prompt and the blinking cursor in the upper left corner of the screen.

Type:
cls
and press ENTER

You can type the clear screen command in all lowercase letters as shown, or in uppercase letters (CLS), or in any mixture of uppercase and lowercase letters (Cls).

The DIR Command

You can use the DIR command to display a directory of files on the disk in any disk drive. To obtain a directory of files on the disk in the default drive, do the following:

Type:
dir
and press ENTER

Figure A-3 shows a directory of files on the PC-Write program disk. This entire directory fits on the screen. However, if a directory is too large to fit on the screen, information will scroll off the top of the screen and you will see only part of the directory. You can "freeze" the screen by using the SCROLL LOCK key. If your computer does not have a SCROLL LOCK key, try holding down the CTRL key and pressing the S key. On the Tandy 1000TX, press the HOLD key to freeze the screen. Press the same key or key combination again to "unfreeze" the screen.

You can tell DOS to print the directory directly to the printer, as follows:

Type:
dir > prn
and press ENTER

You can also tell DOS to print a directory of files on the disk in a designated disk drive. To do so, type the disk drive letter and a colon (:) following the DIR command. For example, to get a directory of files on the disk in drive B, do the following:

Type:
dir b:
and press ENTER

Figure A-3.

```
A>dir

Volume in drive A has no label
Directory of  A:\

GO       BAT        12   5-18-86   8:32p
READ     ME       1012  11-10-88   3:06p
GETYN    COM       161  11-11-88   6:25p
WORKDISK BAT      6241   5-04-89   2:44p
INSTALL  DOC      5865   5-04-89   2:39p
ED       EXE    260912   4-30-89   5:23p
ED       HLP     72684   5-04-89   2:24p
ED       DEF        97  10-26-88   3:47a
ED       TRS      1017   5-04-89   2:22p
ED       SPC       886  10-25-88   2:02a
PROGRAM  DIR       950   5-04-89   2:56p
       11 File(s)     375808 bytes free

A>_
```

A directory of the PC-Write program disk

Appendix A

If you want to display the names of files in a large directory on screen, you can tell DOS to print a wide directory. Figure A-4 shows a wide directory of files on the DOS disk supplied with the Tandy 1000TX. To display a wide directory of the disk in the default drive, do the following:

Type:
dir /w
and press ENTER

Note that in a wide directory, only the file names are printed.

Figure A-4.

```
A>dir /w

Volume in drive A has no label
Directory of  A:\

COMMAND  COM     ANSI     SYS    ASSIGN   COM    ATTRIB   EXE    BASICA   COM
BASIC    EXE     CHKDSK   COM    DISKCOMP COM    DISKCOPY COM    DISKTYPE COM
DRIVER   SYS     FC       EXE    FIND     EXE    FORMAT   COM    GRAPHICS COM
JOIN     EXE     KEYTCF   COM    KEYTFR   COM    KEYTGR   COM    KEYTIT   COM
KEYTSP   COM     KEYTUK   COM    LABEL    COM    LF       COM    LPDRVR   SYS
MODE     COM     MORE     COM    PRINT    COM    REPLACE  EXE    SELECT   COM
SORT     EXE     SUBST    EXE    SYS      COM    TREE     COM    VDISK    SYS
XCOPY    EXE     APPEND   COM    AUTOFMT  EXE    BACKUP   COM    CACHE    COM
CPANEL   COM     DC       COM    DEBUG    COM    DISKOPT  COM    EDLIN    COM
EXE2BIN  EXE     FBACKUP  COM    FDISK    COM    FRESTORE COM    HSECT    COM
KEYCNVRT SYS     LIB      EXE    LINK     EXE    LPSETUP  COM    MLFORMAT COM
MLPART   COM     MLPART   SYS    MOUSE    COM    MOUSE    SYS    PATCH    COM
RCRYPT   COM     RECOVER  COM    RESTORE  COM    SHARE    EXE    SHIPTRAK COM
SPOOLER  COM     SPOOLER  SYS
       67 File(s)       97280 bytes free

A>_
```

A wide directory of files on the DOS disk

Appendix A

The FORMAT Command

Before using a disk, you must first *format* it. If a disk has not been formatted, the computer cannot write information to it or read information from it. Formatting a disk prepares an unused disk for use by your computer. You can also format a previously used disk.

CAUTION Formatting a previously used disk erases all information from the disk. If you accidentally format a disk that contains information, that information will be erased. Use the DIR command to see what files are on the disk before you format it.

To format a disk, use the DOS FORMAT command, followed by a disk drive designation. For example, to format a disk in drive B, put your DOS disk in drive A and the disk to be formatted in drive B. Then, do the following:

Type:
format b:
and press ENTER

The computer will read a formatting program from the DOS disk in drive A, and then prompt you to insert a disk in drive B, as shown here. (The message on your screen might be somewhat different.)

```
Insert new diskette for drive B:
and strike ENTER when ready
```

If you have already put a disk in drive B, just press ENTER. Otherwise, put a disk in drive B and then press ENTER. DOS will format the disk and also test it for certain defects. At the end of the formatting process, you will see a message similar to the following for a 5 1/4-inch disk.

```
Format complete

    362496 bytes total disk space
    362496 bytes available on disk
```

Format another (Y/N)?_

If you format a 3 1/2-inch disk, you will see a slightly different message, as shown here:

```
Format complete

    730112 bytes total disk space
    730112 bytes available on disk
```

Format another (Y/N)?

Occasionally, a disk will have one or more defects. In this case, the formatting process marks the bad *sectors* and tells you about them in the "Format complete" message:

```
Format complete

    362496 bytes total disk space
      5120 bytes in bad sectors
    357376 bytes available on disk
```

Format another (Y/N)?

If you see a "bad sectors" message, as shown, do not use the disk. Discard it. Remove the formatted disk from drive B, and then either press Y and press ENTER to format another disk, or press N and press ENTER to quit. Be sure to label the freshly formatted disk so that you know it is ready to use. If the label is already affixed to the disk, then use a soft felt tip pen so that you do not damage the disk.

If you have only one disk drive, you can tell the computer to format a disk in drive B. Put the DOS disk in drive A and type

format b:. When prompted for the disk to be formatted in drive B, remove the DOS disk, insert the disk to be formatted, and press ENTER. DOS has temporarily renamed drive A as drive B and will format the disk as if your computer actually had two disk drives, A and B.

If you are working from a hard disk (C> _), you can either type **format a:** to format a disk in drive A or type **format b:** to format a disk in drive B.

The DISKCOPY Command

Use the DISKCOPY command to copy the entire contents of a disk to another disk. The two disks must be of the same size and have the same capacity. You can copy a 5 1/4-inch 360K disk to a 5 1/4-inch 360K disk. You can copy a 3 1/2-inch 720K disk to a 3 1/2-inch 720K disk. However, you cannot copy a 3 1/2-inch 720K disk to a 5 1/4-inch 360K disk. If the two disks are incompatible, then DOS will print a message such as the following:

```
Drive types or diskette types
not compatible
Copy process ended
```

To copy a disk in drive A to a disk in drive B, put your DOS disk in drive A, and then do the following:

> Type:
> **diskcopy a: b:**
> and press ENTER

You will see the following (or a similar) message:

```
Insert SOURCE diskette in drive A:
Press any key when ready . . .
```

The disk you are copying *from* is the *source* disk; the disk you are copying *to* is the *target* disk. Remove the DOS disk from drive A. Put the source disk in drive A and press any key (the SPACEBAR is a good choice). You will see a message similar to the following:

```
Copying 40 tracks
9 Sectors/Track, 2 side(s)
```

This message is for a 5 1/4-inch 360K disk. If you are using a 3 1/2-inch 720K disk, the message will read "Copying 80 tracks." In a few moments, you will see this message:

```
Insert TARGET diskette in drive A:
Press any key when ready. . .
```

Put a target disk in drive B and press any key. DOS will make an exact copy of the entire disk in drive A on the disk in drive B. If you should put a disk in drive B that is not formatted, DOS will first format the disk, and then make the copy.

At the end of a DISKCOPY operation, you are asked if you want to make another copy, as follows:

```
Copy another (Y/N)?_
```

If you do not want to make another copy, press N and press ENTER. If you want to make another copy, first remove the copy you just made from drive B, press Y and press ENTER, and then proceed as before.

If your computer has only one floppy drive, then you can still use the DISKCOPY command. You will be prompted to insert the source disk, then the target disk, then the source disk, then the target disk, and so on until the copy is made.

The COPY Command

Use the COPY command to copy individual files from one disk to another disk. For example, suppose you want to copy PC-Write's ED.EXE file from a disk in drive A to a disk in drive B. Make sure the source disk containing the ED.EXE file is in drive A and the target disk on which you want to make a copy is in drive B, and then do this:

> Type:
> **copy a:ed.exe b:**
> and press ENTER

DOS copies the ED.EXE file from the disk in drive A to the disk in drive B. The file is stored on the disk in drive B with the file name ED.EXE. You can use the DIR B: command to verify that the file is now on drive B.

You can copy a file from drive A to drive B so that it appears on drive B under a different file name. For example, suppose you want to copy a file called TWEEDLE.DEE from drive A to drive B and call the copy TWEEDLE.DUM. Do it like this:

> Type:
> **copy a:tweedle.dee b:tweedle.dum**
> and press ENTER

If you want to make a copy of a file on the same disk, you must give the copy a name that is different from the name of the original file. For example:

> Type:
> **copy a:tweedle.dee a:tweedle.dum**
> and press ENTER

The DEL Command

You can use the DEL command to delete (erase) a file from a disk, but be careful. Once you delete a file, it is gone! To delete a file called SCRATCH.PAD from the disk in drive B, do the following:

Type:
del b:scratch.pad
and press ENTER

To delete a file called OLDSTUFF.TXT from drive A, do the following:

Type:
del a:oldstuff.txt
and press ENTER

Remember to be careful about deleting files so that you do not accidentally delete a file that you want to keep.

APPENDIX B

ASCII Codes

This appendix lists the ASCII codes for characters.

Decimal Value	Hexadecimal Value	Control Character	Character
0	00	NUL	Null
1	01	SOH	☺
2	02	STX	☻
3	03	ETX	♥
4	04	EOT	♦
5	05	ENQ	♣
6	06	ACK	♠
7	07	BEL	Beep
8	08	BS	◘

Appendix B

Decimal Value	Hexadecimal Value	Control Character	Character
9	09	HT	Tab
10	0A	LF	Line-feed
11	0B	VT	Cursor home
12	0C	FF	Form-feed
13	0D	CR	Enter
14	0E	SO	
15	0F	SI	
16	10	DLE	
17	11	DC1	
18	12	DC2	
19	13	DC3	
20	14	DC4	
21	15	NAK	
22	16	SYN	
23	17	ETB	
24	18	CAN	↑
25	19	EM	↓
26	1A	SUB	→
27	1B	ESC	←
28	1C	FS	Cursor right
29	1D	GS	Cursor left
30	1E	RS	Cursor up
31	1F	US	Cursor down
32	20	SP	Space
33	21		!
34	22		"
35	23		#
36	24		$
37	25		%
38	26		&
39	27		'
40	28		(
41	29		)
42	2A		*
43	2B		+

Decimal Value	Hexadecimal Value	Control Character	Character
44	2C		,
45	2D		-
46	2E		.
47	2F		/
48	30		0
49	31		1
50	32		2
51	33		3
52	34		4
53	35		5
54	36		6
55	37		7
56	38		8
57	39		9
58	3A		:
59	3B		;
60	3C		<
61	3D		=
62	3E		>
63	3F		?
64	40		@
65	41		A
66	42		B
67	43		C
68	44		D
69	45		E
70	46		F
71	47		G
72	48		H
73	49		I
74	4A		J
75	4B		K
76	4C		L
77	4D		M

Decimal Value	Hexadecimal Value	Control Character	Character
78	4E		N
79	4F		O
80	50		P
81	51		Q
82	52		R
83	53		S
84	54		T
85	55		U
86	56		V
87	57		W
88	58		X
89	59		Y
90	5A		Z
91	5B		[
92	5C		\
93	5D		]
94	5E		^
95	5F		—
96	60		`
97	61		a
98	62		b
99	63		c
100	64		d
101	65		e
102	66		f
103	67		g
104	68		h
105	69		i
106	6A		j
107	6B		k
108	6C		l
109	6D		m
110	6E		n
111	6F		o
112	70		p
113	71		q
114	72		r

Decimal Value	Hexadecimal Value	Control Character	Character
115	73		s
116	74		t
117	75		u
118	76		v
119	77		w
120	78		x
121	79		y
122	7A		z
123	7B		{
124	7C		|
125	7D		}
126	7E		~
127	7F	DEL	⌂
128	80		Ç
129	81		ü
130	82		é
131	83		â
132	84		ä
133	85		à
134	86		å
135	87		ç
136	88		ê
137	89		ë
138	8A		è
139	8B		ï
140	8C		î
141	8D		ì
142	8E		Ä
143	8F		Å
144	90		É
145	91		æ
146	92		Æ
147	93		ô
148	94		ö
149	95		ó
150	96		û
151	97		ù

Decimal Value	Hexadecimal Value	Control Character	Character
152	98		ÿ
153	99		Ö
154	9A		Ü
155	9B		¢
156	9C		£
157	9D		¥
158	9E		Pt
159	9F		ƒ
160	A0		á
161	A1		í
162	A2		ó
163	A3		ú
164	A4		ñ
165	A5		Ñ
166	A6		ª
167	A7		º
168	A8		¿
169	A9		⌐
170	AA		¬
171	AB		½
172	AC		¼
173	AD		¡
174	AE		«
175	AF		»
176	B0		░
177	B1		▒
178	B2		▓
179	B3		│
180	B4		┤
181	B5		╡
182	B6		╢
183	B7		╖
184	B8		╕
185	B9		╣
186	BA		║
187	BB		╗
188	BC		╝

Appendix B

Decimal Value	Hexadecimal Value	Control Character	Character
189	BD		╜
190	BE		╛
191	BF		┐
192	C0		└
193	C1		┴
194	C2		┬
195	C3		├
196	C4		─
197	C5		┼
198	C6		╞
199	C7		╟
200	C8		╚
201	C9		╔
202	CA		╩
203	CB		╦
204	CC		╠
205	CD		═
206	CE		╬
207	CF		╧
208	D0		╨
209	D1		╤
210	D2		╥
211	D3		╙
212	D4		╘
213	D5		╒
214	D6		╓
215	D7		╫
216	D8		╪
217	D9		┘
218	DA		┌
219	DB		█
220	DC		▄
221	DD		▌
222	DE		▐
223	DF		▀
224	E0		α
225	E1		β

Decimal Value	Hexadecimal Value	Control Character	Character
226	E2		Γ
227	E3		π
228	E4		Σ
229	E5		σ
230	E6		μ
231	E7		τ
232	E8		φ
233	E9		Θ
234	EA		Ω
235	EB		δ
236	EC		∞
237	ED		∅
238	EE		∈
239	EF		∩
240	F0		≡
241	F1		±
242	F2		≥
243	F3		≤
244	F4		⌠
245	F5		⌡
246	F6		÷
247	F7		≈
248	F8		°
249	F9		•
250	FA		·
251	FB		√
252	FC		ⁿ
253	FD		²
254	FE		■
255	FF		(blank)

PART V

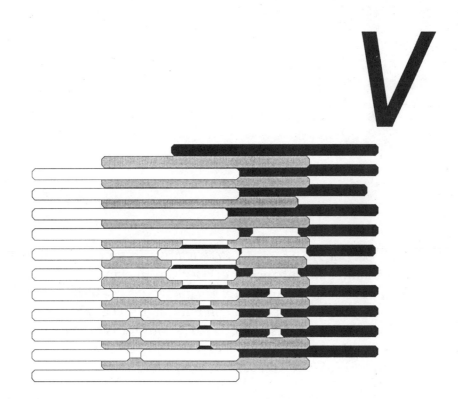

PC-Write Resource Information

This part of *The Shareware Book* consists of four appendixes that streamline and enhance the PC-Write information provided in Part I of this book. Appendix C summarizes PC-Write commands. Appendix D outlines the contents of the PC-Write disk sets. Appendix E provides precise instructions for creating a PC-Write Work Disk. And Appendix F explains how files can be transferred between PC-Write and ASCII, WordStar, and earlier versions of PC-Write.

APPENDIX C

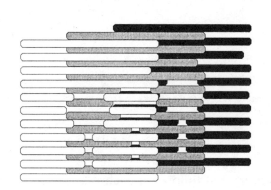

PC-Write Command Summary

PC-Write has a powerful collection of tools you can use to turn your thoughts into words. It provides a rich working environment with hundreds of commands at your fingertips. In Chapters 1 through 5, you learned how to use some of PC-Write's many features. You can continue your learning with the *PC-Write User's Guide*, which concisely presents things you already know how to do (in case you forget), variations of things you know how to do, and many things you can learn to do.

This appendix summarizes information on the PC-Write tools you learned about in this book. It also includes concise information on a few things not covered in the book.

Starting PC-Write

You can load PC-Write's Edit program (ED.EXE) in several ways, depending on what you want to do. Some of these ways are described in the sections that follow. In each description, replace *filename* with the disk drive letter, a colon, and the name of the file you want to use, for example, B:KATHY01.LTR. It is assumed that your work disk is in drive A and that the DOS A prompt (A>) is on the screen. If you are using a hard disk drive, then make appropriate substitutions for the drive designator.

Create a New File Using the Opening Menu

At the DOS prompt, type **ed** and press ENTER.
The Opening menu appears and lists the following options:

F1	Help	Give information about PC-Write operations and features
F2	Exit	Return to DOS, saving the file you were working on
F6	File	Enter the name of a file to edit or create
F7	Print	Enter the name of a file to print

F8   Dir   Get a directory of disk files, pick one to edit or print

Press F6 to create a file. The top line supplies a possible file name (WORK.DOC), as follows:

```
File to load or create (Esc:cancel F8:dir): "work.doc"
```

Type a new file name (*filename*) and press ENTER. The Edit program will search the disk you specified in *filename* to see if the file already exists. Since you are creating a new file, you should see the following message in the top line:

```
File not found.  Esc to retype, or F9 to create "filename"
```

Press F9. The editing screen appears. You can begin creating the new file. (If a file by the name you specified already exists, then you will see a different message in the top line than the one previously shown. See "Load an Existing File Using the Opening Menu" in this appendix.)

Create a New File Without Using the Opening Menu

At the DOS prompt, type **ed** *filename* and press ENTER.
    The Opening menu is bypassed. If the file does not already exist, you will see the following message in the top line:

```
File not found.  Esc to retype, or F9 to create "filename"
```

Press F9. The editing screen appears.

Create a New File, Bypassing the Initial Prompt

At the DOS prompt, type **ed** *filename* **/c** and press ENTER.

The editing screen appears. If the file already exists, then typing **/c** loads the existing file without making a backup file.

Load an Existing File Using the Opening Menu

At the DOS prompt, type **ed** and press ENTER.

The Opening menu appears and lists the following options:

F1	Help	Give information about PC-Write operations and features
F2	Exit	Return to DOS, saving the file you were working on
F6	File	Enter the name of a file to edit or create
F7	Print	Enter the name of a file to print
F8	Dir	Get a directory of disk files, pick one to edit or print

Press F6 to load an existing file. You should see the following message in the top line:

```
File to load or create (Esc:cancel F8:dir): "work.doc"
```

Type the name of the existing file you want to load (*filename*) and press ENTER. The Edit program will search the disk for the file you specified in *filename*. You should soon see the following top line:

```
Press Esc for no backup, F9 to write backup file "backupname"
```

The name supplied for the backup file (*backupname*) is the same as your *filename,* except that the extension is slightly changed. The extension in *backupname* consists of an ampersand (&) followed by the first two characters of the file extension in *filename.* For example, TBT001.LTR is changed to TBT001.&LT

To load the file without making a backup copy, press ESC.

To create a backup copy first, load the file, and then press F9.

In either case, the file you want to edit will appear in the editing screen.

Load an Existing File Without Using the Opening Menu

At the DOS prompt, type **ed** *filename* and press ENTER.

The Opening menu is bypassed. You should see the following message in the top line:

```
Press Esc for no backup, F9 to write backup file "backupname"
```

The name supplied for your backup file (*backupname*) is the same as your *filename,* except that the extension is slightly changed. The extension in *backupname* consists of an ampersand (&) followed by the first two characters of the file extension in *filename.* For example, TBT001.LTR is changed to TBT001.&LT.

To load the file without making a backup copy, press ESC.

To create a backup copy first, load the file, and then press F9.

In either case, the file you want to edit will appear in the editing screen.

Edit a File, Bypassing the Initial Prompt, with No Backup File

At the DOS prompt, type **ed** *filename* **/e** and press ENTER.

Using **/e** is the "express" method of starting an editing session. The opening procedures are bypassed, and you soon see the editing screen with the file you want (*filename*).

Start with a Directory on the Screen

At the DOS prompt, type **ed** *directoryname* and press ENTER.

Directoryname specifies the disk directory you want to see. For example, **a:*.*** specifies the directory of all files on drive A, and **b:*.*** specifies the directory of all files on drive B. The selected directory appears on the screen. You can use the arrow keys to select a file to edit, and then press F9.

Managing Files in the Editing Screen

You will do most of your work in the editing screen. During editing, the top line of the screen is usually the status line. You can issue many commands by pressing two or more keys in succession. In most cases, the screens you obtain will prompt you on how to return to the editing screen.

Obtain a Help Screen

Press F1 to get the System/Help menu. Then, press F1 to get the first help screen.

Save a File and Exit the Edit Program

Press F1 to get the System/Help menu. Then, press F2 to exit the Edit program. If you have changed the file in the editing screen since the last time you saved it, then PC-Write will first save the file, and then return to DOS.

Save a File and Continue Editing

Press F1 to get the System/Help menu. Press F3 to save the file.

Exit Without Saving the File

First, press F1 to get the System/Help menu. Next, press F9 to tell PC-Write not to save the file. Then, press F2 to exit the Edit program and return to DOS.

Load a Different File to the Editing Screen

Press F1 to get the System/Help menu. Then, press F6 to get the following top line:

```
File to load or create (Esc:cancel F8:dir): "filename"
```

Type the name of the file you want to load, and then press ENTER.

Display a Directory

Press F1 to get the System/Help menu. Then, press F8 to get the following top line:

```
Directory to display; can include * and ? (Esc:cancel): "directoryname"
```

Type the *directoryname,* and then press ENTER. For example, to get a directory of all files on drive B, type **b:*.***, and then press ENTER.

Name the File in the Editing Screen

You can change the name of the file in the editing screen to a new name. First, press F1 to get the System/Help menu. Then, press F5 to get the following top line:

```
Name to use for saving (Esc:cancel F8:dir): "filename"
```

Type the new file name and then press ENTER.

Delete a File

Press ALT-F1 to get the Name/File menu. Then, press F7 to get the following top line:

```
File to delete (Esc:cancel F8:dir): ""
```

Type the name of the file you want to delete and press ENTER. Then, either press F9 to complete the delete process, or press ESC to cancel.

Appendix C

Entering, Editing, and Formatting Text

The following sections summarize how to enter, edit, and format text.

Move the Cursor Around a File

To move the cursor	Press
Left one column	←
Right one column	→
Down one line	↓
Up one line	↑
Left one word	CTRL-←
Right one word	CTRL-→
To the left margin	HOME
To the last character in a line	END
Forward one screen	SHIFT-PGUP
Backward one screen	SHIFT-PGDN
To the top of a file	SHIFT-GREY PLUS, ALT-PLUS, or SHIFT-F12
To the bottom of a file	SHIFT-GREY MINUS, ALT-MINUS, or SHIFT-F11

Toggle Automatic Reformatting and Wordwrap

Use SHIFT-F7 to toggle from Wrap+ to Para+, from Para+ to Wrap−, and from Wrap− to Wrap+.

Wrap+	Word wrap is on and automatic paragraph formatting is off
Para+	Word wrap and automatic paragraph formatting are both on
Wrap−	Word wrap and automatic paragraph formatting are both off

Manually Reformat a Paragraph

Position the cursor at the beginning of the paragraph, and then press F7.

Toggle Between Pushright (Push) and Overwrite (Over)

You can either press the SCROLL LOCK key, or press CTRL-V.

Delete Characters, Words, and Lines

To Delete	Press
The character at the cursor	DELETE
The character to the left of the cursor	BACKSPACE
From the cursor to the end of a word	CTRL-ESC

From the cursor to the beginning of the word	CTRL-BACKSPACE
An entire line	SHIFT-CTRL-ENTER

Copy a Block of Text

First, position the cursor at the beginning of the block and press F3. Next, use the arrow keys to move the cursor to the end of the block, and then press F3 to mark the text for copying. Move the cursor to the place where you want to insert the copy and press F3 to insert the copied block.

Delete a Block of Text

First, position the cursor at the beginning of the block to be deleted and press F4. Then, use the arrow keys to move the cursor to the end of the block and press F4 to delete the block.

Move a Block of Text

First, position the cursor at the beginning of the block and press F6. Next, use the arrow keys to move the cursor to the end of the block and press F6 to mark the block for moving. Then, move the cursor to the place where you want to move the block and press F6. The block is moved.

Unmark a Marked Block

To unmark a marked block, simply press F5.

Undelete a Block of Text

When you delete a block of text, the deleted text is retained in a special hold area. To undelete the deleted text, first put the cursor where you want to insert the text that is stored in the hold area, and then press CTRL-F4. The text is inserted and marked. Press F5 to unmark the text.

Changing the Ruler Line

The ruler line controls horizontal text layout in the editing screen, including margins and tabs. You can temporarily display the ruler line on the screen and edit it. You can also embed a ruler line in a file so that it is saved with the file.

Display the Current Ruler Line on the Screen

Position the cursor where you want to display the ruler line and press F2.

Embed a Ruler Line in a File

Place the cursor on the line below where you want the ruler line to be embedded. Press F2 to display the ruler line at the cursor position. Press F4 to embed the ruler line. The ruler line is now part of the file. You can edit and delete it just like normal text.

Change the Left Margin in the Current Ruler Line

First, press F2 to display the current ruler line on the screen. Next, type **L** at the desired left margin position. Then, press F2 to remove the edited ruler line from the screen.

Change the Right Margin in the Current Ruler Line

First, press F2 to display the current ruler line on the screen. Next, type **R** at the desired right margin position. Then, press F2 to remove the edited ruler line from the screen.

Set a Tab Stop in the Current Ruler Line

First, press F2 to display the current ruler line on the screen. Next, type **T** at the desired tab stop position. Then, press F2 to remove the edited ruler line from the screen.

Split the Screen into Columns

First, press F2 to display the current ruler line on the screen. Then, put the cursor at the position where you want to split the screen into columns, and type **V**.

Set left and right margins for each column. Then, press F2 to remove the edited ruler line from the screen.

Formatting Printed Page Layout

The print control file (PR.DEF) on your work disk controls the appearance of text printed to the printer. You can use Dot lines and page breaks in your file to modify the settings in the print control file.

Select a Regular Print Font

First, press ALT-G. Then, type a .R Dot line, **.R:***fontletter*, where *fontletter* is a letter that designates the font you want. The .R Dot line specifies the font for all the text that follows, until another .R Dot line is encountered.

You can override the .R Dot line by embedding a special font character within the text both before and after a block of text. To override the .R Dot line, press ALT-*fontletter*, where *fontletter* is a letter that designates the font you want. A graphics symbol will appear at the place in the text where you press ALT-*fontletter*. Selected font letters, .R Dot lines, font symbols, and ASCII codes for font symbols are shown in Table C-1.

Turn Off a Font

First, press ALT-G. Then, type a .Q Dot line, **.Q:***fontletter*, where *fontletter* is the previously selected font.

Table C-1.

Fontletter	.R line	ALT-fontletter graphics symbol	ASCII code	Font
A	.R:A	♪	014	Align font
B	.R:B	☻	002	Boldface
C	.R:C	♠	006	Compressed
D	.R:D	►	016	Double wide
E	.R:E	♥	003	Elite
F	.R:F	∟	028	Fast
G	.R:G	♂	011	Guide line font
H	.R:H	↑	024	Higher (superscript)
I	.R:I	§	021	Italics
J	.R:J	◘	008	Justify line font
K	.R:K	¶	020	Keep paragraph font
L	.R:L	↓	025	Lower (subscript)
M	.R:M	•	007	Marine blue
N	.R:N	◄	017	Number font
O	.R:O	‼	019	Overstrike
P	.R:P	♣	005	Pica
Q	.R:Q	—	022	Quality
R	.R:R	▲	030	Red
S	.R:S	☺	001	Second strike
T	.R:T	♀ ☼	012	Hard page break
U	.R:U	⊥	023	Underline
V	.R:V	♦	004	Variable
W	.R:W	↕	018	Double underline
X	.R:X	♫	013	X font
Y	.R:Y	▼	031	Yellow
Z	.R:Z	☼	015	Z font

Font letters, Dot lines, ASCII Symbols and Codes

Set Multiple Line Spacing

First, press ALT-G. Then, type a .M Dot line, **.M:***n*, where *n* is the number of lines to advance the printer after printing a line. For example, to obtain double spacing, you would type **.M:2**.

Set a Top Margin

First, press ALT-G. Then, type a .XT Dot line, **.XT:***length*, where *length* is the number of lines you want for the top margin.

Set a Bottom Margin

First, press ALT-G. Then, type a .XB Dot line, **.XB:***length*, where *length* is the number of lines you want for the bottom margin.

Add Leading Spaces to All Printed Lines (Left Margin)

First, press ALT-G. Then, type a .X Dot line, **.X:***number*, where *number* is the number of spaces to print at the left of every line.

Toggle Between Show Mode and Hide Mode

To toggle between show mode and hide mode, simply press ALT-SPACEBAR.

Enter a Hard Page Break (Hard Break)

Position the cursor where you want the hard break to occur. Then, press ALT-T.

Delete a Hard Page Break (Hard Break)

In show mode, put the cursor at the beginning of the hard-break line. Then, press CTRL-ENTER.

Enter a Soft Page Break (Soft Break)

To enter a soft page break, press SHIFT-ALT-T.

Delete a Soft Page Break (Soft Break)

In show mode, put the cursor on the soft-break line. Then, press CTRL-ENTER.

Repage an Entire File

First, press ALT-F7. Next press F5, and then press F5.

Repage and Reformat an Entire File

First, press ALT-F7. Next, press F5, and then press F7.

Create a Header

Move the cursor to the place at which you want the header Dot line to appear, and press ALT-G. Then, type a .H Dot line, **.H:***text*, where *text* is the text you want to appear in the header.

Create a Footer

Move the cursor to the position at which you want the footer Dot line in the file, and press ALT-G. Then, type a .F Dot line, **.F:***text*, where *text* is the text you want to appear in the footer.

Print Automatic Page Numbers

Enter three dollar signs ($$$) where you want the page numbers to occur in the text of a header or footer Dot line.

Print Header or Footer Text Flush Left

Enter three dots (. . .) at the end of the text in a header or footer Dot line.

Print Header or Footer Text Flush Right

Enter three dots (...) at the beginning of the text in a header or footer Dot line.

Center Header or Footer Text

Enter three dots (...) both at the beginning and end of the text in a header or footer line.

APPENDIX

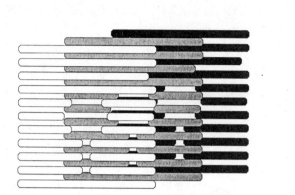

Files Used by PC-Write

Quicksoft, the publisher of PC-Write, distributes PC-Write as a set of either three 5 1/4-inch disks or two 3 1/2-inch disks. This appendix lists the files on both disk sets. The files listed here are for PC-Write version 3.02, as of October 1989. If you have a later version of PC-Write, your disk set may have slightly different files.

Program Disk Files (3 1/2-inch Disk or 5 1/4-inch Disk)

The program disk (disk 1) contains the same files in both the 3 1/2-inch disk set and the 5 1/4-inch disk set. These files are listed and briefly described here:

File	Description
GO.BAT	A program that displays the READ.ME file on the screen
READ.ME	A text file containing information about PC-Write
GETYN.COM	Used by the WORKDISK.BAT program
WORKDISK.BAT	Program used to create a work disk or directory
INSTALL.DOC	A text file that describes how to install PC-Write without using the WORKDISK.BAT program
ED.EXE	PC-Write's main Edit program
ED.HLP	The complete help file
ED.DEF	The edit control file, standard version
ED.TRS	The edit control file for older Tandy 1000s
ED.SPC	The edit control file for noncompatible keyboards and other special cases
PROGRAM.DIR	Text file that contains a directory of files on this program disk

To obtain a similar list of program files, you can use the DOS TYPE command to display the PROGRAM.DIR file on the screen. Insert your DOS disk in drive A and the PC-Write program disk in drive B. Then, do the following:

Type:
type b:program.dir
and press ENTER

You can also use the DOS PRINT command to print the PROGRAM.DIR file to your printer. Insert your DOS disk in drive A and the PC-Write program disk in drive B. Then, do the following:

Type:
print b:program.dir
and press ENTER

Utility Disk Files (5 1/4-inch Disk)

The utility disk is disk 2 in the 5 1/4-inch disk set. It contains the following files:

File	Description
GO.BAT	A program that displays the READ.ME file on the screen
READ.ME	A text file containing information about PC-Write
GETYN.COM	Used by the WORKDISK.BAT program
WORKDISK.BAT	Program used to create a work disk or directory
WORKUTIL.BAT	Program used by the WORKDISK.BAT program
MENUPRT.BAT	Printer picker control program, non-laser printers

MENUPRT1.EXE	Printer picker program, part one, non-laser printers
MENUPRT2.EXE	Printer picker program, part two, non-laser printers
MENULAZ.EXE	Printer picker program, laser printers
PRINT.TST	Used to test printer for font definitions
CHARS.TST	Used to test printer character set
JUSTIFY.TST	Used to test printer for justification
HPDOWN.BAT	Download fonts to HP LaserJet printers
QUADDOWN.BAT	Download fonts to HP DeskJet printers
DESKDOWN.BAT	Download fonts to Quad Laser printers
PSDOWN.INI	Initialize PostScript printer
PSDOWN.FIN	Release PostScript printer
MICSMICE.DEF	Microsoft mouse menu source
MICSMICE.MNU	Microsoft mouse file, earlier versions
MICSMICE.COM	Microsoft mouse version 6.0+ driver
LOGIMICE.DEF	Logitech mouse file
LOGIMICE.MNU	Logitech mouse menu source
MSYSMICE.COM	Mouse Systems mouse driver
MSYSMICE.MSC	Mouse Systems mouse menu source
ED.MDS	Edit control file for MDS Genius
ED.MAC	Edit control file with macro examples
ED.PIF	Used by MS-Windows, DesqView, and so forth
UTILITY.DIR	This text file is a directory of files on this utility disk

To obtain a similar list of utility files, you can use the DOS TYPE command to display the UTILITY.DIR file on the screen. Insert your DOS disk in drive A and the PC-Write utility disk in drive B. Then, do the following:

Type:
type b:utility.dir
and press ENTER

You can also use the DOS PRINT command to print the PROGRAM.DIR file to your printer. Insert your DOS disk in drive A and the PC-Write utility disk in drive B. Then, do the following:

Type:
print b:utility.dir
and press ENTER

Reference Disk Files (5 1/4-inch Disk)

The reference disk is disk 3 in the 5 1/4-inch disk set. It contains the following files:

File	Description
GO.BAT	A program that displays the READ.ME file on the screen
READ.ME	A text file containing information about PC-Write
GETYN.COM	Used by the WORKDISK.BAT program
WORKUTIL.BAT	Program used by the WORKDISK.BAT program
WORDS.MAS	Main spelling checker word list
WORDS.NUL	Empty master word list you can add words to

WORDS.EXE	Program to add user words to WORDS.MAS
EDBEGIN.HLP	Help file for beginners
EDQUICK.HLP	Help file for advanced users
MANUAL1.CRN	Crunched (compressed) PC-Write *Tutorial*
MANUAL2.CRN	Crunched (compressed) PC-Write *Quick Guide*
PRINTMAN.COM	Program to print the *Tutorial* and *Quick Guide*
TYPEMAN.COM	Program to display the *Tutorial* and *Quick Guide*
FILEMAN.COM	Program to uncrunch the *Tutorial* and *Quick Guide*
STORY	Sample text file used with *Tutorial*
QUICK-OR.DER	Quicksoft order form
REFENCE.DIR	Text file that contains the directory of files on this reference disk

To obtain a similar list of reference files, you can use the DOS TYPE command to display the REFENCE.DIR file on the screen. Insert your DOS disk in drive A and the PC-Write program disk in drive B. Then, do the following:

Type:
type b:refence.dir
and press ENTER

You can also use the DOS PRINT command to print the REFENCE.DIR file to your printer. Insert your DOS disk in drive A and the PC-Write program disk in drive B. Then, do the following:

Type:
print b:refence.dir
and press ENTER

Table D-1.

GO	BAT	READ	ME	GETYN	COM	WORKDISK	BAT	WORKUTIL	BAT
MENUPRT	BAT	MENUPRT1	EXE	MENUPRT2	EXE	MENULAZ	EXE	PRINT	TST
CHARS	TST	JUSTIFY	TST	HPDOWN	BAT	QUADDOWN	BAT	DESKDOWN	BAT
PSDOWN	INI	PSDOWN	FIN	MICSMICE	DEF	MICSMICE	MNU	MICSMICE	COM
LOGIMICE	DEF	LOGIMICE	MNU	MSYSMICE	COM	MSYSMICE	MSC	ED	MDS
ED	MAC	ED	PIF	UTILITY	DIR	WORDS	MAS	WORDS	NUL
WORDS	EXE	EDBEGIN	HLP	EDQUICK	HLP	MANUAL1	CRN	MANUAL2	CRN
PRINTMAN	COM	TYPEMAN	COM	FILEMAN	COM	STORY		QUICK-OR	DER
REFENCE	DIR								

41 File(s)   14336 bytes free

Directory of Utility Reference Disk

Utility/Reference Disk Files (3 1/2-inch Disk)

The utility/reference disk is disk 2 in the 3 1/2-inch disk set. It contains all the files previously shown for the utility disk and reference disk in the 5 1/4 inch disk set. A wide directory of this disk is shown in Table D-1. For a brief description of each file, look up the file by name in the previous sections of this appendix.

You can obtain information on the files in the utility/reference disk by displaying or printing both the UTILITY.DIR file and the REFENCE.DIR file, as described previously in this appendix.

APPENDIX

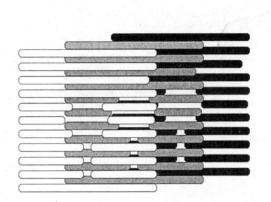

Creating a PC-Write Work Disk

This appendix demonstrates a sample annotated run of PC-Write's WORKDISK.BAT program. It shows the questions, with sample answers, that appear on the screen while making a 5 1/4-inch work disk set consisting of two disks. To begin running the WORKDISK.BAT program, insert a PC-Write program disk in disk drive A and a formatted empty disk in drive B. Then, do the following:

Type:
workdisk b:
and press ENTER

You see the following information and question:

```
Now Making a PC-Write Work Disk
This will NOT affect CONFIG.SYS or AUTOEXEC.BAT files.
 .
If you have DOS 3.0 or a limited "environment", this won't work.
The file INSTALL.DOC tells you how to install PC-Write manually.
 .
Do you have 5.25 inch floppy disks? (Y if so, N if 3.5 inch) (y/n) _
```

If you press Y and then press ENTER, then you are presented with a series of questions. Here are the questions with the answers given in this sample run:

```
Do you want to make backup copies of the PC-Write Diskettes? (y/n) n
Are you installing on a hard disk? (Y if so, N if on floppy) (y/y) n
 .
Do you have 2 blank, formatted diskettes to make work disks? (y/n) y
Work diskettes will be made on the b: drive, ok? (y/n) y
 .
Do you want to put your registration number on the front screen? (y/n) n
Do you want to put your own special message on the front screen? (y/n) n
```

The next question prompts you to put a blank disk in drive B. If you have already done so, then press Y. If not, then put a formatted blank disk in drive B, and then press Y.

```
Insert blank disk to become the Work Disk in drive b:, press Y. (y/n) y
        1 File(s) copied
```

Note that one file has been copied from the program disk in drive A to the work disk in drive B. The next few questions will prompt you with either "Press Y if unsure" or "Press N if unsure." In most cases, you will press the suggested key, as shown here:

```
Do you want to copy the main PC-Write program? Press Y if unsure. (y/n) y
        1 File(s) copied
```

The WORKDISK.BAT program now copies the large ED.EXE file from the program disk in drive A to the work disk in drive B. This takes a little while. You will see the disk drive lights alternately go on and off as this large file is copied. Then, the following question appears on the screen:

```
Older PC-Write versions used the PR command to print from DOS.
  Now the ED command with /P switch is used to print from DOS.
  You can have a PR.BAT file to still print with a PR command.
Do you want this PR command to print from DOS? Press N if unsure. (y/n) n
```

You are next asked if you want to copy PC-Write's extensive main help files. You should say "yes," unless your computer has a small memory. If you must say "no," then you will have an opportunity to load smaller help files.

```
Main Help file has 45 help screens but takes 75K of disk space.
 There are smaller beginner and advanced Help files available.
Do you want this main PC-Write Help file? Press Y if unsure. (y/n) y
        1 File(s) copied
        1 File(s) copied
```

Next, you are asked if you want to load the edit control file (ED.DEF), and you are asked two questions about your keyboard. Users of the Tandy 1000TX, 1000SL, and 1000TL keyboards can answer "no" to the keyboard questions.

```
Do you want to make an Edit Control File? Press Y if unsure. (y/n) y
        1 File(s) copied
Are you using a Tandy 1000/3000 keyboard? Press N if unsure. (y/n) n
Is your keyboard sometimes "incompatible"? Press N if unsure. (y/n) n
```

This sample annotated run uses a color monitor. If you use a monochrome monitor, however, answer "no" to the following question:

```
Do you want to edit on a color monitor? Press N if unsure. (y/n) y
```

Answer "yes" to the next three questions, so that the appearance of text on the screen and text printed to the printer will be the same as that shown in many of the figures and illustrations provided in Chapters 1 through 5.

```
Do you want the three reminder lines on?     Press Y if unsure. (y/n) y
Do you want automatic save every 5 min.?     Press Y if unsure. (y/n) y
Press Y to get one inch margins by default; N for no margins. (y/n) y
```

The WORKDISK.BAT program is ready to copy files from the PC-Write utility disk, disk 2 in the 5 1/4-inch set. At the prompt shown here, remove the program disk from drive A and insert the utility disk. Then press Y.

```
Do you have a copy of the PC-Write Utility diskette? (y/n) y
Insert PC-Write Utility diskette in default drive, press Y. (y/n) y
```

Answer the following question as appropriate. (N was pressed in the sample run.)

```
Do you use Windows, DesqView, or other program using a PIF file? (y/n) n
```

The utility disk contains three files which you can use to test your printer (PRINT.TST, CHARS.TST, and JUSTIFY.TST). Tell WORKDISK to copy these files to your work disk, as shown here:

```
Do you want to copy the 3 printer test files? Press Y if unsure. (y/n) y
    1 File(s) copied
    1 File(s) copied
    1 File(s) copied
```

PC-Write supports a multitude of printers. Tell WORKDISK to create a print control file (PR.DEF) customized for your printer. If you do not have a laser printer or Hewlett-Packard DeskJet, then answer the questions as shown in the following illustration. If you do have a laser printer or HP DeskJet, then press Y for the appropriate question. If you press Y, then you will see a series of questions related to your printer, instead of the questions shown here.

```
Do you want to create the Print Control File? Press Y if unsure. (y/n) y
Do you have a laser printer? Press N if unsure. (y/n) n
Do you have an HP DeskJet with soft fonts? (y/n) n
```

You now see a list of printers, as shown in Table E-1. Look for your brand and press the appropriate letter. In the sample run, P was pressed to choose Radio Shack. After pressing a letter, you will see a list of printer models for the brand you chose. In the sample run, the screen displayed the list of Radio Shack printers shown in Table E-2. Press the letter that corresponds to your printer model, as listed on your screen.

PC-Write then creates a print control file for the printer you select and tells you of its selection. For example, in the sample run, the following message was displayed:

```
File has been created for Radio, DMP-130/130A, IBM mode
Menuprt Version 3.02 - Release Date: 12/06/88
```

The next question asks if you use a mouse. If you do use a mouse, a series of questions follows, prompting you for the type of mouse you use.

The WORKDISK program is ready to install the master word list for the spelling checker on your work disk. If you are creating 5 1/4-inch work disks, as assumed here, then you must put the word list on a second 5 1/4 -inch disk. If you are creating a 3 1/2-inch work disk, then you could put the word list on the same disk that contains the other work disk files. The word list is on the PC-Write reference disk, disk 3 in the 5 1/4-inch disk set.

Table E-1.

1. Alps/Anadex	D. Epson	P. Radio Shack (Tandy)
2. Apple	E. Fujitsu	Q. Roland/Royal
3. AT&T/Axiom	F. Genicom	R. Seikosha/Silver Reed
4. Brother	G. Hewlett-Packard	S. Smith Corona
5. C. Itoh	H. IBM	T. Star Micronics
6. Canon	I. JDL/Juki	U. Swintec
7. Centronics/CIE	J. Mannesmann-Tally	V. Texas Instruments
8. Citizen	K. NEC	W. Toshiba
9. Comrex	L. Okidata	X. Xerox
A. Dataproducts/Datasouth	M. Olivetti/Olympia	Y. Other, Adeus - JCM
B. Diablo	N. Panasonic	Z. Other, Kaypro - Wang
C. Digital (DEC)	O. Printek	

Printer Picker. Press letter or digit for your printer group: ―

Printers Supported by PC-Write

Table E-2.

1. CGP-220
2. Daisy Printer II
3. Daisy Printer II-B
4. DMP-105
5. DMP-106, IBM mode
6. DMP-106, Tandy mode
7. DMP-110
8. DMP-120
9. DMP-130/130A, IBM mode
A. DMP-130/130a, Tandy
B. DMP-200
C. DMP-400
D. DMP-420
E. DMP-430, IBM mode
F. DMP-430, Tandy mode
G. DMP-440, IBM
H. DMP-440, Tandy
I. DMP-500
J. DMP-2100/2120, IBM
K. DMP-2100/2120, Tandy
L. DMP-2100P/2110
M. DMP-2200, IBM mode
N. DMP-2200, Tandy mode
O. DWP-210
P. DWP-220
Q. DWP-230, IBM mode
R. DWP-230, Tandy mode
S. DWP-410
T. DWP-510
U. DMP-520, IBM mode
V. DWP-520, Tandy mode
W. DWP-1120
X. Lineprinter V
Y. Line Printer VIII

Radio Shack Printers Supported by PC-Write

```
Do you have a copy of the PC-Write Reference diskette? (y/n) y
Insert PC-Write Reference diskette in default drive, press Y. (y/n) y
  .

The master word list is a large (110 KB) file used to check spelling.
Your computer must have at least 448 KB to use this master word list.
Do you want this word list? Press Y if unsure. (y/n) y
The PC-Write program and word list file won't fit on
one diskette. Insert your Extra disk in drive b:, press Y. (y/n) y
        1 File(s) copied
```

Your work disk is almost complete. The last two questions give you the option of using smaller help files and of typing (on the screen) and/or printing (on the printer) the *Tutorial* and *Quick Guide,* as shown here:

```
Smaller help files for beginners and advanced users are available.
Do you want either of these two help files? Press N if unsure. (y/n) n
After you type and/or print the Tutorial and Quick Guide,
remove the PC-Write Reference disk from the default drive.
Then place all original and backup diskettes in a safe place.

Insert your new Work Disk in the default drive.
  .

PC-Write Work Disk Is Now Ready
  .

Do you want to type or print the Tutorial and Quick Guide? (y/n)
```

If you do not want either to type or to print the *Tutorial* and *Quick Guide,* then press N.

The creation of your work disk set is now complete. Label your work disks and begin using PC-Write, as described in Chapter 1.

APPENDIX

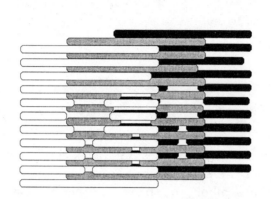

Transferring Files Between PC-Write Version 3 and Other Programs

You can use PC-Write to create files to *export* to other programs. You can also *import* some types of files from other programs to

PC-Write. A few examples are shown in this appendix. For more information, look in the *PC-Write User's Guide* index under the headings "Conversion Menu," "Conversion, customizing commands for," and "Converting."

ASCII Files

The standard ASCII character set uses ASCII codes 32 through 127 to represent uppercase letters, lowercase letters, the digits 0 through 9, punctuation symbols, the space, and special characters such as the dollar sign ($), number sign (#), and ampersand (&). PC-Write uses the codes from 0 through 31 for non-ASCII purposes, such as for font characters and editing functions. PC-Write recognizes the code pair, 13 and 10, as a return followed by a line feed, also called a *line boundary*. These characters are also used in sequential ASCII files to mark the end of a record.

The IBM extended character set uses codes 128 through 255 for graphics characters, foreign alphabets, and other purposes. These are considered non-ASCII characters by PC-Write. However, some of these characters are used by PC-Write for special purposes. For example, the Greek letter "phi" (Φ) is used as the cursor marker in the ruler line. This character has the ASCII code 232.

Export an ASCII File from PC-Write

You can use PC-Write to create an ASCII file that can be read by another program, for example, another word processing program. You can even use PC-Write to create a program file to be used by a programming language such as GW-BASIC or Quick-BASIC. In writing this book, the authors sent ASCII files of chapters to the publisher. These files were then read and used by a computer-based publishing system.

PC-Write uses characters with the codes 00 through 31 for non-ASCII purposes. To prepare an ASCII file for export to another program, you must *strip off* (remove) all of these characters, as follows:

    Press ALT-F4   (to get the Misc-Ops menu)

The Misc-Ops menu appears on the top line, as shown here:

```
Esc F1  F2.Ins-find  F3.Count  F4.Markpair  F5.Date-ins  F6:Nonascii  F7:Repeat
```

The Misc-Ops menu indicates that you can press the F6 key to obtain information on non-ASCII characters.

    Press F6

The top line now provides the following information:

```
Esc:Cancel  F9:Scan to next non-ascii  F10:Strip all non-ascii
```

You can press F10 to strip all non-ASCII characters from the file. This includes PC-Write ruler lines, Dot lines, break lines, font characters, and soft spaces. If the file contains characters with ASCII codes greater than 127, then you are asked if you want to strip them or keep them, as follows:

```
Some character codes above 127; Esc:cancel, F9:keep them, F10: delete them
```

Unless you have a good reason to do otherwise, press F10.

For more information, look in the *PC-Write User's Guide* index under the heading "Stripping non-ASCII characters."

Import an ASCII File to PC-Write

If an ASCII file contains only characters with ASCII codes 32 through 127 and the code pair 13 and 10, you can load the file into PC-Write as you would a file created by PC-Write.

If the imported file contains non-ASCII characters, you can tell PC-Write to find them so that you can delete them. Use the Misc-Ops menu for this purpose:

    Press ALT-F4   (to get the Misc-Ops menu)

The Misc-Ops menu appears on the top line. It provides several options, as shown here:

```
Esc F1  F2.Ins-find  F3.Count  F4.Markpair  F5.Date-ins  F6:Nonascii  F7:Repeat
```

The Misc-Ops menu indicates that you can press the F6 key to obtain information on non-ASCII characters.

    Press F6

The top line provides the following information:

```
Esc:Cancel  F9:Scan to next non-ascii  F10:Strip all non-ascii
```

Transferring Files Between PC-Write Version 3 and Other Programs   **641**

Appendix F

To strip all non-ASCII characters from the file, press F10. Alternatively, you can press F9 to scan to the next non-ASCII character, press ESC to cancel the Misc-Ops menu, and then delete the non-ASCII character.

For more information, look in the *PC-Write User's Guide* index under the heading "Stripping non-ASCII characters."

WordStar Files

You can import WordStar files to PC-Write, and then convert them to a format that PC-Write can use. You can also prepare a PC-Write file for export to WordStar.

Import a WordStar File to PC-Write

After reading a WordStar file into the editing screen, convert it to PC-Write format, as follows:

   Press ALT-F5   (to get the Conversion menu)

The Conversion menu shown here has several file conversion options:

```
Esc F1 F2:Highbits F3:Dots  F4:Tabs F5:Spaces F6:Lines F7:Breaks
```

To convert a WordStar file, use the Highbits option.

   Press F2

The top line now provides the following information:

```
Esc:Cancel F9:Clear high bits, fix Wordstar
```

Press F9 to convert the WordStar file to PC-Write format.

 NOTE This conversion does not substitute PC-Write equivalents for WordStar enhancements like boldface, underlining, and so on.

Export a File from PC-Write to WordStar

To prepare a PC-Write file for export to WordStar, first remove the right margin setting (R) from the ruler line, and then reformat the file. This removes the return character (ASCII 13) and line feed character (ASCII 10) from each line, except the last line of each paragraph. After doing this, you can read the file into WordStar, reformat it, and edit it using WordStar's tools.

For more information on converting WordStar files, look in the *PC-Write User's Guide* index under the heading "WordStar."

Files from Early Versions of PC-Write

Use the Conversion menu to convert files from early versions of PC-Write to version 3 format. In versions of PC-Write prior to version 2.6, there were no guide lines (such as the ruler line). Dot commands were used instead of guide lines. If you have a file created with a version prior to version 2.6, you must put an ALT-G character in front of each Dot command, called a "Dot line" in version 3. You can convert an entire file, as follows:

    Press ALT-F5   (to get the Conversion menu)

The Conversion menu appears as shown here:

```
Esc F1 F2:Highbits F3:Dots F4:Tabs F5:Spaces F6:Lines F7:Breaks
```

The option to convert between Dot commands and Dot lines is "F3:Dots."

    Press F3

The top line now provides the desired information, as follows:

```
Esc:Cancel   F9:Fix format lines (ALT-G to dot lines, text off break lines, etc)
```

Press F9 to insert an ALT-G character in front of every Dot command. This will not, however, insert an ALT-G character in front of dots used for other purposes. For example, it will not insert an ALT-G character in front of .37.

F9 can also perform other conversions, as follows:

- Line boundary errors (line feed without return).
- Empty Dot lines (ALT-G without text is deleted).
- Dot lines and page breaks that do not start in column 1 are moved to column 1.
- Old-style page breaks are converted to version 3 format.

The F7:Breaks option on the Conversion menu converts old-style page breaks to version 3 format. You can also convert version 3 format to old-style page breaks, in case you want to export a file to a version of PC-Write prior to version 3.

Appendix F

    Press ALT-F5   (to get the Conversion menu)

    Press F7   (to obtain page break information)

The top line now offers the following options:

```
Esc F1  Breaks:  F7.Old to new  F8.New to old  F9.Remove all  F10.Remove soft
```

If you are importing a file created by a version of PC-Write prior to version 3, then press F7. If you want to export a file created by version 3 to an older version, then press F8.

PART VI

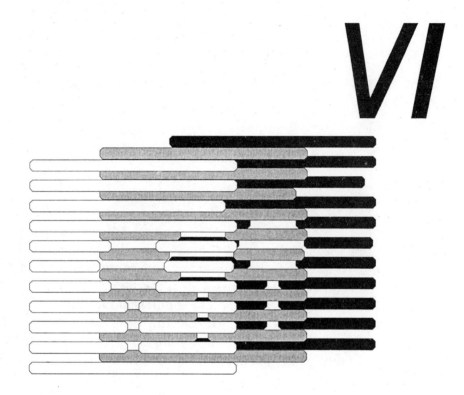

PC-File+ Resource Information

Part VI of *The Shareware Book* contains three PC-File+ appendixes. Appendix G is a complete keystroke and command summary for PC-File+. Appendix H discusses all of the files and programs used by PC-File+ and how to interpret the different file name extensions. Appendix I tells you about transferring files between PC-File+ version 3 and other programs, including early versions of PC-File+ (versions 1 and 2), PC-File:dB, PC-File III (versions 2, 3, and 4), and PC-File/R (version 1).

APPENDIX

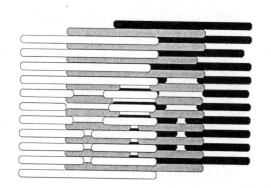

G

PC-File+ Keystroke and Command Summary

You can control many of PC-File+'s features by pressing keys that cause PC-File+ to take specific actions. In addition to the many PC-File+ keystroke operations, PC-File+ also has commands that automatically assist you in creating data, calculating results, producing reports, and manipulating your databases. The following sections provide an annotated summary of all the PC-File+ keystrokes and commands that are available to you.

Special Keys for Use When Typing

The following keys control cursor movement while you are typing within PC-File+.

Key	Function
CTRL-←	Moves the cursor one word to the left
CTRL-→	Moves the cursor one word to the right
↓	Moves the cursor to the following field or line
END	Moves the cursor to the right, past the last character
HOME	Moves the cursor to the left, to beginning of the field
LEFT	Moves the cursor to the left, one position
PGDN	Moves the cursor to last field or next page
PGUP	Moves the cursor to first field or previous page
RIGHT	Moves the cursor to the right, one position
SHIFT-TAB	Moves the cursor to prior field or the window one field to the left
TAB	Moves the cursor to the next field or the window one field to the right
UP	Moves the cursor to the preceding field or line

The following keys control specific PC-File+ features that you can activate from almost anywhere within the PC-File+ program:

Key	Function
CTRL-A	Accepts current data (same as pressing F10)
ENTER	Accepts data or moves the cursor to the next field
F10	Accepts data
ALT-C	Activates the on-screen calculator
CTRL-B	Deletes everything to the right of the cursor
ALT-H	Brings up a context dependent help message
ESC	Cancels the current activity
DELETE	Deletes the character at the current cursor position
BACKSPACE	Deletes the character to the left of the cursor
CTRL-Z	Displays program batch date
CTRL-F	Duplicates field from previous record
CTRL-D	Duplicates the previous record
ALT-M	Loads a smart key file
~(tilde)	Marks where the field contents can be "flipped"
CTRL-L	Prints a "snapshot" label
CTRL-P	Prints the current screen (same as ALT-P)
ALT-P	Prints the current screen
ALT-D	Puts you into DOS so you can issue DOS commands
CTRL-R	Reads field data at the cursor position into memory
ALT-Y	Starts and stops memorization of a smart key sequence
INSERT	Toggles the Insert mode on and off
ALT-T	Toggles the PC-File+ Teach mode on and off
CTRL-W	Writes data from memory into the current field

Special Keys for Use in the PC-File+ Editor

Key	Function
CTRL-END	Moves the cursor to lower left corner of the window
CTRL-HOME	Moves the cursor to upper left corner of the window
CTRL-←	Moves the cursor to beginning of the previous word
CTRL-PGDN	Moves the cursor to left of the last line of text
CTRL-PGUP	Moves the cursor to left of the first line of text
CTRL-→	Moves the cursor to beginning of the next word
↓	Moves the cursor down one line
END	Moves cursor past last character on the current line
ENTER	Moves the cursor to the next line; creates a new line
HOME	Moves the cursor to first position on the current line
←	Moves the cursor one position to the left
→	Moves the cursor one position to the right
PGDN	Scrolls down to the next screen
PGUP	Scrolls up to the previous screen
SHIFT-TAB	Moves the cursor one tab position to the left
TAB	Moves the cursor one tab position to the right
↑	Moves the cursor up one line

Editing Commands

Key	Function
F3	Activates the Editor menu
CTRL-C	Copies a marked text block to the cursor location
CTRL-D	Deletes a marked text block
F5	Deletes the current line
CTRL-V	Enables/disables the "Whoops" key
CTRL-E	Erases from cursor location to end of the document
F6	Erases from the cursor to the end of the line
F10	Exits and saves all changes
ESC	Exits from editor or inserts ESCAPE character into text
CTRL-F	Fills a marked text block with a selected character
ALT-*nnn*	Keys in ASCII character *nnn* (*nnn* is decimal number)
CTRL-L	Marks a block of lines in the document
CTRL-B	Marks the corners of a text block
CTRL-M	Moves a marked text block to the cursor location
CTRL-O	Overlays a marked text block at the cursor location
CTRL-W	Recalls previously changed data ("Whoops" key)
CTRL-R	Reformats a marked text block or current paragraph
CTRL-\	Splits the current line at the cursor position
CTRL-A	Toggles automatic paragraph wrap on and off
CTRL-U	Unmarks a marked text block

Smart Key Simulation Codes

Type	To Simulate
[2]	CTRL-B
[4]	CTRL-D
[6]	CTRL-F
[9]	TAB
[12]	CTRL-L
[18]	CTRL-R
[23]	CTRL-W
[271]	SHIFT-TAB
[288]	ALT-D
[291]	ALT-H
[302]	ALT-C
[315]	F1
[316]	F2
[317]	F3
[319]	F5
[320]	F6
[321]	F7
[322]	F8
[323]	F9
[324]	F10
[327]	HOME
[328]	↑
[329]	PGUP
[331]	←
[333]	→
[335]	END
[336]	↓
[337]	PGDN
[338]	INSERT
[339]	DELETE
^n	Embed smart key #n (0 - 9 supported)
^K	Get keyboard input

Edit Masks, Automatic Fields, Constants, and Calculations

Edit masks, automatic field masks, constants, and calculations are created using the Name command on the Utilities menu. When you activate the Name command, you are asked what kind of modification you want to make (name, mask, constant, or calculation). Picking one of these options lets you specify (or modify) that attribute for a particular field. If you pick the Name option, you can change the name of a particular field. If you pick one of the other options (Mask, Constant, or Calculation), you can create (or alter) the corresponding field attribute.

Edit masks restrict the kind of data that can be entered into a field. Edit masks begin and end with the colon (:) character. Between the two colons, you enter pairs of characters. Each character pair defines a valid range for the kinds of characters that can be input into a field. Here are some examples of edit masks and the range of characters allowed by each mask:

Edit Mask (Example)	Allows These Characters
:AZ:	Only uppercase characters A through Z
:az:	Only lowercase characters a through z
:AB:	Only uppercase characters A and B
:BB:	Only uppercase character B
:09:	Only the numbers 0 through 9
:AZaz09:	All uppercase/lowercase letters; numbers 0 through 9
:--// :	Only dash, slash, and space

Automatic field masks automatically supply the following kinds of data whenever you use these masks to add or modify database records:

Automatic Field Mask	Automatically Supplies
:DATE*:	Date in mm-dd-yy format
:DD/MM/YY*:	Date in dd/mm/yy format
:DUPE*:	Duplicate field from previous record
:DY*:	Day (dd)
:MM/DD/YY*:	Date in mm/dd/yy format
:MO*:	Month (mm)
:TIME*:	Time in hh:mm format
:UNIQUE*:	Unique record number
:YR*:	Year(yy)
:YYMMDD*:	Date in yymmdd format

You can combine edit masks and automatic field masks to control and filter the kinds of characters you want to appear in automatic fields. To add an edit mask to an automatic field mask, place the edit mask character pairs after the asterisk in the automatic field mask. Here are two examples of combining edit masks with automatic edit masks:

Example	Allows These Characters
:DATE*09:	Date—numbers only; exclude dashes
:DUPE*Az:	Duplicate—letters only

When you have a field that always contains a specific set of characters, you can save a lot of typing by specifying a constant to go into that field. You specify a constant by enclosing the characters you want in quotation marks when you assign the constant to the field. For example, suppose you are creating a group of records that have the same ZIP code, 94301. If you assign the constant **"94301"** to the ZIP code field, the characters

94301 will automatically appear in the ZIP code field every time a new record gets added.

Calculated fields can generate results based on arithmetic, date, and relational calculations, and on combinations of these calculation types. Calculations are made up of combinations of field names, arithmetic operators, logical operators, comparison operators, special calculation functions, and relational lookups. The various operators used in calculations are denoted by the following symbols:

Arithmetic		Logical		Comparison	
+	Addition	&	And	=	Equal
−	Subtraction	|	Or	!=	Not equal
*	Multiplication			>	Greater than
/	Division			>=	Greater than or equal
%	Modulo (remainder)			<	Less than
^	Exponentiation			<=	Less than or equal

An example of an arithmetic calculation that computes the difference between the contents of a field called Revenues and a field called Costs, and divides the difference by 1000, would look like this:

((Revenues −Costs)/1000)

Date calculations rely on a set of special PC-File+ functions. These special functions appear in calculations enclosed in a set of parentheses, with an "at" sign (@) preceding the function keyword:

Special Function	Performs This Operation
(@RANDOM#)	Generates a random number between 0 and 1
(@TODAY#)	Creates today's day number relative to 01/01/1901
(@DAY#,mask)	Gets a date from the calculation stack and converts it to a day number. The mask indicates the date format, for example, *ymd ydm mdy myd dmy dym yymmdd*
(@DATE,mask)	Gets a day number from the calculation stack and converts it to date. The mask indicates the date format, for example, *mdy/ dmy dmy-*

The following is an example of a date calculation that computes the date 60 days from the date stored in a field called Payment:

((Payment(@DAY,mdy)+60)(@DATE,mdy))

Relational calculations utilize a PC-File+ special function called *relational lookup*, which has the following form:

(@key1,dbase,key2,item)

In this form of the relational lookup, *key1* is the field in the current database; *dbase* is the name of the database to be searched; *key2* is the field to be matched in the database being searched; and *item* is the field that contains the information to be retrieved when a match is made. An example relational lookup that matches a part number in the current database with a part number in a master file, and then extracts the corresponding price from the master file, would look like this:

(@PartNo,master,PartNo,Price)

Report Commands and Controls

When you create your own custom reports, the report specification is organized into sections. Within each section, you can include any number of report commands which determine what information gets printed and how that information is organized on the printed page.

A report specification may have up to six sections. Each section controls a specific part of the printed report. Report sections are optional. If you omit a section, then that part of the report is not printed. A report specification must contain at least one section, otherwise nothing will be printed.

Section	Controls Printing Of
:COVER	The cover page, or other information printed only at beginning of report
:HEADING	Information at the top of each page
:DETAIL	Information for each record
:SUBTOTAL	Data at each subtotal break
:TOTAL	Data at the end of the report
:FOOTING	Information at the bottom of each page

The commands that you use in a report specification are shown in the following list. These commands can also be embedded in form letters which you can create with PC-File+'s letter-writing feature. Commands used in form letters are associated with the mail-merge report generation capabilities.

Command	Command Interpretation
[xxx]	Database field *xxx*
<xxx>	Field *xxx* (remove excess spaces)

Command	Command Interpretation
[xxx,s,l]	Partial field; (s)tart, (l)ength
"xxx"	A constant
(#)	Relative record number
(a+b)	Calculation
(@f1,DB,f2,f3)	Relational lookup
=nn	Tab to column *nn*
/n	Insert *n* newlines
.FF	Form feed to new page
.CP nn	Conditional skip to new page
.GROUP	Start a group to have no blank lines
.EGROUP	End a group; do not replace blank lines
.EGROUP R	End a group; replace blank lines after
A nn,nn	ASCII printer control codes
.IF (calculation spec)	Do next commands(s) if true
.ELSE	Do next commands(s) if .IF was false
.ENDIF	End of .IF .ELSE sequence
[COUNT*]	Number of records printed
[DATE*]	Today's date
[KEYIN*prompt]	Let user input directly from keyboard
[PAGE*]	Current page number
[RECORD*]	Record number of current record
[RECORDS*]	Number of records in database
[SELECT*]	Selection criteria for report
[SORT*]	Current index or primary sort field name
[SUBCOUNT*]	Number of records in subtotal group
[SUBFLD*]	Field name of subtotal break field
[SUBID*]	Data from subtotal break field
[TIME*]	Current time

When you print data in a report, you can use output report masks to control the formatting of printed information. The masks are placed directly after the field names or calculations that you want to format. Here are some examples of different kinds of masks you might use:

Example	Use
:@@@@@@@@@:	Character mask that prints up to 9 characters
:#####:	Numeric mask that prints 5 digits
:zz,zz#.##:	7 digits; zero suppress; comma; decimal point
:$$$$$$.##:	Floating dollar sign
:******.##:	Check protection; leading zeros print as *
:=12,0,100,* :	Bar chart mask; 12 print positions; minimum value is 0; maximum value is 100; use * to fill in the bars of the chart; use space (character after *) to fill in rest of space outside the bars
::	No output (do not print this field)

APPENDIX H

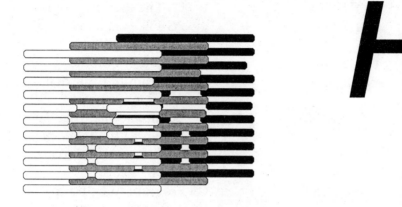

Files on the PC-File+ Disks

Your PC-File+ disks contain many different data files and programs. Some of these are files that you copied from the original distribution disk sets. Many others got created as you started running PC-File+ and as you used the program's various options and capabilities. This appendix helps you to identify each data file and program by providing a brief annotated description of the files on your disks.

Program Files	Description
PCF.EXE	PC-File+ main program
PCLABEL.EXE	PC-File+ mailing label program
PCG2.EXE	PC-File+ graphics program
FPRPT.EXE	Program to print database definition reports
MSHERC.COM	Command file to initialize a system with a monochrome monitor and a Hercules graphics card
PCFIX.EXE	Program to help repair a damaged database

Data Files	Description
dbasename.DTA	File that contains the data
dbasename.HDR	Contains information about the structure of the database
dbasename.INX	The index to the database is in this file
dbasename.KEY	Smart key storage file for the database
dbasename.PRO	Configuration file for a particular database
filename.ANS	Holds your Report menu responses
filename.LTR	Mail merge letter file data
filename.REP	File that contains a report format
PCF.HLP	Help message file
PCFILE.PRO	Configuration file for entire PC-File+ program

Data Files	Description
GRAPH.ME	Work file created by PCG2.EXE
DELETE.ME	Temporary file created by report and letter writing activities
JUNK.*xxx*	Temporary work files created during sort operations. Possible names are JUNK.OLD and JUNK.1 through JUNK.25
PEOPLE*.*	Sample database, eleven files in all

Resource Files	Description
READ.ME	File of information about product and shareware
CHANGES	List of changes to current product version
TECHINFO	How to get file format technical information
CARD	PC-File+ reference card
VENDOR.DOC	Shareware guidelines for vendors
PRODUCTS	Product order form

APPENDIX

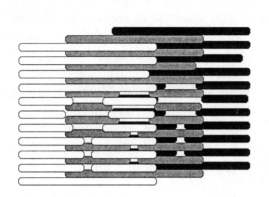

Transferring Files Between PC-File+ and Other Programs

PC-File+ has powerful import and export features which allow you to transfer data between PC-File+ version 3 and many other programs. For example, you can export and import PC-File+ data to and from dBASE (II and III), PC-File:dB (DBF format files), DIF format files (for example, VisiCalc), fixed length (random) format files, mail-merge files (comma-delimited files), PeachText, text editor (SDF format) files, user-defined files, WordPerfect 4.2 merge files, and PC-File compressed format files.

In addition to these import/export capabilities, you can also use PC-File+ to export (but not import) Lotus PRN format files and SYLK format files. Chapter 24 of the *PC-File+ User's Manual,* "PC-File+ & Other Programs," contains detailed information about the use of the PC-File+ Import and Export commands. These two commands operate in a straightforward manner, and you should encounter no problems in trying to import or export data between PC-File+ and the previously mentioned programs and file formats.

If you have data files that were created by earlier versions of PC-File+ (versions 1 and 2), PC-File III (versions 2, 3, and 4), or PC-File/R (version 1), then you should look at Chapter 3, "Compatibility with Previous Versions," in the *PC-File+ User's Manual* (version 3).

To briefly summarize the information from Chapter 3 of the *PC-File+ User's Manual,* most data files from previous versions of PC-File+ either can be read directly by PC-File+ version 3 or can be easily prepared so that they are readable. In most cases, smart key definitions from earlier versions have to be revised, and PC-File+ version 3 cannot read any files that have been encrypted.

Data files created or altered by PC-File+ version 3 can only be transferred to these other PC-File+ programs by exporting the files in text editor format. PC-File+ version 3 adds an extra line to the HDR, REP, LTR, and graphics format files that makes those files unsuitable for use by earlier versions of the product.

For the exact steps you take to exchange data files between PC-File+ version 3 and previous versions, refer to Chapter 3 of the *PC-File+ User's Manual*.

PART VII

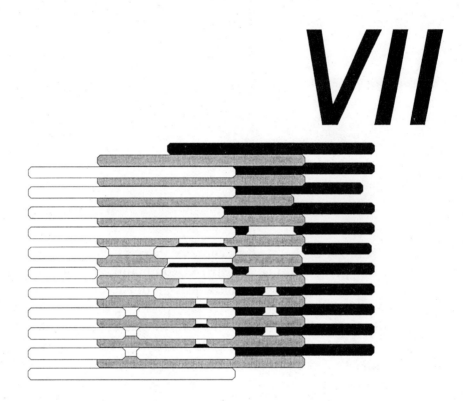

PC-Calc+ Resource Information

Part VII of *The Shareware Book* contains three PC-Calc+ appendixes. Appendix J is a complete keystroke, command, and function summary for PC-Calc+. Appendix K lists all of the files and programs used by PC-Calc+ and how to interpret the different file name extensions. Appendix L tells you how to convert spreadsheets and files created by versions of PC-Calc previous to PC-Calc+ version 2. Appendix L also discusses converting PC-Calc+ files to and from other file formats.

APPENDIX

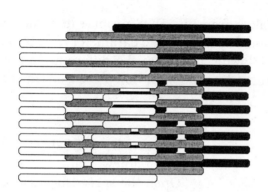

J

PC-Calc+ Keystrokes, Commands, and Functions

PC-Calc+ responds to a variety of keystrokes, command options, and functions as it performs spreadsheet computation, editing, printing, and cell organization tasks. The following lists summarize what PC-Calc+ does as you use specific keys, commands, and functions.

Different Ways to Start PC-Calc+

You can start PC-Calc+ from the DOS prompt in several ways and with several optional command line parameters and file name specifications. The following list shows the different parameters that you can type and a description of how PC-Calc+ interprets each option.

Type	To Start Up PC-Calc+ and...
pcc	Open a new, blank spreadsheet
pcc *filespec*	Open the spreadsheet *filespec*
pcc /e=h	Set EGA screens to 43 lines; VGA to 50
pcc /e=m	Set EGA screens to 35 lines; VGA to 40
pcc /e=l	Set EGA screens to 25 lines; VGA to 25
pcc /green	Override any color settings
pcc /h=drive:subdirectory	Set path to help file
pcc *filespec* /m=x	Load spreadsheet *filespec* and execute macro x

You can combine command line parameters as long as you separate each parameter by a space character. For example, the following command line entry starts PC-Calc+, loads the BUDGET spreadsheet, sets an EGA screen to 35 lines (or VGA screen to 40 lines), and tells PC-Calc+ that the help file is on drive D in the subdirectory HELPFILE.

pcc budget /e=m /h=d:helpfile

PC-Calc+ Keystrokes, Commands, and Functions **673**

Appendix J

PC-Calc+ *Special Command Keys*

You can activate many PC-Calc+ features directly by using the special command keystrokes shown in the following list:

Key	Function
F1	Context sensitive help screen displayed
F2	Summary help screen displayed
F6	Delete data to the right of the cursor
F3	Edit mode activated (also activated by typing)
CTRL-E	EGA/VGA screen modes toggle
F8	Enable block marking feature (CTRL-B)
CTRL-B	Mark beginning and end of range on screen
CTRL-R	Re-mark the last marked range
CTRL-U	Unmark the marked range
CTRL-C	Fill character selection (Used with CTRL-P)
CTRL-P	Fill character write (Used with CTRL-C)
CTRL-F	Formula display option toggle
CTRL-G	Goto command activated
ALT-Y	Macro definition (start and end)
CTRL-K	Pauses macros for keyboard entries
CTRL-Y	Temporary macro executed
/	Main menu displayed
F9	Quick calculator activated
F10	Recalculate spreadsheet
CTRL-S	Switch to other screen when in split screen mode
CTRL-T	Screen synchronization toggle (in split screen mode)
ESC	Stops or cancels the current operation

Keys that Move the Cell Pointer

The following sets of keystrokes control the movement of the cell pointer within the worksheet area on the screen:

Cells

Key	Function
↑	Move cell pointer up one row in current column
↓	Move cell pointer down one row in current column
←	Move cell pointer left one column in current row
→	Move cell pointer right one column in current row
ENTER	Move cell pointer one cell in Smart Cursor direction
CTRL-G	Go to specific cell

Screen

Key	Function
PGUP	Scroll one screen towards top of spreadsheet
PGDN	Scroll one screen towards bottom of spreadsheet
+	Scroll one screen to the right (use numeric keypad)
−	Scroll one screen to the left (use numeric keypad)

Key	Function
HOME	Move to left column of screen, then top row of screen, then left column of spreadsheet, then top row of spreadsheet
END	Move to right column of screen, then bottom row of screen, then right column of spreadsheet, then bottom row of spreadsheet
ALT-5	Move to middle cell on screen (5 on the numeric pad)
ALT-↑	Move to top row of screen in the current column
ALT-↓	Move to bottom row of screen in the current column
ALT-←	Move to leftmost active screen column; current row
ALT-→	Move to rightmost active screen column; current row
ALT-HOME	Move to upper left active screen cell
ALT-END	Move to lower left active screen cell
ALT-PGUP	Move to upper right active screen cell
ALT-PGDN	Move to lower right active screen cell

Spreadsheet

Key	Function
CTRL-5	Move to center cell of spreadsheet (5 on numeric pad)
CTRL-↑	Move to top active spreadsheet row; current column
CTRL-↓	Move to bottom active spreadsheet row; current column

CTRL-←	Move to leftmost active spreadsheet column; current row
CTRL-→	Move to rightmost active spreadsheet column; current row
CTRL-HOME	Move to upper left active spreadsheet cell
CTRL-END	Move to lower left active spreadsheet cell
CTRL-PGUP	Move to upper right active spreadsheet cell
CTRL-PGDN	Move to lower right active spreadsheet cell

Keys That Move the Cursor on the Edit Line

The following keystrokes move the cursor on the edit line:

Key	Function
←	Move the cursor one character to the left
→	Move the cursor one character to the right
TAB	Move the cursor five characters to the right
SHIFT-TAB	Move the cursor five characters to the left
HOME	Move the cursor to the first character on edit line
END	Move the cursor to the right of the last character

Key	Action
F6	Delete from the cursor to the end of the edit line
BACKSPACE	Delete the character to the left of the cursor
INSERT	Insert mode on and off toggle
DELETE	Delete the character at the cursor position
ESC	Return to worksheet area without saving changes
ENTER	Return to worksheet area saving changes to current cell and move the cell pointer one cell in the Smart cursor direction
↑	Accept data and move the cell pointer up one cell
↓	Accept data and move the cell pointer down one cell
CTRL-←	Accept data and move the cell pointer one cell to the left
CTRL-→	Accept data and move the cell pointer one cell to the right
CTRL-↑	Accept data and move the cell pointer up one cell
CTRL-↓	Accept data and move the cell pointer down one cell

PC-Calc+ Menu Command Summary

PC-Calc+ has over 80 primary commands that you can activate from the PC-Calc+ menu structure. The following list presents a summary of all of the command names, organized according to

Main menu command sections. The keystroke that automatically activates each command is shown enclosed in parentheses. You can activate commands either by moving the menu highlight to a command and pressing ENTER or by typing keystroke command sequences. Each command sequence begins with the slash character (/) to activate the Main menu. For example, to set a (B)lock of cells to (B)lanks, you would type **/bb** followed by the block definition.

MAIN MENU COMMANDS
(B)lock, (C)onfigure, (D)OS, (E)dit, (F)ormat, (G)oto, (I)mport, (L)oad/Save, (M)acros, L(O)ops, (P)rint/Graph, (S)plit screen, (T)itle locking

(B)lock Commands
(B)lank, (C)opy, (F)ill, (M)ove, (R)ange, (S)ort, (T)ransform, (Z)ap

(C)onfigure Commands
(A)uto-backup, (C)alculate, (D)isplay, (E)quation delimiter, (F)licker, (G)lobals, (I)mport paths, (L)oop settings, (P)rinter setup, (S)mart, (W)idth, Sort Field (T)ypes, (Z) ASCII sort order

(F)ormat Commands
(C)ells, (D)elete, (F)ormulas, (I)nsert, (W)idth

(I)mport Commands
(C) Load part of PC-Calc+, (U) Update CALC table, (D) Load PC-File:dB, (1) Load PC-File:dB sum, (F) Load PC-File+, (2) Load PC-File+ sum, (T) Load PC-Type/ASCII, (M) Load MailMerge, (E) External files import table

(L)oad/Save Commands
(L) Load spreadsheet, (S) Save spreadsheet, (2) Save condensed spreadsheet, (P) Load print codes, (O) Save print codes, (C) Load configuration, (D) Save configuration, (M) Load macros, (N) Save macros

(M)acro Commands
These commands appear only when a macro has been defined and you select an existing macro to be edited or executed: (C)opy, (D)elete, (E)xecute, (M)odify, (N)ame, (R)eassign

L(O)op Commands
(L)oop processing, (D)isplay loops, (I)terate loops

(P)rint/Graph Commands
(P)rint, (M)odify/run saved reports, (N)umber of copies, (E)scape codes, (R)eport setup, (T)ranslation table, (G)raph, (C)hange/run saved graphs

(S)plit Screen Commands
(H)orizontal, (S)witch, (V)ertical, (U)nsplit

(T)itle Locking Commands
(R)ow, (C)olumns, (B)oth, (U)nlock

PC-Calc+ Computational Functions

PC-Calc+ comes with many pre-programmed functions that assist you in developing sophisticated spreadsheet calculational models. PC-Calc+ functions are organized by computational task into the following eight function groups: Date and Time, Financial, Mathematical, Logical, Special, Statistical, String, and Trigonometric. Most PC-Calc+ functions have a fixed number of arguments. One special function (SELECT) and several statistical functions (AVG, COUNT, MAX, MIN, STDEV, and SUM) can have variable numbers of arguments. The argument lists for functions with variable numbers of arguments contain an ellipsis (. . .).

Date and Time Functions

Function	Result
DATE(*month, day, year*)	Computes number of days between December 31, 1900 and the given date
DAY(*days*)	Computes day of month given number of days since December 31, 1900
HOUR(*seconds*)	Computes hours since midnight
MINUTE(*seconds*)	Computes minutes since midnight
MONTH(*days*)	Computes month given number of days since December 31, 1989
NOW	Computes seconds since midnight
SECOND(*seconds*)	Computes number of seconds remaining after total seconds are converted to minutes
TIME(*hours, minutes, seconds*)	Computes seconds since midnight
TODAY	Computes days between December 31, 1900 and current date

WKDY(*days*)   Computes the day of week given the number of days since December 31, 1900 (Sunday = 0)

YEAR(*days*)   Computes the year given the number of days since December 31, 1900 (1987 = 87)

Financial Functions

Function	*Result*
DB(*scrap%,life,period,amt,type*)	Declining balance depreciation
EQUITY(*loan, payment,rate,p1,pN*)	Equity buildup between period *p1* and period *pN*
FV(*payment,rate,periods*)	The future value of an annuity
IRR(*guess,cash flow*)	Internal rate of return
NPV(*interest,cash flow*)	Net present value
PAYMENT(*principal, rate,periods*)	Payment computation
PERIODS(*principal,payment,rate*)	Number of periods
PRINCIPAL(*payment, rate,periods*)	Principal computation
RATE(*principal,payment, periods*)	Interest rate computation
SLN(*scrap%,life,period*)	Straight line depreciation
SYD(*scrap%,life,period*)	Sum of years digit depreciation

Mathematical Functions

Function	*Result*
ABS(*value*)	Returns absolute value

Function	Result
CEIL(*value*)	Rounds up to next integer
COMB(*value1,value2*)	Computes combinatorials
EXP(*value*)	Calculates exponential
FACT(*value1,value2*)	Computes factorial
FIX(*value*)	Returns integer closest to zero
FLOOR(*value*)	Rounds down to next integer
INT(*value*)	Rounds down to next integer
LN(*value*)	Computes the natural logarithm
LOG(*value*)	Computes logarithm to base 10
MOD(*value1,value2*)	Returns remainder or modulus of the two values
PERM(*value1,value2*)	Computes the permutations
RANDOM(*value1,value2*)	Generates random number between the given values
RMNDR(*value*)	Returns the fractional portion
ROUND(*value,n*)	Rounds value to n decimal places
SGN(*value*)	Returns the sign of the value
SQRT(*value*)	Calculates the square root

Logical Functions

Function	Result
FALSE	Sets value of cell to FALSE (0)
IF(*condition,expr1,expr2*)	If *condition* is TRUE, then *expr1*, else *expr2*

SMOD(*string,type*)	Modify case of string characters and trim excess spaces
SPART(*string,n,type*)	Partial string modification
XFREP(*str1,str2,start,t*)	Multipurpose string function used to compare strings, find substrings, and replace parts of strings

Trigonometric Functions

Function	*Result*
ACOS(*value*)	Arc cosine
ACSC(*value*)	Arc cosecant
ASEC(*value*)	Arc secant
ASIN(*value*)	Arc sine
ATN(*value*)	Arc tangent
ATN2(*value1,value2*)	Arc tangent (4 quadrants)
COS(*radians*)	Cosine
COSH(*value*)	Hyperbolic cosine
CSC(*radians*)	Cosecant
CTN(*radians*)	Cotangent
DEG(*value*)	Degrees converted from radians
PI	Value of pi (3.1415...)
RAD(*value*)	Radians converted from degrees
SEC(*radians*)	Secant
SIN(*radians*)	Sine
SINH(*value*)	Hyperbolic sine
TAN(*radians*)	Tangent
TANH(*value*)	Hyperbolic tangent

APPENDIX

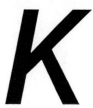
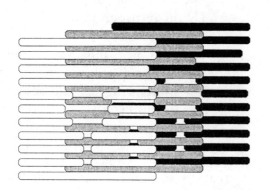

Files on the PC-Calc+ Disks

The distribution disks in registered copies of PC-Calc+ contain a set of "compressed" files. These files are unpacked during the installation process to become the files that you use when you first run PC-Calc+. After you run PC-Calc+, the program creates other files (data, resource, and temporary files) which appear in your directory. The information in this appendix lists the various files that you will find as you install and use PC-Calc+. The first list of files are the ones you will find on your distribution disks.

Distribution Files	Description
INSTALL.EXE	PC-Calc+ installation program
PKUNZIP.EXE	The file extraction utility program
PCCP.ZIP	The main program files (compressed)
READ.ME	The PC-Calc+ information file
VENDOR.DOC	Disk dealer/distributor information
PCCU.ZIP	The utility program and resource files (compressed)

Once you install PC-Calc+ using the INSTALL.EXE program and run PC-Calc+ to create a spreadsheet, you will find the following files in the PC-Calc+ directory.

Program Files	Description
PCC.EXE	The PC-Calc+ main program
CONVERT.EXE	The PC-Calc+ import/export program
PCG2.EXE	The PC-Calc+ graphics program
P90.EXE	Program to print spreadsheets sideways
MSHERC.COM	Command file to initialize a system with a monochrome monitor and a Hercules graphics card

Data Files	Description
spreadsheet.PCC	File that contains the spreadsheet data
spreadsheet.MAC	File that contains macro definitions
spreadsheet.PRO	Configuration file for a particular spreadsheet
printer.PRN	Files that contain printer information
PCC.HLP	Help message file

PCCALC.PRO	Configuration file for overall product
COLOR.PRO	Profile for running PC-Calc+ on a color monitor
GRAPH.ME	Work file created by using PCG2.EXE
GRAPH.ME2	Work file created by using PCG2.EXE
PCG2.ASP	Aspect ratio file created by using PCG2.EXE
LOAN.PCC	Sample spreadsheet
TUTORIAL.PCC	Sample spreadsheet discussed in *PC-Calc+ User's Guide*
SAMPLE.MAC	Sample macro file

Resource Files	**Description**
FILES	List of PC-Calc+ files
RESPONSE	Copy of the User Response Form
PRODUCTS	Product order form

APPENDIX

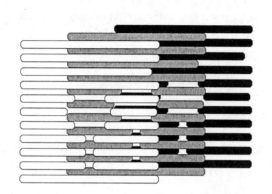

L

Transferring Files Between PC-Calc+ and Other Programs

PC-Calc+ (version 2) stores spreadsheet files in a format that differs from the way files are stored by earlier versions of the program. To use spreadsheets created by earlier versions of PC-Calc+, you must run the PC-Calc+ Convert program. The

Convert program also lets you transfer PC-Calc+ version 2 spreadsheets to and from a variety of other file formats.

For the exact steps that you take to transfer data files between PC-Calc+ version 2 and other file formats, you can either refer to the first appendix of the *PC-Calc+ User's Guide,* "Convert," or you can run the Convert program and use the simple menu options that are presented.

The Convert program supports the following types of file transfers and conversions:

- PC-Calc spreadsheets to PC-Calc+ version 2 spreadsheets
- PC-Calc+ version 1 spreadsheets to PC-Calc+ version 2 spreadsheets
- PC-Calc+ version 1 PRO, MAC, and PRN files to PC-Calc+ version 2 files
- PC-Calc+ version 2 spreadsheets to comma-delimited files
- PC-Calc+ version 2 spreadsheets to DIF files
- DIF files to PC-Calc+ version 2 spreadsheets
- PC-Calc+ version 2 spreadsheets to Lotus 1-2-3 and Symphony files
- Lotus 1-2-3 and Symphony files to PC-Calc+ version 2 spreadsheets

The Convert program will not alter your original files except for conversions that involve files from PC-Calc+ version 1. When converting version 1 files, if you attempt to save the converted file to the original file name, Convert will change the extension of the original file to create a backup version of the original. Again, refer to the first appendix, "Convert," in the *PC-Calc+ User's Guide* for details.

PART VIII

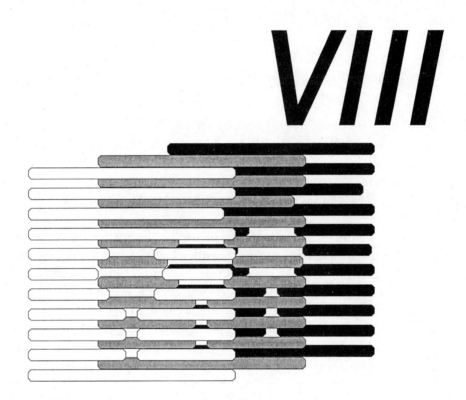

Other Useful Resource Information

The appendixes in this section of *The Shareware Book* provide you with information about three separate topics. Appendix M covers the different ways you can transfer files between the shareware programs discussed in this book. By following specific conventions, you can move files back and forth between PC-Write, PC-File+, and PC-Calc+.

Appendix N lists a number of useful shareware utility packages, many of which can augment and extend your ability to use the programs in this book. In addition, several other packages are listed which offer you shareware alternatives for word processing, database management, and spreadsheet calculations.

Appendix O contains a representative sampling of names, addresses, and contact information for a small number of user groups throughout the world. The goal of this section is to give you a starting point (in your state or country) from which you can reach into the extensive network of support organizations dedicated to helping people use technology. The user group network represents one of the major conduits through which the shareware revolution continues to grow and evolve.

APPENDIX

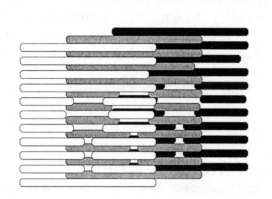

Transferring Files Between PC-Write, PC-File+, and PC-Calc+

If you use all three of the shareware packages discussed in this book, then you may occasionally want to move data back and forth between the programs. The following sections outline how to transfer files between PC-Write, PC-File+, and PC-Calc+, simply and directly. In general, most of the file transfers take place by having one program write or export an ASCII (text only) file, and having another program read or import that ASCII file. In some cases, the programs reading the data provide additional features that let you tailor or process the imported information. PC-File+ and PC-Calc+ can read data from each other directly.

Transfer Files to and from PC-Write

PC-Write can load any ASCII file created by any other program, including ASCII files from PC-File+ and PC-Calc+. When PC-Write saves a file, the file is saved as an ASCII file. ASCII files saved by PC-Write can be imported or read by both PC-File+ and PC-Calc+, as long as the data in the PC-Write file can be meaningfully interpreted by the two programs. PC-File+ and PC-Calc+ can be forced to import an arbitrary PC-Write file. However, if the data organization in the PC-Write file is not meaningful to the two programs, they will create a scrambled database and scrambled spreadsheet, respectively.

Most of the time, you will probably want to output information from PC-File+ or PC-Calc+ and read the data into PC-Write to be edited and printed. Occasionally, you might want to use PC-Write to edit particular files, save the edited versions, and import the edited data back into PC-File+ or PC-Calc+. In this last situation, you will need to carefully study the formats of the files that are output by PC-File+ and PC-Calc+, so that your editing changes do not create problems when the files are imported.

Transfer Files to and from PC-File+

PC-File+ can output ASCII files that can be read by PC-Write in two ways. The first way is to export the data from a database using the Utility menu Export command. The exported ASCII file can be output as either a *comma-delimited* file or a standard *fixed-length editor* file. A comma-delimited file consists of the contents of data fields, separated by commas, with a carriage return and an optional line feed at the end of each record. (This file format is used by many word processing and mail-merge programs.) On the PC-File+ Export menu, the comma-delimited output option is listed as "Mail-merge."

A fixed-length editor file consists of the contents of fixed-length fields with no separators. The end of each record contains a carriage return and an optional line feed. Fixed-length editor files are also used by many word processors, and are often an import/export option in database programs. PC-Write can read, edit, and print both of these kinds of PC-File+ files.

The second way that PC-File+ can output an ASCII data file is to print a report to the disk. When the program prints a report to the disk, an ASCII image of the entire report is saved. You can use PC-Write to read, edit, and print the saved report.

If you use PC-Write to edit a comma-delimited or fixed-length editor file, PC-File+ can import the file back into a database as long as the editing changes do not disrupt the way the PC-File+ database interprets the incoming data streams.

PC-File+ version 3 (the version discussed in this book) can import PC-Calc+ version 1.0 files by using the Utility menu Import command. To import data to PC-File+ from PC-Calc+ version 2 (the version discussed in this book), you first must use the PC-Calc+ Convert program to convert the file to version 1 format. To import data from a PC-Calc+ file, you must also predefine a database in PC-File+ to accept the incoming data. PC-File+ does not automatically create a database from the imported data.

PC-File+ also exports a PC-Calc+ version 1.0 compatible file. PC-Calc+ version 2 can import these files with an import command. Additionally, the two programs can interchange data by using comma-delimited files.

Transfer Files to and from PC-Calc+

PC-Calc+ creates comma-delimited and printed report files that can be read by PC-Write, but it does not create fixed-length editor files. The restrictions that apply to PC-File+ also apply to the editing of PC-Calc+ comma-delimited files that are to be imported back into PC-Calc+. If you disrupt the structure of the data elements in the file, PC-Calc+ may produce a jumbled form of the intended spreadsheet.

PC-Calc+ does not have an export function. The program relies on a standalone routine called Convert to create alternate file structures. As was mentioned in the previous section, Convert must be used to create PC-Calc+ files that can be directly read by PC-File+.

PC-Calc+ supports an import command from the Main menu which allows the program to read PC-File+ files directly and to extract the sum of particular data fields. The import feature also handles comma-delimited files created by any program, including PC-Write and PC-File+.

APPENDIX N

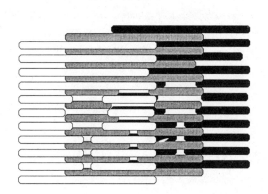

Other Shareware Programs

The number of programs available as shareware products totals into the thousands. Shareware programs are distributed through networks of authorized dealers, through user groups, on electronic bulletin boards, directly from the software developers, and by people sharing useful products with other people.

The following shareware product list represents a small sample of the many good shareware products available on a "try before you buy" basis. For additional information about these and other shareware products, look at the *PC-SIG Encyclopedia of Shareware*, published by PC-SIG, Inc., 1030D East Duane Ave., Sunnyvale, CA 94086. The *PC-SIG Encyclopedia of Shareware* is an alphabetized and annotated guide to over 1500 shareware programs that you can order and evaluate directly from the PC-SIG Library.

Word Processing Programs and Utilities

The following list gives you the names of a few shareware resources and products that can help you deal with word processing and document preparation tasks. For detailed information on ordering and evaluating these products, refer to either the *PC-SIG Encyclopedia of Shareware* or any certified shareware vendor.

- **DCA Conversion for PC-Write** Lets you convert PC-Write files to mainframe computer file formats and mainframe files to ASCII so that they can be used on your microcomputer.

- **Galaxy** A powerful and easy-to-learn word processing program designed around the concept of how people use word processors. Comes with a full array of standard word processing features, such as a spelling checker, macros, and simultaneous printing and editing.

- **MindReader** A program that is part word processor and part automated typist. The program learns the words and phrases that you use repeatedly and tries to guess what you are about to type. MindReader comes with a spelling checker and an address book for mail-merge operations.

- **New York Word** A word processor that lets you do split-screen editing, block moves of text between windows, tables of contents, footnotes, automatic indexing and hyphenation, and mail-merge operations.

- **PC-Outline** An "idea generator" and thought organizer. PC-Outline operates as a "pop-up," RAM-resident accessory which you can activate from within other programs, such as your word processor.

- **PC-Type II** A word processor distributed by the same people who distribute PC-File+ and PC-Calc+. PC-Type II has numerous features, including the Fault Finder module which helps you spell check over 100,000 words, graphics, a "whoops" option which lets you recover up to 15 lines of deleted text, newspaper-style multiple columns, and visual line-up of columns and rows with a "cross hair" function. A combination standard and advanced word processing package.

- **PC-Write Font Selector** Lets you select and use laser fonts in PC-Write documents that will be printed on HP LaserJets or compatible printers.

- **PC-Write Macros** A library of PC-Write macros that help you streamline many editing and document creation tasks.

- **PC-Write PageMaker Import Filter** Lets you transfer PC-Write documents into PageMaker and retain most of the documents' formatting.

- **RGB^Techwriter** A word processor for engineers and scientists. You can create documents that include scientific notation, equations, and symbols, including superscripts and subscripts. The program uses a color coding scheme to help you decode screen information that will be printed in scientific formats.

- **Writer's Heaven** Alters PC-Write, using PC-Write's macro capability, so that you can type, edit, and perform PC-Write tasks more quickly and efficiently.

Database Programs and Utilities

The following list presents several shareware programs that deal with the management of databases:

- **File Express** A database management tool that handles up to 16 million records with 120 fields per record and 250 characters per field. File Express is menu driven and suitable for both the novice and the advanced user.

- **FreeFile** A relational database that handles 2 billion records with 100 fields per record, calculated fields, and the ability to import and export data between other file formats.

- **Muse** A database management program to help authors track submissions to publishers, especially multiple and simultaneous submissions. The program tracks all aspects of the submission process, including queries, actual submissions, responses, acceptances, publications, and mailings.

- **PC-File:dB** The database program that operates like PC-File+ (menu-driven options with no need to use a complex command structure or language) and that handles dBASE file formats directly. The product includes all of the features of PC-File+ (graphics, text editor, mail merge, paint options, macros, smart keys, calculated fields, and sophisticated search operations). PC-File:dB is an easy-to-use alternative to working with dBASE or a dBASE-compatible program.

- **ZoomRacks** A program that uses a patented "card and rack" structure to help you organize virtually anything. ZoomRacks has similarities to various other "hypertext" products, such as HyperCard. (ZoomRacks predates HyperCard and most of the current hypertext products by several years.) With Zoom-Racks, you can zoom in on portions of the screen and access additional data, including graphics. The product has several starter kits which contain templates, forms, and predefined cards and racks. Starter kits are available for business, home, and small business operations. The home starter kit is available for the price of the disks.

Spreadsheet Programs and Utilities

The following list presents several shareware programs that deal with electronic spreadsheets.

- **AsEasyAs**   An electronic spreadsheet program that maintains compatibility with some of the Lotus 1-2-3 commands, that uses on-screen menus, and that accepts Lotus 1-2-3 files directly. AsEasyAs lets you build spreadsheets with up to 256 columns and 2048 rows. The program supports several features that let you plot your data.
- **Instacalc**   A memory-resident electronic spreadsheet that you can pop up over other applications. Instacalc is full featured and can import and export Lotus 1-2-3, dBASE, and DIF files.
- **Lotus Learning System**   Lotus 1-2-3 for beginners. This version of the program contains a comprehensive tutorial that teaches you how to use the program and its menu structures.
- **Power Sheets**   Lets you create massive, three-dimensional spreadsheets of up to 16 million cells. You can rotate the data cube and view "slices" of the spreadsheet in different orientations. Power Sheets is fully programmable and has its own programming language, including numerous functions and pre-programmed features. Cell references in Power Sheet can be lists made up of combinations of ranges, individual cell references, and formulas.

APPENDIX

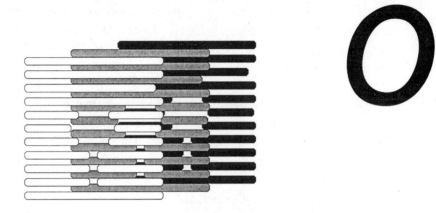

User Groups

You can find computer user groups all over the world. User groups support nearly every conceivable niche within the computing community. Most user groups were founded and persist in order to provide a timely exchange of technical information about a rapidly changing technology. If you want to know how to install your newest piece of software, then take your computer to a user group meeting. If your faithful word processing program suddenly develops "bugs" where none existed before, then take a copy to a user group meeting and ask some of the "wizards" to help you solve the mystery.

User groups form a network of thousands of dedicated computer owners who, formally and informally, influence the development of today's and tomorrow's technologies.

The following list, organized by geographic area, provides a starting point for you to begin your contacts with a user group. More extensive lists of user groups can be found in publications such as the *Computer Shopper* from Coastal Associates Publishing, L.P., One Park Avenue, New York, NY 10016. You can find out about local groups by going on-line to an electronic bulletin board system and browsing around for user group information. The *Computer Shopper* user group list is comprehensive and is maintained by *Fog*, an international nonprofit computer user group. You can contact *Fog* at P.O. Box 3474, Daly City, CA 94015.

Alabama
Huntsville PC User Group, Inc.
P.O. Box 13016
Huntsville, AL 35802
(205) 539-5940

Alaska
Ankor-Guide Computer Group
P.O. Box 210089
Anchorage, AK 99521-0089
(907) 278-3138

Arizona
Phoenix IBM PC Users Group
P.O. Box 44150
Phoenix, AZ 85046
(602) 943-7907

Arkansas
Central Arkansas PC User Asso.
P.O. Box 2095
Little Rock, AR 72203
(501) 225-9304

California
Fresno PC Users Group
P.O. Box 5987
Fresno, CA 93755
(209) 226-0558

IBM PC Users Group of California
P.O. Box 4136
Los Angeles, CA 90028

1st FOG of Silicon Valley
3462 Kirkwood Dr.
San Jose, CA 95117
(408) 371-8699

Stanford/Palo Alto PC Users
P.O. Box 3736
Stanford, CA 94309
(415) 322-3850

San Francisco PC Users Group
3145 Geary
San Francisco, CA 94118-3316
(415) 221-9166

IBM PC Users' Group of the Redwoods
P.O. Box 5055
Santa Rosa, CA 95402-5830
(707) 727-8737

Riverside IBM Computer Club
7860 Live Oak Dr.
Riverside, CA 92509-5339
(714) 685-5407

Kern Independent PC User Group
P.O. Box 2780
Bakersfield, CA 93303
(805) 327-1866

Santa Barbara PC Users Group
281 Oak Rd.
Santa Barbara, CA 93108
(805) 969-9961

Sacramento PC Users Group
P.O. Box 685
Citrus Heights, CA 95611-0685
(916) 332-1944

Colorado
Metro Area Computer Enthusiasts
P.O. Box 440247
Aurora, CO 80012
(303) 830-9143

Connecticut
Business and Professional Micro User Group
363 North Quaker Lane
West Hartford, CT 06119
(203) 233-5571

District of Columbia
Capital PC Users Group
51 Monroe Street
Plaza East Two
Rockville, MD 20850
(301) 762-6775

Florida
Gold Coast Computer Group
P.O. Box 661456
Miami, FL 33266-1456
(305) 258-4334

Space Coast PC Users Group
P.O. Box 396
Titusville, FL 32781-0396
(407) 773-5191

EpSuncoast Users' Group
1237 79th St. S
St. Petersburg, FL 33707
(813) 343-2668

Coast PC Users Group
6017 Rossevelt Blvd. #70
Jacksonville, FL 32201
(904) 633-4750

Georgia
Asso. of Small Computer Users
P.O. Box 54532
Civic Center Station
Atlanta, GA 30308-9998
(404) 221-3331

Hawaii
Aloha Computer Club, Inc.
P.O. Box 4470
Honolulu, HI 96812-4470
(808) 537-2153

Idaho
Idaho PC Users Group
P.O. Box 9136
Boise, ID 83707
(208) 939-9120

Illinois
Chicago Computer Society
P.O. Box 8681
Chicago, IL 60680-8681
(312) 794-7737

Indiana
Indianapolis Computer Society
P.O. Box 2532
Indianapolis, IN 46206
(317) 862-5967

Iowa
Quad-City All Computers Users Group
1005 Canterbury Court
Davenport, IA 52806
(319) 386-3484

Midwest FOG
P.O. Box 2222
Ames, IA 50010-2222
(515) 769-2223

Kansas
Topeka PC Users Club
P.O. Box 1279
Topcka, KS 66601
(913) 272-7832

Kentucky
Heartland Users Group
155 Highland City
Paducah, KY 42003-1206
(502) 898-2489

Louisiana
New Orleans Personal Computer Club
P.O. Box 8364
Metairie, LA 70011
(504) 455-5849

Maine
Island/Reach Computer Users Group
P.O. Box 73
Deer Isle, ME 04627
(207) 348-9917

Maryland
Computer Users of Baltimore
P.O. Box 23510
Baltimore, MD 21203
(301) 442-1190

Massachusetts
Western Mass Computer Club
P.O. Box 363
West Springfield, MA 01089
(413) 533-1888

Boston Computer Society
One Center Plaza
Boston, MA 02108

Michigan
Washtenaw IBM PC User Society
P.O. Box 7508
Ann Arbor, MI 48107
(313) 487-5610

Minnesota
TC/PC
P.O. Box 3163
Minneapolis, MN 55403

Mississippi
North Bay Computer Users Club
456 Oaklawn Place
Biloxi, MS 39530

Missouri
McDonnell Douglas Recreational Computer Club
28 Redwood
Florissant, MO 63031

Nebraska
Lincoln LOG
139 North 11th #704
Lincoln, NE 68508
(402) 477-9233

New Hampshire
Pemi-Baker Computer Group
RFD #2 Box 399
Plymouth, NH 03264
(603) 536-3880

New Jersey
New Jersey PC Users Group
P.O. Box 14
Paradum, NJ 07653-0014
(201) 664-3311

PC Club of South Jersey
P.O. Box 427
Cherry Hill, NJ 08003
(609) 983-1519

New York
New York Amateur Computer Group
P.O. Box 3442
Church Street Station
New York, NY 10008
(212) 505-6021

Long Island Computer Asso.
P.O. Box 71
Hicksville, NY 11802
(516) 293-8368

North Carolina
PC Club of Charlotte
709 Madras Lane
Charlotte, NC 28211
(704) 364-1635

North Dakota
Fargo IBM-PC User Group
P.O. Box 9121
Fargo, ND 58109
(701) 232-3332

Ohio
Northern Ohio Business Users Group
571 East 185th St.
Euclid, OH 44119
(216) 944-5800

Toledo PC Users Group
P.O. Box 13085
Toledo, OH 43613-3085
(419) 245-3701

Dayton Microcomputer Asso., Inc.
2629 Ridge Ave.
Dayton, OH 45414-5499
(513) 252-1230

Oklahoma
OKC-PC Users Group
P.O. Box 12027
Oklahoma City, OK 73157-2027
(405) 340-7099

Oregon
Eugene PC Users Group
P.O. Box 11436
Eugene, OR 97440
(503) 683-1379

Pennsylvania
Three Rivers FOG
P.O. Box 23152
4th Ave. Station
Pittsburgh, PA 15222
(412) 661-2446

Tennessee
Music City PC Users Group
P.O. Box 210171
Nashville, TN 37221-0171
(615) 662-0322

Memphis PC Users Group, Inc.
P.O. Box 241756
Memphis, TN 38111-1736
(901) 386-8452

Texas
Golden Triangle PC Club
7360 Concord Road
Beaumont, TX 77708
(409) 898-2191

Houston Area League of PC Users, Inc.
1200 Post Oak Blvd. #106
Houston, TX 77056
(713) 623-4251

Utah
Utah Blue Chips Society
P.O. Box 510811
Salt Lake City, UT 84151
(801) 571-3433

Virginia
Tidewater's IBM PC Users Group
1001 Edgewood Ave.
Chesapeake, VA 23324-1114
(804) 545-3510

Washington
Pacific NW IBM PC User Group
P.O. Box 3363
Bellevue, WA 98009
(206) 885-6597

West Virginia
Personal Computer—Huntington University
P.O. Box 2173
Huntington, WV 25722-2173
(304) 526-5189

Wisconsin
Eau Claire PC User Group
P.O. Box 1369
Eau Claire, WI 54702
(715) 834-1022

Wyoming
Big Horn Basin Computer User's Group
P.O. Box 2353
Cody, WY 82414

Australia
Australasian Micro Users Society Ltd.
P.O. Box C 530
Clarence Street
Sydney, NSW 2000
Australia
02-439-7084

Canada
Greater Victoria PC Users Asso.
P.O. Box 5309
Station B
Victoria, B.C. V8R 6S4
Canada
(604) 382-3934

PC Users Group of Winnipeg
401-1025 Grant Ave.
Winnipeg, MANI R3M 1YA
Canada
(204) 474-8319

LOG Computer Users Group
80 Nathaniel Court
London, ONT N5X 2N5
Canada
(519) 660-0710

Montreal Micro Computer Society
3463 Ste Famille Apt. 1010
Montreal, P.Q. H2X 2K7
Canada
(514) 526-9940

Indonesia
Jakarta Computer Society
U.S. Embassy Box R
A.P.O.
San Francisco, CA 96536-5000
Indonesia
62-21-750-2371

Mexico
Computer Operators of Lakeside
Apartado Postal #95
45920 Ajijic
Jalisco
Mexico
(91-376) 5-30-16

West Germany
Computer Club Deutschland
Allewind 51
7900 Ulm
West Germany
07-304-3724

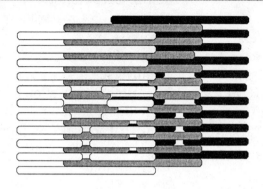

Trademarks

Anadex®	Anadex
Apple®	Apple Computer, Inc.
AsEasyAs®	Trius, Inc.
AT&T®	American Telephone & Telegraph
Axiom™	Axiom Corporation
Brother®	Brother International Corporation
ButtonWare®	ButtonWare, Inc.
C. Itoh™	C. Itoh & Company, Ltd.
Canon®	Canon USA, Inc.
Centronics®	CompuServe, Inc.
Dataproducts®	Dataproducts Corporation
dBASE II®	Ashton-Tate
dBASE III®	Ashton-Tate
DeskMate®	Tandy Corporation
DESQview®	Quarterdeck Office Systems

Diablo®	Xerox Corporation
Epson®	Seiko Epson Corporation
File Express™	Expressware
Fujitsu®	Fujitsu Ltd.
Galaxy®	Omniverse®
GW-BASIC®	Microsoft Corporation
Hercules®	Hercules Computer Technology
Hewlett-Packard®	Hewlett-Packard Company
IBM®	International Business Machines Corporation
Instacalc™	FormalSoft
Juki™	Juki Industries
Kaypro™	Kaypro Corporation
LaserJet™	Hewlett-Packard Company
Logitech™	Logitech, Inc.
Lotus®	Lotus Development Corporation
MailMerge®	MicroPro International Corporation
Microsoft®	Microsoft Corporation
MindReader™	Brown Bag® Software, Inc.
Mouse Systems®	Mouse Systems Corporation
MS-DOS®	Microsoft Corporation
MUSE™	OSM Computer Corporation
NEC®	NEC Corporation
New York Word®	Magma Software Systems
Okidata®	Okidata, and OKI America
Olympia®	Olympia USA, Inc.
1-2-3®	Lotus Development Corporation
Panasonic®	Panasonic
PC-Calc®	ButtonWare, Inc.
PC-File®	ButtonWare, Inc.
PC-Outline™	Telemarketing Resources
PC-SIG®	PC-SIG, Inc.
PC-Type®	ButtonWare, Inc.
PC-Write®	Quicksoft

PC-Write Macros™	Simple Productions
PeachText®	Peachtree Software, Inc.
PostScript®	Adobe Systems, Inc.
QuickBASIC®	Microsoft Corporation
Quicksoft®	Quicksoft
Radio Shack®	Tandy Corporation
Silver Reed®	Silver-Reed America, Inc.
Star Micronics®	Star Micronics
Symphony®	Lotus Development Corporation
Tandy®	Tandy Corporation
Texas Instruments, Inc.®	Texas Instruments, Inc.
Toshiba®	Toshiba America, Inc.
Visicalc®	Visicorp
Wang®	Wang Laboratories, Inc.
WordPerfect®	WordPerfect Corporation
WordStar®	MicroPro International Corporation
Writer's Heaven™	Simple Productions
Xerox®	Xerox Corporation
ZoomRacks™	Quickview Systems

Time Saving DISK AVAILABLE NOW

The Shareware Book Convenience Disk contains all the examples used in this book and can save you hours of time.

➡ You don't need to type in
- ➡ PC-Write documents
- ➡ PC-File+ databases
- ➡ PC-Calc+ spreadsheets

With *The Shareware Book* Convenience Disk, you can spend your valuable time perfecting your control of these programs instead of your typing skills.

➡ **EASY INSTALLATION INSTRUCTIONS ARE PROVIDED!**

Order Today!

Only $19.95 plus $2.00 shipping/handling for 5 1/4" Disk
$21.95 plus $2.00 shipping/handling for 3 1/2" Disk

Toll Free **800-227-0900** ← Call

(Monday-Friday 8:30 A.M. — 4:30 P.M. Pacific Standard Time)
Pay by check or money order, or use your American Express, VISA, or MasterCard.

Or fill out the coupon below, clip out and send to:
Osborne/McGraw-Hill, 2600 Tenth Street, Berkeley, CA, 94710, Attention: Supplementary Disk

---

➡ Please send me:

☐ copies of *The Shareware Book* Convenience Disk — 5 1/4"
at $19.95 each plus $2.00 per disk for postage and handling.   ISBN: 0-07-881607-6

☐ copies of *The Shareware Book* Convenience Disk — 3 1/2"
at $21.95 each plus $2.00 per disk for postage and handling.   ISBN: 0-07-881608-4

Name: _____
Company: _____
Address: _____
City: _____ State: _____ ZIP: _____

➡ Indicate method of payment.

☐ Check or Money Order # _____
(Please include shipping charge.)

☐ VISA   ☐ MasterCard   ☐ American Express _____

Expiration Date _____

➡ Signature _____

Allow 2 weeks for delivery — Prices subject to change without notice

This order subject to acceptance by McGraw-Hill — Offer good only in the U.S.A.

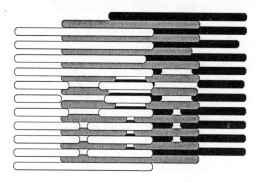

Index

PC-Write

♀☼ hard-break characters, 118
¶, end-of-paragraph mark, 79
Φ, ruler line cursor marker, 77, 143
♀, soft-break character, 116
↨, underline font character, 86
$$$, to print page numbers, 130, 618
., 44
+, in ruler line, 77, 144
&LT, file name extension, 62
.F Dot line, 125, 128, 618
.H Dot line, 125, 126, 618
.M Dot line, 125, 616
.Q Dot line, 614
.R Dot line, 91, 615
.X Dot line, 141, 616
.XB Dot line, 122, 616
.XT Dot line, 121, 616
/s, in FORMAT command, 17

A

A:*.*, 44
A>_, 12
ALT-B key combination, 89
ALT-F5 key combination, 117
ALT-F7 key combination, 116
ALT-G key combination, 91, 614
ALT-I key combination, 89
ALT-K key combination, 79
ALT-*letter* font selections, 89

ALT-Q key combination, 89
ALT-SPACEBAR key combination, 90, 116, 119
ALT-T key combination, 118
ALT-WHITE MINUS (−) key combination, 66
ALT-WHITE PLUS (+) key combination, 65
ASCII file, 638
Automatic pagination, 108, 109
Automatic paragraph formatting, 53, 79, 609

B

B:*.*, 46, 51
BACKSPACE key, 46, 59
Backup file, 61, 605
BASIC Teacher, The, 74, 150
Block of text
    copying, 96, 611
    deleting, 99, 611
    marking, 94, 97, 611
    moving, 92, 611
    undeleting, 100, 612
    unmarking, 95, 98, 611
Boldface font (ALT-B), 89
Bottom margin, 108
    setting, 122, 616
Break, page, 115-118, 617
    hard, 118, 617
    soft, 115, 617
Business letter, 75
Business Letters the Easy Way, 73
Button, Jim, xxvi

C

Centering text, 102
Changing a file name, 103
Character, deleting, 58
COLUMN.NBR file, 138
Columns, multiple, 159, 613
COMMAND.COM file (DOS), 17
Computer Shopper, 706

Convenience Disk, *Shareware Book*, 106, 136
Conversion menu, 117, 641
Converting earlier PC-Write files, 642
COPY command (DOS), 6
Copying a block of text, 96, 610
Copying a disk, 14
CTRL-BREAK key combination, 18
CTRL-ENTER key combination, 117, 617
CTRL-ESC key combination, 610
CTRL-F4 key combination, 100
CTRL-← key combination, 64, 609
CTRL-→ key combination, 64, 609
Cursor, 26, 63
    marker (Φ), in ruler line, 77, 143
    moving. *see* Moving the cursor

D

Default settings
    font, 137
    margin, 137
    work disk, 135, 137
DELETE key, 46, 58, 610
Deleting
    block of text, 99, 611
    character, 58, 610
    file, 608
    hard-break line, 120, 617
    line of text, 92, 611
    soft-break line, 117, 617
    word, 83, 610
DIR command (DOS), 6, 12, 17
Directory
    displaying, 25, 34, 606, 608
    files, 12
    selecting a file, 86
    work disk, 22
Disk
    copying, 14
    labeling, 21

Disk, *continued*
>   program, 9, 16, 622
>   reference, 9, 625
>   source, 15
>   target, 15
>   utility, 9, 623
>   utility/reference, 9, 628

Disk sets, 8, 621
DISKCOPY command (DOS), 6, 15
DOS
>   CLS command, 581
>   COMMAND.COM file, 17
>   COPY command, 6, 589
>   default drive, 579
>   DEL command, 590
>   on different systems, 585
>   DIR command, 6, 12, 17, 582
>   DISKCOPY command, 6, 15, 587
>   essentials, 573
>   file names, 48
>   FORMAT command, 6, 15, 18, 574
>   loading from a hard disk, 577
>   loading from drive A, 575
>   prompt, 12
>   returning to, 24, 40, 607
>   root directory, 44
>   starting, 574
>   TYPE command, 13

Dot command. *See* Dot line
Dot line
>   .F, 125, 128, 618
>   .H, 125, 126, 618
>   .M, 125, 616
>   .Q, 614
>   .R, 91, 615
>   .X, 141, 615
>   .XB, 122, 615
>   .XT, 121, 615

Dot lines in PR.DEF file, 158
Double-spaced printing, 123
DOWN ARROW (↓) key, 63

Draft print mode, 91
DragonSmoke, 86

E

ED.DEF file, 136, 622
>   editing, 155

ED.EXE program, 9, 24, 622
Edit control file (ED.DEF), 136, 155, 622
Editing
>   edit control file (ED.DEF), 155
>   print control file (PR.DEF), 157
>   ruler line, 143, 161

Editing screen, 31, 49
Elite print mode, 91
Embedding ruler line in a file, 150, 153, 612
END key, 64
End-of-paragraph mark (¶), 79
ENTER key, 26
ESC key, 26
Exiting from PC-Write, 24, 40
Exporting a file, 637
>   to Wordstar, 642

F

F1 function key, 27, 32
F2 function key, 24, 144
F3 function key, 33, 59, 97
F4 function key, 100
F5 function key, 95, 98, 100, 116
F6 function key, 29, 49, 94
F7 function key, 36, 78, 112, 117, 147, 149
F8 function key, 25, 34, 114
F9 function key, 30, 50, 112

F10 function key, 37, 117
Family Computer Club Newsletter, 159
Fast print mode, 91
FCC001.NSL file, 160
File
    ASCII, 638
    backup, 61, 605
    changing the name, 103, 608
    converting earlier PC-Write, 642
    creating, 29, 49, 603
    deleting, 608
    exporting, 637
    importing, 637
    load existing, 604
    printing, 35, 68, 108
    reformatting, 618
    repaging, 116, 617
    saving, 32, 59
    WordStar, 641
File name, 48
    changing, 103
Files
    directory, 12
    program disk, 622
    reference disk, 625
    utility disk, 623
    utility/reference disk, 628
Fluegelman, Andrew, xxxiii
FOG, 706
Font character, underline (↨), 86
Font characters
    default settings, 137
    hiding, 90
    making visible, 90
    table of, 89, 615
Footer Dot line, 128, 618
FORMAT command (DOS), 6, 15, 18
Function keys, 24

G

GO.BAT program, 13

Gregg Reference Manual, The, 73

H

Hard disk system, 19
Hard-break characters (♀☼), 118
Hard-break line, deleting, 120, 617
Hard-break line, inserting, 118, 617
Header Dot line, 126, 618
Help system, 27, 606
Hide mode, 90, 116, 119, 616
Hold area for deleted text, 100
HOME key, 64

I

Importing a file, 637
Importing a WordStar file, 641
Inserting a hard-break line, 118, 617
Italic font (ALT-I), 89

K

KATHY01.LTR file, 48, 156

L

L, in ruler line, 77, 143, 161, 613
Labeling disks, 21
Laran Stardrake, 101, 150
LEFT ARROW (←) key, 32, 63
Left margin, ruler line, 54, 76, 143, 161
Left printer margin, setting, 141
Letter to Kathy, 55
Letter-quality print mode, 91

Index 727

Letterhead, creating, 101
Line, deleting, 92, 610
Line, multiple-spacing, 123, 616
LINE.NBR file, 106
Loading an existing file, 604
Loading the edit program
   (ED.EXE), 24, 42, 60, 602
LSHEAD.LTR file, 101
LTR, file name extension, 48

M

Margin
   bottom, 108, 616
   default settings, 137
   left printed, 141, 616
   ruler line, 54, 76, 145, 147,
     613
   top, 108, 616
Marking a block of text, 94, 97
Menu
   Conversion, 117, 641
   Misc-ops, 639
   Opening, 602
   Page break, 116
   Print, 113
   System/help, 34, 606
Microsoft Disk Operating System
   (MS-DOS), 6
Misc-ops menu, 639
Moving a block of text, 92, 611
Moving the cursor
   backward one screen, 609
   beginning of a file, 65, 609
   beginning of a line, 64, 609
   beginning of a word, 63, 609
   bottom of a file, 65, 609
   down one line, 63, 609
   end of a file, 65, 609
   end of a line, 64, 609
   forward one screen, 609
   left one character, 63, 609

Moving the cursor, *continued*
   right one character, 63, 609
   top of a file, 65, 609
   up one line, 63, 609
MS-DOS, 6
Multiple line spacing, 123, 616

O

Opening menu, 25, 602
Opening screen, 25

P

Page break
   automatic, 108, 109
   deleting, 117, 120, 617
   hard, 115, 118, 120, 617
   Hide mode, 116, 119, 616
   menu, 116
   Show mode, 116, 119, 616
   soft, 115, 117, 617
Page numbers, 130
   in footer, 132
   in header, 131
Pagination, automatic, 108, 109
Para+, 53, 56, 79, 609
Paragraph reformatting, 78, 147,
   149, 609
PC-DOS, 6
PC-SIG Encyclopedia of Shareware, 163
PC-Write 3.0 Quick Guide, 7
PC-Write described, 7
PC-Write, files, 621
PC-Write User's Guide, 7
PCW hard disk directory, 20
Pica print mode, 91
PR.DEF file, 137, 622
   Dot lines, 158

PR.DEF file, *continued*
    editing, 157
PRACTICE.LTR file, 103
Print control file (PR.DEF), 137, 157, 622
Print menu, 38, 69, 113
Print mode
    draft, 91
    Elite, 91
    Fast, 91
    letter-quality, 91
    Pica, 91
    Quality, 91
Printing the *Tutorial* and *Quick Guide*, 636
Printing
    double-spaced, 123
    file, 35, 68, 108
    multiple copies, 112
    multiple-spaced, 123, 616
    page numbers, 130
    selected pages, 110, 114
    single-spaced, 123
    skipping pages, 114
PRINTMAN.COM program, 9
Program disk, 9, 16, 622
Prompt, DOS, 12

Q

Quality font (ALT-Q), 89
Quality print mode, 91
Quick Guide, printing, 636
Quicksoft, 7, 621

R

R, in ruler line, 77, 143, 161, 613
READ.ME file, 13, 622

Reference disk, 9, 625
Reformatting
    file, 618
    paragraph, 78, 147, 149
Registering PC-Write, 7
Repaging, 116, 617
Returning to DOS, 24, 40, 607
RIGHT ARROW (→) key, 32, 58, 63
Right margin, ruler line, 54, 76, 143, 161, 613
Root directory of a disk, 44
Ruler line, 54, 76
    change left margin, 147, 613
    change right margin, 145, 613
    editing, 143, 161, 612
    embedding in a file, 150, 153, 612
    left margin (L), 54, 76, 143, 161
    multiple column (V), 613
    right margin (R), 54, 76, 143, 161
    tab stops (T), 77, 143, 612
    two-column, 160, 612

S

Saving a file, 32, 59, 607
Screen, splitting, 159, 613
Selecting a file from directory, 86
Selecting a font, 91
Self-booting work disk, 16
Setting
    bottom margin, 122, 616
    left printer margin, 141, 616
    top margin, 121, 615
Shareware, history of, xxxiii
Shareware Book Convenience Disk, 106, 136
SHIFT-CTRL-ENTER key combination, 611

SHIFT-F7 key combination, 53, 77, 609
SHIFT-F8 key combination, 102
SHIFT-F11 key combination, 65, 609
SHIFT-F12 key combination, 65, 609
SHIFT-GREY MINUS (−) key combination, 65, 609
SHIFT-GREY PLUS (+) key combination, 65, 609
SHIFT-PGDN key combination, 609
SHIFT-PGUP key combination, 609
Show mode, 90, 116, 119, 616
Single-spaced printing, 123
Skipping pages, 114
Soft-break
    character (♀), 116
    line, deleting, 117
    line, inserting, 115, 117, 617
Source disk, 15
Splitting the screen, 159, 613
Stardrake, Laran, 101, 150
Starting an edit session, 24. 42, 60, 602
Status line, 50, 52
System/help menu, 34, 606

T

T, in ruler line, 77, 143, 613
Tab stops in ruler line, 77, 143, 613
Tandy 1000TL computer, 21
Target disk, 15
TBT001.LTR file, 74
Text
    centering, 102
    copying a block, 96, 611
    deleting a block, 99, 611
    deleting a line, 92, 610
    marking a block, 94, 97, 611
    moving a block, 92, 611
    undeleting a block, 100, 612
    unmarking a block, 95, 98, 611

Toggle switch, 90
Top margin, 108
    setting, 121, 615
Tutorial, printing it, 636
Two-column ruler line, 160, 613
TYPE command (DOS), 13

U

Undeleting a block of text, 100
Underline font character (_), 86
Unmarking a block of text, 95, 98
User groups, 707
UP ARROW (↑) key, 58, 63
Utility disk, 9, 623
Utility/reference disk, 9, 628

V

V, in ruler line, 161, 613

W

Wallace, Bob, xxxiii
Word, deleting, 83, 610
Word processing, 5
Word Processor for Kids, 164
Word wrap, 53, 78, 613
WordStar files, 641
Work disk, 16
    creating, 629
    default settings, 137
    directory, 22
WORK.DOC file, 23, 29
WORKDISK.BAT, program, 9, 16-20, 54, 629
Wrap+, 53, 78, 609
Wrap−, 53, 609
Write-protecting a disk, 9

PC-File+

~ search character, 202
# character, 319, 656
.<DATE*>, 268, 271
.<field>, 268, 270
.<KEYIN*>, 268, 271, 281, 283
.[field], 268, 270
.EGROUP, 268, 272, 283
.FF, 272
.FORMFEED, 268, 272
.GROUP, 268, 272, 283
: character, 653
? mark, 300
?????? message, 271, 285
@ character, 300, 656
[ ] characters, 221-224, 317
\PCF directory, 178
_ character, 259

A

Activating calculations, 334
Active commands, Master menu, 196
Add a new record command, 196
Aligning fields with TAB key, 221-224
Alter data command, 256-257
Altering
    location of fields, 206
    the data entry screen, 206
ANS file extension, 662
Arithmetic calculations, 655
ASCII, 591, 697
Attributes in fields, 328, 331
Automatic fields, 653-654

B

Backing up
    5 1/4-inch disks, 172-174

Backing up, *continued*
    MailList, 234
    PC-File+, 171
    PhoneLst, 211
    3 1/2-inch disks, 175-177
Backup disks, 171, 175, 204, 234
Bar chart mask, 659
Bar charts
    horizontal, 345, 357, 368, 371
    vertical, 345, 348, 367
Blank disk, 179
BookStor database, 312, 322
    data records, 324-325
    screen layout, 314, 316
Browse control keys, 210
Bulletin board technical support, 171
Button, Jim, xxvi
ButtonWare, 170
    bulletin board, 171
    PC-File+ User's Manual, 171
    technical support, 255

C

c:1, 215
Calculated fields, 326, 655
Calculation order, 329, 332, 655
Calculation rules, 327, 653, 655
Calculations, 311, 655
    arithmetic, 655
    date, 656
    relational lookup, 656
    special function, 656
CARD file, 173, 176
CHANGES file, 173, 176
Character mask, 659
Check protection mask, 659
Clone command, 206, 211

Cloning a database, 206, 214
Cloning individual records, 231
Column indicator, 215
Commands report format, 245-246, 657-659
Complex search method, 200
Computer Shopper, 706
CONFIG.SYS file, 185-186
Constants, 326
Context sensitive help, 181, 204
Control keys, 649
Convenience Disk, 207, 234, 242, 266, 315
Copying a database, 207
Copying database files, 212
CopyMail database, 235
CopyPhon database, 214
Correcting mistakes, 193
Cursor controls keys, 648

D

Damaged database, repairing, 173, 176
Data creation area, 215
Data entry order in fields, 195
    setting, 229
Data entry screen, 197
    grid sheet, 219
Data records
    MailList database, 243-244
Database disk, 180
Database elements
    fields, 188, 204
    files, 188
    index, 188
    names, 188
    record number, 197
    records, 188, 204

Database
    and cloning, 206
    concepts, 187-188
    copying, 207
    damage to and repair of, 173, 176
    defining, 191
    definition, 169, 188
    drive designation, 181, 184
    and files, 183
    management, 169
    modifying records, 234, 238-242
    path name, 183
    retrieving records, 237
    selecting, 209
    types of, 169-170
Databases
    BookStor, 313, 322
    CopyMail, 235
    CopyPhon, 214
    MailList, 214, 218, 231, 265, 288
    PhoneLst, 190
Date calculations, 656
Default printer type, 251
Defining a database
    Fast method, 191
    Paint method, 191
Definition options screen, 191
Deleting database files, 212
Deleting records, 260
Designating a field, 215
DISK ONE, 172-178, 180, 186
DISK THREE, 172-174, 178
DISK TWO, 172-178
Disk sets,
    5 1/4-inch, 171-174
    3 1/2-inch, 171, 175-177
Display length
    definition, 193
    of a field, 193, 204

Distribution disks, 173
    contents of (5 1/4-inch disks), 173
DOS
    default drive, 579
    on different systems, 574
    essentials, 573
    loading from a hard disk, 577
    loading from drive A, 575
    starting, 574
DOS commands, 580
    change directory, 178
    clear screen, 581
    copy, 178, 208, 234, 339, 589
    delete, 590
    directory, 582
    diskcopy, 172, 175, 587
    files, 186
    format, 179, 585
    graphics, 338, 363
    make directory, 178
Drive designation of database, setting, 183
DTA file extension, 173, 176, 208-209, 662
Duplicate data command, 256-257

E

Edit masks, 326, 653, 659
Editing commands, 206, 651
Editing keys, 238-242, 650
Editing window, 215-216
Editor menu, 216-217
Erase to end of file, 216-217
Erasing the editing window, 217
Error message at start up, 184

Exiting the graphics program, 361
Exiting the program, 185, 204
Expanded Master menu, 199
Export data command, 256-257, 665, 697
Extending field lengths, 207
Extensions, file, 173, 176

F

Fast method of screen design, 191, 215
Fields
    with # character, 319
    and attributes, 328, 331
    automatic, 653-654
    calculated, 326, 655
    and calculation rules, 326, 653, 655
    and constants, 326, 653
    in databases, 188
    definition screen, 192
    designating, 221
    display lengths of, 193
    and edit masks, 326, 653, 659
    extending, 207
    how accessed, 195
    numeric, 319
    order of data entry in, 195
    regular, 193, 227
    selecting report, 246-247
    shortening, 207
    shortening names of, 329
    superfield, 193
    trigger, 344
    window, 194, 227

File extensions, 173, 176, 213, 662
   ANS, 213, 662
   DTA, 173, 176, 208-209, 662
   GR, 213
   HDR, 173, 176, 208-209, 298, 662
   INX, 173, 176, 208-209, 662
   KEY, 173, 176, 662
   LBL, 302
   LTR, 213, 662
   PRO, 173, 176, 662
   REP, 173, 176, 662
Files
   copy options, 213
   copying database, 212
   and databases, 183, 188
   deleting database, 212
   profile, 251
Files on distribution disks
   CARD, 173, 176, 663
   CHANGES, 173, 176, 663
   FPRPT.EXE, 173, 176, 662
   MSHERC.COM, 173, 176, 341, 662
   PCF.EXE, 173, 176, 662
   PCF.HLP, 173, 176, 662
   PCFILE.PRO, 173, 176, 662
   PCFIX.EXE, 173, 176, 662
   PCG2.EXE, 173, 176, 338-340, 662
   PCLABEL.EXE, 173, 176, 662
   PEOPLE*.*, 173, 176, 663
   PRODUCTS, 173, 176, 663
   READ.ME, 173, 176, 663
   TECHINFO, 173, 176, 663
   VENDOR.DOC, 173, 176, 663
Files on PC-File+ disks, 662
Final totals in reports, 250

Find a record command, 199
   browse control keys, 210
5 1/4-inch disk set, 172
   contents of distribution disks, 173
   DISK ONE, 172-177
   DISK THREE, 172-177
   DISK TWO, 172-177
Fluegelman, Andrew, xxxiii
FOG, 708
Form letters, 265, 273-278
Format
   blank disk, 179, 204
   database disk, 179-180
FPRPT.EXE file, 173, 176
Free form report format, 245-246

G

Global command, 256-260
GR file extension, 173, 176
Graph formats
   bar charts, 312
   line graphs, 312, 351, 369
   pie charts, 312, 353
   scatter diagrams, 345, 358
Graphics program
   and calculations, 359
   charting multiple fields, 362-371
   counts, 342
   data summaries, 342
   default graph type, 344
   dependent variable, 344
   exiting, 361
   graphing order, 343

Graphics program, *continued*
    independent variable, 344
    menus, 350
    PCG2.EXE, 173, 176, 338-340
    specifying graphs, 341-347
    trigger fields, 346
    troubleshooting, 341
    values, 342
    (X)chg command, 369
Graphing data, 311
Grid sheet, data entry screen, 219

H

Hard disks and PC-File+, 177-179
HDR file extension, 173, 176, 208-209, 298, 662
Help feature, 181, 190
Help messages file, 173, 176, 182
Help window, 182
Horizontal bar charts, 345, 357, 368, 371

I

Import data command, 256-257, 665, 697
Index to database, 188
    files with INX extensions, 173, 176, 208
INX file extension, 173, 176, 208-209, 662

K

KEY file extension, 173, 176, 662
Keystroke summary, 647

L

Label setup screen, 296
LBL extension, 302, 662
Letter editing window, 267-269
    size, 269
Letter writing command, 266, 286
Line graphs, 312, 351, 369

M

Mail merge
    commands, 268, 270-273
    problems, 285
    reminder labels, 280
Mailing label program
    PCLABEL.EXE, 173, 176
Mailing labels, 265, 293
    alignment, 306
    formats, 308-309
    layout screen, 299
    1-up, 304
    positioning, 305
    printer escape codes, 299
    printing, 303-307
    standard, 304
    2-up, 304
MailList database, 214, 218, 231, 265, 288
    data records, 243-244
    screen layout, 220, 224
MailList layout, 220
Main program
    PCF.EXE, 173, 176
Maintenance command, 212
Maintenance operation, 212
Making corrections, 193
Mapping existing data during cloning, 225

Marking window fields, 228
Masks
    bar chart, 659
    character, 659
    check protection, 659
    editing, 326, 653, 659
    numeric, 659
    zero suppress, 659
Master menu, 196
    active commands, 196
    "Add a new record" command, 196
    expanded, 199, 210
    "Find a record" command, 199, 204
    Letter writing, 266
    for new database, 197
    Reports command, 245
Master profile files, 251
Memory requirements, 171
Modifying records, 234, 238-242
Moving a window, 183
MSHERC.COM file, 173, 176

N

Name command, 256-257
NamePhon report format file, 250
Naming fields, 193
Numeric fields, 319
Numeric Mask, 659

P

Path name of database, setting, 183
"Please reply" portal, 181
Page report format, 245-246

Paint method of screen design, 191, 206, 215, 221, 315-321
    and [ ], 221-224, 317
    how to use, 218, 221-224
    and TAB key, 221-224, 317
PC-Calc+, 293, 373, 691, 695
PC-File+, 169, 573, 695, 697
    backup copies, 171
    evaluating, 170
    and hard disks, 177-179
    license, 170
    memory requirements, 171
    program requirements, 171
    starting, 180
    the package, 170
    unregistered copy, 170
    User's Manual, 170, 172, 242, 251, 308, 326, 666
    version number, 170
PC-File:dB, 293, 665
PC-Label and color monitors, 293
PC-Label program, 266, 293
    Main menu, 295
PC-SIG Encyclopedia of Shareware, 700
PC-SIG, Inc., 702
pcf, 180, 186, 189, 208, 313, 340, 363
PCF.EXE file, 173, 176
PCF.HLP file, 173, 176
PCFILE.PRO file, 173, 176
PCFIX.EXE file, 173, 176
PCG2.EXE file, 173, 176, 338-340
PCLABEL.EXE file, 173, 176
PEOPLE*.* file, 173, 176
PhoneLst database, 190, 204, 207
Pie charts, 312, 353
Previewing letters, 278
Printer
    default, 251
    Diablo, 254

Printer, *continued*
    EPSON, 251, 254, 338
    HP LaserJet, 254
    IBM, 251, 254, 338
    Itoh, 254
    LaserJet compatibles, 254
    NEC, 254
    Okidata, 254
    problems, 255
    Radio Shack (Tandy), 254
    Toshiba, 254
Printer configuration screen, 253
Printing letters, 285-293
Printing mailing labels, 303-307
Printing reports
    to a disk, 248-249, 290-292
    to the printer, 204, 248-249
    to the screen, 204, 248-249, 279-280
PRO file extension, 173, 176, 662
PRODUCTS file, 173, 176
Profile configuration screen, 253
Profile files
    for individual databases, 251
    master, 251
Profile files command, 251
Profile options menu, 252
Program commands
    active commands, 196
    "Add a new record", 196
    "Find a record", 199
    Letter writing, 266
    Reports, 245
    summary, 647
    Utilities, 245
Program elements
    "Please reply" portal, 181

Program elements, *continued*
    control keys, 649
    cursor controls, 648
    data entry screen, 197
    database selection screen, 209
    Definition options screen, 191
    editing commands, 206, 651
    editing keys, 238-242, 650
    editing window, 215-216
    Editor menu, 216-217
    Field definition screen, 192
    help feature, 181
    help messages file, 182
    help window, 173, 176, 182
    letter editing window, 267-269
    Master menu, 196
    printer configuration screen, 252
    Profile options menu, 252
    profile configuration screen, 252
    replacement data screen, 258
    report format options screen, 245-246
    search data screen, 236
    search option list, 199
    smart keys, 199, 652
    start up error message, 184
    title screen, 181
    Utilities menu, 211
Program requirements, 171
Programs
    graphics, 173, 176
    mailing label, 173, 176
    main, 173, 176
    repair, 173, 176
    report, 173, 176

R

r:1 c:1, 215, 218, 269, 317
r:1, 215
Re-describe command, 256-257
Reading charts, 347
READ.ME file, 173, 176
Record number, 197
Records
    BookStor database, 324-325
    in databases, 188, 204, 231
    deleting, 260
    MailList database, 243-244
    modifying, 234, 238-242
    retrieving, 236
    undeleting, 261
Regular fields, 193, 227
Relational lookup calculations, 656
REP file extension, 173, 176, 662
Repair program, PCFIX.EXE, 173, 176
Repairing damaged database, 173, 176
Replacement data screen, 258
Report fields, selecting, 246-247
Report format file, NamePhon, 250
Report formats
    commands, 245-246, 657-659
    free form, 245-246
    page, 245-246
    row, 245-246
Report format option screen, 245-246
Report program, FPRPT.EXE, 173, 176
Report
    description, 248
    format, 248
    totals, 250
    work file, 248
Reports command, 245

Retrieving records, 236
Row indicator, 215
Row report format, 245-246
Row/column indicators, 215

S

Scatter diagrams, 345, 358
Screen design
    Fast method, 191, 215
    Paint method, 191, 215, 221, 315-321
Screen layout
    BookStor database, 314, 316
    MailList database, 220, 224
Search criteria, 204
Search data screen, 236
Search methods
    complex, 200
    simple, 200-203
    using tilde (~), 202
Search option list, 199
Setting
Shareware
    advantages of, 171
    agreement, 170
    history of, xxxiii
    license, 171
    other programs, 701
Shareware Book Convenience Disk, 207, 234, 242, 266, 315
Shortening field lengths, 207
Simple search method, 200-203
Skip over character, 259
Smart keys, 652
Smart keys command, 256-257
Source disk, 172
Special function calculations, 656
Specifying graphs, 341-347
Superfield, 193

T

TAB key
    to align data fields, 218, 221-224, 317
    use of, 218
Target disk, 172
TECHINFO file, 173, 176
Technical support, 171, 255
Termination screen, 205
3 1/2-inch disk set, 175
    contents of distribution disks, 176
    DISK ONE, 175-177
    DISK TWO, 175-177
tilde (~) and searches, 202
Title screen, 181
Trigger fields, 344

U

Undelete command, 256-257
Undeleting records, 261
User groups, 705
User's Manual, 170, 172, 242, 251, 308, 326, 666
Using PC-File+
    with 5 1/4-inch disks, 172-174
    with a hard disk, 177-179
    with 3 1/2-inch disks, 175-177
Utilities command, 210
Utilities menu, 211
Utilities menu commands
    Alter data, 256-257
    Clone, 211, 257

Utilities menu commands, *continued*
    Duplicate data, 256-257
    Export data, 256-257, 665, 697
    Global, 256-260
    Import data, 256-257, 665, 697
    Maintenance, 212, 257
    Name, 256-257
    Profile files, 251, 257
    Re-describe, 256-257
    Smart keys, 256-257
    Undelete, 256-257

V

VENDOR.DOC file, 173, 176
Vertical bar charts, 345, 348, 367

W

Wallace, Bob, xxxiii
Window fields, 194, 227
    creating, 227-228
    marking, 228

X

X option, 198

Z

Zero suppress mask, 659

PC-Calc+

", 476, 483
/, 402, 411, 422, 426, 439, 446, 452
\\PCCALC directory, 387, 422, 442, 482, 543

A

ASCII, 591

B

BACKPACK spreadsheet, 466-504
    backup copy, 508
    column headings, 469
    data, 467, 475-487
Bar charts
    horizontal, 556
    vertical, 547, 556, 564
Block definition, 426
Block option list, 426, 437, 446, 452, 678
BPACK spreadsheet, 509
BUDGET spreadsheet, 426, 431-460
    column headings, 433-436
    row labels, 439-440
    titles, 433
BUDGRAPH spreadsheet, 538
Building a spreadsheet, 421-461
Bulletin board and technical support, 377
Button, Jim, xxvi
ButtonWare, 376
    bulletin board, 377

ButtonWare, *continued*
    PC-Calc+ User's Guide, 376, 378, 495, 568, 692
    technical support, 568

C

Calculation functions, 679-685
Cell pointer, 396-397
    movement of, 397, 408, 674-676
Cell range definition, 426
Cell references
    fixed, 448
    relative, 447
Cells
    changing column widths, 472
    formatting, 470, 477
    justification, 471
Changing column widths, 472
Column headings, 433-436, 469
Columns, 396-398
Commands, 421, 671
    from keystrokes, 673
    summary of menu, 677-679
Computer Shopper, 706
Computing a column of data, 444
CONFIG.SYS file, 390
Configure option list, 434, 439, 468, 678
Context sensitive help, 398, 404
Convenience Disk, 424, 454, 466, 483, 508
Copying
    cells, 437-439
    formulas, 446-449, 452
    functions, 452
Correcting mistakes, 408

D

Date and time functions, 680-681
Disk sets
    5 1/4-inch, 378-381
    3 1/2-inch, 381-383
Displaying cells
    as formulas, 455-456
    as values, 455-456
DOS commands, 580
    change directory, 384, 394, 406, 422, 431, 468, 510
    clear screen, 581
    copy, 509, 589
    delete, 590
    directory, 582
    diskcopy, 379, 382, 587
    files, 390
    format, 585
    graphics, 544
DOS
    and different systems, 574
    default drive, 579
    loading from a hard disk, 577
    loading from drive A, 575
    starting, 574
DOS essentials, 573

E

Edit line, 396-397
    cursor movement on, 676-677
Electronic spreadsheet, 375, 394
    applications, 376
    definition, 375, 394
Entering a column of data, 443
Entering data, 408-410

Entering a formula, 408
Entering labels, 408-409
Entering values, 409-410
Exiting the graphics program, 560
EXPENSES spreadsheet, 407, 424

F

File extraction utility
    PKUNZIP.EXE file, 379, 381
File name extensions, 688-689
File selection box, 417, 431
Files on distribution disks, 688
    INSTALL.EXE, 379, 381, 383, 688
    PCCP.ZIP, 379, 382, 688
    PCCU.ZIP, 379, 382, 688
    PKUNZIP.EXE, 379, 381, 688
    READ.ME, 379, 382, 688
    VENDOR.DOC, 379, 382, 688
Fill option list, 485
Financial functions, 681
5 1/4-inch disk set, 378
    contents of distribution disks, 379
    DISK ONE, 378-381, 384
    DISK TWO, 378-381, 388
Fixed cell references, 448
Fluegelman, Andrew, xxxiii
FOG, 706
Format option list, 455, 678
Formatting cells, 470, 477
Formulas
    and functions, 450-454
    copying, 446-449, 452
    entering, 408, 410, 444-445, 495-499
Free memory, 396

Functions, 421-422, 671, 679-685
    copying, 452
    date and time, 680-681
    financial, 681
    logical, 682-683
    mathematical, 681-682
    special, 683-684
    statistical, 684
    string, 684-685
    SUM, 450-454
    trigonometric, 685

G

Goto command, 470
Graph data table, 561
Graph formats
    bar charts, 556
    line graphs, 550-552
    pie charts, 552-556, 566-567
    scatter diagrams, 557
Graphics program
    and calculations, 557-559
    charting multiple fields, 560-567
    default graph type, 546
    exiting, 560
    menus, 549
    PCG2.EXE,
    PCG2.EXE, 542
    specifying graphs, 545-546
    (X)chg command, 565

H

Help
    context sensitive, 398, 404
    general, 399-402
    message, 398
Horizontal bar charts, 556

Horizontal screen splits, 510-516
    using 515, 518

I

Import option list, 539, 678
INSTALL.EXE file, 379, 381, 383
Installation of PC-Calc+, 383-393
Installation requirements, 383

K

Keys that move cell pointer, 674-676
    around screen, 674-675
    around spreadsheet, 675-676
    within cells, 674
Keys that move edit cursor, 676-677
Keystrokes, 671
Keystrokes, special command, 673

L

Labels, creating, 408-409, 483, 486
Line graphs, 550-552
Load/Save option list, 423, 679
Loading a spreadsheet, 430
Logical functions, 682
Loop option list, 679

M

Macro option list, 679
Main menu, 402-403, 422, 426, 439, 446, 452, 470, 678
Main program files
    compressed, 379, 382
    PCCP.ZIP file, 379, 382
Masks, 479, 503
Mathematical functions, 681-682

Memory requirements, 377
Message line, 396-397
Mistakes, correcting, 408
Move option list, 481
Moving the cell pointer, 397
MSHERC.EXE file, 543
Multi-cell sorting, 525-529

P

Page layout destination screen, 489
PATH request, 423
PC-Calc+, 375, 671, 695
    backup copies, 377-383
    commands, 421, 677-675
    evaluating, 377
    and floppy disk systems, 383
    functions, 421-422, 679-685
    and hard disks, 383
    installation, 383-393
    installation requirements, 383
    memory requirements, 377
    program requirements, 377
    Quick Calc feature, 459
    quitting the program,
      402-405, 418, 460
    shareware agreement, 377
    starting, 393-394, 672
    the package, 376
    User's Guide, 376, 378, 495,
      568, 692
    version number, 376
PC-Calc+ files, 392-393, 688-689
    data, 688-689
    on distribution disks, 688
    extensions, 688-689
    programs, 688
    resource, 689

PC-File+, 169, 573, 695, 697
PC-SIG Encyclopedia of Shareware, 700
PC-SIG, Inc., 700
PC-Write, 7, 601, 697
pcc, 394, 406, 422, 431, 442, 468,
    482, 510
PCCP.ZIP file, 379, 382
PCCU.ZIP file, 379, 382
PCG2.EXE file, 543
Pie charts, 552-556, 566-567
Print/Graph option list, 411, 544,
    679
Printers
    Epson, 543
    HP LaserJet, 543
    IBM, 543
    Okidata, 543
Printing spreadsheets, 412-415,
    488-495, 529-536
Problem-Solver's Backpack, 464-466
Program elements
    Block option list, 426, 437,
      446, 452, 678
    cell pointer, 396-397
    columns, 396-398
    Configure option list, 434,
      439, 468, 678
    edit line, 396-397
    Fill option list, 485
    Format option list, 455, 678
    general help screens, 399-402
    Goto command, 470
    help messages, 398
    Import option list, 539, 678
    Load/Save option list, 423,
      679
    Main menu, 402-403, 411,
      422, 426, 446, 452, 470,
      678
    message line, 396-397

Program elements, *continued*
   Move option list, 481
   Page layout and destination screen, 489
   Print/Graph option list, 411, 544, 679
   Reports option list, 413
   rows, 396-398
   Smart feature, 433-436, 440, 468
   Sort option list, 521-529
   Split screen option list, 509-521, 679
   startup screen, 395-397
   status line, 396-397
   Title locking option list, 487-488, 500, 679
   window controls, 395
   worksheet area, 396-397
Program requirements, 377
PKUNZIP.EXE file, 379, 381

Q

Quick Calc feature, 459
Quitting PC-Calc+, 402-405, 418, 460

R

Reading charts, 547-548
READ.ME file, 379, 382
Relative cell references, 447
Relative or Fixed option list, 447-448
Reports option list, 413
Reports table, 533-535
Row labels, creating, 439-440
Rows, 396-398

S

Saving spreadsheets, 416-417, 428, 441, 475
Scatter diagrams, 557
Shareware Book Convenience Disk, 424, 454, 466, 483, 508
Shareware
   advantages of, 377
   agreement, 377
   history of, xxxiii
   license, 377
   other programs, 699
Situational lessons, 465
Smart feature, 433-436, 440, 468
Sort option list, 521-529
Sorting spreadsheet data, 521-529
   ascending order, 523
   descending order, 523
Sorting spreadsheet multi-cell sorts, 525-529
Source cell definitions, 437
Special functions, 683-684
Specifying graphs, 545-546
Split screen option
   horizontal splits, 510-516
   syncronization, 518-520
   unsplitting, 521
   vertical splits, 516-518
Split screen option list, 509-521, 679
Spreadsheet
   building, 421-461
   cell location, 408
   cell pointer, 396-397, 408
   cells, 408
   changing column widths, 444
   changing data values, 411
   computing a column of data, 472
   copying cells, 437-439
   copying formulas, 446-449
   creating column headings, 433

Spreadsheet, *continued*
    creating row labels, 439-440
    creating titles, 433
    displaying cells as formulas, 455-456
    displaying cells as values, 455-456
    entering a column of data, 443
    formatting cells, 470, 477
    formulas, 410, 444-445, 495-499
    functions, 679-685
    and keystroke commands, 673
    and keystroke controls, 674-676
    labels, 408-409, 483, 486
    loading, 430
    multi-cell sorts, 525-529
    printing, 412-415, 488-495, 529-536
    saving, 416-417, 428, 441, 475
    sorting data on a, 521-529
    titles, creating, 433
    values, 409-410
    "What if?" questions, 456-460
    zapping, 426-428
Spreadsheets
    BACKPACK, 466-504
    BPACK, 509
    BUDGET, 426, 431-460
    BUDGRAPH, 538
    EXPENSES, 407, 424
    LOAN, 424
    TUTORIAL, 424
Startup screen, 395-397
Statistical functions, 684
Status line, 396-397
String functions, 684
SUM function, 450-454

T

Target cell definitions, 438

3 1/2-inch disk, 378, 381-383
    contents of distribution disk, 381-382
    DISK ONE, 381, 384
Title locking option list, 487-488, 500, 679
Transferring PC-Calc+ files, 691-692, 697-698
Trigonometric functions, 685

U

Unsplitting the screen, 521
User groups, 705
User's Guide, 376, 378, 495, 568, 692
Using masks, 479, 503
Utility program files
    compressed, 379, 382
    PCCU.ZIP file, 379, 382

V

Values, entering, 409-410
VENDOR.DOC file, 379, 382
Vertical bar charts, 547, 556, 564
Vertical screen splits, 516-518

W

Wallace, Bob, xxxiii
"What if?" questions, 456-460
Window controls, 395
Worksheet area, 396-397

Z

Zapping a spreadsheet, 426-428

The manuscript for this book was prepared and submitted to Osborne/McGraw-Hill in electronic form. The acquisitions editor for this project was Elizabeth Fisher, the technical reviewer was Johanna Jones, and the project editor was Dusty Bernard.

Text design by Marcela Hancik, using Baskerville for text body and Swiss boldface for display.

Cover art by Bay Graphics Design, Inc. Color separation and cover supplier, Phoenix Color Corporation. Screens produced with InSet, from Inset Systems, Inc. Book printed and bound by R.R. Donnelley & Sons Company, Crawfordsville, Indiana.